The Consequences of Social Movements

Social movements have attracted much attention in recent years, both from scholars and among the wider public. This book examines the consequences of social movements, covering such issues as the impact of social movements on the life-course of participants and the population in general, on political elites and markets, and on political parties and processes of social movement institutionalization. The volume makes a significant contribution to research on social movement outcomes in three ways: theoretically, by showing the importance of hitherto undervalued topics in the study of social movement outcomes; methodologically, by expanding the scientific boundaries of this research field through an interdisciplinary approach and new methods of analysis; and empirically, by providing new evidence about social movement outcomes from Europe and the United States.

Lorenzo Bosi is an assistant professor at the Institute of Humanities and Social Sciences of the Scuola Normale Superiore.

Marco Giugni is a professor in the Department of Political Science and International Relations and Director of the Institute of Citizenship Studies (InCite) at the University of Geneva.

Katrin Uba is a senior researcher and lecturer at the Department of Political Science, Uppsala University.

The Consequences of Social Movements

Edited by

Lorenzo Bosi, Marco Giugni, and Katrin Uba

CAMBRIDGE
UNIVERSITY PRESS

CAMBRIDGE
UNIVERSITY PRESS

University Printing House, Cambridge CB2 8BS, United Kingdom

Cambridge University Press is part of the University of Cambridge.

It furthers the University's mission by disseminating knowledge in the pursuit of education, learning and research at the highest international levels of excellence.

www.cambridge.org
Information on this title: www.cambridge.org/9781107116801

© Cambridge University Press 2016

First published 2016

Printed in the United States of America by Sheridan Books, Inc.

A catalogue record for this publication is available from the British Library

Library of Congress Cataloguing in Publication data
The consequences of social movements / edited by Lorenzo Bosi,
Marco Giugni, Katrin Uba.
  pages cm
ISBN 978-1-107-11680-1 (hardback) – ISBN 978-1-107-53921-1 (paperback)
1. Social movements.   2. Social movements – Political aspects.
3. Social movements – Economic aspects.   I. Bosi, Lorenzo, editor.
II. Giugni, Marco, editor.   III. Uba, Katrin, editor.
HM881.C654   2016
303.48'4–dc23

2015032000

ISBN 978-1-107-11680-1 Hardback
ISBN 978-1-107-53921-1 Paperback

Contents

Part II Policies   157

Part III Institutions   261

Conclusion   361

Figures

Tables

Contributors

Philip Balsiger is an assistant professor of sociology at the University of Neuchâtel, Switzerland. His research studies the interactions between social movements and corporations, the rise of moral markets, and the transformations of contemporary capitalism. He is the author of *The Fight for Ethical Fashion* (2014).

Karen Beckwith is Flora Stone Mather Professor in the Department of Political Science of Case Western Reserve University. A co-editor of *Women's Movements Facing the Reconfigured State* (Cambridge, 2003), she has research interests in comparative women's movements, the comparative politics of gender, and gender and political party leadership. Her work on social movements has been published in the *European Journal of Political Research*, the *Journal of Politics, Mobilization*, and *Politics & Society*, among others. Her current research focuses on social movement loss and its consequences.

Kathleen M. Blee is Distinguished Professor of Sociology at the University of Pittsburgh. She studies both mainstream and extreme-right activism and activist groups. Her recent books include *Democracy in the Making: How Activist Groups Form* and *Inside Organized Racism: Women in the Hate Movement*.

Lorenzo Bosi is Assistant Professor at the Institute of Humanities and Social Sciences of the Scuola Normale Superiore. His research interests include social movements and political violence. By focusing on contentious politics as a specific object of analysis, his research escapes traditional disciplinary boundaries. He is a member of COSMOS.

Jennifer Earl is Professor of Sociology at the University of Arizona, where she studies social movements, information technologies, and the sociology of law, with research emphases on Internet activism, social movement repression, and legal change. She is a member of the MacArthur Research Network on Youth and Participatory Politics and co-authored *Digitally Enabled Social Change*.

Marco Giugni is a professor in the Department of Political Science and International Relations and Director of the Institute of Citizenship Studies (InCite) at the University of Geneva. His research interests include social movements and collective action, immigration and ethnic relations, unemployment, and social exclusion. He is the European editor of *Mobilization*, an international quarterly.

Maria T. Grasso is Lecturer in Politics and Quantitative Methods at the Department of Politics, University of Sheffield. Her research interests are political participation, social movements, and social change. She is a PI on the Living with Hard Times: How European Citizens Deal with Economic Crises and Their Social and Political Consequences (LIVEWHAT) EU FP7 project.

Brayden G. King is a professor of management and, by courtesy, sociology at Northwestern University's Kellogg School of Management. His research focuses on how social movement activists influence corporate social responsibility, organizational change, and legislative policy making. He has published articles in the *American Journal of Sociology, American Sociological Review, Administrative Science Quarterly, Organization Science*, and numerous other academic journals. He is currently a senior editor at *Organization Science*.

Joseph E. Luders is the Gottesman Associate Professor of Political Science at Yeshiva University. His research interests include contentious politics, racial violence, and American political development.

Camille Masclet is a PhD student in Political Sociology at the University of Lausanne and the University of Paris 8. Her research deals with the questions of the biographical consequences of feminist activism and the intergenerational transmission of feminism. She is also participating in the project SOMBRERO, a research project on the outcomes of the 1970s activism in France, in which she is leading the team working on the women's movement.

Abby Peterson is Professor of Sociology at the Department of Sociology and Work Science, University of Gothenburg, Sweden. Peterson has published extensively within the fields of political sociology, cultural sociology, and criminology.

Daniela R. Piccio is a research fellow at the University of Turin. She received her PhD at the European University Institute of Florence and worked as a research associate at Leiden University. Her work has appeared in *South European Society and Politics, Representation, International Political Science Review*, as well as in several edited book volumes. Her research interests include comparative politics, political representation, social movements, and party (finance) regulation.

Katrin Uba is a senior researcher and lecturer at the Department of Political Science, Uppsala University. Her recent research focuses on labor movements' use of online mobilization strategies, political consequences of protest events in Sweden, and citizens' resilience at times of economic crisis.

Mattias Wahlström is a senior lecturer at the department of sociology and work science, University of Gothenburg, Sweden. He has a PhD in sociology from the University of Gothenburg. His research mainly concerns social movements, protest, and the policing of social protest.

Nancy Whittier is Professor of Sociology at Smith College. She is the author of *The Politics of Child Sexual Abuse: Emotion, Social Movements, and the State, Feminist Generations*, and numerous articles on women's movements, collective identity, and culture. Her forthcoming book analyzes feminist and conservative influence on US federal policy on sexual violence.

INTRODUCTION

1 THE CONSEQUENCES OF SOCIAL MOVEMENTS

Taking stock and looking forward

Lorenzo Bosi, Marco Giugni, and Katrin Uba

Citizens of both democratic and authoritarian countries seem to become less supportive of those in power and more willing to use non-conventional forms of collective action for putting pressure on authorities. This was the case, for example, during the past few years, with the major upsurges of protest, in Eastern Europe (Coloured Revolutions), in the Middle East (Arab Spring), in Southern Europe (the *Indignados* in Spain, the *Agonaktismenoi* in Greece), in the United States (Occupy Wall Street), in Chile (the *Pinquinos*), as well as anti-government protests in Hong Kong, Thailand, and South Africa. Such waves of mobilization, comparable in their size to those of the 1960s and 1970s, bring to the fore some important questions for social movement research and call for a deeper understanding of social and political change: When and how does mobilization make a difference? When and how do activists achieve their goals? Is protest a necessary and/or sufficient condition for producing social and political change? Do social movements have any long-term legacies on our societies? Do they change the life choices of those participating in protest activities? How does all this vary both across contexts and across different movements?

These and related questions are not new, but until the 1970s scholars paid little attention to the consequences of social movements as

We would like to thank all the authors contributing to this volume and the Swedish Riksbankens Jubileumsfund for its generous support of the MOVEOUT network and its activities, especially the workshop held at Uppsala University in September 2012. We would also like to thank the reviews of this volume for their valuable feedback and the editing and proof-reading team at the Cambridge University Press protest was mainly regarded as an irrational action with no instrumental goals (Buechler 2004). Since then, also thanks to some pioneering works (Gamson 1990; Piven and Cloward 1979; Schumaker 1975), a new research field emerged slowly and allowed one of the present authors to note as late as in 1998 that "we still lack systematic empirical analyses that would add to our knowledge of the conditions under which movements produce certain effects" (Giugni 1998: 373). The field was revamped, amongst other things, also thanks to two edited collections entirely devoted to the study of different kinds of the effects of social movements (Giugni et al. 1998, 1999). This sudden focus on social movement outcomes could be related not only to the wave of democratization in the Eastern Europe and Latin America in the 1990s, but also to the fact that sufficient time had passed from the mobilization of the 1968 generation in Western Europe and civil rights mobilization in the United States. While research on social movements can study ongoing events, research on their outcomes has to wait for some changes to take place before being able to inquire into their causes. Even if the immediate political outcomes of Colored Revolutions or the Occupy movement seem self-evident, to find out about the broader cultural outcomes of such recent events one has to wait for a longer time.

Since the late 1990s, a wealth of studies have improved our knowledge of how collective mobilizations and protest activities may bring about social and political change. Scholarship has in particular focused on three broad types of outcomes. First, scholars interested in the personal and biographical consequences of social movements have studied "effects on the life-course of individuals who have participated in movement activities, effects that are at least in part due to involvement in those activities" (Giugni 2008: 1588–1589, see Giugni 2004a for a review). Second, cultural change or changes in the social norms and behaviors in which political actors operate, have been studied the least (see review in Earl 2004). The third, political change, or those effects of movement activities that alter in some way the movements' political environment, have been studied most often (see reviews in Amenta and Caren 2004; Amenta et al. 2010; Burstein and Linton 2002; Giugni 1998, 2008; Uba 2009). Research on the biographical, cultural, and political outcomes of social movements has provided a number of important insights into the conditions and processes through which movements succeed or fail. At the same time, however, there remain a number of silences that must be voiced. This book expressly addresses such silences. It challenges conventional studies of the consequences of social movements by covering issues on which there has been little or no research at all.

The volume covers such issues as the impact of social movements on the life-course of movement participants and the population in general (Part I: People), on political elites and markets (Part II: Policies), and on political parties and processes of social movement institutionalization (Part III: Institutions). We believe this volume makes a significant contribution to research on social movement outcomes by achieving three aims: (1) *theoretically*, by showing the importance of hitherto undervalued topics in the study of social movements outcomes; (2) *methodologically*, by expanding the scientific boundaries of this research field through an interdisciplinary approach and new methods of analysis; and (3) *substantially*, by providing new empirical evidence about social movement outcomes from Europe and the United States, such as mobilization for ethical fashion, protest against school-closures, institutionalization processes in deeply divided societies, and effects on activists of far-right and LGBT movements.

In the remainder of this chapter we introduce the contributions included in the volume. In doing this, we point to theoretical, methodological, and substantial developments made by scholarly work on each of the three issues mentioned above, on the one hand, and to remaining blind spots on all three counts, on the other. We conclude with some directions for future research.

People

Previous work on social movements and personal change

People might change for a variety of reasons over their lifetime: because they go to school, because they go through the army, because they find a partner (or split up from one), because they find a job (or lose a job), have children, move from where they live (neighborhood, city, country), because they meet new friends, because they go through particular transformative events. And among other reasons, people might change in part due to their involvement in social movement activities. This type of personal change is what interests us in this section. If contentious politics scholars have spent quite an amount of energy trying to explain why, when, and how people join social movements activities – with competing analytical approaches – it is also true that the post-movement lives of former activists have received some attention (see Giugni 2004a for a review).

Scholars focusing on the long-term biographical impact of movement participation have suggested through their empirical works, mainly concerning highly committed activists within the New Left in the United States, that activists in their post-movement lives tend to continue to espouse political attitudes close to those they embraced during their mobilization, and to show a high level of socio-political commitment and to pursue different lifestyles (jobs and structure of families) in concert with their beliefs (Fendrich 1993; McAdam 1988; Jennings 1987; Taylor and Raeburn 1995; Whalen and Flacks 1989; Wilhelm 1998; Whittier 1995). Further studies examining participation in other types of movements (Klatch 1999), less committed activists (Sherkat and Blocker 1997), and movements embracing political violence (Kampwirth 2004; Viterna 2013) have shown similar results, confirming that participation in social movements has long-term powerful and enduring effects on the political and personal lives of those who have been involved.

A more recent trend in the literature, rarely mentioned in relation to biographical outcomes, examines "institutional activists" (Grodsky 2012; Pettinicchio 2012; Santoro and McGuire 1997), also labeled "inside agitators" (Eisenstein 1996), "insider activists" (Banaszak 2010), "unobtrusive activists" (Katzenstein 1998), and "activists in office" (Watts 2006). Following this literature, past participation in social movements might continue to influence political action inside the institutions (Kim et al. 2013). In pursuing the movement's goals through conventional bureaucratic channels, "institutional activists" show their long-term commitment to the cause. For example, in the period spanning from the Kennedy to the Clinton administration, women's commitment to the feminist cause in the United States "creat[ed] concrete policy changes that altered the social landscape" of the country (Banaszak 2010: 4). Similar processes occurred in the north of Europe when environmentalists went into the political institutions through green parties (Rootes 2004).

In the case of regime changes, the impact of "institutional activists" is even clearer (Bosi, Chapter 14; Della Porta, forthcoming). Furthermore, activists retaining their commitments in their post-movement lives can also continue to participate politically and join new movements during their life-course. In doing so, they are "direct routes" in the spillover effect of frames, discourses, tactics, organizational structure, and identities occurring among different movements across time (Meyer and Whittier 1994; Whittier 2004).

In transforming individuals, social movements may also engender broad processes of social change. Social movement scholars have investigated, even if to a lesser extent, the aggregate-level change in life-course patterns, where social movements activism has much broader social and cultural consequences on society at large behind former social movement activists (McAdam 1999; Wilhelm 1998). Alternative lifestyle patterns, stripped of their original political or counter-cultural content, are diffused and adapted through socialization processes across new cohorts as new life-course norms in the long term. As Rochon notes, "the microfoundations of movement mobilization thus create new patterns of social thought and action, contributing to the breadth and pace of change in cultural values . . . The ripple effects of movement activism also have an impact on family, friends, and fellow members of a group" (1998: 162). The biographical consequences affect then not only those who were active participants in a cycle of protest, but also "many casual participants" (Polletta and Jasper 2001: 296).

Social movements are often presented in the literature as transforming their activists and societies in unintended ways. The category of unintended consequences has been attached to these types of outcomes because it has been said that social movements publicly claim policy changes. But social movements, through their everyday politics, publicly contest cultural values, opinions and beliefs with the aim of self-changing societies through "educating as well as mobilizing activists, and thereby promoting ongoing awareness and action that extends beyond the boundaries of one movement or campaign" (Meyer 2003: 35).

The chapters in Part I of the book

The five chapters that form Part I of this volume extend beyond existing research on biographical outcomes at the empirical, methodological, and analytical levels. Unlike the bulk of the literature on social movement outcomes, which is primarily interested in examining successful mobilizations, in Chapter 2, Karen Beckwith examines why social movement activists persist after experiences of loss. To address this question, the author examines two coalfield communities and women's activist experience in the National Union of Mineworkers (NUM) strike against the National Coal Board in Britain in the 1984–85 period, and compares remobilization efforts in the same communities in the NUM's 1992–94 anti-pit closure campaign. Testing competing explanations of political opportunity, political resources, and political learning, in her work Beckwith hypothesizes that the impact of loss upon future remobilization chances may be less dependent on the actual material circumstances of the actors or even on the issues involved than on the nature of the collective experience of the campaign. Former activists' experience in the course of a campaign – whether they have won or lost in the past – can lead to political learning that can instruct and inspire second attempts or lead to the decision to never try again.

In Chapter 3, Kathleen Blee uses extensive life history narratives with an innovative model that infers causal mechanisms from narrated counterfactual processes to understand, from the perspectives of activists themselves, the steps by which social movement involvement changes the lives of activists. In doing so, she draws on four fields of research in order to build her conceptual framework, the scholarships on narrative, on political imagination, on turning points, and on interpretive processes. Blee draws her empirical research from two rightwing women activists (a current member and a former activist of the US racist movement), analyzing their self-definitions before they entered the racist movement, their experiences of mobilization and participating in a racial movement, and their assessments of how they were affected by such activism.

In Chapter 4, Marco Giugni and Maria Grasso test the relationship between engagements in social movement activities, measured through participation in demonstrations, and the subsequent political life of participants (i.e., political interest, self-positioning on the left-right scale, voting for the left, membership in environmental organizations, and party membership). They use panel data on Switzerland to inquire whether low-degree engagement in social movement activities also has the strong impact observed by previous work on strongly committed activists. They find that previous participation in demonstrations in Switzerland significantly affected the participants' political attitudes and behaviors in the long term, namely fifteen years later. Their findings suggest that the results found on New Left activists in the United States are broadly generalizable to other countries, other cohorts, non-New Left activism, and lower levels of involvement.

In Chapter 5, Camille Masclet examines the unexplored topic of the intergenerational influence of social movements by looking at the specific case of feminist activists and their children. The analysis is based on a case study of women who took part in the French Women's

Liberation Movement in the 1970s and their offspring. Drawing on the political socialization and biographical outcomes literatures, in her chapter Masclet focuses on two main aspects: first, the study of the second generation and the issue of family transmission can add to our understanding of the activists' careers and the long-term effects of activism on their lives; second, the content of the political inheritance of the activists' children. The analysis reveals the existence of effects of the feminist movement on the children's political socialization. This chapter suggests another way of looking at aggregate-level changes through the study of the children of former social movements activists.

Finally, in Chapter 6, Nancy Whittier analyses aggregate-level biographical outcomes of the LGBT movement in the United States (specifically the gay and lesbian movements), focusing on collective identity as a biographical outcome in the broader population, the impact of cultural and policy change on life-course outcomes, and generational/cohortial variations. Whittier focuses first on collective identity definition and diffusion as conditioned by cohort for both participants and non-participants. She then looks at how cultural and policy outcomes affect the life-course of the beneficiary constituency, LGBT people. She focuses on the following life-course outcomes: employment and earnings, couplehood and marriage, and parenting.

Avenues for future research on social movements and personal change

The five chapters in this part of the book introduce unresearched themes, alongside new methodological and analytical approaches, which we hope will be developed further in future research on social movements and personal change. Yet, a number of avenues for future research on social movements and personal change may be mentioned as well. First, it is necessary for future research to focus on the life-course patterns of movements' targets, in addition to movements' activists and participants. Here the literature on victims of armed groups can be particularly helpful, specifically as it entails the trauma experienced by victims in both the short term and the long term (Bosi and Giugni 2012).

Second, more attention should be placed on variation among different types of biographical outcomes (Stewart et al. 1998; Corrigall-Brown 2012; Viterna 2013; Blee, Chapter 3; Masclet, Chapter 5). Once we have established that participating in social movements has a lasting effect on individuals, we should investigate differences among those who participate as we have looked at such differences in the mobilization process, for example, on their level of involvement, closeness to the leadership or previous biographical characteristics, etc. Jocelyn Viterna suggests in her important work (2013) that the arena where an activist demobilizes determines his/her post-movement activist life.

Third, if it is true that research on biographical consequences has been mainly biased toward studying social movements and personal change in Western countries among progressive movements, we should broaden our knowledge by starting to look at biographical outcomes in "awkward" movements (Viterna 2013; Blee, Chapter 3) and in non-Western societies (Hasso 2001; Viterna 2013).

Finally, we need to recognize the structure–agency dynamic shaping participants' post-movement lives (Bosi 2014), connecting biographical outcomes "to the historical contexts where they are developing" (Fillieule and Neveu 2014). If the literature on social movements has started progressively to move beyond the movement-centric approach explanations, this has not yet happened in the sub-field of research that examines biographical outcomes. Micro-level analyses are still very much concerned with how individual experience in social movements is fundamental for participants' post-movement lives, so they lose the rest of the picture. The rest of the picture concerns in particular the determining power of the modern state within the political and social environment, which is able to produce the external factors and forces that channel and mitigate contentious politics and thus ultimately shapes the post-movement lives of activists (Bosi 2014). In order to do this, we need to re-locate our studies on personal change at the intersection of thematic focus on disengagement/transformation/outcomes. This means we ought to study biographical outcomes together with conflicts' decline and post-conflict transformation of societies and institutions (Bosi 2014).

Policies

Previous work on social movements and policy change

Research on the consequences of social movement has long focused on political, and even more narrowly, policy outcomes, and still often does so (see Amenta and Caren 2004; Amenta et al. 2010 for reviews). Nearly twenty years ago, one of the present authors distinguished between two waves of scholarly work on the political outcomes of social movements and protest activities (Giugni 1998). The first wave, chronologically situated in the late 1960s and early 1970s, was mainly interested in the ability of social movements to be successful by focusing on movement-controlled variables. He then depicted the literature from this first wave, perhaps a bit simplistically, as being characterized by a double tension, or by two interrelated debates: one about the role of disruption versus moderation and another about the effectiveness of strongly organized movements versus loosely organized ones (see Gamson 1990).

Around the late 1990s, a second wave of scholarship on the policy outcomes of social movements emerged. With this new wave, attention shifted from an interest in the impact of movement-controlled variables to the role of the context, especially the political-institutional context. In this vein, a number of studies have shown that the political impact of social movements is conditional and contingent on political opportunity structures (e.g., institutional allies, state structures, political regimes) and public opinion (Agnone 2007; Amenta 2005, 2006; Amenta et al. 1992, 1994; Cress and Snow 2000; Huberts 1989; Kane 2003; Olzak and Soule 2009; Schumaker 1978; Soule and Olzak 2004; Uba 2009). In addition, some have shown that the impact of social movements varies across different stages of policy making, being more effective at the stages of agenda setting and less influential at the stages of adoption and implementation of policies (King et al. 2005; Soule and King 2006). The increased attention to context and exogenous factors did not mean that strategies of movements were neglected, rather it was emphasized that strategies and tactics should be seen in its cultural settings. Thus, for example, Banaszak (1996) has shown how movement tactics, beliefs, and values are critical in understanding why political movements succeed or fail.

Since then, scholars have made a lot of progress. For instance, they recognized that policies are not only adopted by state authorities, but also by businesses, and there is a growing research field on how social movements influence change of corporate practices and policies (see King and Pearce 2010 for a review). This scholarship also suggests that the impact of social movements is often conditional on movement controlled factors, such as stakeholders' activism, and contextual factors such as the type of enterprises (Bartley and Child 2011; King 2008; Vasi and King 2012).

Apart from progress made because of the broadened empirical scope of these studies, as well as availability of more sophisticated techniques, the major progress of the field is related to the "episodes-processes-mechanisms" turn proposed by McAdam et al. (2001; see further Tarrow and Tilly 2007). A number of scholars have started to identify and unveil the causal mechanisms that allow movements to have an impact on policy. Among the pieces that we consider valuable in this respect are Andrews' (2004) study of the impact of the civil rights movement on poverty programs and Kolb's (2007) comparison of the political outcomes of the civil rights movement and anti-nuclear energy movements. Both these works explicitly address mechanisms linking movement action to political outcomes. Andrews (2001) argues that movements must be able to create leverage through multiple mechanisms, such as disruption, persuasion, and negotiation, in order to be successful. Kolb (2007) stresses a number of causal mechanisms of political change, such as the disruption, public preference, political access, judicial, and international politics mechanisms.

But others have wandered along this path as well. For example, in their effort to put forward their political mediation model, Amenta and his collaborators (Amenta et al. 1992; see further Amenta 2005) distinguished between four different models of social movement formation and outcomes, which can be seen as four potential mechanisms of influence: economic models, social movements models, political opportunity models, and the political mediation model. Others have distinguished between three main models of movement influence: the direct-effect, indirect-effect, and joint-effect models (Giugni 2004b, 2007). Again, we may look at these models as possible mechanisms relating protest to policy change. The way these mechanisms work, however, is contingent upon context. Thus, for example, while Giugni (2004b) did not find much direct effect of disruption in the United States, Italy, or Switzerland, Uba (2005) showed that for explaining the varying impact of anti-privatization protests in India, the disruption mechanism is more useful than the persuasion one. Yet, these efforts were not explicitly putting forward mechanisms and processes. Quite on the contrary, they were quite static in their emphasis on political-institutional conditions.

The chapters in Part II of the book

The four chapters forming Part II of this volume all attest to the importance of comparisons and, above all, mechanisms in the study of social movement outcomes. Katrin Uba looks in Chapter 7 at policy makers' attitudes vis-à-vis different forms of protest. She examines more specifically the extent to which politicians accept protest against school closures in Sweden. She maintains that relating effectiveness to targets' attitudes helps understand why the political context plays a role in explaining the varying outcomes of disruptive protests. The underlying assumption here is that politicians who have positive attitudes toward protest are more likely to listen to activists' claims and be more responsive to their arguments. Combining survey and protest event data pertaining to Swedish municipalities, her study suggests that both personal background and the power position of the targets of social movements are key to the explanation of their attitudes on protest actions as well as on how they respond to such actions. Attitudes and perceptions here can be seen as a crucial mechanism allowing us to account for why and how policy makers positively respond to social movements' demands.

In his contribution in Chapter 8, Joseph Luders raises the question of why do the targets of social movements and other benefit-seekers groups concede to their demands at center stage. He rightly sees the answer to this question as key to understanding the policy impact of movements. In order to provide an answer to this question, he outlines a general explanation for the influence of benefit-seekers – a term that includes both social movements and interest organizations – on political actors. The fundamental mechanism in this explanation, in his view, lies in how targets assess the costs of acceding or resisting: variation in exposure to costs accounts for different responses of targets and bystanders. He then illustrates empirically the proposed explanation through the case of the contemporary women's movement, looking at its multiple demands. The latter aspect is important as it shows that, in addition to cross-national and cross-movement comparisons, it is also important to compare across different demands made by a given movement. Additionally, his study points, among other things, to the need for a more fine-grained inspection of movements as diverse entities with multiple agendas.

The other two chapters shift the focus of the analysis from political-institutional targets to economic ones, looking at the responsiveness of corporate actors and of fashion-market actors. Brayden King looks in Chapter 9 at business corporations as potential targets of social movements. Starting from the observation that activists are often able to pressure corporate targets to reform their practices and policies, but that the mechanisms whereby activists influence corporate behavior are still largely unknown, he proposes a theory of social movement effectiveness in corporate campaigns stressing two economic mechanisms that give movements leverage to influence corporate targets: reputational threats and creations of risk perceptions. On the one hand, movements may generate reputational threats by using tactics to communicate negative image claims about their corporate targets that undermine the firms' cultivated reputations. On the other hand, they may create perceptions that a firm's actions are financially risky. He concludes by arguing that a theory of corporate-targeted movement outcomes should consider the effects of movement tactics on these intangible sources of economic value.

Finally, Philip Balsiger examines in Chapter 10 the rise of ethical fashion in Switzerland as an example of the impact of social movements on markets, an aspect that has long been overlooked by students of social movements until recently. He addresses the role of tactical competition, asking how the interplay of different tactics used by different movement players shape market change such as the emergence of niches. He looks more specifically at three different approaches adopted by social movement to promote ethnical fashion: launching campaigns targeting fashion brands, developing ethnical labels, and promoting an alternative ethical fashion niche. He shows, based on ethnographic materials, that the transformations of the clothing market in Switzerland are the result of the interplay between such different approaches. His analysis points to the importance of a dynamic approach to the study of the consequences of social movements, one which takes into account the interplay of movement actors using different tactics and, more generally, the diversity within the social movement arena. This may provide important insights into the mechanisms and processes through which social movements bring about social change.

Avenues for future research on social movements and policy change

Notwithstanding the major advances provided by scholarship in the past fifteen years or so, including those offered in this book, there is still much margin for improvement. In this regard, a number of avenues for further research can be outlined. We already mentioned two of them: embedding the study of the political consequences of social movements in a comparative research deign and looking at the mechanisms and processes connecting movement actions to observed outcomes. No need to come back to that. But there are other paths that future research could and should take. Perhaps the most important one comes out forcefully from the four chapters in this part of the book: focusing on targets. All four chapters put at center stage not only what movements do and how they do it, but also which are the targets of protest, how they see the protest as well as the movements, and how they react to them. This implies redefining the political consequences of social movements in two directions. On the one hand, a closer attention to the target of protest requires thinking of social movement outcomes in terms of responsiveness. On the other hand, and related to that, in order to better understand how social movements can obtain responsiveness, one needs to refocus the analysis on the targets of protest, that is, those who are supposed to respond. These are often represented by policy makers – which is the main focus of much research in this field – but they can also be other actors, including economic actors, as shown by the chapters in this part of this book. In brief, one should not only look at what movements do and how they do it, but also to who the targets of the challenges they pose are, what they do, and why.

In addition to multiplying comparative analyses (across countries or other political-administrative levels, movements, and movement demands), shifting the focus from conditions to mechanisms and processes, and especially paying more attention to targets, a few other suggestions for further research, mainly methodological, may be made. Four of them are worth mentioning, as they promise to push the boundaries of research on the policy impact of social movements a step farther. The first consists in considering the interplay of different levels of analyses. Research so far has most often focused on a single level – the macro-level or the meso-level, in case of policy outcomes – paying only little attention or no attention at all at the other two levels. Scholars should acknowledge that, in the end, those who can respond to the challenges and demands by social movements are individual policy makers. One therefore needs to consider how collective action (macro-level) can lead to policy change (macro-level) through the intervention of individual decisions (micro-level).

A second suggestion that can be made originates in the very early days of research on the political outcomes of social movements, namely in Gamson's (1990) seminal work. His study was based on a random sample of US challenging groups, albeit a small one made of fifty-three groups. In spite of its innovative character at the time, this approach was almost completely ignored by scholars interested in the consequences of social movements (while it was of course adopted repeatedly by those addressing individual participation in social movements). Sampling was recently given new legitimacy by Burstein (2014), who maintains that this is a key methodological device one should adopt when studying social movements and in particular their policy outcomes. Sampling was also adopted, in combination with more qualitative techniques such as fuzzy set / Qualitative Comparative Analysis and process tracing, by McAdam and Boudet (2012) in their study of opposition to energy projects in the United States. The lesson we draw from these efforts is that, unless one cannot examine the entire population of policies (Uba 2005), which, however, limits external validity, this research strategy proves extremely helpful if one is interested in causal inference.

A third suggestion is to combine rigorous quantitative methods of analysis (e.g., multi-level modeling, event history analysis) with more qualitative techniques (e.g., in-depth interviews, process tracing) in order to move from the search for simple correlations to causal thinking. This also requires that scholars do not focus only on short-term processes, but evaluate as well the long-term consequences of mobilization.

A fourth and final suggestion consists in making more extended use of experimental data. Experimental designs have been used to study the effectiveness of interest groups (Richardson 2013), but to our knowledge they have never been applied to the analysis of the policy impact of social movement tactics. Again, this would help moving from a correlational to a causal approach. For example, one could conduct lab experiments allowing to effectively establish causal relationship or, even better, field experiments (i.e., experimental designs in "real world" situations), thus avoiding the well-known shortcomings of the former. Quasi-experiments would be a good compromise when truly experimental designs are not possible.

Institutions

Previous work on social movements and institutional change

Institutional change takes a central place in political science and sociology alike. Not surprisingly, there are different definitions of change as well as different approaches to the role of social movements in this process (Amenta and Ramsey 2010; Clemens 1998; Schneiberg and Lounsbury 2008). Defining institutions as the basic rules of the game, one can mention changes in formal institutions such as state structure, political regime, legislation, corporations and their policies, and informal institutions such as unwritten rules (Helmke and Levitsky 2004). The following discussion leaves aside institutions in terms of norms or social practices. The role of social movement in changing such institutions is the best covered by research on cultural consequences of social movements (see Earl 2004 for review). Another approach to study institutions is looking at them as state organizations (government, parliament, bureaucracy) and non-state organizations (religious, cultural, medical, or educational organizations). Institutional change is also examined in various ways. Some scholars focus on the incremental change of power relations or on the sequential change of formal and informal institutions or on slowly changing norms (see Mahoney and Thelen 2009 for a review). Others, on the other hand, investigate the abrupt transformation of organizations, regime changes via revolutions, or significant policy changes during instances of crisis (Greenwood and Hinings 1996; Goldstone 2001; Kriesi and Wisler 1999).

The role of agency in explaining institutional change has become increasingly popular, for instance, many have studied the role of political leaders and their ideas for institutional change (Beland 2007). The explicit impact of social movements on institutional change has been examined much less (see Scheinberg and Lounsbury 2008 for a review). Many such studies focus on changes in state or corporate policies, but a few also look at changes in state structures, for example, changes in party systems (Hanagan 1998) or political regimes (Hipsher 1998).

One of the first systematic attempts to examine the impact of social movements on institutional change was made by Kitschelt (1986) in his already mentioned comparative study on anti-nuclear movements. He showed that the emergence of Green parties is related to the mobilization of anti-nuclear power movements, which thereby have influence on political opportunity structures in general and party systems more specifically. Since his influential work, there has been a steady increase in the number of studies investigating the relationship between social movements and institutional change.

An important mechanism facilitating such interaction is the institutionalization of social movements. This means that social movements can achieve their goals by becoming more professional, hierarchal, and cooperating closely with authorities such as political parties, international organizations, or state bureaucracies (Banaszak 2010; Costain 1981; Giugni and Passy 1998; Gusfield 1955; Meyer 2007; Ruzza 1997; Seippel 2001; Suh 2011; Zald et al. 2005). For example, Staggenborg (1988) showed how the pro-choice movement in the United States created new opportunities for influencing policy change via institutionalization. Similarly, Cowell-Meyers (2014) demonstrates how the women's movement in Northern Ireland created its own political party and increased thereby women' access to political system. However, the consequences of institutionalization vary and a recent comparative study on women's movements shows that autonomous movements rather than insider lobbying were instrumental for the adoption of legislation to combat violence against women (Htun and Weldon 2012). This variation is not surprising because such a close cooperation with authorities involves a threat of co-optation and de-mobilization (Coy and Hedeen 2005; Meyer and Minkoff 2004; Meyer and Tarrow 1998; Piven and Cloward 1979).

Despite the significant importance of the question of institutionalization, there are only a few studies that empirically examine how the factors external to movements influence this process. For example, Suh's (2011) analysis of Korea's women's movement demonstrates international organizations and regime responsiveness facilitated the institutionalization process of this movement. Similarly to the argument on political consequences institutionalization is not determined by structural factors, but contingent to many different contextual factors.

Another approach for studying how social movements influence institutions consists in investigating radical institutional change, particularly regime change via revolution or a slow transition to democracy (Goldstone 1998; Goodwin 2001; Hipsher 1998; Tilly 1978) or the outcomes of self-determination movements (see Gurr 2015 for a review). There are also many studies about how regime change influences social movements (Maney 2007; Pickvance 1999), the two processes being obviously related to each other. However, we focus here on the consequences of mobilization in the first place. Several studies have shown that the achievement of movements' revolutionary goals – that is, regime change – is facilitated by coalition building across different movements (Schock 2005) and elites (Slater 2009). Movement tactics are also an important factor. Based on a large sample of cases,

Chenoweth and Stephan (2011) show that nonviolent strategies or civil resistance tends to be more successful in achieving regime change than violent strategies. On the other hand, revolutionary movements might be successful at some point in time, but fail later on. For instance, Meirowitz and Tucker (2013) look at the cases of Arab Spring and Coloured Revolutions, showing that the actions of the initial governments after democratization can easily bring about new mobilizations and new radical change of institutions. Considering the recent events in the world, the role of movements in the process of regime change is an increasingly important question and emerging studies focus particularly on the impact of new media in this process (Breuer et al. 2015).

The chapters in Part III of the book

Similarly to the challenges posed by the study of other types of consequences of social movement actions (Earl 2000; Jenkins and Form 2005), investigating the impact of social movements on regime change, or institutional change more generally, requires careful analysis of other possible explanatory factors than mobilization itself and detailed tracking of entire, often even repeated, processes of change. The four chapters forming Part III of this volume address some of these challenges successfully.

In Chapter 11, Daniela Piccio, addresses a much neglected issue in the studies of the consequences of social movements. The chapter investigates how social movements interact with formal political institutions, such as political parties, in a comparative perspective. She explains the varying impact of ecology movements on the Dutch Social Democratic Party and the Italian Christian Democratic Party. The impact is measured as the changed discourse and organization of these political parties. The results of her detailed comparative analysis show that electoral benefits and ideological distance between the movement and party, that is, the factors usually emphasized in prior research, are not enough to explain the variation in movement impact on parties. The movement had small, but still noteworthy, discursive and organizational impact on the least likely case of Italian Christian Democrats, while in the most likely case, the Dutch Social Democrats, the party adopted an unexpectedly small amount of ecological claims.

In Chapter 12, Mattias Wahlström studies how protests and related police actions influenced the change of one of the most stable institutions – a state's bureaucracy. His careful comparative analysis shows how the changes in practices of police organizations followed the failed protest policing in Sweden, Denmark, the United Kingdom, and the United States, but not in Italy. This investigation shows that for better understanding of changed bureaucratic practices, we need to look beyond the factors emphasized by social movement scholars, particularly the political opportunity structures, or the well-known arguments from the research on institutional change, namely international learning process. The change in police practices was more related to characteristics of police organization and the triggering protest events.

In Chapter 13, Abby Peterson examines another rigid institution, looking at how social movements influence party systems. She investigates how the Swedish Neo-Nazi movement transformed into a political party – the Swedish Democrats. She provides a detailed theory-driven empirical description of important events and relationships that helps us to understand how a relatively small movement can affect the entire party system. Her analysis also shows the benefits of combining research on social movement institutionalization to the theories of political party institutionalization, particularly emphasizing the interplay between emerging parties and established parties. The empirical case has a significant importance for Swedish politics today, as in the parliamentary elections of 2014 the party received 13% of votes.

Finally, in Chapter 14, Lorenzo Bosi examines the complex interplay of regime change and social movements, focusing on the shifting balance of power relations at different stages of the movements' institutionalization process. He provides a detailed empirical description of the institutionalization of the Northern Ireland Civil Rights Movement and shows how the transformation of this movement affected the incremental regime change in Northern Ireland. Bosi's work does not tend to fall in the trap of creating a rigid and deterministic vision of development sequences toward institutionalization process, but rather to suggest a dynamic strategic-relational approach capable of recognize the shifting complex web of sociopolitical relations. The method he uses – process tracing – not only helps the reader to trace the complicated interactions between the movement and democratizing authorities, but also shows the usefulness of this method for the study of the consequences of social movements.

Avenues for future research on social movements and institutional change

All the chapters in this part of the book address the structural impact of social movements from a new angle. However, there are a few aspects that may be pushed further in future research. First, it is worth following the example discussed by Bosi in Chapter 14, and examine further why some strands of the movement institutionalize and others not. How this affects the relations between these two strands, the movement in general, and how the differences of state regime affect such developments. Such knowledge helps us better understand the development of social movements, but also the emergence of political parties. One interesting case study could be the institutionalization of the Spanish movement M15, which gave roots to three different political parties – Podemos, Ganemos, and Partido X.

Second, the thin line between co-optation and institutionalization has been examined before, but we need to learn more about the reasons why party members and bureaucrats listen to movements' claims. While, in the case of decision-makers, one can refer to their interest in being re-elected, this should not matter for those working in the state's bureaucracy. However, as shown by Wahlström (Chapter 12), bureaucratic institutions do change as a result of mobilizations. Similarly, the motives of political parties for listening and responding movements' claims also require more analysis than the present research provides. Scholars interested in this issues might learn a lot from the literature on political party and party system development (Mair 1997), as well as from research on public administration and planning (Thomas 2013).

Third, and related to the previous point, more attention should be paid on the content of the claims formulated and framed by activists. This has been shown to be important for policy change (McCammon 2009), but it is likely that clear problem formulations, new information for solving the problems at hand, or proposed alternative solutions play an important role for the movements' impact on institutional change. While elected officials care about votes, those working in bureaucracy, appointed officials, might be more interested in information that helps to solve particular problems (Besley and Coate 2003).

Fourth, and more closely related to regime change, students of the consequences of social movements would benefit much from paying

more attention to the wide literature on transition to democracy, revolutions, as well as the outcomes of self-determination movements (Della
Porta, forthcoming). This has benefited research on civil resistance
(Chenoweth and Stephan 2011), and would also help us better explain
the complex interrelations between movements and state authorities,
especially in non-democratic contexts. The last aspect also emphasizes
the importance of thinking beyond the electoral interests of decision-
makers when explaining the reasons why targets respond to activists'
demands.

Fifth, although some of the chapters in Part III use comparative
case-studies (Piccio, Wahlström), we still know little about how structural factors affect the impact movements have on institutional change.
The same applies for different types of movements and their claims.
Hence, future research would benefit from comparative analyses, both
across countries and across movements as well as over time. The latter is
particularly important for understanding how the consequences of
mobilization change in time and whether the effects are the same regardless of prior experiences.

Toward greater synergy

All the chapters in this volume fill some important research gaps in the
study of the consequences of social movements and help us better understand how movements may bring about personal, policy, and institutional
change. These contributions, however, are still largely confined to a given
type of movement outcome, each one addressing one type of outcome at a
time. Furthermore, when presenting the chapters, we also indicate some
avenues for future research, but again remaining within the specific types
of outcome examined in the chapter at hand. We believe it is now time to
go beyond such a segmented approach – for all the benefits it provided
and will keep providing – and try to move to greater synergy in the field.
By that we mean moving from an approach that looks only at one type of
movement outcome to a new perspective that embraces different types at
the same time and that look at how one type of outcome may "spill over"
another type (Bosi 2011).

To be sure, this has already been done to some extent. For
example, Rochon and Mazmanian (1993) maintained as far back as in
the early 1990s that substantial policy effects, or "new advantages," are

more easily obtained once a movement or movement organization has first obtained "acceptance," that is, a procedural effect. Along similar lines, Camille Masclet (Chapter 5) in looking at the intergenerational influence of social movements implicitly addresses the interrelated agenda by showing how the biographical effect on the activists has a lasting effect on their children. However, these works are still confined to one single kind of outcome (political or biographical), however large it is. We need to move beyond that, if we are to open up new avenues for future research and push the boundaries of our knowledge from the consequences of social movements to how social movements are capable to generate processes of social change.

The final chapter does precisely so. Jennifer Earl refers in Chapter 15 to four different types of outcomes – policy, cultural, internal to the movement, and biographical – in relation to Internet activism. She discusses various ways of understanding and evaluating the potential impacts of different forms of Internet activism. More specifically, she presents and reviews research on four broad types of Internet activism and discusses how effective or ineffective these forms of actions could be, also compared to the consequences of similar offline mobilizations. For instance, online participation has arguably the highest potential for achieving independent consequences.

The approach suggested by Jennifer Earl in her contribution, which she applies to Internet activism, can be made more general. One way to do so consists in looking at the interrelated effects of social movements and question. Both Nancy Whittier (Chapter 6) and Lorenzo Bosi (Chapter 14), without explicitly taking forward the interrelated outcomes agenda, suggest trajectories of change through which social movement outcomes may mutually affect each other: political-biographical and political-cultural (Whittier) and biographical-political (Bosi). By giving a short example of what we mean, we might suggest to look at how cultural outcomes "spill over" political ones. *In the long term, cultural changes can be translated into different policies, or in the short term introduce new problems from the private realm to the public agenda.* Social movements have the ability to raise the salience and public profile of a particular set of issues by introducing changes in cultural values, opinions, and beliefs to social and political public discourses (Rochon and Mazmanian 1993; Rochon 1998; Meyer 1999, 2005; Polletta and Jasper 2001). Therefore, movements that win victories in terms of political culture, even where they have suffered immediate defeats on policy issues, can obtain public policy gains in the long term. Strong and clear changes in public opinion that are favorable to the movement's "message" provide the opportunity to significantly influence the process of public policy change, albeit indirectly. Elected officials will, where they see prospects of electoral success and/or support for their mission, follow changes in public discourses by placing a movement's "message" on the political agenda, co-opting it for the governmental agenda, and initiating a change in legislation (Baumgartner and Jones 1993; Burstein 1998, 1999; Burstein and Freudenburg 1978; Burstein and Linton 2002). "[L]egislators – [as Burstein writes] – must become convinced that the issue is so important to the public that its votes will be affected by what the legislature does, or fails to do. And it is important that the shift be large and clear because legislators want to be sure that their votes reflect real changes in public opinion – changes not likely to be reversed before the next election, when their votes may be held against them" (1998: 37). Therefore, policy makers pay much attention to the public perceptions of an issue, and are likely to respond in a way that will satisfy such perceptions, especially if they are considered to reflect a majority opinion. For example, Kane (2003) finds that public opinion, which she sees as a form of cultural opportunity, has helped gay and lesbian movements in decriminalizing sodomy laws in American states.

What needs to be determined accurately is how, when, and where interrelated effects are likely to take place (Bosi 2011). We have to ask more complex questions about the extent and operation of interrelated effects of social movement outcomes. For example: How do different types of effects of protest activities relate to each other? What are the processes and mechanisms underlying the interrelations between different types of effects or between the same types of effect over time? Under what conditions does each interrelation of effects work, fail to occur, or even reverse? Are some types of interrelations more frequently observed than others? How do such interrelations vary across different types of non-electoral behavior (for example, between right-wing and left-wing movements)? Which kinds of methodological developments are required for studying these interrelated processes and mechanisms?

Answering these questions makes the research on the consequences of social movements even more challenging, both theoretically and methodologically. Still, it is worth taking up the challenge.

References

Agnone, Jon. 2007. "Amplifying Public Opinion: The Policy Impact of the U.S. Environmental Movement." *Social Forces*, 85: 1593–1620.

Amenta, Edwin. 2005. "Political Contexts, Challenger Strategies, and Mobilization: Explaining the Impact of the Townsend Plan." In David S. Meyer, Valerie Jenness, and Helen Ingram (eds.), *Routing the Opposition*. Minneapolis: University of Minnesota Press, 29–64.

Amenta, Edwin. 2006. *When Movements Matter: The Townsend Plan and the Rise of Social Security*. Princeton: Princeton University Press.

Amenta, Edwin and Kelly M. Ramsey. 2010. "Institutional Theory." In Kevin T. Leicht and J. Craig Jenkins (eds.), *Handbook of Politics: State and Society in Global Perspective*. New York: Springer, 15–39.

Amenta, Edwin and Neal Caren. 2004. "The Legislative, Organizational, and Beneficiary Consequences of State-Oriented Challengers." In David A. Snow, Sarah Soule, and Hanspeter Kriesi (eds.), *The Blackwell Companion to Social Movements*. Oxford: Blackwell, 461–488.

Amenta, Edwin Amenta, Neal Caren, Elizabeth Chiarello, and Yang Su. 2010. "The Political Consequences of Social Movements." *Annual Review of Sociology*, 36: 287–307.

Amenta Edwin, Bruce G. Carruthers, and Yvonne Zylan. 1992. "A Hero for the Aged? The Townsend Movement, the Political Mediation Model, and U.S. Old-Age Policy, 1934–1950." *American Journal of Sociology*, 98: 308–339.

Amenta, Edwin, Katleen Dunleavy, and Mary Bernstein. 1994. "Stolen Thunder? Huey Long's 'Share our Wealth,' Political Mediation, and the Second New Deal." *American Sociological Review*, 59: 678–702.

Andrews, Kenneth T. 2001. "Social Movements and Policy Implementation: The Mississippi Civil Rights Movement and the War on Poverty, 1965 to 1971." *American Sociological Review*, 66: 71–95.

Andrews, Kenneth. 2004. *Freedom is a Constant Struggle: The Mississippi Civil Rights Movement and Its Legacy*. Chicago: University of Chicago Press.

Armstrong, Elizabeth A. and Mary Bernstein. 2008. "Culture, Power, and Institutions: A Multi-Institutional Politics Approach to Social Movements." *Sociological Theory*, 26: 74–99.

Banaszak, Lee Ann. 2010. *The Women's Movement Inside and Outside the State*. New York: Cambridge University Press.

Bartley, Tim and Curtis Child. "Movements, Markets and Fields: The Effects of Anti-Sweatshop Campaigns on U.S. Firms, 1993–2000." *Social Forces*, 90: 425–451.

Baumgartner, Frank R. and Bryan D. Jones. 1993. *Agendas and Instability in American Politics*. Chicago: University of Chicago Press.

Beland, Daniel. 2007. "Ideas and Institutional Change in Social Security: Conversion, Layering, and Policy Drift." *Social Science Quarterly*, 88(1): 20–38.

Bennett, Andrew. 2010. "Process Tracing and Causal Inference." In Henry E. Brady and David Collier (eds.), *Rethinking Social Inquiry*, Second edition. Lanham, MD: Rowman and Littlefield.

Besley, Timothy and Stephen Coate. 2003. "Centralized versus Decentralized Provision of Local Public Goods: A Political Economy Approach." *Journal of Public Economics*, 12: 2611–2637.

Bosi, Lorenzo. 2011. "Movimenti e cambiamento sociale: l'interrelazione delle conseguenze." *Società degli Individui*, 42: 69–78.

Bosi, Lorenzo. 2014. "Contextualizing the Biographical Outcomes of Provisional IRA Former Activists: A Structure-Agency Dynamic." unpublished paper, presented at the conference *Actvists Forever? The Long-term Impacts of Political Actvisim in Various Contexts*. Rennes, France.

Bosi, Lorenzo and Marco Giugni. 2012. "The Study of the Consequences of Armed Groups: Lessons from the Social Movement Literature." *Mobilization*, 17(1):85–98.

Breuer, Anita, Todd Landman, and Dorothea Farquhar. 2015. "Social Media and Protest Mobilization: Evidence from the Tunisian Revolution." *Democratization*, 22, 764–792.

Buechler, Steven M. 2004. *The Blackwell Companion to Social Movements*, edited by David A. Snow, Sarah Soule, and Hanspeter Kriesi. Oxford: Blackwell, 47–66.

Burstein, Paul. 1998. *Discrimination, Jobs, and Politics*, Second edition. Chicago: University of Chicago Press.

Burstein, Paul. 1999. "Social Movements and Public Policy." In Marco Giugni, Doug McAdam, and Charles Tilly (eds.), *How Social Movements Matter*. Minneapolis: University of Minnesota Press, 3–21.

Burstein, Paul. 2014. *American Public Opinion, Advocacy, and Policy in Congress: What the Public Wants and What It Gets*. Cambridge: Cambridge University Press.

Burstein, Paul and William Freudenburg. 1978. "Changing Public Policy: The Impact of Public Opinion, Anti-War Demonstrations and War Costs on Senate Voting on Vietnam War Motions." *American Journal of Sociology*, 84: 99–122.

Burstein, Paul and April Linton. 2002. "The Impact of Political Parties, Interest Groups, and Social Movement Organizations on Public Policy: Some Recent Evidence and Theoretical Concerns." *Social Forces*, 81:380–408.

Busby, Joshua. 2010. *Moral Movements and Foreign Policy*. Cambridge: Cambridge University Press.

Chenoweth, Erica and Maria J. Stephan. 2011. *Why Civil Resistance Works: The Strategic Logic of Nonviolent Conflict*. New York: Columbia University Press.

Clemens, Elisabeth S. 1998. "To Move Mountains: Collective Action and the Possibility of Institutional Change." In Marco Giugni, Doug McAdam, and Charles Tilly (eds.), *From Contention to Democracy*. Lanham, MD: Rowman and Littlefield, 109–123.

Corrigall-Brown, Catherine. 2012. "From the Balconies to the Barricades, and Back? Trajectories of Participation in Contentious Politics." *Journal of Civil Society*, 8(1):17–38.

Costain, Anne N. 1981. "Representing Women: The Transition from Social Movement to Interest Group." *The Western Political Quarterly*, 34: 100–113.

Costain, Anne N. and Steven Majstorovic. 1994. "Congress, Social Movements and Public Opinion: Multiple Origins of Women's Rights Legislation." *Political Research Quarterly*, 47:111–135.

Cowell-Meyers, Kimberly. B. 2014. "The Social Movement as Political Party: The Northern Ireland Women's Coalition and the Campaign for Inclusion." *Perspectives on Politics*, 12(01):61–80.

Coy, Patrick G. and Timothy Hedeen. 2005. "A Stage Model of Social Movement Co-optation: Community Mediation in the United States." *The Sociological Quarterly*, 46(3):405–435.

Cress, Daniel M. and David A. Snow. 2000. "The Outcomes of Homeless Mobilization: The Influence of Organization, Disruption, Political Mediation, and Framing." *American Journal of Sociology*, 105: 1063–1104.

Della Porta, Donatella. Forthcoming. *Where Did the Revolution Go? The Outcomes of Democratization Paths*. Cambridge: Cambridge University Press.

Earl, Jennifer. 2000. "Methods, Movements, and Outcomes. Methodological Difficulties in the Study of Extra-Movement Outcomes." *Research in Social Movements, Conflicts and Change*, 22:3–25.

Earl, Jennifer. 2004. "The Cultural Consequences of Social Movements." In David A. Snow, Sarah Soule, and Hanspeter Kriesi (eds.), *The Blackwell Companion to Social Movements*. Oxford: Blackwell, 508–530.

Eisenstein, Hester. 1996. *Inside Agitators*. Philadelphia: Temple University Press.

Fendrich, James. 1993. *Ideal Citizens*. Albany: State University of New York Press.

Fillieule, Olivier and Erik Neveu. 2014. "Actvists Forever? The Long-term Impacts of Political Actvisim in Various Contexts." Unpublished paper, Conference, Rennes, France.

Finkel, Steven E. and Edward N. Muller. 1998. "Rational Choice and the Dynamics of Collective Political Action: Evaluating Alternative Models with Panel Data." *American Political Science Review*, 92:37–49.

Gamson, William A. 1990. *The Strategy of Social Protest*, Second edition. Belmont, CA: Wadsworth Publishing.

Gamson, William A. and Emilie Schmeidler. 1994. "Organizing the Poor." *Theory and Society*, 13:567–585.

Giugni, Marco. 2004a. "Personal and Biographical Consequences." In David A. Snow, Sarah Soule, and Hanspeter Kriesi (eds.), *The Blackwell Companion to Social Movements*. Oxford: Blackwell, 489–507.

Giugni, Marco. 2004b. *Social Protest and Policy Change*. Lanham, MD: Rowman and Littlefield.

Giugni, Marco. 2007. "Useless Protest? A Time-series Analysis of the Policy Outcomes of Ecology, Antinuclear, and Peace Movements in the United States, 1975–1995." *Mobilization*, 12: 101–116.

Giugni, Marco. 2008. "Political, Biographical, and Cultural Consequences of Social Movements." *Sociology Compass*, 2: 1582–1600.

Giugni, Marco and Lorenzo Bosi. 2012. "The Impact of Protest Movements on the Establishment: Dimensions, Models, Approaches." In Kathrin Fahlenbrach, Martin Klimke, Joachim Scharloth, and Laura Wong (eds.), *The Establishment Responds: Power, Politics, and Protest since 1945*. New York: Palgrave, 17–28.

Giugni, Marco and Florence Passy. 1998. "Contentious Politics in Complex Societies." In Marco Giugni, Doug McAdam, and Charles Tilly (eds.), *From Contention to Democracy*. Lanham, MD: Rowman and Littlefield, 81–108.

Giugni, Marco, Doug McAdam, and Charles Tilly (eds.). 1998. *From Contention to Democracy*. Lanham, MD: Rowman and Littlefield.

Giugni, Marco, Doug McAdam, and Charles Tilly (eds.). 1999. *How Social Movements Matter*. Minneapolis: University of Minnesota Press.

Giugni, Marco, Lorenzo Bosi, and Katrin Uba. 2013. "Outcomes of Social Movements and Protest Activities." *Oxford Bibliographies Online: Political Science*. doi:10.1093/obo/9780199756223–0037.

Goldstone, Jack. A. 1998. "Social Movements or Revolutions?" In Marco Giugni, Doug McAdam, and Charles Tilly (eds.), *From Contention to Democracy*. Lanham, MD: Rowman and Littlefield, 125–145.

Goldstone, Jack. A. 2001. "Toward a Fourth Generation of Revolutionary Theory." *Annual Review of Political Science*, 4(1): 139–187.

Goldstone, Jack A. (ed.). 2003. *States, Parties, and Social Movements*. Cambridge: Cambridge University Press.

Goldstone, Jack A. and Doug McAdam. 2001. "Contention in Demographic and Life-Course Context." In Ronald Aminzade, Jack Goldstone, Doug McAdam, Elizabeth Perry, William H. Sewell Jr., Sidney Tarrow, and Charles Tilly (eds.), *Silence and Voice in the Study of Contentious Politics*. Cambridge and New York: Cambridge University Press, 195, 195–221.

Goodwin, Jeff. 2001. *No Other Way Out: States and Revolutionary Movements, 1945–1991*. Cambridge, UK: Cambridge University Press.

Greenwood, Royston, and Christopher R. Hinings. 1996. "Understanding Radical Organizational Change: Bringing Together the Old and the New Institutionalism." *Academy of Management Review*, 21(4): 1022–1054.

Grodsky, Brian K. 2012. *Social Movements and the New State: The Fate of Pro-Democracy Organizations When Democracy is Won.* Stanford, CA: Stanford University Press.

Gurr, Ted Robert. 1980. "On the Outcomes of Violent Conflict." In Ted Robert Gurr (ed.), *Handbook of Political Conflict, Theory and Research.* New York: Free Press, 238–294.

Gurr, Ted Robert. 2015. *Political Rebellion. Causes, Outcomes and Alternatives.* London: Routledge.

Gusfield, Joseph R. 1955. "Social Structure and Moral Reform: A Study of the Woman's Christian Temperance Union." *American Journal of Sociology*, 61: 221–232.

Hanagan, Michael. 1998. "Social Movements, Incorporation, Disengagement, and Opportunities – A Long View." In Marco Giugni, Doug McAdam, and Charles Tilly (eds.), *From Contention to Democracy.* Lanham, MD: Rowman and Littlefield, 3–30.

Hasso, Frances S. 2001. "Feminist Generations? The Long-Term Impact of Social Movement Involvement on Palestinian Women's Lives." *American Journal of Sociology*, 107(3): 586–611.

Helmke, Gretchen and Steven Levitsky. 2004. "Informal Institutions and Comparative Politics: A Research Agenda." *Perspectives on Politics*, 2(04): 725–740.

Hipsher, Patricia L. 1998. "Democratic Transition and Social Movement Outcomes: The Chilean Shantytown Dwellers Movement in Comparative Perspective." In Marco Giugni, Doug McAdam, and Charles Tilly (eds.), *From Contention to Democracy.* Lanham, MD: Rowman and Littlefield, 149–168.

Htun, Mala and Laura Weldon. 2012. "The Civic Origins of Progressive Policy Change: Combating Violence Against Women in Global Perspective, 1975–2005." *American Political Science Review*, 106(03): 548–569.

Huberts, Leo. 1989. "The Influence of Social Movements on Government Policy." *International Social Movement Research*, 2(1): 395–426.

Isaac, Larry and William R. Kelly. 1981. "Racial Insurgency, the State, and Welfare Expansion: Local and National Level Evidence from the Postwar United States." *American Journal of Sociology*, 86: 1348–1386.

Jenkins, Craig and William Form. 2005. "Social Movements and Social Change." In T. Janoski, R. Alford, A. Hicks, and M. Schwarts (eds.), *The Handbook of Political Sociology*. Cambridge: Cambridge University Press, 331–349.

Jennings, M. Kent. 1987. "Residues of a Movement: The Aging of the American Protest Generation." *American Political Science Review*, 81: 367–382.

Kampwirth, Karen. 2004. *Feminism and the Legacy of Revolution: Nicaragua, El Salvador, Chiapas, Cuba*. Athens: Ohio University Press.

Kane, Melinda D. 2003. "Social Movement Policy Success: Decriminalizing State Sodomy Laws, 1969–1998." *Mobilization*, 8: 313–334.

Katzenstein, Mary Fainsod. 1998. "Stepsisters: Feminist Movement Activism in Different Institutional Spaces." In David S. Meyer and Sidney Tarrow (eds.), *The Social Movement Society: Contentious Politics for a New Century*. Lanham, MD: Rowman and Littlefield, 195–216.

Kim, Sookyung, Paul Y. Chang, and Gi-Wook Shin. 2013. "Past Activism, Party Pressure, and Ideology: Explaining the Vote to Deploy Korean Troops to Iraq." *Mobilization: An International Quarterly*, 18(3): 243–266.

King, Brayden G. 2008. "A Political Mediation Model of Corporate Response to Social Movement Activism." *Administrative Science Quarterly*, 53: 395–421.

King, Brayden G. and Nicholas A. Pearce. 2010. "The Contentiousness of Markets: Politics, Social Movements, and Institutional Change in Markets." *Annual Review of Sociology*, 36: 249–267.

King, Brayden G., Maria Cornwall, and Eric Dahlin. 2005. "Winning Woman Suffrage One Step at a Time: Social Movements and the Logic of the Legislative Process." *Social Forces*, 83(3): 1211–1234.

Kitschelt, Herbert. 1986. "Political Opportunity Structures and Political Protest: Anti-Nuclear Movements in Four Democracies." *British Journal of Political Science*, 16: 57–85.

Klatch, Rebecca. 1999. *A Generation Divided*. Berkeley: University of California Press.

Kolb, Felix. 2007. *Protest and Opportunities*. Frankfurt/New York: Campus.

Kriesi, Hanspeter and Dominique Wisler. 1999. "The Impact of Social Movements on Political Institutions: A Comparison of the Introduction of Direct Legislation in Switzerland and the United States." In Marco Giugni, Doug McAdam, and Charles Tilly (eds.), *How Social Movements Matter*. Minneapolis: University of Minnesota Press, 42–65.

Luders, Joseph. 2010. *The Civil Rights Movement and the Logic of Social Change*. New York: Cambridge University Press.

Mahoney, James and Kathleen Thelen (eds.). 2009. *Explaining Institutional Change: Ambiguity, Agency, and Power*. Cambridge: Cambridge University Press.

Mair, Peter. 1997. *Party System Change: Approaches and Interpretations*. Oxford: Clarendon Press.

Maney, Gregory. 2007. "From Civil War to Civil Rights and Back Again: The Interrelation of Rebellion and Protest in Northern Ireland 1955–1972." *Research in Social Movements, Conflict, and Change*, 27: 3–35.

McAdam, Doug. 1988. *Freedom Summer*. New York: Oxford University Press.

McAdam, Doug. 1989. "The Biographical Consequences of Activism." *American Sociological Review*, 54: 744–760.

McAdam, Doug. 1999. "The Biographical Impact of Activism." In Marco Giugni, Doug McAdam, and Charles Tilly (eds.), *How Social Movements Matter*. Minneapolis: University of Minnesota Press, 117–146.

McAdam, Doug and Hilary Schaffer Boudet. 2012. *Putting Social Movements in Their Place: Explaining Opposition to Energy Projects in the United States, 2000–2005*. Cambridge: Cambridge University Press.

McAdam, Doug and Sidney Tarrow. 2010. "Ballots and Barricades: On the Reciprocal Relationship Between Elections and Social Movements." *Perspectives on Politics*, 8: 529–542.

McAdam, Doug, Sidney Tarrow, and Charles Tilly. 2001. *Dynamics of Contention*. Cambridge: Cambridge University Press.

McAdam, Doug and Yang Su. 2002. "The War at Home: Antiwar Protests and Congressional Voting, 1965 to 1973." *American Sociological Review*, 67: 696–721.

McCammon, Holly J. 2009. "Beyond Frame Resonance: The Argumentative Structure and Persuasive Capacity of Twentieth-Century US Women's Jury-Rights Frames." *Mobilization*, 14(1): 45–64.

Meirowitz, Aadam and Joshua Tucker. 2013. "People Power or a One-Shot Deal? A Dynamic Model of Protest." *American Journal of Political Science*, 57(2): 478–490.

Meyer, David S. 2003. "How Social Movements Matter." *Contexts*, 2(4): 30–35.

Meyer, David S. 1999. "How the Cold War Was Really Won: The Effects of the Antinuclear Movements of the 1980s." In Marco Giugni, Doug McAdam, and Charles Tilly (eds.), *How Social Movements Matter*. Minneapolis: University of Minnesota Press, 182–203.

Meyer, David S. 2005. "Social Movements and Public Policy: Eggs, Chicken, and Theory." In David S. Meyer, Valerie Jenness, and Helen Ingram (eds.), *Routing the Opposition: Social Movements, Public Policy, and Democracy*. Minneapolis: University of Minnesota Press, 1–26.

Meyer, David S. 2007. *The Politics of Protest: Social Movements in America*. New York: Oxford University Press.

Meyer, David and Debra Minkoff. 2004. "Conceptualizing Political Opportunity." *Social Forces*, 82(4): 1457–1492.

Meyer, David S. and Sidney Tarrow. 1998. "A Movement Society: Contentious Politics for a New Century." In David S. Meyer and Sidney Tarrow (eds.), *The Social Movement Society: Contentious Politics for a New Century*. Lanham, MD: Rowman and Littlefield, 1–28.

Meyer, David S. and Nancy Whittier. 1994. "Social Movement Spillover." *Social Problems*, 42(2): 277–297.

Micheletti, Michele. 2003. *Political Virtue and Shopping: Individuals, Consumerism, and Collective Action*. New York: Palgrave.

Muller, Edward N., Henry A. Dietz, and Steven E. Finkel. 1991. "Discontent and the Expected Utility of Rebellion: The Case of Peru." *American Political Science Review*, 85: 1261–1282.

Nagel, Joane. 1995. "American Indian Ethnic Renewal: Politics and the Resurgence of Identity." *American Sociological Review*, 60: 947–965.

Oberschall, Anthony. 1973. *Social Conflict and Social Movements*. Englewood Cliffs, NJ: Prentice-Hall.

Olzak, Susan and Sarah A. Soule. 2009. "Cross-Cutting Influences of Protest and Congressional Legislation in the Environmental Movement." *Social Force*, 88: 210–225.

Pettinicchio, David. 2012. "Institutional Activism: Reconsidering the Insider/Outsider Dichotomy." *Sociology Compass*, 6(6): 499–510.

Pickvance, Christopher G. 1999. "Democratisation and the Decline of Social Movements: The Effects of Regime Change on Collective Action in Eastern Europe, Southern Europe and Latin America." *Sociology*, 33(02): 353–372.

Piven, Frances Fox and Richard A. Cloward. 1979. *Poor People's Movements*. New York: Vintage Books.

Piven, Frances Fox and Richard A. Cloward. 1993. *Regulating the Poor*, Second edition. New York: Vintage Books.

Polletta, Francesca and James M. Jasper. 2001. "Collective Identity and Social Movements." *Annual Review of Sociology*, 27: 283–305.

Richardson, Liz. 2013. "We Need to Decide!': A Mixed Method Approach to Responsiveness and Equal Treatment." In Peter Esaiasson and Hanne Marthe Narud (eds.), *Between-Election Democracy: The Representative Relationship After Election Day*. Colchester: ECPR Press, 171–188.

Rochon, Thomas. 1998. *Culture Moves*. Princeton, NJ: Princeton University Press.

Rochon, Thomas R. and Daniel A. Mazmanian. 1993. "Social Movements and the Policy Process." *Annals of the American Academy of Political and Social Science*, 528: 75–87.

Rootes, Christopher. 2004. *Environmental Protest in Western Europe*. Oxford: Oxford University Press.

Rucht, Dieter. 1992. "Studying the Effects of Social Movements: Conceptualization and Problems." Paper for the ECPR Joint Session, Limerick (Ireland).

Ruzza, Carlo. 1997. "Institutional Actors and the Italian Peace Movement: Specializing and Branching Out." *Theory and Society*, 26(1): 87–127.

Santoro, Wayne A. and Gail M. McGuire. 1997. "Social Movement Insiders." *Social Problems*, 44: 503–520.

Schneiberg, Marc and Michael Lounsbury. 2008. "Social Movements and Institutional Analysis." In Royston Greenwood, Christine Oliver, Roy Suddaby, and Kerstin Sahlin-Andersson (eds.),

The SAGE Handbook of Organizational Institutionalism. Sage: London, 6648–6670.

Schock, Kurt. 2005. *Unarmed Insurrections: People Power Movements in Non-Democracies.* Minneapolis: University of Minnesota Press.

Schumaker, Paul D. 1975. "Policy Responsiveness to Protest-Group Demands." *Journal of Politics*, 37: 488–521.

Schumaker, Paul D. 1978. "The Scope of Political Conflict and the Effectiveness of Constraints in Contemporary Urban Protest." *Sociological Quarterly*, 19: 168–184.

Seippel, Ørnulf. 2001. "From Mobilization to Institutionalization? The Case of Norwegian Environmentalism." *Acta Sociologica*, 44(2): 123–137.

Sherkat, Darren E. and T. Jean Blocker. 1997. "Explaining the Political and Personal Consequences of Protest." *Social Forces*, 75: 1049–1070.

Slater, Dan. 2009. "Revolutions, Crackdowns, and Quiescence: Communal Elites and Democratic Mobilization in Southeast Asia." *American Journal of Sociology*, 115(1): 203–254.

Snyder, David and William R. Kelly. 1976. "Industrial Violence in Italy, 1878–1903." *American Journal of Sociology*, 82: 131–162.

Soule, Sarah A. 2004. "Diffusion Processes within and across Movements." In David Snow, Sarah Soule and Hanspeter Kriesi (eds.), *The Blackwell Companion to Social Movements.* Oxford: Blackwell, 294–310.

Soule, Sarah A. and Brayden G. King. 2006. "The Stages of the Policy Process and the Equal Rights Amendment, 1972–1982." *American Journal of Sociology*, 111: 1871–1909.

Soule, Sarah A. and Susan Olzak. 2004. "When Do Movements Matter? The Politics of Contingency and the Equal Rights Amendment." *American Sociological Review*, 69: 473–497.

Staggenborg, Suzanne. 1988. "The Consequences of Professionalization and Formalization in the Pro-Choice Movement." *American Sociological Review*, 53: 585–605.

Stewart, Abigail J., Isis H. Settles, and Nicholas J. G. Winter. 1998. "Women and the Social Movements of the 1960s: Activists, Engaged Obeservers, and Nonparticipants." *Political Psychology*, 19(1): 63–94.

Suh, Dowoon. 2011. "Institutionalizing Social Movements: The Dual Strategy of the Korean Women's Movement." *The Sociological Quarterly*, 52(3): 442–471.

Tarrow, Sidney and Charles Tilly. 2007. *Contentious Politics*. Boulder, CO: Paradigm Publishers.

Taylor, Verta and Nicole C. Raeburn. 1995. "Identity Politics as High-Risk Activism: Career Consequences for Lesbian, Gay, and Bisexual Sociologists." *Social Problems*, 42: 252–273.

Thomas, John Clayton. 2013. "Citizen, Customer, Partner: Rethinking the Place of the Public in Public Management." *Public Administration Review*, 73(6): 786–796.

Tilly, Charles. 1978. *From Mobilization to Revolution*. New York, NY: Random House.

Tilly, Charles. 1999. "From Interactions to Outcomes in Social Movements." In Marco Giugni, Doug McAdam, and Charles Tilly (eds.), *How Social Movements Matter*. Minneapolis: Minnesota University Press, 253–270.

Tipaldou, Sofia and Katrin Uba. 2014. "The Russian Radical Right Movement and Immigration Policy: Do They Just Make Noise or Have an Impact as Well?" *Europe-Asia Studies*, 66(7): 1080–1101.

Uba, Katrin. 2005. "Political Protest and Policy Change: The Direct Impacts of Indian Anti-Privatization Mobilizations, 1990–2003." *Mobilization*, 10: 383–396.

Uba, Katrin. 2009. "The Contextual Dependence of Movements Outcomes: A Simplified Meta-Analysis." *Mobilization*, 14: 433–448.

Vasi, Ion Bogdan and Brayden G. King. 2012. "Social Movements, Risk Perceptions, and Economic Outcomes." *American Sociological Review*, 77: 573–596.

Viterna, Jocelyn. 2013. *Women in War. The Micro-Processes of Mobilization in El Salvador*. Oxford: Oxford University Press.

Watts, Nicole. 2006. "Activists in Office: Pro-Kurdish Contentious Politics in Turkey." *Ethnopolitics: Formerly Global Review of Ethnopolitics*, 5(2): 125–144.

Whalen, Jack and Richard Flacks. 1989. *Beyond the Barricades*. Philadelphia, PA: Temple University Press.

Whittier, Nancy. 1995. *Feminist Generations*. Philadelphia: Temple University Press.

Whittier, Nancy. 2004. "The Consequences of Social Movements for Each Other." In D. Snow, S. Soule, and H. Kriesi (eds.), *The Blackwell Companion to Social Movements*. Oxford: Blackwell, 531–551.

Wilhelm, Brenda. 1998. "Changes in Cohabitation across Cohorts: The Influence of Political Activism." *Social Forces*, 77: 289–310.

Zald, Mayer N., Calvin Morrill, and Hayagreeva Rao. 2005. "The Impact of Social Movements on Organizations." In Gerald F. Davis, Doug McAdam, W. Richard Scott, and Mayer N. Zald (eds.), *Social Movements and Organization Theory*. Cambridge: Cambridge University Press, 253–279.

PART I

PEOPLE

2 ALL IS NOT LOST

The 1984-85 British miners' strike and mobilization after defeat

Karen Beckwith

Outcomes have impacts. Social movement scholars, as this volume attests, have turned their attention to the analysis of social movement outcomes, primarily, and unsurprisingly, in terms of victory and defeat.[1] Outcomes of success or failure have additional consequences. For example, success in a social movement campaign can transform the terrain for future campaigns.[2] A social movement's success can shape, positively or negatively, the political opportunity structure by changing, for example, labor law or electoral law; forcing elected or appointed public officials to resign; setting the issue agenda for a national election or referendum; extending political rights upon which new rights can be built; and provoking opposition and counter-movement mobilization. In addition, success – whether attributable or incidental to the social movement – can encourage further, future activism among its adherents. Success can create and strengthen collective identity, inspire additional campaigns on related issues, increase social movement "standing," and promote alliances.

Loss in social movement campaigns can also shape opportunities for future attempts. Loss can confirm and reinforce existing hostile political opportunity structures, strengthen opponents, exclude the movement's issues and demands from the political agenda, and

---

[1] As Tilly notes, however, "'success' and 'failure' hardly describe most of the effects" of social movements (1999, 268).

[2] This chapter employs a specific distinction between "social movement" and "social movement campaign," a distinction developed in della Porta and Rucht 1991; see also Beckwith 2013.

constrict political rights. Loss can demobilize activists, dispel potential supporters, and undermine collective identity and group solidarity. Depending on the nature of the loss, defeat in a social movement campaign can result in the eradication of a movement cohort, through persecution, imprisonment, and/or murder of leaders, activists, and sympathizers.

Ironically, as Gupta (2009, 420) suggests, success in a social movement campaign can also have negative consequences, depressing involvement as activists experience "a sense of satiety" and "find themselves less willing to continue devoting scarce resources and time to the movement." Conversely, social movement loss may have mobilizing impacts. "Under a satiety scenario," as Gupta argues (2009: 420), potential activists may "mobilize in order to prevent a total policy rout."

This chapter examines a case of social movement defeat and asks about a potential positive impact of loss: do social movement activists remobilize after loss and, if so, how? Employing a single, cross-time case-study design, the chapter examines the experience of the coalfield communities associated with Parkside Colliery across two anti-pit closure campaigns in Britain, focusing on women's activism in the anti-pit closure campaigns.

Two major campaigns of resistance to pit closures were provoked, in Britain, by the National Coal Board (NCB) and the British Coal Corporation (British Coal) announcements of targeted pit closures, in 1984 and 1992, respectively. In 1984, the announcement that Cortonwood Colliery (South Yorkshire) would be shut down provoked the National Union of Mineworkers (NUM) into a nationwide strike that lasted more than a year, and ultimately involved thousands of striking miners and their supporters in coalfield communities, and internationally. Women were active in strike support, including joining men in picketing, and founded a national organization, Women Against Pit Closures. In 1992, British Coal issued a similar announcement, that as many as thirty collieries would be closed, provoking, again, a nationwide anti-closure campaign by the NUM and its supporters ("Collieries under Threat"). In many – but not all – cases, women remobilized, reactivating Women Against Pit Closures and establishing "pit camps" as bases for resistance and publicity.[3]

---

[3] For a discussion of the pit camps established in 1992–93, see Beckwith 1996, 1997.

This chapter analyzes loss in the context of the 1984–85 strike at Parkside Colliery in Lancashire and subsequent remobilization of activist women in response to the renewed threat of pit closures in 1992–93. The 1984–85 strike and the 1992–93 anti-pit closure campaign approximates a natural or "found" experiment; that is, an act of nature or "some external force intervenes and creates comparable treatment groups in a seemingly random fashion" (Robinson et al. 2009: 346). In this case, the external intervention was the post-strike announcement of a new round of pit closures that created a subset of collieries, active in the 1984–85 strike, that were potentially available for remobilization. Why and how did some groups of women remobilize after their defeat in the 1984–85 strike? What encouraged mobilization after loss?

The focus on Parkside Colliery and Lancashire Women Against Pit Closures (LWAPC), in a cross-time, single case study, offers advantages in assessing the impact of loss. First, it permits a close, detailed focus on a single colliery – Parkside – and the miners and communities that were involved in defending it against government closure. Second, across the two campaigns, actors and issues remain constant. In each campaign, the precipitating actor was the British government agency responsible for managing the coal industry: in 1984, the NCB and, in 1992, British Coal.[4] The threat was the same in 1984 and 1992: closure of multiple collieries. Finally, the responding actors at Parkside, defending against pit closures, were also the same: the NUM and activist women in the extended coalfield communities of Lancashire.

Third, the NUM strike against the NCB in 1984–85 resulted in a clear, indisputable defeat. Victory and defeat are relative terms, and, as Suh argues, "it is not *objective consequences* but *perceived or interpreted subjective outcomes* that are causal to movement dynamics...; subjective outcomes do not always mirror objective ones" (2012: 2; emphasis in original). As Gupta claims (2009: 417), "most outcomes typically stop far short of the kind of decisive victory or abject defeat that might otherwise trigger movement demobilization." The impact of outcomes should be clearest, however, in exactly such cases; that is, in campaigns where a social movement has been completely triumphant or has thoroughly failed to achieve its goals. In these cases, the objective

---

[4] In 1987, the National Coal Board became the British Coal Corporation; in 1994, British Coal's responsibilities were transferred to the Coal Authority, which thereafter oversaw the privatization of the British coal industry.

outcome is undeniable and "subjective outcomes" (Suh 2014: 4) face substantial constraints in interpretation.

Again, clear, "objective" outcomes in social movements are relatively rare. More common are "smaller battles in a larger war [with] interactions between movements, policy makers, and the public [being] protracted and iterative" (Gupta 2009: 417). In addition, social movements more typically experience a combination of minor successes and defeats in the context of a social movement campaign; "these incremental outcomes from prior rounds of contention can open up or close off avenues for contention, win or lose access to new institutional channels, divide or unify elites, and fragment or solidity movement groups – outcomes that can radically alter a movement's environment and strategic options" (Gupta 2009: 418). The choice of this unambiguous case of objective loss, described later, mitigates the confounding impact of interpreted outcomes and permits strong conclusions about the impact of loss upon remobilization.

Fourth, the focus on women offers an additional, strong test of mobilization after loss. Men in the British mining industry had the NUM and the National Association of Colliery Overmen, Deputies and Shotfirers (NACODS) to organize and to represent them. The unions' organizational structures were in place before the two campaigns, and NUM members had a well-established strike repertoire. Because women were not miners, they had to mobilize themselves and establish their own organizational structures. Unlike NUM members, working-class women in coalfield communities had not participated in mining strikes and had not experienced direct loss as a result of their own campaign efforts before 1985;[5] hence, the effects of loss on remobilization should be most evident among activist women.

Evidence concerning women's activism during the 1984–85 strike and the 1992–93 anti-pit closure campaign is based on field research I undertook in Britain from 1992 to 1994, and during the 1992–93 anti-pit closure campaign. Field research involved surveys and structured individual interviews with activist women and with NUM local officials at Parkside Colliery, among others, including women who had been active

---

[5] NUM members and activist women interviewed for this project were explicit that women had not been involved in strike picketing before 1984 (and, moreover, that their involvement required considerable adjustment by all involved: miners, women, and police). None of the women whom I interviewed had any historical knowledge or memory of women's activism in earlier mining strikes.

in strike support during the 1984–85 strike. In addition, I photocopied activists' speeches and notes from the 1984–85 strike and the 1992–93 anti-pit closure campaign, among other primary documents. These data were supported by secondary sources, newspaper articles, and local and national union publications. Finally, my research involved similar inter-viewing and data collection at Point of Ayr Colliery (North Wales) and Houghton Main Colliery (South Yorkshire), with members of Sheffield Women Against Pit Closures, and with activists in Women Against Pit Closures at the NUM Headquarters in Sheffield.[6] I also visited pit camps established by activist women at Grimethorpe Colliery at Barnsley, South Yorkshire, and at Trentham Colliery near Stoke-on-Trent.

In the following sections, I describe the precipitating event: National Coal's threatened closure of twenty coalmines in March 1984, and the NUM's strike response. I discuss (1) the strike conduct and context at Parkside, (2) women's organized activism in support of striking miners, and (3) the strike outcome. This section evidences the nature and extent of loss in the 1984–85 strike at Parkside as the baseline for assessing post-loss remobilization. The chapter then describes, and evaluates, a second campaign in 1992–93, in response to similar threats. Again, I outline the precipitating event, British Coal's announced closure of thirty coalmines, and the NUM's response in its anti-pit closure campaign, the campaign context at Parkside, and women's involvement. The chapter's final section examines the consequences of campaign loss: how the experi-ence of women, mobilized for strike support in the mid-1980s, effected their remobilization more than half a decade later.

The strike against the National Coal Board, 1984–85

The 1984–85 miners' strike began quickly. On March 1, 1984, the NCB announced their decision to close Cortonwood Colliery in South Yorkshire, with threats to close additional pits. In immediate response, Yorkshire miners struck. An estimated 55,000 Yorkshire miners were called out on strike (Reed and Adamson 1985, np), and within weeks, thousands of miners were on strike in Scotland, South Wales, and Kent, with additional pits subsequently stopping work, as miners were

---

[6] Results of the broader field research are part of a larger project; for discussion of Lancashire Women against Pit Closures, see Beckwith 1996, 2013.

picketed out by "flying pickets" of strikers and supporters. No national ballot of all NUM members was held, although individual pit locals balloted their members. Many local pits voted to join the strike; others were successfully picketed out; others, in North Wales and Nottinghamshire, voted against striking and continued to work.

As the NUM struggled to maintain the strike nationally, the government instituted a series of policies to deprive the families of striking miners of social security (i.e., welfare) benefits and to employ directed violence against strikers and supporters. By June 1, 1984, an estimated 3,200 people had been arrested in strike-related incidents; multiple mass rallies, involving thousands of demonstrators, took place at Haworth Colliery, Orgreave coke depot, and elsewhere; and the police employed what was seen at the time to be shocking violence against strikers and residents of pit villages.[7] On August 11, a massive march and demonstration were held in London, organized under the banner of National Women Against Pit Closures, a federal organization of women that had only recently been established; an estimated 20,000 people participated (Reed and Adamson 1985, np).

Large numbers of striking miners began to return to work, crossing picket lines to do so, and by December, several thousand miners had returned, while nearly 10,000 strike-related arrests had been made. On March 1, without any national agreement between the NUM and the NCB, miners in South Wales, Lancashire, and Durham voted to return to work and did so, with miners in other areas soon following. The last striking miners to return to work were the Kentish miners, in mid-March. Issues concerning the sequestration of NUM monies and amnesty for convicted miners marked the post-strike period, and, in July 1985, the Nottingham miners began their formal disaffiliation from the NUM to form a new miners' federation, the Union of Democratic Mineworkers, made formal on December 6, 1985 (Winterton and Winterton 1989: 227–231).

Lasting a year, the strike failed to prevent the closure of any targeted mines. It resulted in job loss for thousands (Winterton and Winterton 1989: 44) and in millions of pounds in lost wages. More than 9,700 persons were arrested (Reed and Adamson 1985, np). The strike was followed by a series of legal prosecutions against the NUM, its

---

[7] A particularly distressing example was the police attack on villagers in Armthorpe, Yorkshire.

leadership, and some of the striking miners. Characterized as "loss without limit" (Adeney and Lloyd 1989), the NUM strike against the NCB was a clear defeat.

The strike at Parkside Colliery

Strike context and conduct

Parkside Colliery was one of eight working pits in Lancashire at the onset of the 1984–85 strike. On March 6, a premature work stoppage was the first evidence of the strike at Parkside. Given the previous record of pit closures in Lancashire, the NUM Lancashire leadership was reluctant to take strike action against pit closures; as the result of several leadership and local union meetings, the strike at Parkside was not officially initiated at the beginning of the strike wave in Yorkshire. As flying pickets came from South Yorkshire and elsewhere in an attempt to picket out Parkside and other Lancashire collieries, the NUM local leadership declared that the strike was still unofficial and took the position that crossing picket lines was an individual decision. According to one Parkside NUM official, four strike votes were taken at Parkside Colliery, at the pit and at the local level, with inconclusive results. With no clear leadership to resolve the situation, what one official called " a complete state of confusion" lasted for almost ten weeks, as some miners and even union officials carried on working, crossing a picket line of striking Parkside miners and NUM members. A meeting in Sheffield, national NUM headquarters, and a decision by the national leadership to declare an official national strike, clarified the situation. Parkside Colliery joined the national strike, with most miners honoring the picket line.

Sylvia Pye, Chair of National Women Against Pit Closures, described the initial onset of the strike at Parkside:

> At most of the other pits, there was like a lot out and a lot stayed in
> for the first couple of weeks because they were very indecisive.
> We're on strike. We're not on strike. You know, one day you're on
> strike and you bring all the lads up out of the pit and off we go
> on strike and then the next thing it would be, well, we're not quite
> on strike yet, you know. So some of the lads would go back in
> and for a couple of weeks it was very indecisive. I mean, this pit,
> here, we had 1600 men at this pit then. And, I would say, that there

was, well, about 1400 of them on strike at the beginning. And 249
people were left at the end.

(S. Pye interview, January 20, 1993)

The conduct of the strike replicated the conventional strike
repertoire of the NUM. Billy Pye, National Delegate to the NUM
Executive and a Parkside miner, explained that Parkside Colliery was
somewhat unusual in having a relatively large number of older miners
still working:

> We were lucky to have a lot of members that had been in this
> situation before, had been on strike before. The majority of people
> that were on strike at this pit, who actually finished out, were my
> age or perhaps a little bit older [early thirties] but they'd been
> [educated] by the older element at the beginning in order to tell
> them what to do and ... how you conduct yourself in the middle of
> a strike ... As it developed, the younger element took over the
> [direction] of the strike and its general organization, but without
> that invaluable assistance in the beginning, those people would
> have not known what to do.
>
> (B. Pye interview, April 13, 1993)

Conventional picketing was initially twenty-four hours a day,
but diminished to eight hours, from early morning until mid-afternoon.
Although the local union always had half-a-dozen or more miners
picketing, on some occasions pickets would include as many as 3,000
people, as miners from Yorkshire and elsewhere would join picketing at
Parkside. At the beginning of the strike, the pickets were successful in
limiting the number of working miners.

Women's activism

Women's initial activism around the strike began informally, as part of a
general community mobilization. With encouragement from the local
NUM and with assistance from the local Labour Party, a women's
support group started up in Newton-le-Willows and in other coalfield
communities in Lancashire. Two soup kitchens were established in
Newton, one in the village civic hall and another in a rented building.
To support the soup kitchens, miners' wives and women and other

supporters in the community began a leafletting campaign to raise funds and to collect food. Coordinating their efforts, the women in the St. Helens area worked with the local Labour Party in establishing a food bank that eventually was able to provide weekly food parcels to striking families and additional parcels to families with children.

Women also participated in picketing. Chris Sumner, chair of LWAPC, suggested that "It must have been one of the first strikes where women were actually made welcome on the picket lines" (Sumner interview, January 7, 1993). With the 1984–85 strike, women on a picket line was a new experience for everyone and was initially resisted by striking miners for a variety of reasons; as the strike progressed, opposition to women picketing subsided. At Parkside, women usually appeared on pickets in the morning and in the evening, given that household and other work occupied the main part of the day for most women. According to women active at Parkside during the 1984–85 strike, women's participation in picketing drew massive police presence. As one activist recounted,

> ... it didn't matter whether it was four or six or thirty women, you would then immediately see a great massive police force ... As soon as they saw women come on to a picket line, I don't know what they thought we were going to do, but we always then were surrounded by hundreds they'd bring in ... [W]e always had a massive force whenever there was women on a picket line for some reason, and they were brutal.
>
> *(Interview, January 20, 1993)*

A Parkside miner confirmed this observation:

> The police developed a system where they would use what we used to call "snatch" clubs because they [would identify specific] people in the crowd. And they went in in a big way, like a battering ram. [In one picket], the ranks of the police opened up ... and they didn't come for us [the miners]; they went straight to the women. And then they just – it was the most disgraceful spectacle I've ever seen in my life. They just attacked this group of women and children ... So we had to stand there and watch for a few minutes ... And they were actually ripping our women's shirts off and things in order to wind the crowd up and it worked. It was a complete ... riot situation.
>
> *(Interview, April 13, 1993)*

Activist women of the Parkside Colliery communities learned political skills as a result of the strike. Although LWAPC was formally established after the strike, it worked closely with the local and national NUM in its function as a support group during the strike. Women picketed; raised money; staffed soup kitchens; and organized food parcels. They held separate weekly meetings, and organized demonstrations and mass meetings, autonomously, that permitted them to invite speakers of their own choice without the intermediary of the local union. Lancashire women supporting the strike at Parkside also traveled throughout Britain, and to Ireland, France, the United States, the Soviet Union, and elsewhere, soliciting financial and political support for the NUM.

As they traveled, activist women gave speeches, frequently at large mass meetings. The claim by several NUM officials that women were speakers on every union platform during the strike is not exaggerated. Women who had been active at Parkside emphasized repeatedly in interviews how terrified they had been initially of speaking in public and how their development as public speakers constituted major personal transformation. Chris Sumner described how substantial such a change could be for women:

> I think it's probably because for a lot of women for the first time in their lives they actually did things without being allowed to do them. I mean that was such a big change for a lot of people ... Well, I came from a very small village in Yorkshire and I would never have dreamed, ever, when I was still living there, of what I might get in involved in ... Many of [the women had] not been out the Yorkshire area except to go on holiday ... Many of the miners' wives that went on international delegations had never been abroad. They had to get passports for the first time, you know. [T]hat was, in itself, that was quite a significant landmark. And, so then, it's quite funny, 'cause I was talking to somebody [who] ... went to France, Sweden, and Germany during the strike, on three separate occasions. She'd never been abroad before. And she said when she looks back now she thinks, "My god, I went to foreign countries where I didn't know a *word* they were saying to me. And I stood up in front of all these people and just spoke to them about what was happening in England. And someone else told them what I was saying." And she said, "When I look back on that now I think, "'God, wasn't I brave!'"

And it's a real bravery! ... You ... just didn't have time to say,
"Oh, I don't think I could do that." 'Cause somebody had to do it.
One girl we brought from Bold in the very early days, she had to
go to the pub and have four brandies before she'd [speak at a
meeting]. She said after, she couldn't remember a word she said. She
was so terrified, but she was really good [because] she was just
speaking about what was happening in her community.

(Sumner interview, January 7, 1993)

   In an interview, Sylvia Pye reflected on her lack of political
involvement prior to the 1984–85 strike.

Up until that time – I was forty-four, forty-five [years old]. I really
hadn't had any experience of strikes or – I'd always known that I
should – my dad said like you should be in the union, you know,
and you should vote Labour. So all my life, I'd been told, you know,
what I should be doing. And I knew that that was the way to be. But,
as far as like, militancy, or anything like that, I just, well, that
wasn't me. You know, I was probably one of these people that
think, "Well, you know, as long as they, you know, it's their fight.
It's not mine." ... All I did in them days was kept my family going
with a lot of support from my own family and [my husband's]
family. And, really, I mean, I had three babies and plenty to do, and
I wasn't really involved in those [earlier] strikes.

(S. Pye interview, January 20, 1993)

   Sylvia Pye recalled the point at which she moved from observer
to active participant:

After ... the first few weeks when my lads kept telling me what was
going on up here. And we used to be actually escorted over the
picket line. We weren't being [told], "No, you're not going." They
were ... allowing us to go over the picket line. But when they kept
coming in saying ... what the police were doing to them at this end,
and they were arrested a couple of times, and I then felt [that]
something's wrong here somewhere. I mean, these are people that,
the police, that we've been taught to respect all our lives, you know.
So, what's going on? I'm quite sure the lads [were not] making these
things up. So, I then started to take an avid interest in what was
going on and then started to say ... I want to be out on strike with
them. And, at that time, there was thirteen of us worked in the

canteen. And there was myself and my sister and my best friend who were all of the same mind and we said that that's it. We're going. You know, we're going out on strike.

(S. Pye interview, January 20, 1993)

Chris Sumner reflected on the transformations of women who had been active in supporting the strike:

I think for the first time women began to actually see . . . I think for the first time, . . . women realized the power of women collectively and it was just a mind-blowing experience for a lot of women . . . Women that at the beginning of the strike would [say], "Oh, no, I couldn't do that and I can't do this, and I'm no good at that" – and you would look at some of them after the strike. They'd been involved in writing books. They'd gone on to further education. They'd taken degrees. They'd become local councilors. And they're actually . . . looking around and saying, "Yes, I've a real role to play here. It's not just kind of washing up and cooking and stuff like that. There's all this world outside.

(Sumner interview, January 7, 1993)

Lancashire women active in the 1984–85 strike not only developed specific political skills and experience; their participation was recalled in positive terms and the efficacy, politicization, and solidarity that resulted from the strike served as potential resources for future similar mobilizations. Female activists at Parkside established a formal organization (LWAPC), led by women, with the organizational autonomy to raise money and to organize events supporting the striking miners.

Strike resolution. The strike at Parkside Colliery ended in early March, 1985, when Parkside miners returned to work. The return to work was formally organized for the day (morning) shift, when the local NUM returned en masse to the colliery, marching behind the local union banner. With supporters from the Parkside community, the return to work at Parkside was organized by the NUM as a demonstration of solidarity and a refusal to present themselves, as a community and as a union, as defeated, even as the strike had failed.

As was the case at other pits, returning striking miners were persecuted by colliery management and put in hostile work situations underground with miners who had worked throughout the strike.

Parkside miners who stayed out for the duration, in many cases, gave as good as they got, and scab miners were sometimes set upon by vengeful former strikers. One Parkside miner recalled his return to work after a year on strike:

> It was strange. You never lose that sense of the pit itself, ... even though ... you can be away for ten years. You go back and it's always there, like in the smell and everything. But the atmosphere was different at the time ... It was hard because you was looking around and talking to people and all the time you're thinking, well, did he scab out? Did he ... go back early? Is he a lad who stayed out all the time? And it was only over a period of time that you got to know who was who, that there was some feeling between certain sections of men, you know. And the thing is the people who did work all the way through obviously was looked after afterwards. They was given the better jobs and better conditions, ... which caused a bit of friction again amongst men ... You got small sections of men who would stare and do – you know, a bit like, but as time passed – As they say, time is a great healer and men got back together again.
>
> *(Sean Topping interview, August 7, 1993)*

At Parkside, activists, supporters, and miners recalled the strike as unsuccessful but did not emphasize it as a defeat. In recollection, miners still employed at Parkside Colliery in the early 1990s had positive memories of the strike. Any bitterness about the strike was reserved for specific instances, for the police, and for the Thatcher government. Despite the inability of Parkside striking miners to protect other pits from closure, to change government policy, or, near the end of the strike, to prevent increasing numbers of their own from returning to work, Parkside miners did not characterize themselves as defeated. Their experience of a losing, even heroic strike was not an experience of defeat. Particularly for the women active in supporting striking Parkside miners, the experience was in many ways a positive one. Activist women could claim their part in having helped to sustain so many miners who stayed on strike until the official end. They could identify their contributions to the solidarity of the strike and to the defense of their community, and the specific personal transformations that they had experienced. As Chris Sumner observed,

> I just think the whole sort of power of people acting collectively and
> particularly the supportiveness of other women, I think that
> makes a difference that is different to men organizing. I mean, I
> know that men have kept sort of contact and when they get together
> again they do talk about what happened and exchange stories ... I
> mean I can't feel what men feel but I don't think there's the same
> spirit of the powerfulness of the strike somehow. And I think that's
> why women would have gone on. I really do think they would have
> carried on ... Many, many women were really disappointed when
> the men went back to work.
>
> *(Sumner interview, January 7, 1993)*

The anti-pit closure campaign, 1992–93

On September 18, 1992, the *Guardian* published a front-page article,
exposing the British government's secret proposal to close thirty collieries ("Collieries under Threat"). Although the possibility of new pit
closures had been recognized before 1992, the proposed closures would
constitute the most extensive shutdown of mines in Britain since the
1984–85 strike, leaving only twenty deep coal mines remaining. The
Guardian reported that "the Government is forcing British Coal to close
30 pits and sack 25,512 miners in a merciless cutback which will reduce
the industry by two thirds almost immediately" (Beavis and Harper
1992). An estimated 752 miners at Parkside Colliery would lose their
jobs in the closure, ending mining in Lancashire. By mid-October, the
closure list identified thirty-one collieries for closure – twenty-seven to
be closed outright and another four to be "moth-balled" – with the
closure program concluding in March 1993 (Harper and Beavis 1992b).

With the possibility of a nationwide miners' strike, the NUM
and the breakaway Union of Democratic Mineworkers leaderships discussed possibilities of coordinating independent efforts by both federa-
tions to resist the pit closures (Harper and Beavis 1992a). The NUM
Executive called a special delegate conference to determine whether or
not to take industrial action in response to the closures. The NUM
suspended its strike action consideration, however, when the British
High Court issued an emergency injunction against the implementation
of any colliery closures or redundancies on the grounds that the man-
dated review process, involving consultation with the NUM, had not

taken place (Harper, Halsall, and Weston 1992). As the NUM and NACODS were successful in seeking an injunction, UDM leader Roy Lynk staged an underground sit-in at his former colliery, Silverhill in Nottinghamshire (Harper, Halsall, and Weston 1992; Clouston 1992). The UDM also sought an injunction against closures of six Nottinghamshire collieries (Weston 1992a), and the Trades Union Congress (TUC) backed plans for a national day of protest (Weston 1992b).

The unions made multiple efforts to delay or to prevent pit closures through a variety of actions. These included successfully seeking injunctions against immediate closures and layoffs, mobilizing public opinion against the closures, arranging buy-out schemes that would permit miners to buy collieries targeted for closure, and engaging in mass protests and occasional sit-ins and occupations of collieries.[8] The miners also had allies in Conservative Party backbenchers (Wintour 1992), British Members of the European Parliament (Milne 1992), and Neil Clarke, chairman of British Coal (Randall 1992). Despite these efforts, the Major government held firm to the pit closure policy. Although the High Court ruled that the government's procedure for the pit closure program was illegal (Mason 1992; "Pit closure plan ruled illegal"), an independent review of the threatened pits supported the government's program (Smith and Owen 1993). By the summer of 1993, most targeted pits had been closed or were closing. Final redundancies were imposed upon Parkside miners by mid-June 1992, and by March 1993, the pit was filled with stone and permanently sealed.

Parkside pit camp and Lancashire Women against Pit Closures

Lancashire Women against Pit Closures was in abeyance from 1988 until 1992,[9] when its leaders reconvened to challenge the government's

[8] A major demonstration was held in London on Sunday, October 25, 1992. The *Guardian* estimated that 150,000 miners and supporters attended the rally (Travis 1992); the *Financial Times* put the number of demonstrators at 200,000 (Adonis 1992).

[9] Note that I use "abeyance" more generally here; LWAPC concluded its activities once it had completed its post-strike efforts supporting miners who had been sacked as a result of the strike or who were fighting legal battles concerning strike-related arrests. Friendship networks, among LWAPC members, established during the strike, were intact in 1992, and hence facilitated remobilization of LWAPC. For a detailed discussion of abeyance structures, see Taylor 1989: 762, 772.

threat to close Parkside Colliery. The leadership structure was still in place, and Sylvia Pye, the mother of a Parkside miner, was National Chair of WAPC. At the last remaining colliery in Lancashire, Parkside Colliery's workforce was more militant than might have normally been expected. Miners who refused redundancy offers when Bold and other pits closed after 1985 went to work at Parkside and, as many interview respondents claimed, only those most committed to mining and to the NUM refused redundancy. Hence, mining militancy may have been concentrated at Parkside Colliery by 1992. With a resistant mining workforce and a women's support group leadership in place, remobilization in opposition to pit closures was available.

As the NUM local membership organized, in coordination with the national NUM leadership, to oppose the closure of Parkside, activist women remobilized as well. In December 1992, LWAPC leaders met to discuss how to organize women in opposition to the closure, and in mid-January a meeting was called at a pub in Earlestown. Almost two dozen women, some of whom had been active during the 1984–85 strike, convened to discuss the possibility of establishing a women's "pit camp" at the colliery, to serve as a base for and symbol of resistance to pit closures. The camp, established with the assistance of Parkside miners, was established within two weeks, when a caravan was moved onto colliery property at the entrance to the pit, just along the A49 in Newton-le-Willows. A brazier was lit, to provide warmth and to attract notice; signs were posted stating opposition to the government's closure program; the LWAPC banner was unfurled.

Space constraints preclude a detailed discussion of the years-long resistance mounted by LWAPC, and I have written elsewhere about the group's contribution to and leadership in the anti-pit closure campaign at Parkside (Beckwith 1997, 1996). Suffice it to say that the pit camp remained the illegal and highly visible center of the resistance to the closure of Parkside Colliery. Staffed twenty-four hours a day, by LWAPC members, Parkside miners, and supporters, it served as the organizing base for mass demonstrations; for press conferences and interviews; for local NUM and LWAPC meetings; and for organizing, mounting, and sustaining several illegal occupations of the colliery itself, including one of the colliery winding towers.

LWAPC activism reflected in many ways its previous involvement in supporting Lancashire miners during the 1984–85 strike. LWAPC organized autonomous actions; it solicited and raised its own funds; members traveled to other organizations to speak about the opposition to pit closures; and they spoke at major mass meetings, including NUM rallies. Although picketing was not a strategy, especially as Parkside Colliery was quickly put on "care and maintenance,"[10] LWAPC activists and leaders were militant and active across the course of the 1992–93 campaign.

The extent and duration of LWAPC remobilization was attributable to their positive experience in the 1984–85 strike. LWAPC activists characterized their remobilization as the result of the skills they developed and politicization they underwent during the strike. Sylvia Pye, speaking of the impact of the 1984–85 strike on the anti-pit closure remobilization, recalled her strike experience positively:

> It was fantastic ... We had some really brilliant times then ... We made a lot of friends. We lost a lot of people that we thought were our friends. We lost a lot of people that we were close to and thought were friends ... So it did a lot of harm. But I think we found out who our friends were. And, I mean, this is what, nearly nine years later, and they're still our friends and still fighting along side us, which is brilliant. I made contacts all over the world and I'm very grateful for that. And I've now realized that, you know, I've really got something to do in my life. I mustn't sort of sit back and think, well, it's okay. It doesn't affect me – because it did affect me, so.
>
> (*S. Pye interview, 20 January 1992*)

Pye also reflected on the general shift of activism and support from miners that gave women a sense of empowerment in their activism during the 1984–85 strike:

> A lot of men really thought we were great, you know, with the support that we gave. I think we actually changed the attitude of a lot of the men during the strike. You know, "We don't want our women involved in this, and we don't want you involved in that" was the general thing at the beginning. But before long they were saying, you know, "Well, come along and get involved and, you

---

[10] Coal-cutting was stopped almost immediately at Parkside Colliery but the pit had to be maintained for safety reasons; hence, a reduced workforce continued to service the mine, checking gas levels and for flooding.

know, get in." So, you know, I think towards the end most of the
women were involved and the men used to think we were
brilliant ... And there were a lot of [women] that didn't go back,
never went back [to the way they'd been before the strike]. I never
went back, never went back to what I was before. I started with it in
'84, '85, realizing that there was a lot to be fought for.

(S. Pye interview, 20 January 1992)

Conclusion

The issues involved in the 1984–85 strike provoked Lancashire women
to organize in support of the striking miners as a generalized commitment to defend the coalfield communities that were created and sustained by mining. Claims that the government was attacking a way of
life and targeting specific working-class communities served as the basis
for justifying activist Parkside women's resistance to pit closures in the
1984–85 strike. Striking in support of other pits was seen as a crucial
component of class, family, and community solidarity.

Although striking miners eventually returned to work, a large
number of militant Parkside miners had resisted to the end. Their return
to work, although bitter, was marked with defiance, interpreted as a
moral victory, and celebrated by their supporters in the community.
The striking Parkside miners also had some understanding of (if not
sympathy for) the reasons that some of their colleagues returned to
work early, unable to remain out for the formal duration of the strike.
Moreover, post-strike retaliation against strikers was apparently matched
by anti-scab vengeance. For women, the pattern was similar: Parkside
women were celebrated in their community for their contributions to
supporting the strike.

Women who had supported striking miners at Parkside during
the 1984–85 strike were available, even after defeat, for remobilization
in 1992. Although there was not a perfect correspondence between
those active in 1984–85 and those still committed to supporting their
coalfield community, many leaders and activists were residing in the
same area, connected to other political activists, and in contact with
each other. When the 1992 pit closures were announced, and Parkside
Colliery was targeted, LWAPC remobilized in the 1992–93 campaign –
despite the failure of their activism in the 1984–85 strike. The loss in the

strike against the National Coal Board was real and considerable: almost a year's lost wages for striking miners and their families; subsequent job loss; legal prosecutions against some striking miners; and damage to friendships, workplace solidarity and social networks. Given that LWAPC women lost their campaign in 1984–85, what were the effects of loss for women at Parkside? What permitted remobilization after loss?

The effects of loss for LWAPC

Although activist women at Parkside Colliery lost their campaign in 1984–85, along with the miners and their communities, they experienced that loss in ways that made remobilization possible. At Parkside, activist women, as well as the NUM and the communities that witnessed the end of the 1984–85 strike and the return of the miners, did not experience the end of the strike as a final defeat. The experience and the framing of the 1984–85 loss at Parkside had several positive effects that left the Lancashire women, and LWAPC, available for remobilization after loss.

First, a clear effect of the 1984–85 loss for LWAPC was social movement abeyance. The defeat of the NUM strike had the eventual effect of concluding LWAPC activism, obviously in terms of strike support after the miners returned to work, but also in terms of active contacts and LWAPC involvement in other issues.[11]

Second, the LWAPC experience of loss in the 1984–85 strike presented an opportunity for political learning (see Beckwith 2015). During the course of the strike itself, LWAPC activists developed important political skills, heightened political consciousness, and were confirmed, in many ways, in their political efficacy. In the context of a supportive community, including supportive NUM national and local leadership, activist women at Parkside emerged from the 1984–85 miners' strike with a sophisticated and solidary collective identity[12] and an appreciation of their new political skills. As Lancashire WAPC

[11] In the strike aftermath, LWAPC was involved in raising money for the defense of miners who were facing prosecution on a variety of strike-related charges, many of which were extremely serious.

[12] For a discussion of collective identity as a process and product, see Flescher Fominaya 2010.

went into abeyance (from approximately 1988 until 1992), their sense of collective identity and achievement was latent, but available for reactivation.

Despite the actual social movement campaign loss, which was substantial, for LWAPC and its members, the effects of loss were not catastrophic. The effect of the campaign loss, in terms of potential remobilization, was to suspend LWAPC activism, which permitted recognition of political learning; and, in concert with the NUM, tactical innovation and a shift in collective action repertoire. As they faced the threat, in 1992, of the closure of Parkside Colliery, LWAPC women's contacts with each other and with the NUM, their positive collective identity, their political skills, and their insights and political learning from the previous campaign, positioned them well for remobilization. Their previous experience, even in loss, empowered them to engage in direct action in establishing illegal women-only pit camps,[13] in maintaining a physical presence at collieries scheduled for closure, and in shifting from a strike repertoire of mass picketing to a (mostly) nonviolent repertoire of trespass, illegal occupation, and mass demonstrations. In short, for LWAPC, one effect of serious campaign loss was positive positioning for remobilization.

Mobilization after loss?

What does this case suggest about the effects of loss for social movements? First, loss in a social movement campaign is not the end of the story. In studying social movement outcomes, social movement scholars must recognize that outcomes are independent as well as dependent variables. As Taylor (1989: 419) wrote more than two decades ago, "existing approaches overlook social movement continuity by neglecting to think about outcomes ... [and by] focusing on short-term gains." Even social movement scholarship that focuses on outcomes, however, focuses primarily on successes rather than failures, and does not examine the effects of these outcomes, on social movements themselves or on future social movement mobilization and campaigns.

---

[13] See Beckwith 1997 for an account of the LWAPC pit camp at Parkside Colliery. During the 1992–93 campaign, women established pit camps at six of the ten collieries listed for immediate closure in 1992, including Grimethorpe, Houghton Main, and Trentham, among others.

Identifying social movement outcomes of victory and defeat is challenging on at least two grounds.[14] The identification of outcomes is dependent, in part, on identification of the movement's goals. A social movement campaign often will have multiple goals, including goals both internal and external to the social movement. Internal goals – those focused on the movement or the campaign itself – include, for example, sustaining collective identity, mobilizing bystanders, reassuring activists, and maintaining solidarity. External goals – exacting specific responses from campaign targets – can be as specific as generating legislation or stopping a dam from being built, and as general as stopping violence against women, ending race and caste discrimination, or expanding citizenship rights. Furthermore, goals change across time. As a social movement campaign adapts strategically, in interaction with its targets and/or opponents, and in response to incremental successes and defeats, a social movement is likely to adjust its original, stated goals (Gupta 2009). As a social movement campaign unfolds, movement leaders and spokespersons are likely to emphasize some goals rather than others and to give increasing attention to a few goals (and to become silent in regard to still others). In short, identification of a social movement's goal is complicated by the number of goals and the movement's shifting commitments to them.

As a result, social movement outcomes are best understood in the context of social movement campaigns. A social movement campaign is likely to be part of a sequence of campaigns launched across time by a social movement, and success and failure are likely to be interdependent and to function as continuous rather than as discrete outcomes. As Suh (2014: 3–4) claims, "The relationship between social movements and movement outcomes is reciprocal, and more important, dialectical." What appears to be a loss – and often is simply that – may also be the foundation for a second, or even third, try.

Third, loss in a social movement campaign, and its impact upon future remobilization chances, beyond political opportunity structures, may be less dependent on actual material circumstances of the actors or even on the issues involved, and more determined by the collective

---

[14] In addition, in terms of success or failure, social movement outcomes can be classified as anticipated or unanticipated; intended or unintended; and objective or subjective (Suh 2012). Unintended consequences – "consequences that social movements generate [that] occasionally deviate from their formal goals" (Suh 2014, 5) can also be positive or negative.

experience of the campaign, the framing of loss, and the identity that binds the actors together. Actual campaign loss that, through political learning, becomes a positive experience of collective identity may serve to explain why some groups remobilize after defeat and others fail – or refuse – to do so. The translation of loss through collective identity may be the key intermediary between the defeat of a particular campaign and future remobilization chances.

Fourth, cases of loss and remobilization after loss should encourage a rethinking of the meaning of social movement abeyance. As Taylor indicates (1989: 761), "The term 'abeyance' depicts a holding process by which movements sustain themselves in nonreceptive political environments and provide continuity from one stage of mobilization to another." In the case of LWAPC, I use abeyance more generally to mean absence of activism. Between 1985 and 1992, LWAPC did not persist in a "holding pattern [continuing] to mount some type of challenge" (Taylor 1989: 772). LWAPC friendship networks persisted after the 1984–85 strike's conclusion, and LWAPC members were available for reactivation around similar issues involving coalfield communities and the NUM, once those issues emerged. LWAPC activists' indirect standing in the 1984–85 strike (Beckwith 1996: 1042–1043), as well as the absence of renewed labor conflict that would elicit their activism, positioned LWAPC members as available for remobilization, rather than as a small group scaling down and retrenching, struggling to maintain solidarity in a hostile political opportunity context (Taylor 1989: 772). Instead, the renewed threat of additional pit closures in 1992 – recasting the political environment as hostile – provided the opportunity context within which LWAPC then remobilized. This suggests that abeyance experience and abeyance structures will differ, depending on whether the movement is advancing or defending claims, that is, whether the movement has initiated claims for reform (e.g., votes for women) or has responded to threats from an opponent (e.g., proposals to close working pits, with dire consequences for miners, their unions, and the coalfield communities).

Finally, a social movement's experience in the course of a campaign – winning or losing – can lead to political learning that can instruct and inspire second tries (or that can lead to the rational decision never to try again). *What* a social movement learns and *how* that learning unfolds are likely to be key factors in explaining and predicting remobilization after loss. A social movement whose activists and supporters learn that they will be pilloried, shunned, and attacked by peers and neighbors in their own communities as the result of their social movement campaign activities are unlikely to make the effort to try again. Those whose community celebrates their valiant efforts, even in failure, learn that their actions were vindicated and valued, and come away, even in loss, not just with the political resources of activist experience but with the belief that they could possibly try again, under different circumstances or on different issues, and prevail. Such activists learn, in sum, that all is not lost when a social movement loses.

References

Adeney, Martin and John Lloyd. 1988. *The Miners' Strike, 1984–85: Loss Without Limit*. London: Routledge.

Adonis, Andrew. 1992. "Estimated 200,000 Join March to Protest against Pit Closures." *Financial Times*, October 26.

Beavis, Simon and Keith Harper. 1992. "Treasury Blocks Aid Funds as 30 Pits Marked for Axe." *Guardian*, September 18: 22.

Beckwith, Karen. 1996. "Lancashire Women Against Pit Closures: Women's Standing in a Men's Movement." *Signs*, 21(4) Summer: 1034–1068.

Beckwith, Karen. 1997. "Movement in Context: Women and Miners' Campaigns in Britain." In Ricca Edmondson (ed.), *The Political Context of Collective Action*. London: Routledge Press, 15–32.

Beckwith, Karen. 2013. "Narratives of Defeat: Explaining the Effects of Loss in Social Movements." Paper presented at the annual meetings of the Midwest Political Science Association, Chicago, IL, April 11–14.

Beckwith, Karen. 2015. "Narratives of Defeat: Explaining the Effects of Loss in Social Movements." *Journal of Politics*, 77(1): 2–13.

Clouston, Erlend. 1992. "Lynk's Light Shines Down the Shaft." *Guardian*, October 17: 5.

"Collieries under Threat." 1992. *Guardian*, October 10: 38.

della Porta, Donatella and Dieter Rucht. 1991. "Left-Libertarian Movements in Context: Comparing Italy and West Germany, 1965–1990." Discussion Paper FS III, no. 91–103. Wissenschaftszentrum Berlin.

Flesher Fominaya, Cristina. 2010. "Collective Identity in Social Movements: Central Concepts and Debates." *Sociology Compass*, 4(6): 393–404.

Gupta, Devashree. 2009. "The Power of Incremental Outcomes: How Small Victories and Defeats Affect Social Movement Organizations." *Mobilization*, 14(4): 417–432.

Harper, Keith and Simon Beavis. 1992a. "National Strike Call Over Pit Closures." *Guardian*, October 9: 6.

Harper, Keith and Simon Beavis. 1992b. "Savage Government Axes Kills 30,000 Mining Jobs." *Guardian*, October 14: 1.

Harper, Keith, Martyn Halsall, and Celia Weston. 1992. "Court Puts Hold on Pit Closures." *Guardian*, October 16: 1.

Mason, John. 1992. "Miners Had Right to Talks, Judge Declares." *Financial Times*, December 22: 4.

Milne, Seamus. 1992. "MEPs Back Campaign against Pit Closures as Unions Continue Fight in High Court." *Guardian*, November 20.

"Pit Closure Plan Ruled Illegal by High Court." 1992. *Financial Times*, December 22: 1.

Randall, Jeff. 1992. "Pit Closures Focus Bosses' Fury on the Government's Failings." *The Sunday Times*, October 18: 11.

Reed, David and Olivia Adamson. 1985. *Miners Strike, 1984–1985: People versus State*. London: Larkin.

Robinson, Gregory, John E. McNulty, and Jonathan S. Krasno. 2009. "Observing the Counterfactual? The Search for Political Experiments in Nature." *Political Analysis*, 17: 341–357.

Smith, Michael and David Owen. 1993. "Government Says Pit Closure Plan Vindicated." *Financial Times*, January 23: 1.

Suh, Doowon. 2014. "What Happens to Social Movements after Policy Success? Framing the Unintended Consequences and Changing Dynamics of the Korean Women's Movement." *Social Science Information*, 53(1): 3–34.

Suh, Doowon. 2012. "*What Happens to Social Movements after Policy Success?*" Seoul: Graduate School of International Studies, Korea University. Unpublished manuscript.

Taylor, Verta. 1989. "Social Movement Continuity: The Women's Movement in Abeyance." *American Sociological Review*, 54(5), October: 761–775.

Tilly, Charles. 1999. "From Interactions to Outcomes in Social Movements." In Marco Giugni, Doug McAdam, and Charles

Tilly (eds.), *How Social Movements Matter*. Minneapolis, MN: University of Minnesota Press, 253–270.

Travis, Alan. 1992. "Tory MPs' Rebellion Widens." *Guardian*, October 26: 1.

Weston, Celia. 1992a. "Pit Closures Delayed by Court Challenges." *Guardian*, October 17: 4.

Weston, Celia. 1992b. "TUC to Back Day of Protest Action." *Guardian*, October 17: 4.

Winterton, Jonathan and Ruth Winterton. 1989. *Coal, Crisis and Conflict; The 1984–85 Miners' Strike in Yorkshire*. Manchester and New York: Manchester University Press.

Wintour, Patrick. 1992. "Tory Majority Evaporates as Backbenchers Revolt." *Guardian*, October 17: 5.

3 PERSONAL EFFECTS FROM FAR-RIGHT ACTIVISM

Kathleen M. Blee

Scholars agree that participating in social movements has significant effects on activists, shaping their attitudes, identities, political involvement, and life choices long into the future. If there is consensus that activism affects a person's life, however, it is less clear *how* this happens. I tackle this issue by focusing on the processes – that is, the steps or causal chains – by which long-term personal consequences flow from participating in social movements. Using an interpretive approach, this study introduces a model of narrative-based counterfactual logic to explore how activists' understandings of themselves and their political involvement mold their sense of alternatives and lead to enduring consequences. While most studies of individual consequences of movement participation focus on those with progressive politics or, at least, democratic agendas (Bosi and Uba 2009), this study looks at the outcomes of participating in far-right movements in the United States, specifically the racist movements of neo-Nazis and the Ku Klux Klan (KKK).

Some studies suggest that personal outcomes might not differ much between rightist activists and those in progressive movements. Movements of the left and right share similar characteristics in how they mobilize participants, frame issues, forge collective identities, create solidarity, and develop goals and strategies (Blee 2002, 2012; Blee and Creasap 2010; Bosi and Giugni 2012), so they should have similar effects on activists. Other studies, however, suggest that the outcomes for far-right activists might be different than for their leftist counterparts, even on the far-left, due to right-wing support for social hierarchies, distrust of democracy, and disdain for the broader public. Because racist groups regard virtually all whites – outside a small set of committed members and those targeted for recruitment – as potential "race traitors" hostile to the white race (Blee 2002) and rarely measure success by public support (Bosi and Giugni 2012; Giugni 1998), they instill in their members a sense of victimization and fear of the larger society that makes it difficult for them to sustain social ties with those outside the far-right or to reenter mainstream life after they leave racist groups (Blee 2009a, 2009b; Simi and Futrell 2010).

Conceptual framework

This chapter argues that the personal outcomes that flow from movement activism can be understood by looking closely at how people experience themselves as activists and post-activists. Four distinct literatures provide the conceptual framework. First, I draw from the extensive scholarship on *narrative*. Initially developed as a tool for literary analysis, narrativity reveals the plot lines of stories through which people understand the trajectories of their lives (Bruner 1991; Ewick and Silbey 2003; Fine 2002; Polletta 1998). I use narrative to analyze activists' stories about their social movement participation and its outcomes.

Second, I use scholarship on *political imagination* to examine how the sense of a desirable and realizable future shapes action (Adam 2009). There is an iterative relationship between how people construct a sense of plausible alternatives and what they decide to do. As Ann Mische (2009: 695) describes, the imagined future "acts on the present [as] it guides our plans and choices, decisions and actions."

Third, I use recent theoretical work on *turning points* in action sequences (Abbott 1997, 2001). Individuals narrate turning points to denote major shifts in life patterns such as self-transformations, conversions, and awakenings (DeGloma 2007). Such narratives reveal what Abby Peterson (2011) terms "critical moments" when actors define the meaningful points of decision and action in their lives. For example, activists commonly describe themselves very differently before and after they become involved in a movement, particularly if their involvement requires intense commitment or creates great risk (Blee 2002; Ferguson 2008).

Finally, I use recent work on social movements and *interpretive processes* (Lichterman 2005) to understand the distinction between actions and interpretations of movement involvement. People can join in social movement events, meetings, and even planning sessions without seeing themselves as participants. Conversely, they can claim membership in a movement group with little involvement (Blee 2002, 2012). The effects of movement involvement thus are conditioned by the activist's interpretation of that involvement.

Data and analytic model

I examine personal outcomes of participating in far-right movements through a parallel case analysis of two life history interviews with racist activists. These interviews elicit details on each activist's steps toward mobilization and what happened afterward, from the point of view of the actors themselves. They provide a lens into how people understand themselves as racist activists and how these understandings orient their life choices.

One interviewee is a current racist activist in a neo-Nazi group, among the most active segments of the US racist movement (Simi and Futrell 2010) and in which women often play visible roles. The other interviewee is a former activist in the Ku Klux Klan, a long-standing part of America's racist history (although now in considerable disarray) and in which men generally serve as leaders and public spokespersons. Both were rank-and-file members of their groups and both are women. I collected these life histories from women racists because, in my experience interviewing male and female racist activists, women are more likely to provide personal information to researchers (Blee 2002). Rank-and-file men racists are loath to reveal details of their lives that might compromise the possibility of becoming a future leader, while men who are currently in leadership positions tend to simply parrot the group's positions as their own experiences. In contrast, racist women realize that they are blocked from leadership positions in the male-dominated world of organized racism and thus are more open in interviews. Moreover, many feel mistreated in their groups and are willing to express ideas that go against movement beliefs.[1]

---

[1] The increasing involvement of women in virtually all segments of right-wing extremism (Blee and Deutsch 2012), it no longer makes sense for studies of far-right male activists to be regarded as producing general findings about rightist movements

I use interviews with a current racial activist and a defected racial activist to capture a broad range of narrated experience. Since the factors, mechanisms, and motivations that bring activists into extremist groups are not simply reversed in the process of leaving these groups (Bjorgo 2011; Bosi 2012), entering, remaining in, and exiting racist groups can have distinct impacts on a member's life. As Lorenzo Bosi and Donatella della Porta (2012; also Harris 2010; Pyrooz et al. 2013) note, someone may join a group for ideological reasons but remain (or leave) for interpersonal ones, underscoring the need to understand motives and personal outcomes at all stages of racist activism.

The current activist was interviewed as part of a larger life-history study of women active in white supremacist groups in the United States in the late twentieth century, using a multi-stage purposive sample to identify interviewees (Blee 2002). The defected activist is from an ongoing study of women who leave the racist movement; this uses a snowball sampling technique. I define defecting as withdrawal from the organized aspects of the racist movement, although it is important to recognize, as Gilda Zwerman and Patricia Steinhoff (2012) find, that exiting members may not reject the ideologies of their former movement (also Bovenkerk 2011; White 2010).

Both women were interviewed multiple times. The interviews began as unstructured discussions to allow the women to frame their life histories without questions or prompts that might shape their narratives. This was followed by a structured elicitation in which I asked each woman to produce a highly detailed chronological account of her life before, during, and (for the former activist) after her racist involvement. The women were then re-interviewed about any discrepancies between their unstructured life history accounts and their structured, chronological histories.

These narratives are analyzed with a model developed by Robert Smith (2012) to infer causal mechanisms by using naturally occurring counterfactual processes captured in ethnographic data. Smith studied how the children of Mexican immigrants to New York City choose one high school over another. He focused on points in which these youth (and their families) express their decisions in counterfactual terms, as they envision competing scenarios for the future based on selecting one school

and activists while studies of female activists are seen as generating findings specific to women.

over another. To take one example, students/families consider whether to choose a school with many other Mexican students, or one with few such students. A school with a large number of Mexican students might be viewed as dangerous by posing the risk of being attacked by or attracted to a gang or being lured away from schoolwork with the temptation of partying and hanging out with friends. However, the same school might be envisioned quite differently, as one in which the large number of other Mexican students would protect the student from dangerous African American gangs. How people choose, and the actions that they undertake after making that choice, are highly dependent on the interpretive frames with which they operate. Put more abstractly, the causal dynamic rests on an interpretation that propels action in one direction or another.

Smith uses moments of counterfactual reasoning – how actors imagine alternative courses of action – as a lens through which to see otherwise-obscure chains of causation, similar to James Mahoney's (2000) use of counterfactual reasoning in historical sociology (also Blee 2012, 2013; Smith 2012). These moments reveal how people develop trajectories of action based on how they interpret their possible choices and the consequences of these choices. Such an analytic model is better able to deal with the complexity of causal processes in social life than is the commonly used, and analogous, method of quantitative net effects based on isolating the effects of one (or several) factor(s) on an outcome.

Smith's model of counterfactual reasoning can generate new insights into the processes that generate personal outcomes of social movement activism. It is an actor-centered model, tracing sequences of action over time from the perspective of the actors themselves. It produces, in Smith's terms, "self-reflexive assessments of causality," creating a method of eliciting the experience of the three distinct stages that are traced in net effects analysis: (1) an actor's self-definition before s/he is mobilized into activism (pre-Treatment categorization); (2) the actor's experience of mobilization and participating in a social movement (Treatment); and (3) the actor's assessment of the mechanisms by which s/he was affected by social movement participation and the nature and extent of these personal outcomes (post-Treatment). Probing the actor's understandings of his/her life processes creates a "biographical logic of analysis" that "takes seriously the informant's theory of causality in their own life, including their counterfactual on how their life would have turned out if ..." (Smith 2012).

Narratives are not simply stories. They reveal the self-understandings that propel action. Coming to understand your life as a trajectory of unfolding spirituality, sexuality, athleticism, or scientific prowess shapes subsequent choices. Such understandings also condition which aspects of life are noticed, remembered, and incorporated into future decisions and narratives. To see the causal mechanisms that produce outcomes from rightist activism, I explore how a current and a former activist see themselves as having been before they were involved in organized racism (pre-Treatment), how they experienced mobilization into and commitment to organized racism (Treatment), and the personal outcomes of their activism (post-Treatment). Moving through the stages of activism (including exit) brings a new interpretive lens to earlier as well as later experiences, understandings, and motivations.

Analysis

The narratives of the racist activist and former activist have several common instances of counterfactual reasoning – that is, critical junctures or turning points at which distinct alternative paths were imaginable. The first juncture, which they described as a shift in their life trajectory, was the point of *mobilization* when they began a plotline that culminated in their entry into organized racism. It is narratively described as the moment after which life was set on a virtually unchangeable path toward racist activism. For both women, this was long before contact with a racist group or activist. Meeting racist recruiters and discovering racist group propaganda were narrated as later events in the plot of mobilization, as midpoints in a longer path into organized racism.

A second critical juncture in both narratives occurred during the point of *commitment*, after embracing racial activism. This was when both women began to envision another way of life for themselves outside of a racist group. Although stayers and leavers made different decisions at this point, their processes were similar. For both women, it was a juncture of considerable more agency than the point of mobilization.

Case # 1: Suzanne (active member)

When I met her, Suzanne was a widely known and powerful activist in an active neo-Nazi group, SS Warriors. SS Warriors were a high-profile group in the American far-right, notorious for violent and provocative demonstrations in favor of racist policing, overt threats against African Americans, and public displays of swastikas and other symbols of the German Third Reich.[2] They staged events in areas within driving distance of their local base to protest the Jewish control of the government, which they, like others in the racist movement, termed Zionist Occupation Government (ZOG) to denote its supposed domination by Jewish elites. SS Warriors' rallies often ended in mayhem, as the group's vicious attacks on Jews, immigrants, and people of color provoked confrontations with counter-demonstrators.

Although she did not hold an official leadership position in the SS Warriors, Suzanne was a frequent speaker at the group's events because of her ability to hold an audience's attention and aggressively confront antiracist protesters and authorities. She claimed to spend virtually all her time with other white supremacists, which seemed likely as her livelihood was based on peddling racist books, videos, and clothing emblazed with swastikas and other Nazi insignia to fellow activists. She also home-schooled her children, teaching them the tenets of her beliefs, including that "if the [race] mixing continues, the white race is gonna die" and that the WWII-era Jewish Holocaust was when Jews "were so high and mighty and took so much that finally somebody got up and stood up for their rights and said, 'that's enough. Enough's enough.'"

Life before racial activism

Suzanne narrated the story of her life in an animated fashion and with careful attention to detail. She situated her current life – as a dedicated racial warrior – in contrast to what it might have been otherwise, the first counterfactual in narrative. Raised in a "nice" city in Indiana, Suzanne recalled that her parents had instilled a sense of racial tolerance. They "used to always tell me, 'Don't be prejudiced, try to get along.'" Such an attitude was possible, Suzanne's story later implied, because whites and nonwhites rarely crossed paths in her city when she was growing up. By the time she was an adolescent, however, things had changed. "More [African Americans] moved in. Then I became a nobody … I always could get along with one, two, three but after three … there was no way I

---

[2] Names and identifying details have been changed to preserve the confidentiality agreements with the interviewees.

could." Racial tensions permeated her school and neighborhood, causing her father (by then, her mother had left the family and moved away) to change his stance on getting along with others. Now he cautioned Suzanne that "if they [nonwhites] fight you, you fight to win, no matter what." And he took a second job so they would have enough money to "get them the hell out of this neighborhood."

Suzanne narrated her early life as a sequence of events over which she had no control. Although she imagined that things might have turned out very differently if the racial composition of her neighborhood had not changed (a moment of counterfactual reasoning), Suzanne did not envision a possibility of acting otherwise. The changing nature of her neighborhood changed her life. She had no choice in the matter.

Mobilization

Looking for an opportunity to leave her increasingly "bad" neighborhood, Suzanne enlisted in the Army and was ordered to report to a base in Nevada. A critical juncture in her story came as she was preparing to leave for the Army base and discovered that she was pregnant. Despite her pregnancy, Suzanne's father encouraged her to enter the Army. Looking back, she imagines that her life would have taken a very different course if she had taken her father's advice. It would have moved her away from the racial conflicts that caused her to see racial minorities in an increasingly negative way:

> I was totally fed up with Indiana . . . I had an opportunity to go out to Nevada . . . I'd be really happy out there . . . establishing myself in an apartment [with] a pool a couple feet away . . . There's not many blacks and if there are, they treat you like they're a human being. It's like, if I left Indiana, they'd be gone . . . I was totally fed up with Indiana, the blacks taking from me . . . This was my escape.

Before reporting to the Army base, however, Suzanne heard about a job opening in an Indiana nursing home. It seemed a way to raise her child and stay near her father. About the same time, she ran into an old friend, Doris, who told her, Suzanne recalled, "Oh, you don't have to go [to the Army base in Nevada]. What do you got out there? Why don't you just stay awhile. You and I could get an apartment together [and] everything will be cool, and I can watch the baby."

Suzanne took Doris' advice, a path she now regrets: "She kind of talked me into staying. And I wish I never listened to her."

This was the only point of choice in Suzanne's narrative of her pre-racist life. After deciding to stay in Indiana, Suzanne told me, things moved inexorably toward racist activism. Foregoing the change to leave Indiana, she became locked into an increasingly "bad" neighborhood where white people were always under attack. In such a situation, Suzanne insisted, she had no choice but to defend herself and her children.

> I started workin' the nursing home and I got robbed already before I even moved in [with Doris]. They done already took my brand new color TV and my clock radio . . . It was bad but I thought 'Oh, I can do this, I'll just be real quiet and they won't mess with me . . . And I think, I gotta get the hell out of this neighborhood. But I can't. I wish I woulda [sic.]went [to Nevada]. Should have went. I mean, still to this day, I'm stuck.

In Suzanne's account, becoming racist wasn't a decision. It was the inevitable outcome of the difficult circumstances in which she lived. The actions of others (violent, criminal African Americans) forced her to relinquish her earlier racial tolerance and develop negative attitudes toward nonwhites.

Suzanne's mobilization story ended with the episode in which she met Frank, the neo-Nazi recruiter who introduced her to organized racism. Suzanne did not recount this meeting as the precipitating event that brought her into the SS Warriors. [Although, in actuality, Frank's role was essential because groups like SS Warriors operate with great secrecy. People cannot join without a personal reference from a member or racist recruiter.] She narrated her meeting with Frank as just another unremark-able event in a life that was preordained to end in racial activism. If not Frank, Suzanne's narrative implied, somebody else would have brought her into organized racism. So, in her words, "I started gettin' into politics [neo-Nazism]. Then the more I got into politics the more I met others." According to Suzanne's narrative, mobilization into racist activism was the inalterable outcome of growing up in the midst of racial tension.

Commitment

A second critical juncture in Suzanne's narrative came when she recounted an episode that occurred after she had been in SS Warriors for some time. The instigating incident happened when Doris, the friend with whom she shared an apartment earlier, tracked her down and expressed dismay at Suzanne's racial activism. "Now Doris knows I'm into politics and Doris is saying, 'No, you don't need to go this far into politics. You don't need this garbage.'"

When Doris questioned her decision, Suzanne considered what might happen if she left the SS Warriors. She would have "no more hassle." She could move to another town where she was not known to the police or the antiracist activists who harassed, pursued, and even violently assaulted her when she spoke at rallies and demonstrations. In another town, "I would be driving a nice car, having a beautiful home to live in. . . . I still woulda been prejudiced to some point, but not [be] mean like I am. . . . I don't need this aggravation." But none of this seemed possible. She had changed. Not only had she became racially prejudiced, but her essential character had shifted. She had become mean, what she described as the product of being a SS Warrior. When she described her comrades – "Some of them can be good people. Some of 'em are assholes. Some of 'em can be idiots. I won't have nothing to do with the idiots, the jerks" – those she calls the "good people" were the newest recruits. Such good people, though, quickly "turn" as they face the reality of life as a racial warrior; they become mean.

Despite the drawbacks, Suzanne saw her many years in neo-Nazism as having given her influence and a measure of esteem among her comrades. "All I have to do is send a flyer and I will have everybody show up [for a rally]. That makes me feel so good because they respect me so much." Yet she envisioned her future as one of unremitting violence, repeating the many episodes of confrontation with hostile protestors in which she had "the shit beat out" of her. If she remained a SS Warrior, she thought she had a good probability of killing or being killed.

Outcomes

Suzanne categorized herself initially as a fundamentally tolerant person with no particular racial animus. In her account, she was pulled into racial activism by decisions (such as where to live) that she made earlier and for no racist reasons. It was deciding to forego the possibility of joining the Air Force that Suzanne retrospectively recounts as what led her on a path to racist activism. She made one choice that stripped away her future choices.

Figure 3.1 Suzanne (current activist).

In Suzanne's interpretation, the main causal mechanism for her move into racial activism was the racial landscape of Indiana. Once she settled there, her future path was determined. Having Frank recruit her into a neo-Nazi group was the outcome of her decision to remain in Indiana. Her trajectory into racism was out of her hands.

In Suzanne's account, the next time she made a real decision about her life was long after her entry into organized racism, when she had an opportunity to leave the SS Warriors but decided to remain. It was not the risks and costs of leaving or her lack of options in main-stream society (Blee 2002; Giugni 2007) that kept Suzanne in the SS Warriors. Rather, she felt that her essential character had been trans-formed; she now belonged there. She had left the outside world in a way that was virtually irrevocable, similar to how Ferguson (2008: 145) says terrorists describe having "crossed a boundary" from which they cannot easily return. For Suzanne, the outcome of racist activism was a transformed self that made other alternatives simply unthink-able. She could only imagine acting in a way that fit her new warrior self (Figure 3.1)

Case # 2: Lisa (former activist)

Lisa was a dedicated member of the KKK for over a decade, following in the footsteps of her Klan father (a police officer) and her racist but unaffiliated mother (a nurse). Unlike Suzanne, she was never a public spokesperson for a Klan chapter, reflecting both her shy personality and the distinctly subordinate role and restrictions placed on women in most Klans. Lisa's description of Klan life was recounted in vague, often disjointed images: "guns appeared ... you just knew that this is the Klan and this is your life" or, speaking of appearing at public rallies, "you took a certain gait in your step, learned to change how you walk." When she left the KKK, Lisa privately renounced her earlier beliefs but would not speak publicly about her time in the racist order. She hid her involvement from virtually everyone she subsequently met, including her current intimate partner, to "protect me from them, from you, from social disparage[ment]." She also insisted that she wanted to avoid what she regarded as the ill-deserved acclaim given to other racist defectors who market their stories for money or public approval. "It prevents me from obtaining any glory for my evolution," Lisa told me.

Life before racial activism

Lisa recounted her life story with far less precision and detail than did Suzanne, although her interviews lasted far longer and produced a transcript of more than 150 pages. Her narrative was strictly segmented in time, which may reflect Lisa's more extensive efforts to reflect critically on the trajectory of her life in the wake of her defection from the Klan. She told her life story as three segments of fifteen years each. Fifteen years of being exposed to Klan ideas and rituals in her family before she joined the Klan; fifteen years in the Klan; and nearly fifteen years since she left the movement.

Unlike Suzanne, whose parents – at least initially – preached racial tolerance, Lisa grew up in a family whose male members were involved in various types of organized racism, from white citizen councils to the KKK. She recalled watching Klan ceremonies from the perspective of a child for whom outdoor cross burnings – intended to assert the power of white supremacy and terrorize nonwhites – were no more significant than any other "kinds of gatherings, like church on a Sunday." To Lisa, racist affiliation was a natural – although not inevitable – outgrowth of how she grew up.

According to Lisa, most adult Klan members had Klan parents, a pattern that is indeed far more common in the insular, geographically concentrated KKK than in other segments of the US racist movement: "It seems that the Klan members who join as adults were exposed as a child, such that they felt invited and finally embraced the fledgling beliefs in their hearts, much like an adult who chooses to become baptized." Yet, Lisa recounts, she wasn't fated to be in the Klan simply because her father, grandfather, and uncles had been. Certainly, they "sort of pushed me in the direction of the Klan," she acknowledged when recounting her years being homeschooled by a racist mother. But she could envision, however vaguely, the possibility of choosing a life outside the Klan. An outside observer might trace her racial activism to her early socialization and childhood experiences. But that is not Lisa's narrative. She saw these as influencing, but not determining, the racial activist she later became.

Mobilization

Lisa narrated her trajectory into racist activism by beginning with a story of being molested as a young teen by an African American man.[3] Despite her parents' racist beliefs and her family's active involvement in racist groups, she insisted that "had I not been molested, I wouldn't have been in the Klan. I would have gone to college and had a different life. I would have made better choices ... The molestation led to [my sexual] promiscuity too." There are two causal stories here, both drawing on explanatory narratives familiar in the United States. One is that the sexual violation of young white girls by African American adult men is commonplace. This tale, repeated by racists and racist groups in every era of US history, cautions that whites are vulnerable to the depravities of nonwhites and indicates the needs for whites to band together for their self-protection. The other is the narrative that women who have multiple sexual partners do so because they have been the subject of sexual abuse in their childhoods. Had the molestation not occurred, in Lisa's interpretation, she would have been on a different path both sexually and racially. Even though she was homeschooled (to shield her from nonwhite students and from messages of racial tolerance in public schools), she claimed that she "would have sought out more diverse friends and not have fallen into" the life of the Klan and would have had a more stable intimate life.

---

[3] Even more than other parts of Lisa's narrative, this incident is likely to have been elaborated and made particularly salient in her memory by the Klan which, since its origin in the aftermath of the Civil War, has positioned itself as defending innocent white womanhood against the predatory intentions of nonwhite men (Blee 1991).

Lisa grew up around the Klan, but nonetheless described her move into racial activism in fairly passive terms, as a choice made with little reflection. "I'm having a hard time explaining how I got involved . . . it seemed more reasonable at the time." Once in the Klan, she changed. "I made new friends and started to become obsessed with race . . . I thought about race 24/7." Not surprisingly since Lisa had left the Klan, she described this life in largely negative and even bleak terms. She blamed the Klan for her rapid downward mobility: "I wound up very poor, laden with debt . . . I could not accept staying poor." And she insisted that being in the Klan made her more socially isolated ("the only life is the Klan") and dependent on the Klan for protection ("they convince you that they have more power than you'll ever have").

Leaving

Lisa provided much detail on her decision to leave the Klan, reflecting the difficult process this entailed. She traced her turning point to the birth of her daughter, which allowed her to see new possibilities for her future, breaking the pattern in which life in the Klan seemed normal and unchangeable. The counterfactual moment for Lisa was realizing that she could provide a secure life for her daughter if she left the Klan, but could not hold a "good job" if she stayed. Her sense of the future, which had been short and attenuated during her Klan years, was now envisioned in longer terms, as the length of her soon-to-be-born daughter's lifetime. Deciding to end her involvement with the Klan, Lisa started to pull away. In contrast to the passive way that Lisa experienced entry into the Klan, she presented her exit as the result of a conscious and careful decision: "people won't get out until they are ready. I left because I was ready."

Like others who leave the far-right, Lisa took steps to bring her beliefs in line with her new non-Klan reality, recalling that she "did things to deprogram myself" like deliberately seeking out negative evaluations of the Klan and other racist groups. But defection from the Klan is as incremental, dynamic, and ambiguous as mobilization into the Klan. As she drew away, Lisa realized how much she had internalized and come to depend on the Klan: "I departed from the Klan slowly . . . feeling their pervasive grip around me getting tighter the more I pulled away." She also realized that her place in the Klan was less central than she had imagined: "when I did defect it seemed as if my grand

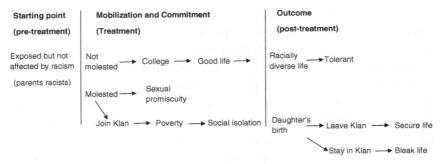

Figure 3.2 Lisa (former activist).

departure was as bland as my grand arrival ... What bothered me was that they didn't miss me."

Outcomes

Despite the deep immersion of her family in the Klan and other racist groups, Lisa presented herself as initially largely unaffected by the racism that swirled around her. Against the common assumption that children raised in racist families will inevitably become racist themselves, Lisa positioned herself as fully capable of moving her life in a different direction. It was only a later act, her sexual molestation by a nonwhite man, which destroyed her ability to choose a future direction different from the racist world in which she was raised. Until then, racism was an external force that surrounded but did not control her.

In her narrative, molestation was a critical turning point that moved Lisa's life in a direction that she neither actively chose nor could she alter it. A life that earlier had been open to many possibilities was now set on an externally imposed path. She was swept into sexual promiscuity and active participation in the Klan, automatically and without a sense of alternatives. Even as she experienced the outcomes of life in the Klan as negative, condemning her to a life of economic and social marginality and exclusion, she saw no choice except to continue on. Only an unrelated event, the birth of a daughter, broke the trajectory. Imagining life as a mother, Lisa saw the possibility of leaving the Klan as a viable option and one that would improve life for her and her child. It was this, she recounted, that made it possible for her to leave the Klan (Figure 3.2).

Conclusion

Although this study of two narratives captures a limited range of possible interpretive trajectories, it speaks to four silences in the study of personal consequences of social movements. The first is the attenuation of time. Studies of social movement outcomes generally look no further back than when an actor joins a movement. As Suzanne and Lisa's narratives show, however, personal outcomes can be shaped by interpretive trajectories that begin much earlier than the point of mobilization. Social movement participants see themselves as set on trajectories that may have been set long before they joined an activist group, and that continue to shape the possibilities they regard as salient, plausible, and even inevitable. Scholars can deepen the understanding of personal outcomes by starting analysis earlier in an activist's life.

A second blind spot is the tendency to restrict personal outcomes of social movements to easily measured changes in life-course patterns, behaviors, and attitudes. As this study shows, less visible interpretive outcomes are also important. Suzanne and Lisa both regarded racist activism as having changed their essential character, making them more sensitive to victimization and immune to violence, as well as meaner and more passive. It also shifted their political imaginations, making alternative courses of action seem increasingly or decreasingly feasible. Future scholars can extend this finding by analyzing other activist narratives to understand a broader array of biographical consequences that flow from social movement participation.

A third blind spot is the search for uniformity of experience. Studies that focus on commonalities in the personal outcomes of social movements have made important contributions, but they overlook the significance of variation and divergence in these outcomes. Social movement scholars can enrich the study of outcomes by attending to the idiosyncrasies and distinctive routes of causality in biographical trajectories. Methodological approaches that trace trajectories in fine detail over lengthy periods of time may prove particularly useful in this effort.

A final blind spot is the predominant focus on visible, fixed outcomes. As this study shows, interpretation is both an outcome and a cause of future outcomes. When Lisa thought she was fated to join the Klan after being molested, her earlier set of choices was extinguished and a new trajectory was set. Scholars can build the study of social movement outcomes by considering outcomes not as final states, but as provisional points along longer chains of causation.

References

Abbott, Andrew. 1997. "On the Concept of Turning Point." *Comparative Social Research*, 16: 89–109.

Abbott, Andrew. 2001. *Time Matters: On Theory and Method*. Chicago: University of Chicago Press.

Adam, Barbara. 2009. "Cultural Future Matters: An Exploration in the Spirit of Max Weber's Methodological Writings." *Time & Society*, 18(7): 7–25.

Bjorgo, Tore. 2011. "Dreams and Disillusionment: Engagement in and Disengagement from Militant Extremist Groups." *Crime, Law, and Social Change*, 55(4): 277–285.

Blee, Kathleen M. 1991. *Women of the Klan: Racism and Gender in the 1920s*. Berkeley, CA: University of California Press.

Blee, Kathleen M. 2002. *Inside Organized Racism: Women in the Hate Movement*. Berkeley, CA: University of California Press.

Blee, Kathleen M. 2009a. "Trajectories of Action and Belief in U.S. Organized Racism." In Assaad E. Azzi, Xenia Chryssochoou, Bert Klandermans, and Bernd Simon (eds.), *Identity and Participation in Culturally Diverse Societies: A Multidisciplinary Perspective*. London: Blackwell, 239–255.

Blee, Kathleen M. 2009b. "The Stigma of Racial Activism." In Fabrizio Butera and John Levine (eds.), *Coping with Minority Status: Responses to Exclusion and Inclusion*. Cambridge: Cambridge University Press, 222–242.

Blee, Kathleen M. 2012. *Democracy in the Making: How Activist Groups Form*. New York: Oxford University Press.

Blee, Kathleen M. 2013. "How Options Disappear: Causality and Emergence in Grassroots Activist Groups." *American Journal of Sociology*, 119(3): 655–681.

Blee, Kathleen M. and Kim Creasap. 2010. "Conservative and Right-Wing Movements." *Annual Review of Sociology*, (36): 269–286.

Blee, Kathleen M. and Sandra McGee Deutsch, co-editors. 2012. *Women of the Right: Comparisons and Interplay Across Borders*. State College, PA: Penn State University Press.

Bosi, Lorenzo. 2012. "Explaining Pathways to Armed Activism in the Provisional Irish Republican Army, 1969–1972." *Social Science History*, 36(3): 347–377.

Bosi, Lorenzo and Donatella della Porta. 2012. "Micro-mobilization into Armed Groups: Ideological, Instrumental and Solidaristic Paths." *Qualitative Sociology*, 35(4): 361–383.

Bosi, Lorenzo and Marco Giugni. 2012. "The Study of the Consequences of Armed Groups: Lessons from the Social Movement Literature." *Mobilization: An International Journal*, 17(1): 85–98.

Bosi, Lorenzo and Katrin Uba. 2009. "Introduction: The Outcomes of Social Movements." *Mobilization: An International Journal*, 14(4): 409–415.

Bovenkerk, Frank. 2011. "On Leaving Criminal Organizations." *Crime, Law, and Social Change*, 55(4): 261–276.

Bruner, Jerome. 1991. "The Narrative Construction of Reality." *Critical Inquiry*, 18(1): 1–21.

DeGloma, Thomas. 2007. "The Social Logic of 'False Memories': Symbolic Awakenings and Symbolic Worlds in Survivor and Retractor Narratives." *Symbolic Interaction*, 30(4): 543–565.

Ewick, Patricia and Susan S. Silbey. 2003. "Narrating Social Structure: Stories of Resistance to Legal Authority." *American Journal of Sociology*, 108(6): 1328–1372.

Ferguson, Neil. 2008. "Crossing the Rubicon: Deciding to Become a Paramilitary in Northern Ireland." *International Journal of Conflict and Violence*, 2(1): 130–137.

Fine, Gary Alan. 2002. "The Storied Group: Social Movements as Bundles of Narratives." In Joseph E. Davis (ed.), *Stories of Change: Narrative and Social Movements*. Albany, NY: SUNY Press, 229–245.

Giugni, Marco G. 1998. "Was it Worth the Effort? The Outcomes and Consequences of Social Movements." *Annual Review of Sociology*, 24(1): 371–393.

Giugni, Marco G. 2007. "Personal, Biographical, and Other Consequences of Social Movements." In David A. Snow, Sarah A. Soule, and Hanspeter Kriesi (eds.), *The Blackwell Companion to Social Movements*. Malden, MA: Wiley-Blackwell, 489–507.

Harris, Kira J. 2010. "Entitativity and Ideology: A Grounded Theory of Disengagement" *Proceedings of the 1st Australian Counter Terrorism Conference*, Edith Cowan University, Perth, 81–87.

Lichterman, Paul. 2005. *Elusive Togetherness: Church Groups Trying to Bridge America's Divisions.* Princeton, NJ: Princeton University Press.

Mahoney, James. 2000. "Path Dependence in Historical Sociology." *Theory and Society,* 29(4): 507–548.

Mische, Ann. 2009. "Projects and Possibilities: Researching Futures in Action." *Sociological Forum,* 24(3): 694–704.

Peterson, Abby. 2011. "The 'Long Winding Road' to Adulthood: A Risk-Filled Journey for Young People in Stockholm's Marginalized Periphery." *Young,* 19(3): 271–289.

Polletta, Francesca. 1998. "It Was Like a Fever: Narrative and Identity in Social Protest." *Social Problems,* 45(2): 137–159.

Pyrooz, David C., Gary Sweeten, and Alex R. Piquero. 2013. "Continuity and Change in Gang Membership and Gang Embeddedness." *Journal of Research in Crime and Delinquency,* 50(2): 239–271.

Simi, Pete and Robert Futrell. 2010. *American Swastika: Inside the White Power Movement's Hidden Spaces of Hate.* Lanham, MD: Rowman & Littlefield.

Smith, Robert Courtney. 2012. "Ethnography, Epistemology, and Counterfactual Causality." Paper presented at *American Journal of Sociology* Conference on Causality and Ethnography (Chicago, March).

White, Robert W. 2010. "Structural Identity Theory and the Post-Recruitment Activism of Irish Republicans: Persistence, Disengagement, Splits, and Dissidents in Social Movement Organizations." *Social Problems,* 57(3): 341–370.

Zwerman, Gilda and Patricia Steinhoff. 2012. "The Remains of the Movement: The Role of Legal Support Networks in Leaving Violence while Sustaining Movement Identity." *Mobilization: An International Journal,* 17(1): 67–84.

4 THE BIOGRAPHICAL IMPACT OF PARTICIPATION IN SOCIAL MOVEMENT ACTIVITIES

Beyond highly committed New Left activism

Marco Giugni and Maria T. Grasso

Introduction

Studying the outcomes of social movements is important if we want to elucidate the role of collective action in society. While most works have addressed aggregate-level political outcomes such as changes in laws or new policies, a relatively small but substantial body of literature deals with the personal and biographical consequences of social movements at the micro-level, that is, effects on the life-course of individuals who have participated in movement activities, due at least in part to involvement in those activities (see Giugni 2004 for a review). In general, these studies converge in suggesting that activism has a strong effect both on the political and personal lives of the subjects. Most of the existing studies, however, share a number of features that limit the scope of their findings. First, they focus on a specific kind of movement participants, namely movement activists, most often New Left activists, who are strongly committed to the cause. Yet, as suggested by McAdam (1999a), not more than between 2% and 4% of the American population took part in New Left activism of the 1960s. As a result, we cannot directly generalize from these findings to the biographical impact of participation in

We thank Lorenzo Bosi and Katrin Uba, as well as the participants of the MOVEOUT workshop held at Uppsala University on September 6–8, 2012, for the useful comments on previous drafts of this chapter. We also thank James Laurence and Alessandro Nai for the advice with the data analysis.

social movements by less strongly committed people who, in addition, might belong to other ideological areas, not necessarily to the New Left. Second, they use only a limited number of subjects and often do not analyze non-activists. The possibility of generalizing the findings is therefore very limited due to the small samples used and the lack of a control group of non-activists. Third, they look at a specific geographical and area and historical period, namely the United States (or often even more circumscribed geographical areas) in the late 1960s and early 1970s. As such, we do not know from these studies how movement participation may affect the lives of people more generally. Thus, overall, in spite of the crucial insights that these works provided, they have little to say about the effects of more "routine" forms of participation.

In this chapter we try to go beyond the traditional focus on highly committed New Left activism to investigate the impact of protest participation on political life-course patterns amongst the general population. Our main research question is the following: Does participation in social movement activities, such as participation in protest activities, have an enduring impact on the subsequent political life of individuals? This question is linked to two more specific research questions: Does run-of-the-mill activism have an effect on the political attitudes and behaviors of participants in movement activities? Does the strong impact of activism found among New Left activists in the United States hold in another country and across generations? To answer these questions, we test the relationship between engagement in social movement activities, namely participating in mass demonstrations, on the one hand, and a number of indicators of political life-course patterns in terms of political attitudes and behaviors, on the other.

Our study has three main features, which, combined, we believe can lead us beyond existing scholarship on this topic. First, unlike most previous works in this field, we not only look at the biographical impact of participation by strongly committed activists of the New Left, but we examine whether run-of-the-mill activism, such as participating in mass demonstrations, has an effect on the political life of participants at the general population level as well. Second, unlike most of the existing studies, we conduct an analysis of such effects in a European country, namely Switzerland. Third, avoiding issues with retrospective data, we use a panel survey to disentangle the relationships between participation in demonstrations and in social movements more generally, on the one hand, and its individual-level effects, on the other. Panel data allow us to make a stronger case for a causal relationship between movement participation and its effects, since we measure the outcomes at a later time point than participation and control for the outcome variables at the time of participation also. By following over time the personal lives of people involved in social movement activities we can make a stronger case for the causal effect of participation in movements on the political life of individuals.

The biographical impact of activism: cornerstones, blind spots, and promises

Scholarly work on the biographical consequences of involvement in social movements has most often focused on New Left activists in the United States. A number of researchers have independently studied the long-term impact that involvement in protest activities has on both the attitudes and behaviors of those involved. The first major follow-up study of New Left activists was done by Demerath et al. (1971) in 1969, when they interviewed part of the volunteers they had surveyed four year earlier before and after the latter took part in a voter registration effort sponsored by the Southern Christian Leadership Conference. Some of the volunteers were then surveyed once again years later in order to gauge the long-term effects of their participation (Marwell et al. 1987). Similarly, Fendrich and his collaborators have studied a sample of activists involved in the civil rights movement in Tallahassee, Florida, in the early 1960s to show the biographical impact of activism (Fendrich 1974, 1977; Fendrich and Tarleau 1973). Here too, the subjects were surveyed once again at a later stage in order to assess the impact of their involvement in the long run (Fendrich 1993; Fendrich and Lovoy 1988). Other important studies of former New Left activists were conducted by Jennings and Niemi (1981), Nassi and Abramowitz (1979; see further Abramowitz and Nassi 1981), and Whalen and Flacks (1980, 1984, 1989).

One of the most well-known works in this field is McAdam's (1988, 1989) study of participants in the 1964 Mississippi Freedom Summer project. McAdam's study was aimed to assess both the short-term and long-term political and personal consequences of movement participation. Most importantly for our present purpose, it compared participants with a sample of "no-shows," that is, individuals who applied, were accepted, but did not take part in the project. As a result, the researcher had at his disposal a control group of non-participants against which to assess the impact of participation. He found a strong and enduring effect of engagement on the political life of the participants.

As summarized elsewhere (Giugni 2004; McAdam 1989), these follow-up studies of New Left activists provide consistent evidence that prior involvement in social movements and protest activities has a powerful and enduring impact of participation in movement activities on the biographies of participants. Specifically, activism had a strong effect both on the political and personal lives of the subjects. On the political side, former activists: (1) had continued to espouse leftist political attitudes (e.g., Demerath et al. 1971; Fendrich and Tarleau 1973; Marwell et al. 1987; McAdam 1989; Whalen and Flacks 1980); (2) had continued to define themselves as "liberal" or "radical" in political orientation (e.g., Fendrich and Tarleau 1973); and (3) had remained active in contemporary movements or other forms of political activity (e.g., Fendrich and Krauss 1978; Fendrich and Lovoy 1988; Jennings and Niemi 1981; McAdam 1989). On the personal side, former activists: (1) had been concentrated in teaching or other "helping" professions (e.g., Fendrich 1974; Maidenberg and Mayer 1970; McAdam 1989); (2) had lower incomes than their age peers; (3) were more likely than their age peers to have divorced, married later, or remained single (e.g., McAdam 1988, 1989); and (4) were more likely than their age peers to have experienced an episodic or nontraditional work history (e.g., McAdam 1988, 1989).

While this body of scholarly work forms an invaluable cornerstone for research on the biographical consequences of participation in social movements, not least because of the consistency of findings across studies, there remain some blind spots. A number of such shortcomings are worth mentioning here (see Giugni 2004 for a more detailed discussion), as our study aims to go beyond them. In a way, they all refer to methodological issues in a broad sense. However, while some of them deal with the substantive focus of the study, others concern the methodological design of the research. On the substantive level, first, they all deal with a specific kind of movement participants, namely strongly committed activists, sometimes involved in high-risk political activities. As a result, they can say nothing about the personal consequences of more "routine," low-risk forms of participation. Second, they study activists from a specific side of the political spectrum, namely New

Left activists. Little can be said about participants in other movements. Third, they focus on a given historical period, namely the 1960s cycle of contention. This makes it hard to determine to what extent certain features of the life-course observed in follow-up interviews are due to individual involvement in political activities rather than a product of the special era that forms the background of the research. Fourth, they draw their subjects from a specific national situation, namely that of the United States, and often from even narrower geographical areas. We do not know whether the patterns found for activists in this country and these areas hold also in other places.

In addition to the shortcomings related to the narrow focus, which undermines the representativeness of the samples, these studies suffer from some methodological problems more strictly defined, which prevent them from establishing a causal relationship between activism and its biographical effects. In particular, these studies often rely on retrospective data (but see the studies by Demerath et al., Jennings and Niemi, Marwell et al., and McAdam), with all the problems this entails in terms of potential biases when one relies on people's recollection of previous attitudes or opinions, are done on non-representative samples, hence making empirical generalizations impossible, lack a control group (but see the studies by Fendrich, Fendrich and Lovoy, Jennings and Niemi, and McAdam), and are limited to a small number of subjects, going from a minimum of 11 in Whalen and Flacks' study to a maximum of 330 in McAdam's research.

Overall, all these shortcomings weaken the follow-up studies of New Left activists to a considerable extent, in particular with regard to the cause–effect nexus and the generalization of empirical findings. More recently, scholars have addressed this topic on other kinds of movement participants and with new methods. In doing so, they have tried to address one or the other of the shortcomings of previous works, offering some important promises for further research. For example, Klatch (1999) studied the long-standing personal and biographical consequences of both people "on the left" and people "on the right" of the political spectrum. Taylor and Raeburn (1995)looked at the career consequences of high-risk activism by lesbian, gay, and bisexual sociologists.

The most relevant work for our present purpose has been done by Sherkat and Blocker (1997). This study takes us beyond highly committed New Left activism to inquire into the individual-level effects of involvement in social movements by not-so-committed participants. Sherkat and Blocker (1997) investigated the political and personal consequences of participation in antiwar and student protests of the late 1960s using data from the Youth-Parent Socialization Panel Study. They found that ordinary involvement in these movements had an impact on the lives of those who had participated. They showed that demonstrators differed from non-activists in both their political orientations and certain life-course patterns, and that such differences were still present about a decade after their movement experiences. In particular, former protesters held more liberal political orientations and were more aligned with liberal parties and actions, selected occupations in the "new class," were more educated, held less traditional religious orientations and were less attached to religious organizations, married later, and were less likely to have children.

Our analyses follows Sherkat and Blocker's (1997) footsteps in aiming to ascertain the effects of participation in mass demonstrations on the political-life of participants, but we do so in a context other than the United States. Compared to their study, we also look at how participating in demonstrations and more generally joining a social movement has an impact on individuals' subsequent political life. We contribute to the literature in several important ways. First, we show that this effect holds also for participants other than those belonging to the New Left of the 1960s and 1970s. Second, we show it is true also of another country in addition to the United States, namely Switzerland. Third, we show this effect with time-ordered data measuring participation in demonstrations in 1999 and expected attitudinal and behavioral outcomes about fifteen years later thus avoiding the problems with retrospective data. Fourth, we show that this effect is net of the previous state of such outcomes.

In brief, our study draws on some of the advances made by these works in order to examine the potential impact of participation in social movements by not-so-committed participants who do not necessarily belong to the New Left in a country other than the United States. To do so, we make use of panel survey data. These data have two crucial features for our study. First, they are survey data, that is, they consist in a representative sample of the general population. As a result, they include both people who have participated in social movement activities as well as people who have not. Second, they are panel data, that is, they follow the same subjects over time. This allows us to make a stronger case for a causal effect of participation on the political life of participants. In addition, we are using panel survey data bearing on a country other than the United States, namely Switzerland. Is the consistently strong and durable impact of activism on the political life of New Left activists in the United States found in previous research also observed among run-of-the-mill movement participants in Switzerland? This is the question we will try to answer below. Before doing this, however, we need to discuss in more detail our data and operationalization.

Data and methods

To test our hypothesis that not only strong activism by a specific cohort in a specific country, but also less committed participation in social movements by a wider range of cohorts elsewhere has an impact on the subsequent political life or participants, we use data from the Swiss Household Panel. This is a yearly panel study of a random sample of private households in Switzerland. While its main goal is to observe social change, in particular the dynamics of changing living conditions and representations in the Swiss population, it also includes a number of indicators of political attitudes and behaviors, including participation in mass demonstrations. This panel has started with the first wave in 1999, the most recent available wave being that of 2013. We limited that sample to those born between 1934 and 1984, so that respondents in 2013 would have been younger than eighty and respondents in 1999 would have been older than fifteen, to allow for opportunities to participate in demonstrations without the restriction of too young age or mobility.

In the 1999 wave, respondents were asked whether they engaged in a demonstration in the last twelve months. We use two panel waves: 1999 and 2013. The 1999 wave provides the measure of movement participation we wish to assess the impact of as well as an initial measurement of our dependent variables that we can use as a "lagged" control. The 2013 wave allows us to ascertain whether participating in demonstrations has an effect on the subsequent political life of participants, as compared to non-participants, and gives us a sense of how durable such an effect (if any) is. By testing for political-life outcomes of protesters about fifteen years later, we can see whether even run-of-the-mill activism has an impact on the subsequent political life of individuals and whether it is an enduring impact.

While these data are very useful in that they provide panel observations for a country other than the United States, they have several limitations that need to be mentioned. The most important one is that the question about participation in demonstration was asked only in the first wave. As a result, we do not know whether respondents who said in 1999 that they had participated in the last twelve months continued to attend afterwards, so that we cannot exclude that the observed effect is reinforced by protest in later years. Therefore, it may be that protesting in 1999 leads individuals to continue protesting and that this "protest life" leads to differences in values. Ideally, we would have liked to use methods for panel data analysis involving measures of all variables in all waves. However, the time-ordering of the data is still a large improvement on cross-sectional methods of analysis since it allows us to follow respondents over time and therefore avoids relying on retrospective data. In addition, it is possible to include measures of the dependent variables as observed in the first wave, so as to be able to examine effects net of previous levels. Hence, in each model we control for a measure of the dependent variable in 1999, whereas the latter is measured in 2013.[1] This allows us to see whether demonstration participation in a previous wave distinguishes individuals in terms of their political-life outcomes in a subsequent wave, net of where they were at the previous point in time. This method is called the lagged dependent variable measure (Johnson 2005).

In order to counter the risks of finding spurious relationships, in addition to including a lagged dependent variable in the models, we conducted two types of sensitivity analysis to provide supporting evidence for our conclusions from the main analysis. First, we also ran a model for each dependent variable in which we included all five lagged dependent variables. This test allows us to further control whether we see the effect of demonstrating due to some underlying unobserved variable common to both participants and non-participants. Second, we ran models in which we included an interaction term between attending demonstrations in 1999 and the lagged dependent variable

---

[1] It should be noted that membership in environmental organizations and party membership are measured in 2011 instead of 2013 since these questions were not asked in the 2013 nor in the 2012 panel waves.

at hand also measured in 1999. This test allows us to control whether the effect of demonstrating is the same across values of the lagged dependent variables.

The variables we use in our analyses are the following. Concerning the main independent variable, we coded engagement in protest in the last twelve months as 1 and other responses as 0. The specific indicator we use is participation in demonstrations. This is only one among a broader range of protest activities in which one may be involved. However, it is perhaps the most typical form, one that has become "modular" over time (Tarrow 2011), that is, used by a variety of actors for a variety of aims. When some have spoken of the "institutionalization of protest" (van Aelst and Walgrave 2001) or of the "social movement society" (Meyer and Tarrow 1998), they indeed refer to the widespread use of demonstrations as the archetypical social movement activity nowadays. Thus, while we cannot generalize beyond this specific form without testing empirically the effect of participating in other forms, this is a form that captures much of the social movements' activities and political engagement therein.

As for our dependent variable, we focus on five potential outcomes, covering both attitudinal (the first two) and behavioral (the last three) aspects. First, we look at the impact of participation in demonstrations on political interest. The latter is measured through a 0–10 scale, where 0 is lowest and 10 highest interest. Second, we have an indicator of self-placement on the left–right scale, where 0 is the Left and 10 the Right. This is meant to ascertain whether those who have demonstrated are more likely to change (or radicalize) their political ideology. Third, we consider voting behavior, more specifically voting for the left, as a first behavioral indicator. This is a dummy variable, whereby those who have voted for the left are coded 1, while those who have not are coded 0. We focus on left voting as movement participants are often characterized in the extant literature as being closer to the left (Dalton et al. 2010). Fourth, we examine membership in environmental organizations to see whether movement participation impacts on organizational membership. This is a dummy variable, whereby members are coded 1, while non-members are coded 0. Fifth, we have a measure of party membership, so as to include institutional, in addition to non-institutional organizational involvement. Again, this is a dummy variable, whereby members are coded 1 and non-members 0.

The regression analyses below include a number of controls relating to sociodemographic characteristics of respondents and their value orientations as identified as important in the literature on political participation: generation (WWII, baby boomers, and post-baby boomers), gender, education (degree), and socioeconomic class (having a manual job) as sociodemographic controls (Grasso 2014). We also control for biographical availability, using marital status as a proxy (code 1 for being married, 2 for cohabiting, and 3 for being single). Controlling for these aspects is crucial to our test as they might affect the relationship between the fact of having demonstrated in 1999 and the political-life outcomes in 2013 (2011 for membership in environmental organizations and party membership).

Findings

Figure 4.1 shows our main findings. We present the results in graphical form in order to make them as readable as possible also to those not familiar with quantitative and especially regression techniques. We show five graphs, one for each dependent variable, or political life-course outcome.[2] The graphs plot markers for coefficients and horizontal spikes for confidence intervals. The point estimates are unstandardized regression coefficients or log odds (depending on the regression model) based on lagged dependent variable models. When the segment indicating the confidence interval does not overlap with the vertical line, this means that the variable at hand is significantly different from zero, that is, the variable has a statistically significant effect. Of course, we are most interested in the variable concerning attendance of demonstrations in 1999.

As we can see, demonstrating in 1999 has a significant effect on four out of five indicators of political-life outcome in 2013 (2011 for membership in environmental organizations and party membership), net of their levels in 1999. These are: left–right self-placement, left voting, membership in environmental organizations, and party membership. For all four variables the horizontal spikes representing the standard errors do not overlap with the vertical line representing the null effect. Thus, people who said in 1999 that they had demonstrated in the twelve months prior to the interview were more likely than non-participants to vote for the left and to be members of an environmental organization

[2] Table 4.1.A in the appendix shows the full results of the regression analyses.

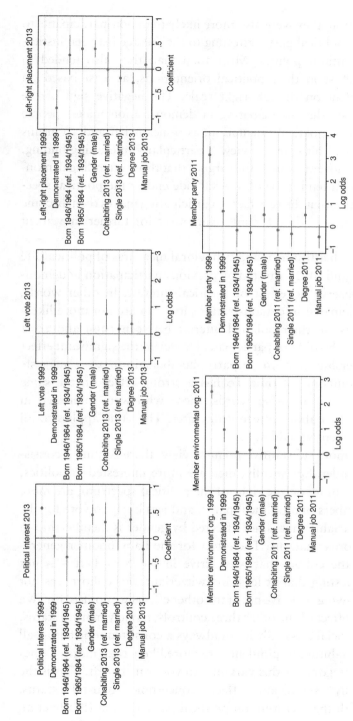

Figure 4.1 Effect of participation in demonstrations in 1999 on selected indicators of political-life outcomes in 2011/2013.

in 2011. In addition, they were also more likely than non-participants to be members of a political party, attesting to the linkage between institutional and contentious politics. More than that: they also tended to become more leftist in their political orientations, at least based on their self-placement on the left–right scale. The negative sign of the coefficient suggests that participating in demonstration makes people more leftist in their political orientation, as 0 means left and 10 means right on this scale. This is in our view a particularly interesting finding. While the social movement literature argues that those attending demonstrations in general tend to be on the left-side end of the political spectrum, here we show that the very fact of participating makes them become even more leftist, providing a reinforcing effect for further movement participation.

While both attitudinal and behavioral measures of political-life outcomes are significantly affected by previous participation in demonstrations, we observe no effect on political interest. In other words, those who participated in demonstrations in 1999 are not more likely to see an increase in their political interest between 1999 and 2013 relative to those who did not participate. However, the significant effect of party membership in 1999 on party membership in 2011 suggests that a certain outcome at time T_0 has a strong effect on the same outcome at time T_1. In other words, those who were interested in politics remained so about fifteen years later. The same applies to all four other dependent variables.

From a more substantive point of view, there is quite a consistent effect of gender. Specifically, men are more interested in politics, place themselves more on the right of the political spectrum, are more likely to be members of a political party, and less likely to vote for the left. The only variable that is not affected by gender is membership in environmental organizations. The effect for the baby boomer generation – that is, the cohort that was active in the New Left – is not significant, suggesting that at least in Switzerland this cohort was not particularly left-wing or active net of the other effects we control for. We also observe an effect of the other three controls, namely marital status, education, and social class, albeit not always a consistent one across all five models. Cohabiting respondents are more likely than married ones (the reference category for this variable) to vote for the left. This is the only statistically significant effect concerning marital status. Consistently with the literature on political participation (Brady et al.

1995; Verba et al. 1995), education has a positive impact on all the dependent variables, that is, on all the measures of political engagement. Finally, social class plays a role as well, as respondents who have a manual job are more likely to vote for the left and to be members of an environmental organization, as compared to other professions. Overall, these effects are in line with the mainstream literature on political participation and more specifically individual engagement in social movements.

We thus find an impact of participation in demonstrations on a number of political attitudes and behaviors about fifteen years later. As we said in the methodological section, in order to check for the robustness of our results, we performed two additional sensitivity analyses. First, we ran the same models but with the inclusion of all lagged dependent variables in each model. So, for example, the model predicting political interest in 2013, in addition to political interest in 1999, also includes self-placement on the left–right scale, voting for the left. Membership in environmental organizations, and party membership, all measured in 1999. The results (not shown) point in the same direction as the main analysis: three out of four indicators of political-life outcomes – self-placement on the left–right scale, voting for the left, and membership in environmental organizations – remain statistically significant below the standard 5% threshold, while the fourth one – party membership – is significant but only at the 10% level.

Second, we ran models including an interaction term between attending demonstrations in 1999 and the lagged dependent variable. Again, the results (not shown) of this further check underline the robustness of our results, as none of the interactive terms is statistically significant. This means that the effect of demonstrating was the same across values of our lagged dependent variables.

Finally, we also ran the same models as in our main tests, but on the dependent variables measured one year later only, in 2000. If we found the effect of attending demonstrations in 1999 on our five dependent variables one year later to be smaller than those observed for 2013 or even inexistent, we can conclude, at least tentatively, that the impact of participation in demonstrations is a long term one. Under control of the lagged dependent variable, the coefficients are all smaller than in the analysis for the 1999–2013 time span, and the effect for one of the dependent variables – party membership – disappears. Furthermore, when controlling for all lagged dependent variables in each model, only the effect for self-placement on the left–right scale remains significant, while the one for voting for the left remains significant but only at the 10% level. This provides further evidence of a long-term impact of attending demonstrations.

Overall, our findings confirm what was found by previous research on the biographical consequences of activism in the United States, hence strengthening them to the extent that one can start generalizing beyond the specific national case. They also confirm in particular the findings of Sherkat and Blocker (1997). They suggest that previous participation in mass demonstrations has a significant and enduring impact on the political life of participants. In other words, even low-risk activism distinguishes people on political-life outcomes of movement participation. Most importantly, these effects are durable, as they are observed after fifteen years or so.

Conclusion

This chapter has explored the question of the biographical outcomes of activism. In particular, it employed panel data from a general population household survey from a country other than the United States to examine whether participation in protest activities has an impact on the subsequent political life of participants. Results showed that it does. Specifically, previous participation in demonstrations in Switzerland significantly affected participants' political attitudes and behaviors when they were interviewed a year later. Most importantly, we found that impact to be visible later in time, namely fifteen years later. Thus, according to our analysis, demonstrating has an important and durable effect on such political-life outcomes as self-placement on the left–right scale, voting for the left, membership in environmental organizations, and party membership. The only indicator for which we found no evidence is political interest.

We have understood attending a demonstration as a marker of deeper political involvement with social movements. Our analysis suggests that participating in demonstrations and, more generally, being active in social movements changes people and has an impact on their subsequent political life, both at the attitudinal and the behavioral level. We have shown that this effect is net of their previous level of political engagement as well as of their current social characteristics and biographical availability. It stands to reason that joining a social movement would lead individuals to keep their commitment to contentious politics, but also to become engaged in more institutional forms of participation. Furthermore, it also seems to lead them to become more leftist in their political orientations, be it in terms of self-placement on the left–right scale or in terms of voting for the left.

What lessons can we draw from our findings and what avenues for future research do they open up? The first and foremost lesson is that the biographical impact of participation in social movement activities is not limited to highly committed New Left activists. As was discussed in the literature review, previous research has abundantly shown that activism by the American New Left in the late 1960s and early 1970s had a strong effect both on the political and personal lives of participants. Our analysis suggests that not only strongly committed activists, but also run-of-the-mill activists undergo a transformation through participating in social movements. Their political attitudes and behavioral patterns in their later lives are changed through this earlier involvement. Thus, we have contributed to the still rare scholarship on individual-level effects of involvement in social movements by not-so-committed participants (McAdam 1999a; Sherkat and Blocker 1997; Van Dyke et al. 2000; Wilhelm 1998). These studies have used random samples of American citizens to examine the impact of ordinary involvement in social movements on the lives of those who had participated, showing that demonstrators differed from non-activists in both their political orientations and certain life-course patterns. We have replicated this research on a different sample using the Swiss Household Panel and obtained similar findings as far as certain political attitudes and behaviors are concerned. The time-ordered nature of our data avoided issues with retrospective data and problems of recall.

The importance of our findings lies above all in the fact that they allow scholarship to go beyond highly committed New Left activism. Although our analysis should be developed in future research, both theoretically and methodologically, our results suggest that the biographical outcomes of social movements are not confined to a specific generation of strongly committed activists mobilizing during the 1960s and 1970s within the New Left in the United States. Rather, our results show that these findings can be generalized to other cohorts of people involved in social movement activities with much lower intensity and in different countries, at a different point in time.

The fact that we used survey data to generalize existing findings to a new country, other cohorts, and participants in general population samples allows us to draw wider conclusions about whether participation in social movement activities can translate into aggregate-level outcomes, in other words, whether protest participation can be seen to alter the political life of the population more generally and not just those of a handful of highly committed activists living in self-consciously counter-cultural enclaves. As was shown by McAdam (1999a), there is a broader life-course impact of movement activity.

Our findings are important for the study of the consequences of social movements. They suggest that attending a demonstration can change people. Participation in social movement activities influences individuals in certain key aspects of their political life such as their ideology or positioning on the left–right scale, their voting behavior, and also their organizational membership. While such biographical outcomes are readily understandable when it comes to strongly committed social movement activists who dedicate their whole lives, sometimes paying a high price, for the movement, how is it that the simple act of participating in a demonstration can change attitudes for the long-term even amongst the general population? The answer to this question calls for a reflection on the mechanisms linking participation in demonstrations to the political life of participants.

One possible explanation is that attending mass demonstrations works as an initiator of "cognitive liberation" (McAdam 1999b): it allows for individuals to realize the importance of political engagement and action to improve the world we live in, not only through continued activism, but also in joining a social movement organization or, on the institutional side, a political party. The effect may also be more "structural:" attending a demonstration also allows for meeting other, politically engaged, people. So, just as joining a social movement can be explained, at least in part, by pre-existing social ties and interpersonal networks (McAdam and Paulsen 1993; Passy 2003), the very fact of participating puts people in contact with similarly minded individuals, therefore providing a reinforcing mechanism stimulating the deepening of one's political beliefs. Exchanges and communications occurring during or in the aftermath of attending a demonstration would contribute to making the participant more politically aware and committed.

Moreover, this process would also contribute to the formation of a collective identity, crucial in particular for engagement in social movements (Polletta 2001). Additionally, it may be that participation reinforces attitudes that lead to repeated participation. In this way, attendance at a demonstration can initiate one to a new "protest life" that leads to further, more wide-ranging personal changes.

Further research is needed in order to test the internal and external validity of our findings. Concerning the former, as was stressed in the methodological section, panel data with measures available at all points in time would be desirable. Concerning the latter, for example, future research should aim to test whether we observe similar patterns in yet other contexts. Regardless, our findings show that something about participating in protest activities has important effects on political life-course patterns. This could be since individuals engaged in social movement activities have the courage, the mental structures, the resources, and so forth to remain committed to social and political causes or to become even more committed to them. Future research should aim to test and verify these mechanisms.

Appendix

Table 4.1.A *Lagged dependent variable regression models (1999–2011/2013)*

	Political interest 2013	Left–right self-placement 2013	Left voting 2013	Membership environmental organization 2011	Party membership 2011
Demonstrating 1999	0.04 (0.21)	−0.78*** (0.19)	1.22*** (0.30)	0.97*** (0.25)	0.66* (0.31)
Born 1946/1964 (ref.: 1934/1945)	−0.37 (0.24)	0.28 (0.20)	−0.10 (0.35)	0.08 (0.34)	−0.16 (0.38)
Born 1965/1984 (ref.: 1934/1945)	−0.64** (0.25)	0.40 (0.21)	−0.30 (0.36)	0.16 (0.35)	−0.26 (0.40)
Male	0.46*** (0.10)	0.40*** (0.09)	−0.38* (0.15)	0.02 (0.13)	0.51** (0.18)

Table 4.1.A (*cont.*)

	Political interest 2013	Left–right self-placement 2013	Left voting 2013	Membership environmental organization 2011	Party membership 2011
Cohabiting (ref.: married)	0.32 (0.19)	−0.01 (0.17)	0.74** (0.28)	0.26 (0.25)	−0.14 (0.38)
Single (ref.: married)	0.07 (0.16)	−0.18 (0.14)	0.19 (0.24)	0.38 (0.19)	−0.31 (0.30)
Education (degree)	0.37** (0.12)	−0.27** (0.10)	0.37* (0.17)	0.40** (0.16)	0.52** (0.20)
Manual job	−0.21 (0.14)	0.09 (0.13)	−0.52* (0.25)	−0.91*** (0.23)	−0.44 (0.27)
Lagged dependent variable (1999)	0.59*** (0.02)	0.51*** (0.02)	2.64*** (0.15)	2.50*** (0.14)	3.14*** (0.19)
Constant	2.74*** (0.26)	2.16*** (0.23)	−1.90*** (0.36)	−2.21*** (0.35)	−2.85*** (0.40)
N	1569	1307	1324	1797	1796
R-squared / Pseudo R-squared	0.472	0.372	0.294	0.238	0.281
Log likelihood	−3235.74	−2437.19	−563.61	−739.90	−487.32

* $p < 0.05$, ** $p < 0.01$, *** $p < 0.001$
Notes: OLS models for political interest and left–right self-placement. Logit models for left-voting, membership in environmental organizations, and party membership. Standard errors in parentheses. The lagged dependent variables are the same as the dependent variable in each model but measured in 1999, at the same time as demonstrating. Controls are from the same survey year as the dependent variable. The measures of membership in environmental organizations and party membership are from 2011.

References

Abramowitz, Stephen I. and Alberta J. Nassi. 1981 "Keeping the Faith: Psychological Correlates of Activism Persistence into Middle Adulthood." *Journal of Youth and Adolescence*, 10: 507–523.

Brady, Henry E., Sidney Verba, and Kay Lehman Scholzman. 1995. "Beyond SES? A Resource Model of Political Participation." *American Political Science Review*, 89: 271–294.

Dalton, Russell, Alix van Sickle, and Steven Weldon. 2010. "The Individual-Institutional Nexus of Protest Behaviour." *British Journal of Political Science*, 40: 51–73.

Demerath, N.J., Gerald Marwell, and Michael Aiken. 1971. *Dynamics of Idealism*. San Francisco: Jossey-Bass.

Fendrich, James M. 1974. "Activists Ten Years Later: A Test of Generational Unit Continuity." *Journal of Social Issues*, 30: 95–118.

Fendrich, James M. 1977. "Keeping the Faith or Pursuing the Good Life: A Study of the Consequences of Participation in the Civil Rights Movement." *American Sociological Review*, 42: 144–157.

Fendrich, James M. 1993. *Ideal Citizens*. Albany: State University of New York Press.

Fendrich, James M. and A.T. Tarleau. 1973. "Marching to a Different Drummer: Occupational and Political Correlates of Former Student Activists." *Social Forces*, 52: 245–253.

Fendrich, James M. and Elis M. Krauss. 1978. "Student Activism and Adult Left-Wing Politics: A Causal Model of Political Socialization for Black, White and Japanese Students of the 1960s Generation." *Research in Social Movements, Conflict and Change*, 1: 231–256.

Fendrich, James M. and Kenneth L. Lovoy. 1988. "Back to the Future: Adult Political Behavior of Former Political Activists." *American Sociological Review*, 53: 780–784.

Giugni, Marco. 2004. "Personal and Biographical Consequences." In David A. Snow, Sarah Soule, and Hanspeter Kriesi (eds.), *The Blackwell Companion to Social Movements*. Oxford: Blackwell, 489–507.

Grasso, Maria. 2014. "Age-Period-Cohort Analysis in a Comparative Context: Political Generations and Political Participation Repertoire." *Electoral Studies*. 33:63–76.

Jennings, M. Kent and Richard G. Niemi. 1981. *Generations and Politics*. Princeton, NJ: Princeton University Press.

Johnson, David. 2005. "Two-Wave Panel Analysis: Comparing Statistical Methods for Studying the Effects of Transition." *Journal of Marriage and Family*, 67: 1061–1075.

Klatch, Rebecca. 1999. *A Generation Divided*. Berkeley: University of California Press.

Maidenberg, Michael and Philip Meyer. 1970. "The Berkeley Rebels Five Years Later: Has Age Mellowed the Pioneer Radicals?" *Detroit Free Press*, February 1–7.

Marwell, Gerald, Michael Aiken, and N.J. Demerath. 1987. "The Persistence of Political Attitudes among 1960s Civil Rights Activists." *Public Opinion Quarterly*, 51: 359–375.

McAdam, Doug. 1988. *Freedom Summer*. New York: Oxford University Press.

McAdam, Doug. 1989. "The Biographical Consequences of Activism." *American Sociological Review*, 54: 744–760.

McAdam, Doug. 1999a. "The Biographical Impact of Activism." In M. Giugni, D. McAdam, and C. Tilly (eds.), *How Social Movements Matter*. Minneapolis: University of Minnesota Press, 117–146.

McAdam, Doug. 1999b [1982]. *Political Process and the Development of Black Insurgency, 1930–1970*, Second edition. Chicago: University of Chicago Press.

McAdam, Doug and Ronnelle Paulsen. 1993. "Specifying the Relationship Between Social Ties and Activism." *American Journal of Sociology*, 99: 640–667.

Meyer, David S. and Sidney Tarrow (eds.). 1998. *The Social Movement Society: Contentious Politics for a New Century*. Lanham, MD: Rowman and Littlefield.

Nassi, Alberta J. and Stephen I. Abramowitz. 1979 "Transition or Transformation? Personal and Political Development of Former Berkeley Free Speech Movement Activists." *Journal of Youth and Adolescence*, 8: 21–35.

Passy, Florence. 2003. "Social Networks Matter. But How?" In Mario Diani and Doug McAdam (eds.), *Social Movements and Networks: Relational Approaches to Collective Action*. Oxford: Oxford University Press, 21–48.

Polletta, Francesca and James M. Jasper. 2001. "Collective Identity and Social Movements." *Annual Review of Sociology*, 27: 283–305.

Sherkat, Darren E. and Blocker T. Jean. 1997: Explaining the Political and Personal Consequences of Protest. *Social Forces*, 75, 1049–1070.

Taylor, Verta and N. C. Raeburn. 1995. "Identity Politics as High-Risk Activism: Career Consequences for Lesbian, Gay, and Bisexual Sociologists." *Social Problems*, 42: 252–273.

Tarrow, Sidney. 2011. *Power in Movement: Social Movements and Contentious Politics*. Cambridge: Cambridge University Press.

Van Aelst, Peter and Stefaan Walgrave. 2001. "Who is that (Wo)man in the Street? From the Normalisation of Protest to the Normalisation of the Protester." *European Journal of Political Research*, 39: 461–486.

Van Dyke, Nella, Doug McAdam, and Brenda Wilhelm. 2000. "Gendered Outcomes: Gender Differences in the Biographical Consequences of Activism." *Mobilization*, 5: 161–177.

Verba, Sidney, Kay Lehman Schlozman, and Henry E. Brady. 1995. *Voice and Equality: Civic Voluntarism in American Politics*. Cambridge, MA: Harvard University Press.

Whalen, Jack and Richard Flacks. 1980. "The Isla Vista 'Bank Burners' Ten Years Later: Notes on the Fate of Student Activists." *Sociological Focus*, 13: 215–236.

Whalen, Jack and Richard Flacks. 1984. "Echoes of Rebellion: The Liberated Generation Grows Up." *Journal of Political and Military Sociology*, 12: 61–78.

Whalen, Jack and Richard Flacks. 1989. *Beyond the Barricades*. Philadelphia: Temple University Press.

Wilhelm, Brenda. 1998 "Changes in Cohabitation across Cohorts: The Influence of Political Activism." *Social Forces*, 77: 289–310.

5 EXAMINING THE INTERGENERATIONAL OUTCOMES OF SOCIAL MOVEMENTS

The case of feminist activists and their children

Camille Masclet

Introduction

Research on the outcomes of social movements has tended to focus on institutional and political impacts as opposed to individual impacts. Indeed, scholars have generally emphasized the intended consequences of protest activities while leaving the unintended effects, such as biographical consequences, relatively unexamined. However, despite this general trend, several studies conducted since the 1970s have dealt with the impact of activism on the life-course of those who participated in social movements (for a review, see Fillieule 2009; Giugni 2004; Leclercq and Pagis 2011; McAdam 1989, 1999). These studies are characterized by the consistency of their findings, which all point to a "powerful and enduring impact of participation in movement activities on the biographies of participants" (Giugni 2004: 494). Using different methods, the studies show the existence of long-term effects of activism not only on the core participants (McAdam 1988; Whalen & Flacks 1989) but also on the less strongly committed participants (Sherkat & Blocker 1997; Wilhem 1998). More precisely, they demonstrate that three aspects of activists' lives are durably affected by contentious activities: political participation, professional career, and family life. Concerning the last area, various studies highlight that former activists are more likely than their age

I thank Marie Bergström and the editors of this volume for helpful comments on earlier drafts.

peers to have married late in life, divorced, or remained single. Yet despite these findings – which are an incentive to investigate the personal and family spheres of former activists – the issue of activists' children is mostly absent in the majority of studies, or else limited to indicators such as child-bearing rates.[1] Only a few studies have gone further in an analysis of activists' family lives and showed that the education of the activists' children could constitute a way by which former activists could keep working for social change (Whittier 1995). However, the question of the effects on children is generally not tackled. The same can be said about research on political socialization. Although intergenerational transmission within the family lies at the core of investigations on political socialization (Abendschön 2013; Jennings 2007; Jennings et al. 2009), few inquiries have been dedicated to the specific question of the influence of political commitment on activists' children. Thus, we observe that on the whole, intergenerational transmission within the activists' families remains an understudied issue in the field of political socialization as well as in research on the biographical consequences of activism. However, some recent studies have addressed this topic and showed that merging the two areas of study and literature is highly relevant (Pagis 2009, 2014; Quéniart et al. 2008).

The aim of this chapter is to investigate the intergenerational influence of social movement activism by examining the specific case of feminist activists and their children. In an ongoing research project, I examine under what conditions feminist activism has an impact on the "second generation" who grew up and became adults in a political context different from that of their parents. More generally, this contribution argues that developing research on activists' children can provide insights into the issue of social movement outcomes. By focusing on the activists' offspring, this perspective first contributes to the analysis of the biographical changes produced by social movement activism even on those who were not activists. Thereby, it addresses the issue of the aggregate-level changes (Goldstone and McAdam 2001; McAdam 1999; Whittier 2015). The influence of political activism on the socialization of the second generation can be considered as another way by which social movements produce social change in the wake of

---

[1] This absence can also be related to a general tendency in the literature to restrict biographical outcomes to easily measured changes in life-course patterns, behaviors and attitudes, as pointed out by Kathleen Blee (Chapter 3).

the reflections about the diffusion process (McAdam 1999). Finally, the investigation of the second generation also leads to articulate the micro, meso, and macro levels in the analysis of social movements' outcomes.

This investigation draws on a case study of women who took part in the French Women's Liberation Movement (WLM) in the 1970s, and their offspring. The WLM designates the radical second wave feminist groups that emerged in the aftermath of May 1968. These groups struggled for free contraception and abortion among other claims and used contentious repertories of actions such as meetings, demonstrations, and petitions but also practicing illegal abortions (Pavard 2009, 2012). They also railed against the dominant definition of women's roles as mothers and spouses (Bereni 2013). In parallel with these mobilizations, the WLM was also composed by consciousness raising groups in which women collectively analyzed their oppression. These women's groups generally served as an important agent of (re)socialization for their participants (Achin and Naudier 2010; Masclet 2009; Whittier 1995). Through its claims (the women's right to dispose their own body) and its practices (sexual separatism and rejection of hierarchical organization), the WLM contributed to the questioning of gender relations in various spheres and produced a politicization of everyday life with the idea that the personal is political (Picq 1993). Because of these characteristics, I assumed that participation in the WLM has produced effects on the personal and family lives of the feminist activists and that it has therefore influenced their children's socialization. The initial findings of the study confirm this hypothesis and show that participation in the 1970s women's movement is an experience that led feminist activists to question gender norms and roles and to set up according practices in their own lives. Some changes and redefinitions were operated in the areas of sexuality, the couple, and the family. Furthermore, the feminist veterans who became mothers have considered education as a domain where they could continue questioning the gender system in the wake of their political activism and most of them tried to raise their children from a feminist perspective.

This contribution is dedicated to the analysis of the political inheritance of the feminists' children in order to address the issue of the intergenerational effects of social movement activism. To what extent has the political socialization of the second generation been influenced by their mothers' activism? And what are the contents of their political inheritances? To answer these questions, I will first give a general overview of the political inheritances of the children interviewed. I will then focus on two cases of the feminists' children in order to propose an in-depth analysis of their socialization. This would allow us to show the complexity of the transmission process but also to give further empirical evidence of the intergenerational outcomes of the feminist movement.

Presentation of the study

This chapter presents empirical data from my ongoing fieldwork. The research consists of matched in-depth interviews with some women who participated in the 1970s women's movement and their children. The former feminist activists interviewed (n = 42) were involved in one or several groups and organizations that composed the WLM in Lyon and Grenoble – the two French cities selected for the study.[2] The feminists' activist careers are heterogeneous and differ after their participation in the 1970s feminist movement, some of them remaining strongly involved in the feminist organizations while others not. The sample was limited neither to women who have raised children nor to hetero-sexual women, even if this is the profile of the majority of the respondents. The second part of the fieldwork consists of interviews conducted with the children of some of the feminist respondents (n = 24). I decided to interview both daughters and sons and as far as possible several siblings in order to analyze variations in the appropriation of the political legacy. The sample of children included fifteen women and nine men, their age ranging between nineteen and forty-five years old at the time of the interview. Conducting matched interviews with mothers and children is a method already used in some previous studies in the field of political socialization (Percheron 1993). This allows us to independently collect information from mothers and children and to avoid some well-known biases (Niemi 1973). Moreover, an analysis based on the comparison of interviews conducted with different family members produces some interesting data on the socialization dynamics within a specific family. Here I address mainly the findings from the

---

[2] The selection of these two French provincial cities answers different research objectives. In order to articulate the activists' trajectories in the organizational and political context in which they took place, it was necessary to reconstruct and map this context and its evolutions through archival and oral history work (Masclet 2014). This means working on some cities smaller than Paris. On the other hand, this research also aims at investigating the issue of the biographical consequences of feminist activism about some "common" women and not about the great figures of the 1970s women's movement who were mainly Parisian and have already been investigated in previous studies.

interviews conducted with the feminists' children, although I also interviewed their mothers separately. Finally, since this work is based on limited and specific cases, we consider this study to be exploratory.

Do the feminists' children become (feminist) activists? A general overview of the political socialization of the second generation

In a recent study on family transmission based on longitudinal data (Jennings et al. 2009), the authors conclude that "families marked by parental political engagement and frequent political interchanges are families fostering the transmission of political attitudes and identities from parents to child." According to these results, we can assume that the activists' children have inherited political dispositions in relation to their mothers' activism. But what are these political traits? In what follows, we explore the political content of the children's inheritance. This analysis is based here on a classic approach to political socialization. In other words, we will examine the dimensions usually considered as political in the literature on political socialization (Jennings 2007; Maurer 2000).

First, we will focus on the conventional political traits generally investigated in the inquiries on family transmission: political orientation, politicization, and political participation. The data come from the analysis of the interviews and direct questions systematically asked at the end of the interviews.[3]

Regarding the political orientations – assessed notably through a binary Left–Right dimension, which is the basic cleavage and the most suitable indicator in France as demonstrated in previous studies (Percheron and Jennings 1981) – we observed that all the children interviewed except two were left-wing, just like their parents.[4] The majority of

[3] The questions systematically asked were the following: What is the political party that you feel the closest to? What are your practices regarding voting? The other dimensions, such as the political stances of the respondents or their participation in social movement or political organizations, usually emerged during the interviews.

[4] It is not possible to give a detailed presentation of the parents' political socialization here even though this would be necessary. However, we can mention that the majority of the interviewed feminist veterans have maintained their left-wing or far-left stances since the 1970s and, on the whole, keep being very interested in politics whether they are still involved in political organizations today or not. Most of them had children with a partner who was also an activist (but not a feminist one) during the 1970s and all the fathers are left-wing.

the children presented this political orientation as something natural, underlined by the words of one feminist veteran's daughter, Laure (born in 1983): "It has always been something obvious and unquestioned that we are left-wing. I have always known that, it was not negotiable. We were collectively left-wing: our families and all our relatives." Regarding the two individuals who do not identify as left-wing, one declared being "a socialist" but refused to consider this orientation left-wing given that he is "not a progressive"; the other one declared being politically in the center.[5] However, the analysis shows that a significant part of the respondents are not only left-wing but define their political stances as far-left. Indeed, when asked which political party they felt closest to, half of the respondents mentioned a far-left party such as le Nouveau Parti Anticapitaliste (NPA) or le Front de gauche.

Furthermore, the feminists' children interviewed seem to be highly politicized. This is suggested by the interest in politics they reported during the interviews. Only one interviewee reported having little interest in politics, while the rest reported being strongly or quite interested in politics. Pablo (born in 1968), one of the interviewed children, explained for instance that he is "very fond of politics" and added as proof that he has been a subscriber to Le Monde diplomatique (a radical and intellectual French newspaper) for fifteen years. The analysis of the children's voting practices confirms this high level of politicization. Most of them declared that they always or generally vote, even though they often feel uncomfortable with this practice. The two interviewees who declared that they never vote presented this fact as a political choice. Gilles (born in 1988) for example, who was close to certain libertarian groups when he was younger, explained that "[his] abstention comes from the fact that [he] doesn't believe in the way the democratic system is currently functioning." It is also interesting to note that some of the children presented voting as a family practice: "My parents are very critical toward democracy but we go to the polls. We have always gone to the polls and I have kept this habit" (Sandrine, born in 1970). Sandrine's quote underlines the important role that the socialization process within the family plays in her attitude toward voting.

---

[5] This general trend of reproduction is not surprising given that, according to Anne Muxel, the two-thirds of the French can be considered as "political heirs" as their political orientation (left-wing, right-wing, neither left- nor right-wing) is similar to that of their parents (Muxel 2008).

We thus observe that the majority of the children interviewed represent cases of "successful" intergenerational transmission, usually defined in the literature as the reproduction of parental political traits such as partisanship, ideology, and level of political participation. This is not surprising given the fact that their families generally meet several conditions that enhance the transmission of political legacy: homogeneity and visibility of the parents' political choices (Percheron 1993) as well as a high level of parental politicization and stability in their political traits (Jennings et al. 2009; Pagis 2009). This brief overview shows a "successful" transmission regarding the usual and conventional indicators. However, the transmission process is more nuanced when it comes to the specific question of activism.

If we now turn to the relations that the feminists' children have to activism in general, we observe that the majority of the interviewed feminists' children have had an experience of activism. Indeed, eighteen out of twenty-four respondents have already taken part in social movements and/or in political organizations. Beyond this general trend – also related to the broad definition of activism that is used – these experiences turn out to be heterogeneous. They vary in terms of the type of political groups and activities that the respondents have taken part in: trade union ($n = 4$), left or far-left political parties ($n = 4$), radical activist groups and libertarian groups ($n = 7$), social movements and mobilizations ($n = 10$), experiences of professional activism ($n = 3$).[6] More generally, we observe some important differences in terms of "activist career."[7] A few children have had a long and intense activist career. This is seen for example in the case of Rachel (born in 1981), who went to her first demonstration on her own at the age of fourteen, then took part in various social movements, joined a radical feminist group for two years, and finally became a member of a far-left political party (*Le Nouveau Parti Anti-Capitaliste*). However, it is more common among the respondents to have had shorter activist experiences and/or a more distant attitude to political activism. For instance, Benoît (born in 1976) was a member of *le Parti socialiste* for two years when he was a student; Gilles took part in a high-school movement and was connected to some

---

[6] For instance, working in an environmentalist association.

[7] The notion of an "activist career," drawing on the interactionist concept of career, has been elaborated by sociologists of commitment and refers to a conception of activism as "a long-lasting social activity articulated by phases of joining, commitment and defection" (Fillieule 2010: 4).

libertarian groups; Valérie (born in 1975) joined a trade union just three years ago. Moreover, these interviewees do not define themselves as activists. It is also interesting to note that, in this second group as well as among the non-committed children, several respondents highlighted that they feel uncomfortable with political groups and political commitment. Pablo, for example, mentioned his "repulsion toward being a member of a political group," while Gilles explained that he is very apprehensive about identifying with a political label.

If we examine the specific question of feminist activism, we can observe that six children out of twenty-four have already participated in a feminist group and/or mobilization. More specifically, some of them have already participated in a radical feminist group or a lesbian feminist group (n = 4), others have been involved in le Planning familial[8] (n = 2), and two were active in the women's group of their political party or organization. Another one has been active in a radical activist group that is not specifically feminist but holds feminist views and often takes part in feminist mobilizations.

Who are the feminists' children who become feminist activists? A few answers can be found when analyzing these cases. First, it seems that feminist activism does not stand alone. The children who participated in feminist groups or mobilizations also had other activist experiences. More precisely, they are part of those interviewees who have been involved in different political activities and have already had a long activist career. Another characteristic that can be highlighted is that feminist activism remains a female commitment in the second generation. Yet, the political context has changed from the 1970s: men's exclusion from feminist groups is no more the norm within the French feminist movement. On the contrary, the new movements that developed since the 1990s are generally open to men and distinguish themselves from their predecessors by their rejection of sexual separatism (Jacquemart 2015). Nevertheless, all the respondents who reported having had an experience of feminist activism were feminist veterans' daughters. In this respect, it is interesting to analyze the positions of the feminists' sons toward feminism. None of them has been involved in a feminist group. Furthermore, they do not identify with the label "feminist," whereas the daughters – even the non-committed ones – generally do so. For instance, Gilles explained that he "sympathizes with the

---

[8] The French equivalent to the Planned Parenthood Federation.

feminist cause" but that he would not define himself as feminist. Pablo on the other hand responds to this question with another: "Is it possible for a man to be a feminist?" These elements suggest the existence of some effects of gender on the children's relation to the feminist legacy and more precisely regarding two elements: feminist self-identification and feminist activism.

This broad exploration of the second generation's political inheritance suggests that the mothers' feminist activism has influenced the political socialization of their children. It highlights that some traits were passed down from them to their child. More precisely, we observed a "successful" transmission regarding the conventional political traits and a more nuanced process when it comes to the specific question of (feminist) activism. These observations lead us to consider that the 1970s feminist movement has had an impact on the second generation through the transmission process that took place within the feminist veterans' families. Nevertheless, this first analysis based on the comparison of the political attributes of mothers and children – which is the usual method in studies on family transmission – presents some limitations. It is difficult to disentangle what comes from family socialization and the mothers' feminist commitment and what comes from other forces in the children's political socialization. Moreover, this does not allow us to grasp the way in which these political inheritances were transmitted and appropriated by the feminists' children in relation to their own biography. It seems therefore necessary to enter into the complexity of the transmission process through a case study. The in-depth analysis of two feminists' daughters' cases developed in the following section would also enable us to observe some specific contents in the inheritance of feminist veterans' children in addition to the conventional political traits presented in this first part.

Into the complexity of the intergenerational transmission process: a case study of two feminists' daughters

Previous studies have shown that political socialization is not a unilateral process in which children are passive (Percheron 1993). On the contrary, the second generation appropriates the inheritance in relation to their own biography (Darmon 2006; Terrail 2004). This appropriation has taken place in a different political context, which has also

influenced the reception of the inheritance among the second generation. In this section, I will focus on two feminists' children in order to
propose an in-depth and detailed analysis of the political socialization
processes that is attentive to the diachronic dimension. This case study
will enable us to move a step further in the analysis of the effects of
political activism on the second generation. After a brief presentation of
the respondents, I will examine the relations that the feminists' daughters have to feminism and in which conditions they became feminists
themselves. I will then show that their political legacy is also composed
of a specific content that is related to the feminist commitment of their
mothers.

Presentation of the two feminists' daughters

The children I choose to focus on for this case-study are the daughters of
two feminist veterans, Jeanne and Cristina.[9] In the 1970s, both were
strongly involved in the Women's Liberation Movement and they also
took part in far-left groups. They have not had any other strong feminist
commitment since the 1980s but they are still in contact with feminist
veterans today and they maintain a feminist framework (Taylor and
Whittier 1992; Whittier 1997). In both families, the parents met in the
context of their activism during the 1970s and took part in the same far-
left groups. The partners are described by the respondents as "feminist
men" in their political views and everyday practices ("as much as a man
can be" says Jeanne about her husband) and as supportive of their
feminist commitments. Cristina is still with her partner today whereas
Jeanne – whose family life changed in the 1980s when she fell in love
with a woman – is now in a ten-year-long homosexual relationship.

　　The children I present here are their respective daughters:
Sandrine and Laure. Both are the elder sibling of the family but they
grew up in different contexts.[10] Jeanne's daughter Sandrine, born in

---

[9] Names and some biographical elements were changed to preserve the anonymity of
the interviewees. Some general information about Jeanne and Cristina: born in 1945,
Jeanne worked as a high school teacher. Her husband was a scholar and he is
described by both her wife and her daughter as an "intellectual person." Cristina
was born in 1950, she studied social sciences in the university, and after doing
different jobs she created her own business of multimedia with her husband.

[10] The family context in which children grow up, such as their place among siblings, has
been underlined as an important element in the intergenerational transmission of
political legacies (see Pagis 2009).

1970, grew up during the heyday of her parents' activism. She was physically present during several feminist events such as demonstrations, women's group meetings, and parties and remembers having participated in the production of feminist leaflets.[11] Born in 1983, Laure's childhood took place during a period when her parents had withdrawn from political activism and returned to a more conventional life. As a consequence, Laure does not have any memories of activist events. She also mentioned that she did not know the commitments of her parents during the 1970s very well. Laure and Sandrine had successful school careers: both were "good pupils" and studied in French *Grandes Écoles*. After a PhD in computational science, Sandrine made a reconversion when she was thirty years old and is now working in an environmentalist association. At the same time, which is presented as a biographical turning point, she started having homosexual relationships and she is now in a relationship with a woman. Laure, who defines herself as heterosexual, is single and is currently doing a PhD in history.

Concerning their political socialization, Sandrine and Laure both correspond to cases of "successful" intergenerational transmission as presented above. They are both left-wing, as are their parents. They usually vote but feel uncomfortable with this practice. In the presidential election, Sandrine usually votes "far-left" at the first round and "blank" at the second round. Laure emphasizes that she does not feel represented by the established political parties and she defines her political stance as "far-left, radical but non-violent, environmentalist but not the Green party, feminist but not..." Regarding the issue of activism, Laure started participating in social movements and activist groups very early and already has a long activist career. She successively took part in high-school movements, in an activist group in her university, and in the alterglobalist movement by joining a group of alterglobalist activists from 2006 to 2009. All these collectives defined themselves as feminist. Sandrine did not take part in any political activity until the age of thirty. At that time, she started spending time in libertarian spheres and joined a lesbian feminist group. Before that period, she

[11] It is interesting to note that Sandrine's brother, born five years later, was not brought up in the same context (the parental activism was no longer at its peak and the family configuration changed as Jeanne started a homosexual relationship). Both Sandrine and her mother mobilized this argument during the interviews in order to explain the reasons why Sandrine's brother became much more "conventional" and "conformist" than other family members are.

states having been politicized in her everyday life and especially in her search for a nonconformist life.

How do the feminists' children become feminists?

At first glance, the feminists' daughters studied seem to inherit dispositions to activism and even to become feminist activists. Indeed, as presented above, both Sandrine and Laure have already been involved in feminist groups. In this case, we therefore observe a transmission of political engagement and even what seems to be a reproduction of the same kind of activism. I would like to show how a more detailed analysis enables us to go further than the statement of similarity by highlighting some different aspects of the transmission process. To achieve this, I examine the general relations Sandrine and Laure have to feminism as a way of life, as a label, and finally as a political commitment.

The interview analysis first reveals that, before being a political commitment, feminism was primarily considered as "a way of life" (Laure). The feminists' daughters refer to feminism as something they have been immersed in. Both Sandrine and Laure use several expressions to explain the all-pervading nature of feminism in their lives. Sandrine calls it "an incorporated feminism" that is "in her genes" while Laure mentions a "feminism by immersion" with which she was "bottle-fed." Thereby, both daughters underline how their mothers' activism impregnated their everyday life and influenced their socialization. This perception can also be observed in their relation to the feminist label. Both identify themselves by the term "feminist" but not necessarily with an activist meaning:

> I consider myself as a feminist because it is not possible to not identify as such. It's so obvious. I don't understand how you can be anything else but a feminist. But I am a feminist in my everyday life.
>
> *(Laure)*

Sandrine has the same position toward self-identification. She explains that she has "never questioned this legacy, this education, or this theory, so [she has] always defined [herself] as a feminist [...], a kind of everyday feminism." Thus, both respondents recognize feminism as a product of their family inheritance and emphasize its influence on their personal lives.

Feminism appears first and foremost as an everyday legacy. In brief, the feminists' daughters were feminists but not activists before they proceed in a re-appropriation of this inheritance. It is therefore necessary to analyze the conditions in which this everyday feminist legacy turns into an activist one and more specifically how dispositions to feminist activism are activated and how this is related to the children's biography (Lahire 2002).[12]

The beginning of Sandrine's feminist commitment occurred at a biographical turning point. At the end of a job contract when she was thirty years old, Sandrine became unemployed. She decided to take advantage of that opportunity to change her life:

> I tried to find some alternatives. At that moment I was introduced
> by acquaintances to the libertarian scene, to the squat scene and . . .
> I changed sphere. And that's the moment where I constructed my
> own feminism. I tried to look for alternatives, because I felt that
> I was not at the right place neither in the academic sphere nor in the
> engineer one. [. . .] It was at the same time that I became a lesbian . . .
> that I finally decided to live with women.

This biographical turning point can be partly related to the ambivalent contents that Sandrine inherited during her family socialization. These ambivalent contents are on the one hand the valorization of school, studies and also professional and social achievement. On the other hand, they are dispositions to be critical "toward the system," unconventional, and to distinguish oneself. As a result, Sandrine had always felt "in tension" and "on the fringes" of the spheres she was in. The beginning of activism, and more generally the biographical turning point, can be interpreted as an answer to this tension. Changes occurred in every sphere of her life: the professional sphere (with the reconversion toward a new kind of job), the personal sphere, and the political sphere. This also had repercussions on some other spheres such as friendship or family, by creating conflicts or ruptures. Thus, we observe that Sandrine's first commitment took place in a context characterized by an important level of "biographical availability" (McAdam 1988).

---

[12] As emphasized by Bernard Lahire, a disposition – broadly defined as an incorporated product of a socialization process – must be studied in relation to a context: the context in which the dispositions were created and those in which they are transferred (or not), activated, or on the contrary inhibited (see Lahire 1998, 2002).

More precisely, Sandrine entered these libertarian spheres and then a feminist group through a woman she had recently met in other spheres and who later became her partner. Regarding the political context, several libertarian and feminist groups flourished in this city at the end of the 1990s. More generally, feminist protest gained new momentum in France during this period, with the formation of new groups by younger generations of activists and the campaigns for equal political representation in government (Bereni 2013). Sandrine participated in a lesbian feminist group oriented toward political and personal discussions and practices such as self-defense and collective projects. This was an intensive experience that lasted five years. Today, Sandrine is less involved in this group but she explains that she is still involved in a feminist organization dealing with sex workers.

Laure for her part inherited some general dispositions to activism. For instance she explains that her parents transmitted a "capacity of indignation" to her. These dispositions were activated during the first social movement in which she took part, a high-school mobilization at the end of the 1990s in which she engaged "as if it was [her] destiny." Since then, she has been involved in different kinds of far-left groups. All would consider themselves as feminist groups but she emphasizes that feminism was just one of many claims and that they were not "mainly feminist." In her case, we see that dispositions to feminist activism were activated in the context of her general political commitments.

Thus, both Laure and Sandrine inherited dispositions to feminist activism that were activated and turned into an effective feminist commitment in different contexts and moments of their life. As they both have been involved in a feminist group, Sandrine and Laure seem to reproduce their mothers' activism. Yet, a closer examination of their activism shows that they do not proceed in a strict reproduction of their mothers' feminism. Indeed, neither Sandrine nor Laure shares the same feminist perspectives as their mothers'. They establish a distinction between their feminism, oriented toward gender issues, and what they perceived as "a traditional feminism," oriented toward women's liberation. For example, Laure explains that her political group was "more concerned by the LGBT issue," which was considered "as an essential issue today," than by the women issue, which was considered as "more or less resolved." She focused on "gender transgression" and not on "women's rights" as her mother did. Sandrine also mentions the difference between her mother's approach to feminism and the one she discovered in the lesbian feminist group she joined, which she describes as "queer stuff" and "gender stuff."

Sandrine's and Laure's own activist socialization in their respective political groups can explain the differences with their mothers' feminist perspectives. Indeed, Laure and Sandrine were socialized in activist groups that did not carry the same political stances and frameworks than the feminist movement in which their mothers participated (Whittier 1995). We see that while the daughters inherited dispositions to feminist activism within their family, the context in which these dispositions were activated transformed the elements of their feminist legacy. Thus, their activist socialization led them to adopt a different feminist framework, which transformed and renewed the components of their feminist legacy. This process of transformation is also related to the evolutions of the political context, and more precisely the evolutions of the feminist movements and theories since the second-wave feminism. Indeed, both Sandrine and Laure mention elements – such as queer theory, the rejection of the gender binary or the intersectionality of oppressions – that are characteristics of some more recent feminist movements and theories, sometimes called "third-wave feminism" (Bessin and Dorlin 2005; Gillis et al. 2007; Nengeh 2005).

Thus, a closer examination of the relations that the feminists' children have to feminism allowed us to go further than observing the mother–daughter similarity in the political activism in which they engaged. This detailed analysis allowed us to highlight the conditions in which these feminists' daughters became feminists and the way the context in which they activated their dispositions to activism led them to a process of transformation and renewal of their feminist legacy. In what follows, we would like to show that this feminist legacy is not only composed of the conventional political traits we have studied until now, but also of specific content.

The specific content of the feminist legacy

A broad approach to political socialization is adopted in this investigation, which consists of considering that political socialization is not limited to the transmission of explicit political contents (such as partisanship, ideology, level of political participation, etc.) but also includes other representations and practices that compose the individuals' political views of the social world (Maurer 2000). This approach allows us to observe some specific contents in the inheritance of feminist veterans' children. We aim to show through this case study that these specific dispositions are related to the feminist commitment of the interviewees' mothers and that they are characterized by the objective of gender transformation. By gender transformation, we refer to a partial and non-radical modification of gender (Bachmann 2014).

The first specific element I analyze as part of a feminist legacy concerns the children's gendered socialization. Indeed, in both cases we observe that our respondents have incorporated throughout their socialization some dispositions that are partly unconventional in terms of gender. This is especially true in the case of Sandrine. According to her own words, Sandrine "[has] always been a tomboy." During her childhood, she looked like a boy and enjoyed playing with tools and construction sets, as both she and her mother explained. She only had male friends and remembers being the only girl playing football with the boys in primary school. Later she studied traditionally male-dominated disciplines, such as computational science, "areas in which we were always 3 women out of 300," she states. Thus, we observe that Sandrine's socialization led her to build some "dispositions characteristics of the other sex-class[13]" (Court 2010). As Court (2010) demonstrated in her investigation, socialization studies can explain how children constitute not only "typical" but also "atypical" gender dispositions. A detailed analysis of influential institutions of socialization, and the messages they delivered during childhood, allows us to examine how these dispositions are built. Regarding Sandrine, the family played an important part in her atypical gendered socialization. We could mention for example her parents' educational practices in terms of clothing and toys when she was a child; the presence of unconventional female models in her surrounding (her mother, grandmother, and the feminist and lesbian friends of her mother); and also her mother's injunction to be "a strong woman," something that Sandrine presents as "very very important in [her] education."[14] On the other hand, the case of Laure seems to be more ambivalent. She had a more conformist gender socialization that among other things can be related to her mother's relative absence of

---

[13] Martine Court borrows the notion of "sex-class" to Erving Goffman (see Goffman 1977, 303).

[14] During the interview, Sandrine explained that "[her] mother brought her up with the idea that women are strong and should be able do everything, as well as men or even better"; an idea that was explicitly formulated and that "oriented all [her] life choices."

concern, in contrast to Jeanne, regarding the issue of parenting from a feminist perspective. However, she also inherited more "open" dispositions concerning gender roles. A certain distance to the female gender role reveals the coexistence of contradictory elements. Laure mentions that she felt out of step ("a bit marginal") with her female friends when she was a teenager. It is interesting to notice that this problematic relation to the female gender role and femininity appeared in both trajectories. Indeed, Sandrine also pointed out this issue that was mainly important during her teenage years ("Since the first teenagers' parties, I did not feel at-ease with girls' stuff seduction and so on," says Sandrine) but that could have been persistent.

It is also because the female gender role is associated with weakness that both feminists' daughters seem to feel uncomfortable with it. Like Sandrine, who was brought up as "a strong woman," Laure always rejected a certain model of femininity that was perceived as "degrading" and that she presents as the model of "the weak woman." Also, she always reacts when she hears women saying that they are not strong enough to do something "because of their gender." Indeed, being able to do things by themselves appears as something extremely important and valued by both respondents. To give an example, both know how to do DIY.[15] Sandrine developed these skills during her primary socialization as her mother proudly explains: "when she was a child, I offered her some tools. When she started going shopping, she did not go to clothing stores but to hardware ones. She is a handy woman, she is able to do anything." Laure on her part asked her father to teach her a few years ago.

> I asked my father to teach me DIY because I couldn't bear the women around me anymore who were deploring the absence of a male partner that would do stuff in the house. I really often heard that and I found it totally stupid. But the point was that I could not do it either. So I learned and that improved my autonomy.

Not being treated as a "weak woman," having – or giving oneself – the means to not be treated as one by developing a set of skills and to not depend on anyone can be considered as contents of the feminist legacy. These traits can be considered as dispositions to autonomy. Both have incorporated these dispositions but their activation

---

[15] "Do It Yourself."

occurred at different moments in life. Moreover, we observe that these dispositions were also transferred and activated in another context: relationships. Sandrine explains, for example, how she had problems with her "partners' paternalism" when she was in heterosexual relationships. The examples she gives of gallant attitudes such as opening doors show that this criticism of gender roles has been constituted as an instinctive reaction. Laure emphasizes that being autonomous in relationships is an imperative for her ("otherwise it might turn against you") and she also says that the other person's autonomy is a criterion in her choice of partners. These dispositions to autonomy reflect a certain leeway regarding gender norms. Thus, the feminists' daughters inherited dispositions to question gender norms in both symbolic and practical ways, and to enlarge women's possibilities by transgressing gender-based boundaries. This finding supports the argument present in the larger literature on gender and socialization that children raised with less gender stereotyping will develop more complicated and less consistent gender schemes (Bem 1993; Risman and Myers 1997).

Another trait that I identify as part of the feminists' daughters' legacy lies in the existence of an interpretative framework of the social world that is sensitive to gender issues. Indeed, we observe that both respondents have a reflexive capacity to perceive and analyze gender relations. I consider that the vigilance they apply to the world around them is an expression of this framework. This vigilance appears in the context of social relations (both mentioned being shocked by the way some of their friends deal with the division of household labor or with child care) but it is also displayed in the professional sphere.[16] Finally, this framework is also mobilized in their interpretation of political news. During the interview, Laure mentioned the recent "Dominique Strauss Kahn case" and interpreted it as something that "reveals the strength and the persistence of gender relations."[17] This interpretative framework, sensitive to gender issues, was inherited during the

[16] As underlined for instance by Laure's "consciousness" of "the situation of the women having children during their PhD" and her strong criticism of "the absence of concern from the unions' part."

[17] The interview took place in 2011, a short time after the beginning of the "Dominique Strauss-Kahn case." This was a criminal case relating to allegations of sexual assault and attempted rape made by a hotel maid Nafissatou Diallo against Dominique Strauss-Kahn, a French politician and head of the International Monetary Fund at that time. The feminist movements have considered this case and the way it was treated in the French media as an indicator of sexism in French politics (see Delphy 2011).

feminists' daughters' family socialization through mechanisms such as their mothers' regular speeches on women-related topics, their mothers' reactions to news concerning gender issues, and the political discussions that followed. These mechanisms participated in raising awareness and forming reflexive dispositions toward gender relations, but we also see that these dispositions were activated in other contexts. For Laure, the academic world, and more specifically her classes in gender studies, operated as the context of activation. Indeed, she took classes in women's history and gender studies while she was at the university, and I infer from the academic knowledge (and specialized vocabulary) she mobilized that she had read gender theory. Sandrine on her part activated her reflexive dispositions in an activist context that is the lesbian feminist group she joined when she was thirty years old. Finally, it is interesting to notice that this framework can also lead to concrete practices. For instance, Laure's vigilance when it comes to women's visibility brought her to use her two parents' surnames – instead of using only her father's – in everyday life and in administrative matters.[18] The aim being, as she says, to "pay tribute to the two branches of [her] family." It is interesting to note that other feminists' children also declare this practice. But, unlike Laure, they do not give any specific reason for this choice.

The in-depth analysis of these two cases of two feminists' daughters allows us to show the existence of contents in their political legacy that are specific. Their political socialization – characterized by a transmission of partly unconventional gender elements, an enlargement of the scope of women's possibilities, and dispositions to autonomy – brought them to develop an individual agency regarding gender norms and a general framework that is sensitive to gender issues.

Conclusion

The purpose of this study was to investigate the intergenerational influence of social movements by examining the specific case of feminist activists and their children. As the study is based on a few and specific

---

[18] Until the law of 2002, the transmission of family names in France was a patronymic system: children were required by law to take the surname of their fathers. Since 2002, parents are allowed to give their children either the name of their father, mother, or both. Children born before can also ask for using both surnames.

cases, this contribution was exploratory and did not aim to give general results about all the children of feminist activists. We rather tried to use our data to provide some insights into this understudied issue and contribute more generally to address the questions of the long-term and unintended effects of social movements.

The broad exploration of the political inheritances of the studied children suggested some effects of feminist activism on their political socialization. As we have seen, the children's political traits were globally similar to those of their mothers when it comes to political orientation, politicization, and political participation. The case study allowed us to go further than this general analysis of mother–child similarity in order to assess more precisely the effects of political activism on the second generation. Indeed, the transmission process is not an automatic one: some variations can be observed among the second generation in the appropriation of the feminist legacy. Only a detailed study of the children's socialization and trajectories allowed us to understand the conditions in which this inheritance had been appropriated and renewed by the feminists' children.

More generally, this study did not avoid the methodological challenges arising from the analysis of the social movements' outcomes (Earl 2000). In the analysis of the children's political inheritances, it was therefore difficult to disentangle what was related to their family socialization and their mothers' commitment and what came from other forces. We tried to respond to this challenge by proposing an in-depth analysis of two trajectories that aimed at providing some further empirical evidence of the relations between feminist activism and the second-generation political socialization. In this regard, it is interesting to underline that, in this case, the above-mentioned challenge is also partly due to the dissemination of the feminist ideas in the wider society during recent decades (Albenga et al. 2015), which can be regarded as a general outcome of the 1970s feminist movement.

In the wake of the reflections on aggregate-level changes, this investigation of the activists' children appears finally as a different approach from which to think about the broader impact of social movement activity. Intergenerational influence through family transmission can be regarded as another way by which social movements' outcomes spread to the general population. Or, in other words, how alternative patterns of socialization produced by social movements become available and diffused beyond their participants. Thereby, it sheds light on another possible mediation between social movement activity and social and cultural change.

References

Abendschön, S. 2013. *Growing into Politics: Contexts and Timing of Political Socialisation.* Colchester, UK: European Consortium for Political Research Press.

Achin, C. and D. Naudier. 2010. "Trajectoires de femmes ordinaires dans les années 1970. La fabrique de la puissance d'agir féministe." *Sociologie*, 1(1): 77–93.

Albenga, V., A. Jacquemart, and L. Bereni (eds.). 2015. "Appropriations ordinaires des idées féministes." *Politix*, 109.

Bachmann, L. 2014. "Female Friendship and Gender Transformation." *European Journal of Women's Studies*, 21(2): 165–179.

Bem, S.L. 1993. *The Lenses of Gender.* New Haven, CT: Yale University Press.

Bereni, L. 2013. "Women's Movements in Europe." In Snow, D. et al. (eds.), *The Blackwell Encyclopedia of Social and Political Movements.* Oxford: Wiley-Blackwell.

Bessin, M. and E. Dorlin. 2005. "Les renouvellements générationnels du féminisme: mais pour quel sujet politique?" *L'Homme et la société*, 158(4): 11–27.

Court, M. 2010. *Corps de filles, corps de garçons : une construction sociale.* Paris: La Dispute.

Darmon, M. 2006. *La socialisation.* Paris: Armand Colin.

Delphy, C. 2011. *Un troussage de domestique.* Paris: Editions Syllepses.

Earl, J. 2000. "Methods, Movements, and Outcomes. Methodological Difficulties in the Study of Extra-Movement Outcomes." *Research in Social Movements, Conflicts and Change*, 22: 3–25.

Fillieule, O. 2009. "Conséquences biographiques de l'engagement." In O. Fillieule, L. Mathieu, and C. Pechu (eds.), *Dictionnaire des mouvements sociaux.* Paris: Les Presses de Sciences Po, 131–139.

Fillieule, O. 2010. "Some Elements of an Interactionist Approach to Political Disengagement." *Social Movements Studies*, 9(1): 1–15.

Gillis, S., G. Howie, and R. Munford. 2007. *Third Wave Feminism: A Critical Exploration.* Basingstoke: Palgrave Macmillan.

Giugni, M.G. 2004. "Personal and Biographical Consequences." In D. A. Snow, S.A. Soule, and H. Kriesi (eds.), *The Blackwell Companion to Social Movements*. Oxford: Blackwell, 489–507.

Goffman, E. 1977. "The Arrangement between the Sexes." *Theory and Society*, 4(3): 301–331.

Goldstone, J., and D. McAdam. 2001. "Contention in Demographic and Life-Course Context." In R. Aminzade, J. Goldstone, D. McAdam, E. Perry, W.H. Sewell, S. Tarrow, and C. Tilly (eds.), *Silence and Voice in the Study of Contentious Politics*. Cambridge: Cambridge University Press, 195–221.

Jacquemart, A. 2015. *Les hommes dans les mouvements féministes. Socio-histoire d'un engagement improbable*. Rennes: Presses Universitaires de Rennes.

Jennings, M.K. 2007. "Political Socialization." In R. J. Dalton and H.-D. Klingemann (eds.), *The Oxford Handbook of Political Behavior*. Oxford: Oxford University Press, 29–44.

Jennings, M.K., L. Stoker, and J. Bowers. 2009. "Politics across Generations: Family Transmission Reexamined." *Journal of Politics*, 71: 782–799.

Lahire, B. 1998. *L'Homme pluriel. Les ressorts de l'action*. Paris: Nathan.

Lahire, B. 2002. *Portraits sociologiques. Dispositions et variations individuelles*. Paris: Nathan.

Leclercq, C. and J. Pagis. 2011. "Les incidences biographiques de l'engagement." *Sociétés contemporaines*, 84, (4), 5–23.

Masclet, C. 2009. *Les trajectoires personnelles des militantes du Mouvement de libération des femmes sont-elles politiques? Analyse des effets biographiques d'un engagement féministe*. Master thesis.

Masclet, C. 2014. "La quête des féministes. Techniques et enjeux de reconstruction d'un mouvement social." *Genèses*, 95(2): 120–135.

Maurer, S. 2000. "École, famille et politique : socialisations politiques et apprentissage de la citoyenneté. Bilan des recherches en science politique." *Dossier d'étude*, 15, Paris: CNAF.

McAdam, D. 1988. *Freedom Summer : The Idealists Revisited*. New York: Oxford University Press.

McAdam, D. 1989. "The Biographical Consequences of Activism." *American Sociological Review*, 54: 744–760.

McAdam, D. 1999. "The Biographical Impacts of Social Movements." In M. Giugni, D. McAdam, and C. Tilly (eds.), *How Social Movements Matter*. Minneapolis: University of Minnesota Press, 117–146.

Muxel, A. 2008. *Toi, moi et la politique: Amour et convictions.* Paris: Seuil.

Nengeh Mensah, M. (ed.). 2005. *Dialogues sur la troisième vague féministe.* Montréal: Les éditions du remue-ménage.

Niemi, R.G. 1973. "Collecting Information about the Family: A Problem in Survey Methodology." In J. Dennis (ed.), *Socialization to Politics: A Reader.* New York: John Wiley & Sons, 464–490.

Pagis, J. 2009. *Les incidences biographiques du militantisme en Mai 68. Une enquête sur deux générations familiales: des « soixante-huitards » et leurs enfants scolarisés dans deux écoles expérimentales.* PhD in social sciences, ENS-EHESS.

Pagis, J. 2014. *Mai 68, un pavé dans leur histoire.* Paris: Sciences Po, Les Presses.

Pavard, B. 2009. "Genre et militantisme dans le mouvement pour la liberté de l'avortement et de la contraception. Pratique des avortements (1973–1979)." *Clio,* 1 (29): 79–96.

Pavard, B. 2012. *Si je veux, quand je veux. Contraception et avortement dans la société française (1956–1979).* Rennes: Presses Universitaires de Rennes.

Percheron, A. 1993. *La socialisation politique.* Paris: Armand Colin.

Percheron, A. and M.K. Jennings. 1981. "Political Continuities in French Families: A New Perspective on an Old Controversy." *Comparative Politics,* 13(4), July.

Picq, F. 1993. *Libération des femmes. Les années-mouvement.* Paris: Éditions du Seuil.

Quéniart, A., M. Charpentier, and A. Chanez. 2008. "La transmission des valeurs d'engagement des aînées à leur descendance: une étude de cas de deux lignées familiales." *Recherches féministes,* 21(2): 143–168.

Risman, B. and K. Myers. 1997. "As the Twig is Bent: Children Reared in Feminist Households." *Qualitative Sociology,* 20(2): 229–252.

Sherkat, D.E. and J.T. Blocker. 1997. "Explaining the Political and Personal Consequences of Protest." *Social Forces,* 75: 1049–1070.

Taylor, V. and N. Whittier. 1992. "Collective Identity in Social Movement Communities: Lesbian Feminist Mobilization." In Aldon D. Morris and Carol McClurg Mueller (eds.), *Frontiers in Social Movement Theory.* New Haven, CT: Yale University Press, 104–129.

Terrail, J.P. 2004. "Transmissions intergénérationnelles." In H. Hirata, F. Laborie, H. Le Doaré, and D. Senotier (eds.), *Dictionnaire critique du féminisme.* Paris: PUF, 239–243.

Whalen, J. and R. Flacks. 1989. *Beyond the Barricades*. Philadelphia, PA: Temple University Press.

Whittier, N. 1995. *Feminist Generations*. Philadelphia, PA: Temple University Press.

Whittier, N. 1997. "Political Generations, Micro-Cohorts, and the Transformation of Social Movements." *American Sociological Review*, 62(5): 760–778.

Whittier, N. 2015. "Aggregate level biographical outcomes for gay and lesbian movements" in Lorenzo Bosi, Marco Giugni and Katrin Uba (eds.) The Consequences of Social Movements. Cambridge: Cambridge University Press.

Wilhelm, B. 1998. "Changes in Cohabitation across Cohorts: The Influence of Political Activism." *Social Forces*, 77: 289–310.

6 AGGREGATE-LEVEL BIOGRAPHICAL OUTCOMES FOR GAY AND LESBIAN MOVEMENTS

Nancy Whittier

As social change occurs, individuals' lives are altered. Whether produced by social movements or other forces, social change can affect the demography, life-course, and life chances of participants or of populations as a whole (Goldstone and McAdam 2001). Most empirical and conceptual work on how social movements affect biography focuses on effects on movement participants, who experience a range of lasting effects, as the introduction to this section describes. Movements can also shape biographical outcomes for the larger population, or for certain cohorts or demographics, what Guigni and McAdam (Goldstone and McAdam 2001; Guigni 2004; McAdam 1999) term "aggregate biographical outcomes." There has been little research on aggregate-level biographical outcomes. Existing work suggests that they vary according to cohort location, spreading from activists to the general population over time, as activists develop "alternative conceptions of the life-course and related behavioral norms," which then spread to subcultural locations such as college campuses, and finally diffuse to youth in general (Goldstone and McAdam 2001). Such life-course outcomes are generational; cohorts that have already begun trajectories of education, occupation, marriage, or childbearing are less likely to be affected by new norms. Factors such as gender and class also likely shape aggregate biographical outcomes; that is, social movements affect the life-course of different segments of the population in different ways (Hagan and Hansford-Bowles 2005; Van Dyke et al. 2000). As Guigni (2004) points out, such aggregate biographical outcomes are often unintentional.

In contrast to the previous focus on unintended effects on the general population, I focus on how social movements affect the life-course and biography of movement *beneficiaries*, the group on whose behalf the movement seeks change. Such effects can be intentional, although unintended effects also occur. Many social movements hope to change individuals' lives by opening up education, job, and housing opportunities, and changing how people identify, feel, and interact (Whittier 2009). These effects can occur despite the fact that most members of beneficiary groups (such as women, African Americans, or lesbian/gay/bisexual (LGB) people) do not participate in activism on their behalf and need not agree or identify with the relevant movement. Beneficiaries are affected in different ways and through different mechanisms than activists themselves. Participants' biographies are shaped by their immersion in activism and movement networks, collective identities, and ideological commitments; beneficiaries' biographies are shaped by movement outcomes. Ongoing participation in activism and lasting political orientation are outcomes for movement veterans, but not for beneficiaries or the general population. In contrast, when a movement successfully targets life-course patterns, as in the women's movement, changes in those patterns (lower marriage rates, later age of marriage, greater women's employment, norms of equity in relationships) are expected in the beneficiary population as a whole (Gerson 2004).

The LGB movement provides a focused case through which to examine aggregate biographical outcomes for beneficiaries. It targeted policy goals directly related to life-course and biography, including employment and housing discrimination (affecting income, occupation, and residence), marriage and domestic partnership, adoption, and child-bearing. Its cultural goals – to change societal views of LGB people and LGB people's own sense of self – are also relevant to aggregate biographical outcomes. Rapid social change around these issues cannot be attributed solely to the movement (but see Fetner 2008; Stone 2012); however, because the changes coincided closely with movement mobilization with no clear alternative drivers, we can assume that the LGB movement accounts for a good measure of them.

Aggregate biographical outcomes are part of the cultural and individual effects of movements. Social movements attempt to produce change in culture and individuals, but these changes are often very hard to track (Rochon 1998; Whittier 2009). As Guigni (2004) points out, the vast majority of work on biographical outcomes focuses on the United States, the movements of the New Left, and the baby boomer cohort. The aggregate biographical outcomes of the LGB movement are more recent in time and cohort.

The LGB movement emerged in the United States on a large scale in the late 1960s, grew steadily throughout the 1970s, diversified and institutionalized organizationally and in movement communities during the 1980s (partly in response to the AIDS epidemic), and has continued to be vital at organizational, community, and protest levels throughout the 1990s and 2000s (Armstrong 2002; Ghaziani 2008). Substantial change has occurred over time in collective identity (Bernstein 1997; Ghaziani 2011; Taylor and Whittier 1992), the inclusion of women as well as men, bisexual people, and transgender people (Gamson 1995; Ghaziani 2008), tactics (Taylor et al. 2009), goals, and organizational development and institutionalization (Armstrong 2002).

My focus is on the lesbian and gay movement. Despite the inclusion of transgender issues under the acronym "LGBT" and in some movement organizations, the transgender movement and its outcomes proceeded differently and require a distinct analysis (Stone 2009a, 2009b). In contrast, I include bisexuals in "LGB" to recognize that these outcomes affect anyone in a same-sex relationship, regardless of sexual identity. Substantial division exists in the LGB movement over precisely the biographical outcomes under discussion here: whether LGB people ought to seek legal marriage or model relationships differently; whether child-raising, like marriage, represents undesirable assimilation into a mainstream model of family; whether employment in mainstream occupations is desirable; and whether residence in gay enclaves is preferable to residential assimilation. These debates, in general, center around the creation and preservation of a non-normative culture versus assimilation into mainstream culture. These are not simply questions of strategy and ideology, but of life-course.

Consequently, some life-course changes may be similar for activists and beneficiaries as a whole, but many likely differ. For example, continued residence in a gay neighborhood after the mainstreaming of residence patterns may be more likely for movement participants. Identification as "queer" rather than gay or lesbian, or (in the earlier period) as gay or lesbian rather than homosexual or homophile may occur both earlier and to a greater degree among activists versus the general population. Further, the diffusion processes from activists to the general population differs. Activist and subcultural norms for relationships and life-course focused on critiquing conventional family patterns, while the policy outcomes tended to extend access to conventional family forms of marriage and legal kinship bonds with children, rather than non-nuclear families and chosen kin (Weston 1991).

Despite the debates, many movement outcomes have been policies that extend access to normative marriage, family, employment, and residence. In addition to policy change, two kinds of cultural outcomes affect individuals biographically: changing definitions of LBG collective identity and calls to come out; and increased social tolerance, facilitating coming out and entry into integrated social settings. Data for most arenas are imperfect. The US Census and American Community Survey, the best sources of information on most variables of interest, do not measure sexual identity and thus permit assessment of same-sex couples but not single LGB people. Changes over time in how same-sex couples are enumerated further complicates matters. Because few comprehensive data sources on LGB people exist, the paper draws on multiple sources to piece together life-course patterns; I clarify data sources and limitations throughout where relevant.

I will first assess effects of cultural changes and then move to employment, residence, marriage, and parenting. Table 6.1 provides an overview of the evidence for the expected aggregate biographical outcomes associated with each specific movement outcome.

Effects of cultural change on collective identity and coming out

Collective identity is an important biographical outcome for movement participants. For some movements, including gay and lesbian movements, the production, definition, and diffusion of collective identity is also an important biographical outcome in the larger population (Bernstein 1997; Taylor and Whittier 1992). Gay and lesbian movements sought – and largely succeeded – to encourage individuals to define themselves proudly as gay or lesbian and to "come out," disclosing their identity publicly. They saw this as a strategy for changing attitudes about homosexuality, and as a change in itself, enabling individuals to shed shame and live openly. Not only the participants adopted these new collective identities and disclosed them publicly, but LGB people in general did it.

Table 6.1 *Summary of aggregate biographical outcomes*

Movement outcome	Expected aggregate biographical effect	Evidence
Successful promotion of coming out	Increased openness about identity	Polls: more report knowing LGB people; Qualitative work: less closetedness
Cultural change: increased tolerance	Increased coming out; "post-gay" identities	Polls: more report knowing LGB people; Ghaziani (2011)
Production of identity terms and definitions	Self-identification (specific terms, meanings, and degree of similarity/ difference to heterosexuals)	Ethnographic work on changes and meanings of identity; Ngrams (indirect evidence for changing terms and diffusion to general public)
Non-discrimination ordinances (state level);	Decreased wage gap (men); Changing occupational distribution	Wage gap no lower where there are non-discrimination laws; no evidence re occupation
Employer non-discrimination policies and extension of benefits to partners/spouses	Partner health benefits (direct economic benefit)	Increased wellbeing and openness about identity where employers offer benefits
Residential non-discrimination ordinances and increased tolerance	Residential dispersal from gay enclaves	Regional: evidence mixed but increased openness over time in conservative areas; City: gay neighborhood to suburb dispersal
Legal marriage/civil union	Rates of coupling; Rates of marriage; Self-definition as spouses	No evidence about coupling rates; Large increases in rates of self-reporting as spouses; biggest increases where marriage is legal;

Table 6.1 (*cont.*)

Movement outcome	Expected aggregate biographical effect	Evidence
		Also increases in conservative non-marriage states (Definition of relationships changes, not just legal)
Second-parent and joint adoption; adoption agencies and fertility treatment open to same-sex couples	Increased parenting rates; Increased parenting by choice, decreased parenting through prior heterosexual relationships; Increased adoption	No evidence for increased parenting rate for lesbians; some evidence for gay men. Probable increase in parenting by choice; Higher adoption/foster rate in liberal states; Increase in adoption over time

The label and associated meaning of the collective identity produced by LGB movements varies over time, and thus by cohort or generation (Ghaziani 2011; Whittier 1997). A short sampling of identity terms used by lesbian and gay people since the mid-twentieth century exemplifies this: gay, homophile, lesbian, butch, femme, stud, lesbian feminist, gay liberationist, GLBT, queer. The terms carry different meanings about gender, assimilation, sexuality, and commonality with other sexual minorities. "Queer," for example, implies commonalities of sexuality over gender, in contrast to "lesbian," which in turn emphasizes similarities between women who are attracted to other women over the differences in sexual practice and gender presentation highlighted by "butch" or "fem." The identities characterize different periods in the movement and, following the diffusion model, each was first constructed by activists, and later spread to non-participants (Goldstone and McAdam 2001; McAdam 1999). Ultimately, diffusion of identity terms and definitions to the larger culture produces cultural change (Rochon 1998; Whittier 2009). Collective identity has implications for life-course. For example, Ghaziani (2011) suggests that a recent shift toward a "post-gay" collective identity promotes a sense of commonality with heterosexuals and assimilation into mainstream organizations and life paths, in contrast to earlier eras that stressed cultural uniqueness and solidarity.

One way of tapping changes in identity terms over time is through the Google Books data analysis tool Ngrams. A graph of major identity terms shows the change over time. Figure 6.1 shows the terms, "gay, lesbian, queer, LGBT, and GLBT" from 1970 to 2008.[1]

All the terms except "homosexual" increased during this period, with "gay" and "lesbian" following similar patterns; "queer" began a rise in the early 1990s, "bisexual" peaked briefly in 1995, and the acronyms enjoyed only a small, brief rise in the first decade of the twenty-first century. "Homosexual" was replaced as the dominant term by "gay" and "lesbian" by 1992. The publication of books on LGB topics is an outcome of the movement (see Arthur 2009), as is the growth in these books of terms preferred by activists over "homosexual."

Publications are one means by which identity terms diffuse to the larger culture where they are available for adoption by non-participants. "Queer," for example, is commonly adopted as a self-descriptor by college students who encounter it in their course work via "queer theory," whereas, in earlier cohorts, primarily activists adopted it through the work of the groups Queer Nation and ACT UP. Some individuals now choose "queer" if they want an indeterminate, umbrella term (Ghaziani 2008, 2011; Seidman 2002). By producing, redefining, and promulgating collective identities, activists changed the self-definitions available more broadly.

Declaring identity publicly through the process of *coming out* was understood by many as both activism and personal transformation (Whittier 2012). Movement strategy emphasized coming out, not just for activists but for all LGB people, through events such as National Coming Out Day (which became widespread around 1990). These strategies preceded an increase in disclosure of gay/lesbian identity, although causation is hard to establish. Seidman (2002) documents

---

[1] The following terms are omitted from the table but did not change results when included: "homosexuality" (tracks closely with "homosexual" but is not an identity label), "LGB," "GLB," "lesbian women," "gay men" (very low frequency and LGB/GLB appear in other contexts). Results from prior to 1970 are excluded because of the use of "gay" to mean happy and "queer" to mean strange; both usages continued after 1970, but an examination of the results shows that they are rare. Results after 2008 are omitted because the database is incomplete and results are thus unstable.

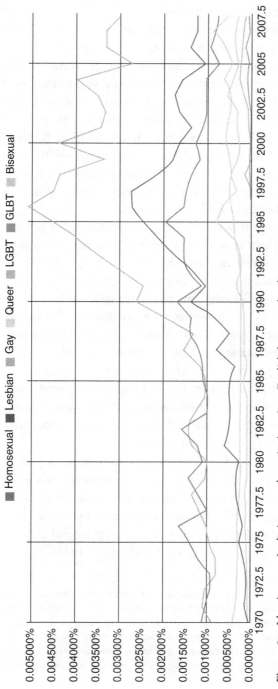

Figure 6.1 Identity terms' relative prevalence in American English-language books, 1970–2008.

increasing openness by LGB people, finding that even people who said they were closeted were out to many people.

Survey data confirm the pattern.[2] Increasing percentages of the US public report knowing someone who is gay or lesbian or having a close friend or family member who is gay or lesbian. Some of this increase is due to greater social integration, but most is due to increased visibility, or coming out. Polls (which use varying wording) show a clear shift from a relatively small number of people who say they know someone who is gay or lesbian to well over half ("Polling Report" 2012; Yang 1997). Prior to the mid-1990s, fewer than one-third of respondents said they knew any gay or lesbian person; by 1998, 59% said they had a family member, close friend, or acquaintance who was gay or lesbian. The number increased to 63% in 2010.

Increased coming out is both a biographical outcome for gay and lesbian people who live their lives more openly and a sign of cultural change more generally. Coming out itself has diverse biographical consequences, ranging from discrimination, rejection or acceptance by family, enhanced sense of personal worth, emotional transformations (from shame to pride), and entry into movement or community institutions (bars, coffee shops, activist organizations) (Seidman 2002). These consequences are conditioned by changes in LBG life more generally. Contact with openly lesbian and gay people is associated with more favorable attitudes toward homosexuality (Lemm 2006). In addition, media visibility of lesbian and gay characters increased during the late 1990s and early 2000s. Some polling suggests that media visibility contributed to increased social tolerance (Brewer 2003; Riggle and Ellis 1996).

Public opinion has shifted steadily in favor of a range of policies related to LGB rights. At the most basic level, the percentage of the US population who say that sexual relations between two adults of the same sex (GSS) are "not wrong at all" fluctuated between 11% and 14% from 1973 to 1991, but then began a steady increase to around 30% by 2002–2006, 36% in 2008, and 41% in 2010 (Smith 2011). Public support

---

[2] Willingness to disclose on a survey is an indicator of coming out. Representative surveys between 1988 and 1996 found that 1% of women and 2.5% of men identified as gay or lesbian (Gates and Ost 2004). An estimate of the lesbian and gay population based on the 2000 US Census is 2.5–3.8% of men and 1.3–1.9% of women. Comparing these estimates to the proportions found in the nationally representative surveys suggest that 25–50% of women and 0–30% of men did not disclose their identity to the survey-takers.

for same-sex marriage has also increased rapidly, from a low of 10.7% (combined strongly agree and agree) when the question was first asked in 1988 to 30% in 2004, 35% in 2006, 39% in 2008, 46% in 2010, and 54% in 2012 (Burns and Harris 2012; Smith 2011). By 2010, half of people age eighteen to twenty-nine said homosexual behavior is not wrong at all, and 64.2% supported same-sex marriage (Smith 2011), a number that increased to 73% in 2012 (Burns and Harris 2012).[3] These cultural outcomes foster biographical change, encouraging further identity disclosure and collective identities that emphasize similarity to rather than difference from heterosexuals (Ghaziani 2011), migration out of LGB enclaves (Ghaziani 2010), and open relationships and child-raising. Because of the marked cohort differences in attitudes toward homosexuality, it is likely that these life-course patterns are more common among younger LGB people than their older counterparts. In a feedback loop, such life-course changes further the cultural shift.

Policy outcomes and the life-course

The central elements of the life-course for LGB people have changed over the past twenty to thirty years in direct response to related policy changes. For each arena, I will first describe the policy changes and then examine evidence of related life-course change. This chapter discusses legal and policy change through 2011. Note that the law, especially regarding same-sex marriage, has continued to expand rapidly since then.

Anti-discrimination ordinances and outcomes for employment and residential patterns

The law barring discrimination against LGBT people, non-existent in the United States before the late 1970s, expanded dramatically from the 1990s to the 2010s. Figure 6.2 shows the number of states with anti-discrimination ordinances covering either sexual orientation alone, or sexual orientation and gender expression.

Similar expansion occurred in companies' internal non-discrimination policies and same-sex spousal benefits. Between 2000 and 2003, 75 Fortune 500 companies added domestic partner benefit

[3] The 2012 youngest cohort was eighteen to thirty-four (Burns and Harris 2012).

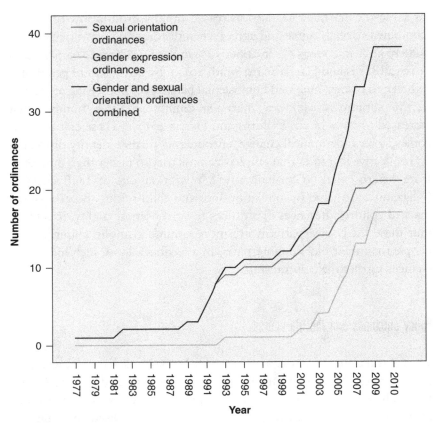

Figure 6.2 US state ordinances prohibiting discrimination on sexual orientation and gender expression, by year.

Source: National Gay and Lesbian Task Force, 2012

coverage; by 2006, half of Fortune 500 companies provided health benefits to same-sex partners and 86% had non-discrimination policies (Badgett 2008). In 2001, while only 15% of gays and lesbians worked in organizations that offered partner health benefits, 52% were in organizations that welcomed same-sex partners at social events, and only 18% in organizations that did not (Ragins and Cornwell 2007).[4] Women, whites, and the more highly educated were most likely to be in jobs that offered partner benefits, but the differences between groups were not large (Ragins and Cornwell 2007).

[4] Study based on random sample of members of gay, gay Latino, and gay African American organizations, stratified geographically.

Because non-discrimination laws and policies affect access to employment, compensation, and housing, we would expect they might produce changes in employment and occupation, income, and residential patterns. Note, however, that a majority of US states have no such law, meaning that discrimination against LGBT people remains legal; as such, life-course effects are limited.

Biographical outcomes: employment and income

Gay men earn less than heterosexual men, with a larger gap relative to married than unmarried heterosexual men. Although some evidence suggests that gay men disproportionately enter lower earning predominantly female occupations, the wage gap is not readily explained by differences in occupation (Badgett and King 1997; Badgett and Frank 2007). In contrast, on average lesbians earn more than or the same as heterosexual women, perhaps because as primary wage earners they work more hours, enter higher-paying gender nonconforming occupations, or are less discriminated against or more closeted than gay men (Badgett and Frank 2007). At the household level, female couples' average household income is similar to that of married heterosexual couples, while male couples' income is about $10,000/year higher.[5] Among same-sex couples, both partners work fulltime more often than in heterosexual couples, explaining their higher combined income, despite lower individual income (Lofquist 2011).

The evidence about the effects of non-discrimination policy on income is inconclusive. An early study showed that the gay–straight wage gap was no lower in places with non-discrimination laws (Klawitter and Flatt 1998). Badgett and Frank (2007) attribute this to lack of enforcement or insufficient time for non-discrimination law to affect income and occupation. At the employer level, company non-discrimination policies and partner benefits appear to affect identity disclosure and well-being, if not earnings (Badgett 2001). Workers were also more likely to be out at work if they perceived their workplace as supportive, partners were welcome at work events, and co-workers' reactions were good (Badgett 2001; Ragins and Cornwell 2007). Regardless of whether workers were out or not, those whose employers offered health benefits were more

---

[5] Unmarried heterosexual couples' income is substantially lower than other groups'. Data, 2010 Census.

committed to and happier at their employer, and even more so when their partners were welcome at work events.

In sum, non-discrimination laws and employment policies seem not to have affected income or occupation, except – importantly – through partner benefits, a form of compensation. Cohorts entering the workforce before the late 1990s established work trajectories without benefit of the ordinances, which would have a stronger effect on more recent cohorts, those now around thirty to thirty-five years old. Over time, we may see stronger effects, particularly if a federal anti-discrimination law is passed.

Biographical outcomes: residence and housing patterns

Although housing is covered by non-discrimination ordinances, residential patterns are driven more by other forces. There are two main types of shifts in LGB residence patterns: regional migration, and migration into and out of gay or lesbian neighborhoods. In both cases, we see over time first a concentration, and then a dispersion as discrimination and cultural disapproval decrease. Well-documented migrations to the coasts and port cities occurred following the Second World War, establishing gay enclaves in many major cities (D'Emilio 1998). Following the policy and cultural changes of the 1980s and 1990s, these patterns may be shifting.

Regionally, while most states' rankings on concentration of same-sex couples remained stable from 1990 to 2006, several states' rankings increased, notably Utah, Delaware, and New Mexico, none of which is historically gay-friendly (Gates 2007). The larger increases in same-sex couples in some regions is due partly to migration, but regional migration for same-sex couples doesn't differ substantially from migration patterns for the US population overall (Gates 2007). The apparent increases more likely reflect an increase in residents' willingness to come out, rather than a true increase in population. Gates (2007) argues that this is why the apparent increase in gay and lesbian population is greatest in conservative areas that historically had "bigger closets," where more people were closeted in earlier surveys and came out in later ones. This suggests a socially significant change in the individual lives of LGB residents in more conservative regions.

Within cities, LGB residents historically formed gay neighborhoods, often distinguished by gender or ethnicity. These enclaves flourished from the 1960s through the 1990s, but may be diminishing more recently (Ghaziani 2010). Many cities still have consistently high concentrations of lesbian and gay residents, and "nine of the top ten cities in concentration of gay and lesbian couples have remained the same from 1990–2006" (Gates 2007; Gates and Ost 2004). However, in some cities, same-sex couples appear to be moving out of the central city and into the suburbs. Gates (2007) shows that in three metropolitan areas (Atlanta, Philadelphia, and Detroit) the numbers of same-sex couples dropped in the central city but increased in the larger metropolitan area, suggesting a move to the suburbs.

In sum, laws prohibiting discrimination in housing may have promoted some LGB migration out of concentrated neighborhoods, but a more likely driver is increasing social acceptance. Given the persistence of LGB concentration by region and city, the recency of the residential shifts, and the evidence that increased identity disclosure explains some of the apparent change, it is premature to conclude that LGB residential patterns are changing dramatically.

Marriage and civil unions

Marriage, as a legal, social, and financial institution, is an important part of the life-course. Age and rate of marriage decreased for heterosexuals overall as an outcome of the New Left movements (Goldstone and McAdam 2001; Guigni 2004; McAdam 1999). For the LGB population, in contrast, marriage rates have increased because access to legal marriage is an outcome of the movement. Figure 6.3 shows the number of states with various forms of legal recognition for same-sex relationships over time: marriage; civil unions or domestic partnerships granting many of the rights of marriage; and limited forms of relationship recognition such as inheritance or hospital visitation.[6]

The biographical outcomes of interest are rates of coupling, rates of marriage, and whether couples consider themselves spouses regardless of legal status. There is no accurate way to tap changing

---

[6] Note that the United States does not recognize same-sex marriage at the federal level, nor do most states recognize same-sex marriages performed in other states. Numbers will be updated before book goes to press.

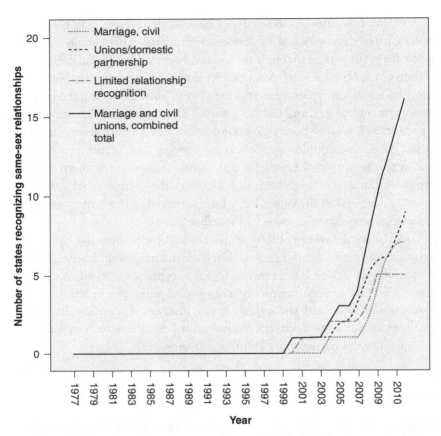

Figure 6.3 US states' legal recognition of same-sex relationships by type and year

Source: National Gay and Lesbian Task Force, 2012

rates of couplehood. The number of same-sex couples who reported themselves on the Census or the American Community Survey increased dramatically between 1990 and 2010, but the increasing numbers of same-sex couples who report themselves as unmarried partners may simply reflect increased willingness to come out on surveys along with the Census's changes in counting methods (Gates 2007; O'Connell and Feliz 2011).

Increases in the percentages of same-sex couples who report that they are spouses rather than unmarried partners is likely due to availability of legal marriage, a social moment outcome. Twenty percent of same-sex couples reported themselves as spouses on the 2010 Census, after the legalization of same-sex marriage in some locales, compared to only 12% in 2000 (O'Connell and Feliz 2011). In states with legal same-sex marriage, 42.4% of same-sex couples reported they were spouses, versus 28.2% for states with domestic partnership or civil unions, and 22.7% in other states (Krivickas and Loftquist 2011; Lofquist 2011). In Massachusetts, the earliest state to legalize same-sex marriage in 2004, 6.5% of same-sex couples listed themselves as spouses in 2000 versus 46.7% in 2010, a dramatic change likely due to both actual legal marriages and changing meanings available for categorizing relationships. The other states that legalized marriage did so in 2008, 2009, and 2010, allowing less time for couples to marry before the 2010 survey, but also showed substantial increases and higher percentages of couples reporting as spouses than the national average.[7]

Couples who reported they were spouses may not necessarily have legally recognized marriages. The overall increase in the percentage of couples who consider themselves spouses also points to a more general change in the cultural templates and labels available to same-sex couples. In fact, several conservative states where same-sex marriage is banned also have higher than average percentages of same-sex couples reporting as married, so reporting a relationship as spousal is not tightly linked to the law (Lofquist 2011).[8]

Biographical outcomes vary among groups and cohorts (Van Dyke et al. 2000; Whittier 1995). As with heterosexual couples, the mean age of married couples is higher for lesbian and gay couples compared to unmarried partners, but the age difference is smaller than for heterosexuals (Lofquist 2011) because most same-sex couples, regardless of age or longevity of relationship, remained unmarried. Some groups are more likely to call their same-sex relationships spousal. Compared to same-sex couples as a whole, higher percentages of Black/African American, American Indian/Alaskan Native, and Asian people, less educated couples, non-interracial couples, and people with children in the household report that they are married (Lofquist 2011). The presence of children in the household makes a particularly dramatic difference for gay male couples: 25% of male couples

---

[7] 12% versus 42.6% in Connecticut, 13.5% versus 32.1% in CA (where marriage was legal only for a few months in 2008), 0 versus 46% in Iowa, 0 versus 46.5% in New Hampshire, 6.7% versus 34.1% in Vermont. States that permit registration of domestic partnership but not same-sex marriage do not generally show a higher than average reporting as spouses.

[8] It is possible that some of these are errors (O'Connell and Feliz 2011).

reporting as spouses have children, versus 6.2% who report being unmarried.[9]

In sum, LGB couples have become more likely to call themselves spouses following legalization of marriage and civil unions. The increase is strongest in states where legalization of marriage occurred, but exists elsewhere as well. Age or cohort differences in rate of marriage, if any, are small, but age patterns in LGB marriages differ from heterosexual marriage. For heterosexuals, marriage is part of a transition to adulthood and first marriage occurs early in life and in the course of a relationship. (Note that there are substantial differences by race in these patterns in the United States.) LGB legal marriage, in contrast, occurred in all stages of relationships, with long-term and newer couples marrying when it became legal. Over time, couples may marry earlier in their relationship; this would be a notable cohort difference.

Child-bearing and adoption

Policy changes related to both adoption and biological child-raising affect LGB parenting. Two policy issues affect LGB people seeking to adopt children. First, couples where one parent is the biological parent seek legal recognition for the second parent ("second-parent adoption"). Second, couples seek to adopt children jointly. In 2012, thirteen states permitted joint adoption by same-sex couples and second-parent adoption. Prior to 1995 none did; most added these rights after 2002. Thus, we see a significant change related to the life-course in a short period of time. In regard to biological parenting, access to donor gametes and assisted reproduction (including surrogacy) varies by agency; the professional associations for medical professionals issued statements in support of access by LGB people in 2006 (Ethics Committee of the American Society for Reproductive Medicine 2009).

If these changes affected aggregate biographical outcomes, we would expect increased rates of parenting among LGB people. It is impossible to get solid numbers on the prevalence of child-raising among lesbians and gay men, especially prior to 2000. Estimates in the 1970s and early 1980s of lesbian mothers ranged from 30% to 45% of lesbians (including biological and non-biological mothers, the

[9] 26.2% of lesbian couples reporting as spouses have children, versus 23% of those reporting being unmarried.

latter of whom would not have had legal relationships to the children). Many of these were raising children from prior heterosexual relationships (Gottler 1984). Virtually all gay fathers during this period had children from heterosexual relationships because adoption by single men (regardless of sexuality) was very difficult and surrogacy was not yet available. Both lesbians and gay men often lost custody battles to former spouses or relatives. Custody cases gradually liberalized in the 1990s, allowing more gay and lesbian parents to retain custody or visitation with children from prior heterosexual relationships. In tandem with larger cultural changes around LGB issues, this permitted a growing number of openly lesbian and gay parents.

By 1990, the Census showed that an estimated "22% of partnered lesbians and about 5% of partnered gay men had children in their households" (Krivickas and Lofquist 2011). By 2008, 13.9% of male and 26.5% of female couples had children under 18 in their households, compared to 43% of male–female couples (Lofquist 2011; see also Gates and Ost 2004). This is a substantial increase over 1990, although the changing methods of counting same-sex unmarried partners make the precise change impossible to determine. Even higher percentages of all lesbians and gay men (including those who are not coupled) have had children (including children not currently living with them). In 2002, 35% of lesbians had given birth and 23% had lived with and had responsibility for a child to whom they had not given birth; 16% of gay men had children by birth or adoption (Gates et al. 2007). The number for lesbians increased to 49% in 2008 (remaining the same for men) (Gates 2011).[10] Many more lesbians and gay men without children wanted to have children. In 2002, 49% of lesbians and 57% of gay men who were not parents wanted children (Gates et al. 2007).[11]

The 2010 Census showed a slight decrease. 17.5% of same-sex couples – 10% of male couples and 24% of female couples – had children in their households (Lofquist 2011; O'Connell and Feliz 2011).[12] Gates (2011) argues that the decrease occurred *despite* dramatic increases in the percentage of lesbians and gay men adopting children. Parenting rates among lesbian and gay people include those

---

[10] GSS data. [11] For bisexuals, the percentages were 75 (women), 70 (men).
[12] Calculated from the supplemental tables in O'Connell and Feliz 2011. Using Census and ACS data on unmarried same-sex partners with children at home, Gates shows a steady increase from 12.5% in 1990 to 18.8% in 2006, and then a decline to 16.2% in 2009.

who had biological children in mixed-sex relationships, before they come out. As LGB people come out younger, they are less likely to have children in heterosexual relationships, reducing the overall parenting rate. Instead, they are more likely to have children after coming out via donor gametes or adoption. Regionally, the highest percentages of same-sex couples who are parents are in the East and West South Central states, and the lowest in the Pacific and South Atlantic regions (Gates 2011). But for same-sex parents through adoption and foster care, the patterns differ, with more in the more liberal New England, Mid-Atlantic, and West Coast states where gay adoption is easier (Gates et al. 2007). African American, Latino, and Native American/Alaskan Native same-sex couples are more likely to have children, but adoptive parenting is much more common among White same-sex couples. Adoptive parenting is more common among same-sex couples with higher education, but parenting overall is more common among those with lower levels of education (Gates 2011). These patterns suggest that parenting by choice through adoption is more common among higher SES couples in more liberal states (which permit adoption by gay or lesbian couples and second-parent adoption), while the reverse is true for having children through prior heterosexual relationships.

Routes to parenthood differ for same-sex and heterosexual couples and have changed over time. Adoption has become more common over time; 10% of same-sex couples with children had adopted children in 2000, compared with 19% in 2009 (Gates 2011). Dramatically more same-sex couples with children had only adopted or step-children (21.2%) or a combination of biological children, step-children, and children from adoption (6%), for a total of 27.2%, than did heterosexual married couples (total 9.2%) or heterosexual unmarried couples (total 12%) (Gates 2007).[13] "Four percent of all adopted children in the United States are being raised by gay or lesbian parents" (Gates and Ost 2004), as are 3% of all children in foster care (Gates et al. 2007). About half of all adoptive same-sex families adopt children through the foster care system, previously impossible, and 60% of adoption agencies will accept applications from LGB parents, although only 40% reported having placed children with LGB parents (Kennedy 2011).

---

[13] Variations in numbers due to different data sources.

Although there are substantial barriers to adoption remaining in a majority of states, very few agencies would have worked with open LGB parents before 1990. Routes to parenthood vary between lesbians and gay men, since biological reproduction for gay men through surrogacy and egg donation is more expensive and complex than for lesbians, who need only use donor sperm. For gay men, adoption is a major route to parenthood. The increasing percentage of gay male couples with children is a clear result of the opening of legal adoption to gay men in some states and agencies and "single" men in others. Adoption remains more difficult for gay men than for lesbians, because of barriers to adoption by male couples and because fewer agencies or countries permit adoption by single men than by single women. Adopted children living with male couples are much more likely to have disabilities and are older than those with female couples, suggesting that male couples may be more likely to adopt harder-to-place children (Gates et al. 2007).[14]

Overall, parenting by choice by same-sex couples has become more common over time, with liberalization of adoption law and availability of reproductive technology. Routes to parenting have changed; biological childbearing through heterosexual relationships prior to coming out has decreased, and adoption and use of donor gametes and surrogacy increased. These trends are strongest in regions where adoption and foster care law and policy is more liberal and where second-parent adoption is permitted. These changes are primarily due to LGB movement policy gains on adoption and access to reproductive technology, as well as cultural changes that led to earlier coming out.

Conclusions

Overall, LGB movement outcomes included many that we would expect to influence biography: the production of specific collective identities, increased cultural tolerance, non-discrimination policies, legal recognition of same-sex couple relationships, and availability of adoption and second-parent adoption. In most arenas, life-course

---

[14] Note, however, that Gates et al. 2007 do not have data on the age at adoption, only the age at the time of the survey. 2000 Census data.

patterns did shift: increased numbers of LGB people disclosed identities publicly to family members, friends, and survey-takers; residential patterns dispersed; rates of legal marriage and the use of "marriage" and "spouse" as terms increased; child-raising through adoption and reproductive technology increased and (probably) child-bearing by LG people in prior heterosexual relationships decreased. Employment non-discrimination ordinances appear to have little or no effect on earnings or occupation, but company policies affect employees' well-being and identity disclosure, and effects on earnings or occupations may emerge over time. Importantly, in the United States, non-discrimination law is not the norm, most locales and the federal government prohibit same-sex marriage, legal parenting remains difficult, and large portions of the public continue to view same-sex behavior as morally wrong. Aggregate biographical outcomes, thus, are limited.

Gay and lesbian movements are similar to other movements that seek to change the social position of disadvantaged groups: their success in doing so changes the life-course of the groups' members. For example, feminist movements contributed to women's access to some categories of employment and perhaps to greater labor force participation, delayed marriage and child-raising, and changes in gender divisions of labor within the household; immigrant rights movements can affect residence, employment, and education. As with other movements, the forces that shape aggregate life-course outcomes for gay and lesbian people include broader changes in norms about relationships, marriage, childbearing, and disclosure of personal identity. Disentangling these forces is a formidable methodological challenge.

Aggregate biographical outcomes among movement beneficiaries are shaped by gender, race, class, and cohort. Because economic inequality plays out differently for lesbians and gay men (with gay men earning more than lesbians, but having a larger wage gap compared to their heterosexual counterparts), any effects of non-discrimination ordinances will likely vary by gender. Because gay neighborhoods and migration to suburbs are sometimes structured by gender, race, and class, residential patterns will vary accordingly. Routes to parenthood differ for gay men and lesbians, and expansion of adoption rights was especially crucial for increased parenting by gay men.

In terms of cohort, non-discrimination ordinances primarily affect people early in their work history and access to parenthood is most relevant to the younger cohorts. Further, the meanings of marriage and parenting may vary by cohort. For earlier cohorts of lesbians, the definition of marriage as a patriarchal institution may lessen desire to enter it; and for earlier cohorts of both genders, alternative relationship arrangements such as non-monogamy and extended kinship/friendship networks that were normative in earlier eras may persist. Many individuals in earlier cohorts of both lesbians and gay men may not have been interested in parenting or may have assumed it was impossible; their attitudes toward increased parenting by younger cohorts, therefore, may be mixed. For the cohorts entering young adulthood now, the expectation of marriage and child-raising may become normative; marriage may be an expected expression of a committed relationship, and parents and peers may ask when to expect babies (Swarns 2012). This is a historically unique life-course experience for LGB people.

Many of these biographical outcomes were explicit goals of the LGB movement, in contrast to the life-course outcomes of the New Left movements, which were largely unintentional (Guigni 2004). Earlier activists were more likely to embrace ideologies critical of mainstreaming, while the policies they achieved led to increased mainstreaming by the general LGB public. Nevertheless, many activists view them with mixed feelings, torn between support for increasing legal and cultural equality and regret at the loss of distinctive cultural patterns and communities, or are critical of what they regard as a mainstreaming and entry into normative heterosexual patterns of family. Biographical outcomes, like other movement successes, are out of the control of the activists who set them in motion (Whittier 2009).

Aggregate biographical outcomes are related to, but distinct from, movements' policy and cultural outcomes. Evident at the individual level, they follow from policy changes related to the life-course and cultural changes in societal views of the group or its issues. My focus on the life-course consequences for movement beneficiaries is distinct from previous work on aggregate biographical outcomes. Whereas changes in the life-course patterns of overall populations may be unintended, changes in beneficiaries' biographies are an important part of many movements' goals. Assessing the degree of such changes is, therefore, crucial to understanding movement outcomes.

References

Armstrong, Elizabeth A. 2002. *Forging Gay Identities: Organizing Sexuality in San Francisco, 1950–1994 / Elizabeth A. Armstrong*. Chicago: University of Chicago Press.

Arthur, Mikaila M.L. 2009. "Thinking Outside the Master's House: New Knowledge Movements and the Emergence of Academic Disciplines." *Social Movement Studies*, 8: 73–87.

Badgett, Mary V.L. 2001. *Money, Myths, and Change: The Economic Lives of Lesbians and Gay Men / M.V. Lee Badgett*. Chicago: University of Chicago Press.

Badgett, M. V. L. 2008. "Bringing all Families to Work Today." In Amy Marcus-Newhall, Diane F. Halpern, and Sherylle J. Tan (eds.), *The Changing Realities of Work and Family : A Multidisciplinary Approach*. Malden, MA; Oxford: Wiley-Blackwell Pub, 140–153.

Badgett, M.V.L. and Jeff Frank. 2007. *Sexual Orientation Discrimination: An International Perspective*. London and New York: Routledge.

Badgett, M.V.L. and Mary C. King, 1997. "Occupational Strategies of Lesbians and Gay Men." In Amy Gluckman and Betsy Reed (eds.), *Homo Economics: Capitalism, Community, & Lesbian & Gay Life*. New York: Routlege, 73–86.

Bernstein, Mary. 1997. "Celebration and Suppression: The Strategic Uses of Identity by the Lesbian and Gay Movement." *American Journal of Sociology*, 103: 531–565.

Brewer, Paul R. 2003. "The Shifting Foundations of Public Opinion about Gay Rights." *Journal of Politics*, 65: 1208–1220.

Burns, Crosby and Burns Harris. 2012. "Infographic: Marriage Equality is Now a Mainstream Value." Center for American Progress, Retrieved July 11, 2012 (www.americanprogress.org/issues/2012/07/marriage_equality).

D'Emilio, John. 1998. *Sexual Politics, Sexual Communities : The Making of a Homosexual Minority in the United States, 1940–1970*. Chicago: University of Chicago Press; 2nd ed.

Ethics Committee of the American Society for Reproductive Medicine. 2009. "Access to Fertility Treatment by Gays, Lesbians, and Unmarried Persons." *Fertility and Sterility*, 92: 1190–1193,

Retrieved May 21, 2013 (www.asrm.org/uploadedFiles/ ASRM_Content/News_and_Publications/Ethics_Committee_ Reports_and_Statements/fertility_gaylesunmarried.pdf).

Fetner, Tina. 2008. *How the Religious Right Shaped Lesbian and Gay Activism*. Minneapolis: University of Minnesota Press.

Gamson, Joshua. 1995. "Must Identity Movements Self-Destruct? A Queer Dilemma." *Social Problems*, 42: 390–407.

Gates, Gary J. 2007. *Geographic Trends among Same-Sex Couples in the U.S. Census and the American Community Survey*. Los Angeles, CA: The Williams Institute, Retrieved August 7, 2012.

Gates, Gary. 2011. "Family Formation and Raising Children among Same-Sex Couples." *NCFR Report* FF51: 1, 1–4.

Gates, Gary, M.V.L. Badgett, Jennifer Macomber, and Kate Chambers. 2007. *Adoption and Foster Care by Gay and Lesbian Parents in the United States*. Los Angeles, CA: Williams Institute, Retrieved August 13, 2012 (http://williamsinstitute.law.ucla.edu/research/parenting/ adoption-and-foster-care-by-gay-and-lesbian-parents-in-the-united- states/).

Gates, Gary J. and Jason Ost. 2004. *The Gay & Lesbian Atlas / Gary J. Gates & Jason Ost*. Washington, DC: Urban Institute Press.

Gerson, Kathleen. 2004. "Understanding Work and Family through a Gender Lens." *Community, Work & Family*, 7: 163–178.

Ghaziani, Amin. 2008. *The Dividends of Dissent: How Conflict and Culture Work in Lesbian and Gay Marches on Washington*. Chicago: University of Chicago Press.

2010. "There Goes the Gayborhood?" *Contexts*, 9: 64–66.

2011. "Post-Gay Collective Identity Construction." *Social Problems*, 58: 99–125.

Goldstone, Jack and Doug McAdam. 2001. "Contention in Demographic and Life-Course Context." In Ronald Aminzade, Jack Goldstone, Doug McAdam, Elizabeth Perry, William H. Sewell Jr., Sidney Tarrow, and Charles Tilly (eds.), *Silence and Voice in the Study of Contentious Politics*. Cambridge and New York: Cambridge University Press, 195, 195–221.

Gottler, Janet M. 1984. "Cultural Pioneers: The New Lesbian Families: A Project Based upon an Independent Investigation / Janet M. Gottler." Master's Thesis, Smith College School of Social Work, Northampton, MA,

Guigni, Marco. 2004. "Personal and Biographical Consequences." In David Snow, Sarah Soule, and Hanspieter Kriesi (eds.), *The Blackwell Companion to Social Movements*. Malden, MA: Blackwell Publishing, 489–507.

Hagan, John and Suzanne Hansford-Bowles. 2005. "From Resistance to Activism: The Emergence and Persistence of Activism among American Vietnam War Resisters in Canada." *Social Movement Studies*, 231–259.

Kennedy, Kelli. 2011. "Adoptions Spiked among Gay Couples in Past Decade." (www.boston.com/news/local/massachusetts/articles/2011/10/20/adoptions_spiked_among_gay_couples_in_past_decade/ [accessed August 14, 2015]).

Klawitter, M.M. and V. Flatt. 1998. "The Effects of State and Local Antidiscrimination Policies on Earnings for Gays and Lesbians." *Journal of Policy Analysis and Management*, 17: 658–686.

Krivickas, Kristy M. and Daphne Lofquist. 2011. "Demographics of Same-Sex Couple Households with Children, SEHSD Working Paper Number 2011–11." Washington, DC: U.S. Census Bureau, Retrieved July 6, 2012 (www.census.gov/hhes/samesex/files/Krivickas-Lofquist%20PAA%202011.pdf).

Lemm, Kristi M. 2006. "Positive Associations among Interpersonal Contact, Motivation, and Implicit and Explicit Attitudes Toward Gay Men." *Journal of Homosexuality*, 51: 79–99.

Lofquist, Daphne. 2011. "Same-Sex Couple Households: American Community Survey Briefs." Washington, DC: United States Census Bureau, Retrieved August 7, 2012 (www.census.gov/prod/2011pubs/acsbr10-03.pdf).

McAdam, Doug. 1999. "The Biographical Impact of Social Movements." In Marco Guigni, Doug McAdam, and Charles Tilly (eds.), *How Social Movements Matter*. Minneapolis: University of Minnesota, 117–146.

O'Connell, Martin and Sarah Feliz. 2011. "Same-Sex Couple Households Statistics from the 2010 Census. SEHSD Working Paper Number 2011–26." Washington, DC: U.S. Census Bureau. Retrieved August 7, 2012 (www.census.gov/hhes/samesex/files/ss-report.doc).

"Polling Report, Same-Sex Marriage, Gay Rights." 2012. Retrieved August 6, 2012 (http://pollingreport.com/civil.htm).

Ragins, Belle and John Cornwell. 2007. "We Are Family: The Influence of Gay Family-Friendly Policies on Gay, Lesbian, and Bisexual Employees." In M. V. L. Badgett and Jefferson Frank (eds.), *Sexual Orientation Discrimination*. London and New York: Routledge, 105–117.

Riggle, Ellen D.B. and Alan L. Ellis. 1996. "The Impact of 'Media Contact' on Attitudes Toward Gay Men." *Journal of Homosexuality*, 31: 55.

Rochon, Thomas. 1998. *Culture Moves*. Princeton, NJ: Princeton University Press.

Seidman, Steven. 2002. *Beyond the Closet: The Transformation of Gay and Lesbian Life Steven Seidman*. New York: Routledge.

Smith, Tom. 2011. "Public Attitudes Toward Homosexuality." Chicago: NORC, Retrieved August 2, 2012 (www.norc.org/PDFs/2011%20GSS%20Reports/GSS_Public%20Attitudes%20Toward%20Homosexuality_Sept2011.pdf).

Stone, Amy L. 2009a. "Like Sexual Orientation? Like Gender? Transgender Inclusion in Non-Discrimination Ordinances." In Scott Barclay, Mary Bernstein, and Anna Marshall (eds.), *Queer Mobilizations: LGBT Activists Confront the Law*. New York: New York University Press, 142–157.

2009b. "More than Adding a T: American Lesbian and Gay Activists' Attitudes towards Transgender Inclusion." *Sexualities*, 12: 334–354.

2012. *Gay Rights at the Ballot Box*. Minneapolis: University of Minnesota Press.

Swarns, Rachel. 2012. "Male Couples Face Pressure to Fill Cradles." *The New York Times*.

Taylor, Verta, Katrina Kimport, Nella Van Dyke, and Ellen A. Andersen. 2009. "Culture and Mobilization: Tactical Repertoires, Same-Sex Weddings, and the Impact on Gay Activism." *American Sociological Review*, 74: 865–890.

Taylor, Verta and Nancy Whittier. 1992. "Collective Identity in Social Movement Communities: Lesbian Feminist Mobilization." In Aldon Morris and Carol Mueller (eds.), *Frontiers in Social Movement Theory*. New Haven: Yale University Press, 104–129.

Van Dyke, Nella, Doug McAdam and Brenda Wilhelm. 2000. "Gendered Outcomes: Gender Differences in the Biographical Consequences of Activism." *Mobilization*, 5: 161, 161–177.

Weston, Kath. 1991. *Families We Choose: Lesbians, Gays, Kinship*. New York: Columbia University Press.

Whittier, Nancy. 1995. *Feminist Generations*. Philadelphia, PA: Temple University Press.

1997. "Political Generations, Micro-Cohorts, and the Transformation of Social Movements." *American Sociological Review*, 62: 760–778.

2009. *The Politics of Child Sexual Abuse: Emotion, Social Movements, and the State*. New York: Oxford University Press.

2012. "The Politics of Visibility: Coming Out and Individual and Collective Identity In Jeff Goodwin, Rachel Kutz-Flamenbaum, Greg Maney, and Deana Rohlinger (eds.), *Making History: Movements, Strategy, and Social Change*. Minneapolis: University of Minnesota, 145–169.

Yang, Alan S. 1997. "The Polls-Trends." *Public Opinion Quarterly*, 61: 477.

PART II
POLICIES

7 PROTEST AGAINST SCHOOL CLOSURES IN SWEDEN

Accepted by politicians?

Katrin Uba

Scholars studying the consequences of social movements have usually focused on movements and activists (Amenta et al. 2010; Giugni 1998). Recently, however, more attention has been paid to targets, who are usually policy makers, and to their motives for listening to contentious actions (e.g., Luders 2006). These studies assume that targets respond to protests on the basis of their rational interest in reelections and stability. Others argue that authorities' responses depend on the perceived legitimacy and worthiness of mobilization (e.g., Tilly 1999). Although these propositions are not mutually exclusive, current scholarship has paid little attention to how authorities actually look upon protest actions. If we assume that targets are more responsive to movements that use strategies they understand and consider legitimate, then it is important to investigate which forms of protest are seen as more or less legitimate. For instance, activists are sometimes concerned about radical groups, whose actions can undermine the legitimacy of their non-disruptive protest strategies. But how warranted is this concern? The few prior studies on targets' attitudes toward protests do not answer this question, because these studies treat all protest strategies

I would like to thank the Mikael Gilljam and David Karlsson for sharing their survey data, Lisa Magnusson for helping me with coding, participants at the international conference "Silence in the Study of Social Movement Outcomes" (Uppsala University, Sweden, September 2012), and the co-editors of this volume for their helpful comments. The writing of this chapter has benefited from a generous funding of the Swedish Riksbankens Jubileumsfond (project number P09-1020:1-E).

as the same type of action. This treatment may be misleading, because the character of petitioning and letter-writing in media is clearly different from that of demonstrations, strikes, occupation of public buildings, or activists' visits to politicians' homes. More disruptive actions also have different political consequences than less disruptive ones (Luders 2006; Uba 2005). On the other hand, studies that examine the outcomes of different protest strategies and relate them to the novelty, militancy, variety, size, and cultural resonance of these actions (see more in Taylor and van Dyke 2004), have not related the question of effectiveness to targets' attitudes toward different protest strategies. This chapter does relate protest effectiveness to targets' attitudes, and suggests that this approach helps us better understand why political context plays a role in the varying outcomes of disruptive protests.

The chapter examines how targets' attitudes toward different forms of protest vary among Swedish decision-makers, and which kinds of targets tend to be more understanding toward petitioning or occupations of public buildings. Mass-level studies show that an individual's approval of a protest action is related to her personal background and to the disruptiveness of the experienced events (Crozat 1998). It is reasonable to expect that similar factors explain the variation in the attitudes of policy makers. However, one also needs to account for the position of power. The only prior study on elite-level attitudes toward protests showed that incumbents have strongly negative reactions toward protesting in general (Gilljam et al. 2012); but this study did not focus on different forms of action. The analysis presented in this chapter improves on prior research in two ways. First, it disentangles the forms of protest as suggested by prior mass-level studies (Crozat 1998; Batel and Castro 2014; Thomas and Louis 2013). Second, it improves the measure of protest experience, which is assumed to affect the attitudes toward different protest strategies. This is done by combining two data-sets: (1) a survey of attitudes toward different forms of protest against school closures among Swedish municipal-level decision-makers; and (2) protest event data on mobilization against school closures in all Swedish municipalities. Although the survey does not provide us with a good measure of the decision-makers' experiences with protests, the event data tell us how many and which kinds of protests have actually taken place in the respondents' municipalities.

Local authorities in Sweden closed 816 primary schools between 1991 and 2009. This number represented about 17% of all schools and 65% of the schools that were originally proposed to be closed. The process involved more than 1,300 protest events, and this issue of school closures has been noted as one of the major reasons for joining local-level protests in Sweden (Solevid 2009). Authorities never used violence or repression in response to protest actions, but the consequences of those actions are still not clear. Some protests achieved the activists' goal and saved the school from closure, while other protests were ignored and met with reactions such as, "One becomes a bit immune towards protests just because these are protests."[1] Such a general negative attitude among the elite toward protesting is not surprising, but targets are not a homogenous group, and their attitudes vary. Knowing more about the factors explaining this variation is relevant for scholars interested in policy makers' responsiveness to contentious actions, and also for activists who might want to know which kinds of targets are more receptive to particular protest strategies.

The chapter continues as follows. The first section discusses the theoretical grounds for the varying degrees of understanding for protests among elite actors. Next, it describes the survey data, the protest event data, and the methods of analysis. The third section presents the findings, which clearly demonstrate that targets' attitudes toward different forms of protest vary, and that the variation is mostly explained by different personal characteristics (gender, ideological leaning) and incumbent status. The conclusion discusses the broader implications of these results. The closure of schools or other public facilities, and protests against such decisions, occur beyond Sweden (see Kearns et al. 2010; Witten et al. 2003). Even though Swedish political culture is often seen as more collaborative and involving little conflict, the factors that explain which targets tend to be more understanding toward petitions or strikes in Sweden should also be applicable elsewhere.

Attitudes toward protests among the political elite

Electoral forms of political actions such as voting, referenda initiatives, or supporting political parties are considered to be necessary characteristics

---

[1] A representative of a right-wing party in Uppsala; the interview was conducted by Malina Abrahamsson, who studied the elite attitudes towards school closures (Abrahamsson 2010) and has kindly shared her transcriptions with the author.

of a well-functioning democracy. Other forms of citizens' actions such as demonstrations, strikes, and occupations of buildings have not always been regarded as a legitimate part of a democratic political system (Teorell 2006). Therefore, it is not surprising that the political elite, the most common target of political protests, often refers to protests as being disturbing and illegitimate. On the other hand, citizens also participate in politics between elections, and such forms of action have become a normal part of the political process (Esaiasson and Narud 2013; Meyer and Tarrow 1997; Walgrave and van Aelst 2001). Some forms of action, such as petitioning, are encouraged today by decision-makers via numerous citizens' initiatives (Bochel 2013). Other more disruptive forms of action, such as occupations of public space, are little accepted or understood by the political elite. Similarly, social psychologists have shown that nonviolent actions more effectively convey a sense of legitimacy and promote support for the actions and for the activists' claims among bystanders (Thomas and Louis 2013). If we assume, reasonably, that decision-makers are more receptive to claims that are made via actions they consider to be legitimate or more worthy, then in order to better understand protest outcomes, we need to know which forms of action are tolerated more than others, and what explains the variance of such attitudes.

The research on attitudes toward protest has mainly focused on the masses (Barnes and Kaase 1979; Crozat 1998). It has been assumed that those who respond more positively toward protests are also more likely to participate in such actions.[2] Very little, however, is known on what the political elite thinks of protests as a form of political participation (but see Gilljam et al. 2012; Marien and Hooghe 2013). This lack of information is probably due to the lack of empirical data, and to the fact that the elite has often been neglected in research on political participation and social movements.[3] Still, the findings that both the public (Barnes and Kaase 1979; Crozat 1998; Teorell et al. 2007; Thomas

---

[2] Mass-level survey studies have shown that those who have positive attitudes towards protesting or participate in different protest actions are usually male, educated, younger than an average citizen, and more close to leftist ideology (Walgrave and van Aelst 2001; Bäck et al. 2011).

[3] The few existing studies have more general focus. For example, Polletta (1998) has studied the effects of mobilization on elite discourse and Skrentny (2006) examined how elite perceptions of social movements (but not of their actions) affect targets' actions and thereby social movement outcomes.

and Louis 2013) and the elite (Turnbull 1973; Gilljam et al. 2012; Marien and Hooghe 2013) respond more positively toward less contentious or nonviolent forms of action are not unexpected. Protests are often considered to be a threat on societal stability, and activists are perceived as illegitimate actors. Take one historical example: the elite's negative attitude toward hunger marches in the United Kingdom in the 1930s was so significant that they even formulated a bill that proposed a ban on such actions, although this bill was never discussed in parliament (Turnbull 1973). Similarly, negative statements toward various forms of protest are common in contemporary democracies. Still, there is a clear variation of such attitudes among the elite. Thus, the research question of this chapter is: what kinds of political elite respond more positively to different forms of protest such as petitioning, writing attacking letters in local media, demonstrating, striking, occupying buildings, or visiting decision-makers in their homes?

Explaining the varying attitudes

Mass-level studies suggest that supporting protest actions is not only a function of an individual's personal characteristics (commonly male, young, and left-wing), but also depends on how the action is described in the media (Detenber et al. 2007). The last can be interpreted as a way of experiencing protest, but its effect on the acceptance of particular forms of action is not uniform (Crozat 1998). The only elite-level study on attitudes toward protesting shows that targets with more perceived experience of citizen protests have higher protest acceptance (Gilljam et al. 2012). However, an even larger role is played by the ideology and parliamentary position of the respondents' party (Ibid., p. 262). Left-wing politicians are more open to protests than their right-wing colleagues; members of the incumbent party respond more negatively than members of the opposition; and respondents who are aware that in their municipality there are more protests than elsewhere were more positive in their response to protests.

Interestingly, Gilljam et al. (2012) found no gender effects on attitudes toward protesting, but noted that younger decision-makers are probably more likely to have a higher acceptance of protests. The lack of a difference between male and female representatives is rather unexpected, because prior mass-level studies demonstrate clearly that women respond more negatively toward protests, and participate less in such actions than men (Teorell et al. 2007). Moreover, women in the United States are shown to be more active in petitioning, while men participate more often in demonstrations (Caren et al. 2011). It is likely that the results of Gilljam et al. (2012) are affected by the fact that they use a general index of "protest acceptance" and do not distinguish between different forms of action such as petitioning, demonstrations, strikes, or occupations of buildings. This lack of differentiation is unfortunate, because protesting involves a wide range of actions, and scholars of social psychology have demonstrated significant differences between both motives and consequences of different forms of action (see Thomas and Louis 2013). Hence, the following analysis looks at attitudes toward different forms of protest separately. With respect to the prior research on mass-level attitudes described above, the expected result is to find that *the effect of gender and age on attitudes toward protests varies across the forms of action.*

Female and elderly members of the political elite, for example, would be expected to be more understanding toward non-contentious forms of action such as petitioning or media campaigns than toward violent or aggressive forms of protest.

As noted earlier, an ideological leaning toward left or right has been shown to be an important predictor of support for protests, in both mass- and elite-level studies. Due to the historical legacy of left-wing parties, that is, their closeness to popular movements, *left-wing decision-makers are expected to be more understanding toward protests.*

It is difficult to expect any variation across the forms of action here, although one could suggest that common strategies of labor movements, such as strikes, might be more accepted by politicians from the left than the right. Similarly, it is very likely that decision-makers in *incumbent positions* are more sensitive to the issues of stability, and therefore have more negative attitudes toward protests than their colleagues from the opposition. This effect should be particularly strong for more contentious or disruptive forms of action such as strikes or occupations of public space.

Finally, attitudes are not stable, but are sensitive to their context (Bohner and Dickel 2011). If people are exposed to information that is relevant for their specific attitudes, then these attitudes can change (Althaus and Coe 2001). This explains why negative media presentation of protests affects attitudes toward such actions negatively (Arpan et al. 2006). Experimental studies demonstrate that reading about violent collective action has no effect on perceptions about the issue at stake. On the other hand, those who read about nonviolent actions become supportive of the activists' claims, perceiving that activists have a power to change the situation, and agreeing that there is need for similar protests in the future (Thomas and Louis 2013). Experimental research is lacking at the elite level, but Skrentny (2006) showed that elite perceptions of a mobilizing group, but not of their strategies or claims, changed after experiencing the mobilization. Gilljam et al. (2012), as noted above, also found a positive relationship between perceived experience and acceptance of protesting in general.[4]

Such a trend could be explained by some sort of "normalization mechanism"; if one encounters protests more frequently, those actions will seem less threatening and more acceptable. On the other hand, it is very likely that the effect of protest experience varies between the forms of action. Petitions, public meetings, and peaceful demonstrations might have a positive effect to the elite's understanding toward such actions, while disruptions caused by strikes, riots, and other more threatening events might have a negative effect instead. There could even be some critical threshold effect: Large campaigns that involve many different actions or so-called sustained mobilization might be less understood than one or two protest events. Hence, the expectation of this study is that *the effect of protest experience on attitudes toward protest vary across the forms of action.*

The "normalization" mechanisms would work in the case of less contentious actions (petitions, media campaigns), while in the case of attitudes toward more disruptive actions (strikes, occupations of public buildings) the effect would be the opposite. The following section provides a short description of the process of school closures in Sweden,

---

[4] Gilljam et al. (2012) even found two interesting interaction effects: (1) Left-wing politicians with protest experience had more positive attitudes towards protesting than their right-wing colleagues, while right-wing politicians were not affected by such experiences; (2) the positive attitude of opposition members of the elite became even more positive when they had some protest experience. These results seem plausible, as it is likely that the negative attitudes of the right-wing or incumbent representatives are so strong that the experience of protest has little effect on it.

before the chapter continues to an explanation of how the proposed hypotheses will be tested.

Swedish school closures

Closing schools as a result of economic difficulties, decreasing number of pupils, or problems with the quality of teaching is nothing new in Sweden or elsewhere (Basu 2007; Björklund et al. 2004). The systematic process of school closures started in Sweden in the early 1990s, just after municipalities received the right to make decisions on the financing of schools. The entire sector was opened for competition, in that non-municipal, independent schools (so-called *friskola*) were now permitted. This competition did not directly cause any closures of municipal schools, but it did increase competition over pupils and resources, which in the long term could have increased the likelihood of closing municipal schools. On the other hand, the opportunity to open an independent school turned out to be an "exit" strategy for many parents who opposed the closure of a municipal school. They could now apply for permission to open a school at the Swedish National Agency for Education. Municipalities rarely manage to stop the opening of these new schools after the Agency's approval has been given.[5] The opening of independent schools was not the only or even the main factor behind the closures of municipal schools. The main reasons were economy and demographics. In times of economic recession, as in the early 1990s, Swedish municipalities had to critically evaluate their budgets and cut all kinds of welfare programs, including school budgets. At the same time, the population in rural regions had significantly decreased, and many of the municipal schools had less than twenty pupils.

The process of closure usually starts with a proposal prepared by municipal bureaucrats on the basis of their own internal analysis, or on a study by an external auditing company. Such studies are obviously ordered by local politicians. The proposal is then discussed in the municipal committee for educational issues,[6] and at this time the

[5] Note that municipalities do not win economically if a closure results in the opening of an independent school, because the school is still financed, but not controlled, by the municipality (Björklund et al. 2004).

[6] All parties that are represented in the municipality have at least one representative in the committee, although the chairperson is a representative of the incumbent party.

proposal becomes public. Sometimes the news "leaks" before this point, as school personnel, parents, or opposition politicians learn about the issue during the internal investigation. This is also the stage during which citizens' protests mobilize against the proposal, and such actions are used in this chapter as the evidence of elite protest experience. The final decision about the closure is usually made by the aforementioned committee. However, in small municipalities, or in the case of significant conflicts in the committee, the decision is made by the general legislative body of the municipality. Hence, all members of the committee are the direct targets of protests against school closures, and in many cases other members of the municipal elite are at least indirect targets of these actions. Mobilization is usually *ad hoc*, but in some cases it is supported by local village societies or trade unions. As no political party has stated that they support or oppose school closures, there are no clear political allies to the activists. Rather, the elite's support of activists' claims is case specific, depending among other things on the position of the decision-makers (i.e., incumbent or not) and their electoral interests (Abrahamsson 2010). In rural areas, however, the Centre Party could be seen as an ally to activists because of their general support for sustainable rural development.

The survey data

Data on attitudes toward protests are taken from a survey that was conducted among local-level decision-makers in all 290 Swedish municipalities from late 2008 to early 2009 (details in Gilljam et al. 2012). This study uses responses from almost 8,000 respondents: 42% women and 58% men; 44% opposition members and 55% from some incumbent party.[7] Still, the general background of the respondents is similar to that of the legislators sitting in municipal councils, and it is acceptable to

---

[7] Respondents not only come from larger parties like the Social Democratic Party (38%) or the Moderate Party (20.1%), but also from the smaller Green Party (3.5%) and the more radical right-wing party of Swedish Democrats (1.3%). One can recall that the elections in 2006 were won by the right-wing block of the Moderate Party, Christian Democrats, Liberal Party, and Centre Party. Smaller municipalities are slightly over represented, because large cities like Stockholm or Gothenburg have roughly the same number of respondents (about fifty) as smaller cities like Linköping or Norrköping.

consider these answers as representing the general view of municipal legislators in Sweden (Gilljam et al. 2012).

The dependent variable of the study is the councillors' attitude toward different forms of protest against school closures. It is examined with the help of the following survey question:

> Imagine a situation where there is a proposal to close one school. To what degree do you have an understanding for the following forms of protest action:
>
> (1) petitioning,
> (2) unauthorised demonstrations,
> (3) school strike (parents refuse to send their children to school),
> (4) occupation of the school,
> (5) illegal teachers' strike,
> (6) parents visit politicians at their homes,
> (7) parents disturb public meetings (e.g., committees),
> (8) parents challenge politicians via local mass media.[8]

The evaluation was done on a scale from 0 (none) to 10 (a great deal of understanding), and responses are described with box plots in Figure 7.1. (All descriptive data are in the Appendix.)

It is not surprising that petitioning is the most understood form of protest (mean 7.8) and that only a few politicians tolerate an illegal teachers' strike (mean 1.7) or the occupation of schools (mean 2.0). Relatively many respondents have little understanding for being challenged by parents via local media (mean 3.6), a result that is probably more a characteristic of local politics, because local elite is less used to media attacks than the national-level representatives.

The presented numbers are well described with the following examples. In 1995, the Swedish school minister noted publicly that pupils' protests against school closures were "silly" actions with "crazy" demands. Another politician added, "A [school] strike is totally unacceptable!"[9] Meetings with parents are a formal way to inform

---

[8] The original question in Swedish was: "*Om du tänker dig en situation där det finns förslag om att lägga ner en skola, hur stor förståelse har du för följande typer av protester?*" The expression "*ha förståelse för*" could be translated and interpreted in various ways – from sympathy (meaning to identify with), acceptance (endorsement or support) to understanding (get the point, but do not necessarily agree with it). The last seems to be the best way to describe politicians' attitudes towards protests in Sweden.

[9] Göteborgs Posten, January 15, 1995.

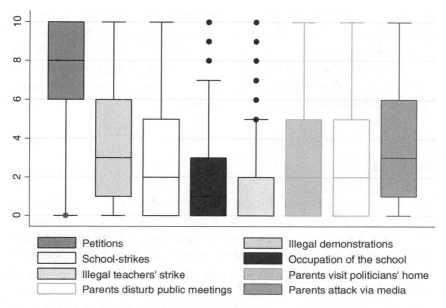

Figure 7.1 Degree of understanding for different forms of protest.

citizens about proposed school closures, but obviously decision-makers do not appreciate these events becoming nasty:[10]

> / ... / we had an information meeting about the closure of a school Y and it was awful ... / ... / pupils threw papers ... / ... / one parent called the member of [X]-party "Hitler" ... / ... / one bureaucrat was attacked on her way home. I would have voted for the closure of this school if this had been the only "dialogue" with the citizens we had.
> / ... / it is good that they protest, show engagement, fight for something they think is good.

> Interviewer: Is it important that they are many?
> Respondent: No, the most important thing is that they do it properly – friendly!

Still, Figure 7.1 demonstrates the significant *variation* of the examined attitudes. Factor analysis (Table 7.3.A in the Appendix) suggests two different components of the attitudes studied. The different forms of

---

[10] A representative of a right-wing party in Uppsala; the interview was conducted by Malina Abrahamsson, who studied the elite attitudes towards school closures (Abrahamsson 2010) and has kindly shared her transcriptions with the author.

protest probably differ in terms of the typical activists involved, and the type of claim formulated for the target. For example, a media article is clearly more elaborated than the slogan of a school strike. Hence, this study examines the attitudes toward different actions separately, but the expectation is that the two dimensions of more and less contentious actions will show some common patterns.[11]

Protest data

The main reason for combining the survey data with event data on protests against school closures in all 290 Swedish municipalities is the need for a better measure of protest experience. Gilljam et al. (2012) asked local politicians to estimate the number of protests (in general) in their own municipality and compare this number to the estimated number of protests elsewhere.[12] It is likely that those representatives who had a more negative attitude toward protests underestimated the number of protests in their municipality or elsewhere, and vice versa. Hence, the relationship of these two variables might be biased. Ideally, a study about the impact of protest experience on attitudes would use panel data, that is, an examination of attitudes toward protest before and after such events. Unfortunately, elite-level panel studies are very rare. The proposed solution of using the records of protest against school closures as discussed in the media significantly improves the measure of protest experience, although one should be aware that different actors might experience the same protest differently.

Data on protest events cover all protests[13] against school closures that were mentioned in Swedish media during 1991–2009. The collection of data was based on two processes: (1) direct contact with municipalities to receive information about which schools they

---

[11] These dimensions are very similar to the ones found by scholars examining the individuals' reported political participation (Teorell et al. 2007).

[12] Their question for measuring protest experience is as follows: "What is your estimation regarding how many citizen protests occur in your municipality?" Answers could vary from (1) "My municipality belongs to the group of Swedish municipalities that have the highest number of protests" to (5) "My municipality belongs to the group of Swedish municipalities that have the lowest number of protests."

[13] Protest is defined as any action by three or more people that clearly states its opposition to the proposed closure of a school/s.

proposed to close and which they actually closed during 1991–2009; and (2) a systematic search for protests and threatened schools in news media reports (print and online media archive Retriever, Swedish Radio, and Swedish TV).[14] Data collection procedures follow the traditions of protest event research and thereby suffer from its classic problem of selection bias; that is, smaller events are often not reported in mainstream media (Ortiz et al. 2005). Some available local newspapers, which are more likely to report small local events, were used, but not all local papers were available for the entire period of study. The information from municipalities was helpful in searching for news of particular schools that did not turn up in the first round of protest event search. On the other hand, as only 60% of the 290 municipalities responded to requests for information, data about threatened schools in missing municipalities were searched for and found in media. In the end, the triangulation process minimized the number of missed protest events; however, all actions that were hidden from the media, such as letters sent directly to the municipalities, obviously cannot be examined here. Considering that school closures are a sensitive and much discussed issue in Sweden, it is likely that the number of missed protests is small.

About 1,300 protest events were observed in the examined 290 municipalities during 1991–2009. These actions ranged from petitions and letters in media (44%) and protests during public meetings (21%), to demonstrations (16%) and school strikes (5%). All actions were peaceful, and police were involved on only a few occasions. The maximum number of participants was about 13,500, with the average number of participants in a protest being 172. Out of the 1245 threatened schools, more than half (57%) faced at least one protest against the proposed closure. However, eighty-five entire municipalities had no recorded protests (forty-seven of these municipalities did not threaten any schools).

The main independent variable in this analysis is the number of protests in a particular municipality. Obviously, the exact protest experience of every respondent is unknown, but this study assumes that each

---

[14] These archives cover the major Swedish national and regional newspapers since the early 1990s, though many of the local newspapers like Uppsala Nya Tidning (UNT) have been included only since the mid-2000s. The digital data have been complemented with the information from several paper-based newspapers all across Sweden: UNT (east), Norrbottens-Kuriren (north), Göteborgs-Posten (west), and Sydsveskan (south). This time-consuming manual search of protest events on microfilms and coding of the events was done by the author and two research-assistants. Details about codebook and raw data are available from the author.

examined protest targeted all the members of the political elite in a municipality. The survey on attitudes was conducted from 2008 to 2009, and Swedish local elections took place in September 2006 and 2002. Many of the decision-makers who participated in the survey were probably reelected in 2006. Considering that attitudes toward protests do not change very fast, this study used two general protest variables: recent protests (2007–2008) and long-term number of protests (2003–2008).[15] The theoretical discussion above suggests that more contentious actions could have different effects on attitudes. Hence, two distinct variables were used in the analysis: the mobilization of any school strike, and the mobilization of any large campaign. The first refers to significant illegal actions, in which parents do not send their children to school. School strikes can last from one day to a week. The second refers to the use of multiple forms of action, usually demonstrations and petitions, which involve more than 1000 people. Large campaigns generally produce a higher degree of conflict and have a stronger impact than more general protest measures.

The individual-level variables used in the model are: respondent's age, gender, ideological self-replacement in the left–right scale, dichotomous measure of incumbent position in the municipality, and dichotomous measure of awareness of school protests. All respondents were asked to note if they recalled any particular protests in their municipality. Those who mentioned school-related protests are considered to be aware of them. Finally, the analysis also uses a control variable for school closures, namely the percentage of schools threatened in that particular municipality during the period from 2003 to 2008.

Results and discussion

Although the data used for this study have a hierarchical character and as such would usually be examined with the help of multi-level models

[15] The survey was done in late 2008 and in early 2009, so it is likely that actions in 2009 did not affect the attitudes. The protest variable is used as a proxy for the protest experience, and it is assumed that all policy makers in the municipality have experienced the same number of events. This is, of course, a serious assumption because those decision-makers who are the members of the committee for school issues are direct targets of the actions, while other representatives are only indirect targets. However, this assumption would not be a problem as party groups discuss these questions internally and all representatives should be aware of protest events.

of analysis (Steenbergen and Jones 2002), there is very little intra-municipality variance. Hence, this study used an ordinary linear regression analysis instead.[16] The analysis was performed separately for two groups of protest types: more and less contentious forms of action (Tables 7.1 and 7.2). The first model, for every form of action, estimates the effect of main individual-level variables as well as the control variable (Null model). The second model (with protests) measures the effect of protest experience on attitudes. The results demonstrate that this effect is present only when considering understanding for strikes, parents' visits to politicians' home, disruptions of public meetings, and protests via media.

The effects of individual-level variables show an interesting variation. While age effects are too small for any substantial impact on attitudes, the effect of gender is large and *varies across the forms of protest*. Female decision-makers have more understanding for petitioning and parents' protests during public meetings than their male colleagues. The situation is opposite for parents' visits to politicians' home and school strikes. Regarding the four remaining forms of action, the effect of gender is very small (protests via mass media, illegal demonstrations, teachers' strike) or insignificant (occupation of school buildings). These effects remain the same when protest experience is accounted for. The varying effect of gender might seem puzzling. It seems that on average, Swedish local-level female decision-makers have more understanding for "peaceful" and "friendly" protests, and prefer to keep their privacy.[17] The results suggest that groups that oppose school closures might improve their impact on the process by targeting male and female decision-makers using different strategies.

Second, the incumbent status and ideological position of the decision-maker appear to be important factors for explaining the varying degrees of understanding for protests. The position of power is particularly important, as those with incumbent status are clearly less understanding toward all examined forms of protest than the opposition members. The effect remains after accounting for ideology and protest experience, and is consistent with prior studies (Gilljam et al.

---

[16] The results remain the same if the multi-level models of analysis are used.

[17] There also are some interesting interaction effects of age and gender status. In the case of petitioning, elderly women respond more positively than elderly men, while in the case of parents' visits to decisions-makers' homes, the situation is directly opposite.

Table 7.1 *Attitudes toward more challenging protests against school closures among Swedish local political elite*

DV: understanding protests: little (0) … a lot (10)	Illegal demonstrations		School strikes		School occupations		Teachers' strike	
	Null model	With protests	Null model	With strikes	Null model	With protests	Null model	With protests
Female	−0.160**	−0.160**	−0.296***	−0.293***	0.030	0.030	−0.104**	−0.106**
Age	−0.036***	−0.036***	−0.017***	−0.017***	−0.031***	−0.031***	−0.036***	−0.036***
Incumbent	−0.650***	−0.650***	−0.756***	−0.757***	−0.633***	−0.635***	−0.737***	−0.736***
Ideology	−0.243***	−0.243***	−0.100***	−0.099***	−0.181***	−0.181***	−0.155***	−0.157***
Awareness	0.374***	0.376***	−0.122**	−0.120**	−0.031	−0.025	−0.223***	−0.219***
% of schools threatened	0.001	0.001	−0.001	−0.001	0.002	0.003	0.001	0.0001
Any protests since 2003								
Any school strikes				−0.201**				
Any large campaigns		0.131				−0.072		0.193**
Constant	7.290***	7.283***	4.725***	4.738***	4.808***	4.820***	4.907***	4.897***
Adjusted R^2	0.096	0.096	0.039	0.040	0.087	0.087	0.093	0.094
# municipalities					290			
N					7898			

Notes: *** $p < 0.01$; ** $p < 0.05$

2012). This effect is particularly strong in the case of more contentious actions (see Table 7.1). These results demonstrate clearly that the character of being a target of protest is unpleasant. Moreover, as elections can easily change the incumbent status, decision-makers might "need" to change their attitudes toward protests every four years.

The position of power has a strong impact even for representatives from the Left or Green Party, although the members of these parties are in general more understanding toward protests than the representatives from right-wing parties (e.g., the Moderate Party). The last is also reflected by the significant, but small, effect of ideological self-replacement on the left–right scale. Right-wing representatives are slightly less tolerant toward protests, especially illegal demonstrations, than their left-wing colleagues. However, there are also interesting differences between the left-wing parties – the Left Party (v) and the Social Democratic Party (s). While representatives from the first are generally more understanding toward protests, decision-makers from the second tolerate all forms of action significantly less. For example, mean acceptance of illegal demonstration for representatives of (v) is 6.5, while for members of (s) it is 4.1. One of the reasons could be the long incumbent experience of Social Democratic representatives in the majority of Swedish municipalities.

These findings have implications for research on social movement outcomes, which often focus on left-wing parties as potential movement allies (e.g., Giugni 2004; Kriesi 1995). Although the claims of such a movement might appeal to left-wing representatives, their attitudes toward the strategies of the social movement become more negative while they are in power, and their attitudes are not always coherent in the group of "left." On the other hand, the results also provide support for arguments that facilitation and help from political parties are more likely when these parties are in opposition. This trend may not only be due to electoral interests (Tarrow 1993), but also to the fact that decision-makers have a more positive attitude toward protest strategies while in opposition. Swedish local political elite is certainly not a representative for all decision-makers in Western Europe, but the results suggest that caution is in order when discussing potential political allies for social movement in countries with multi-party systems. Moving on to the role of protest experience, the results do not provide any solid support for the expectations of this study. Those decision-makers who were aware of school protests in their municipality had, in

Table 7.2 Attitudes toward less challenging protests against school closures among Swedish local political elite

DV: understanding protests: little (0) . . . a lot (10)	Petitioning		Parents' visit politicians' home		Disturbing public meetings		Protesting via mass media		
	Null model	With protests	Null model	With protests	Null model	With # protests	Null model	With # protests	With large campaigns
Female	0.842***	0.842***	−0.363***	−0.365***	0.520***	0.518***	−0.125**	−0.128**	−0.127**
Age	−0.024***	−0.025***	0.009***	0.009***	−0.043***	−0.043***	−0.050***	−0.050***	−0.050***
Incumbent (0;1)	−0.556***	−0.557***	−0.292***	−0.296***	−0.546***	−0.552***	−0.424***	−0.419***	−0.422***
Ideology (Left . . . Right)	−0.055***	−0.056***	−0.052***	−0.052***	−0.132***	−0.133***	−0.031***	−0.031***	−0.031***
Awareness (0;1)	0.142**	0.145**	−0.043	−0.027	0.164**	0.188**	0.222***	0.214***	0.226***
% of schools threatened	−0.003	−0.002	0.004	0.007***	−0.001	−0.003	−0.002	−0.004**	−0.003
Any protests since 2003				−0.215***		−0.324***		0.068	
Any large campaigns		−0.048							0.230**
Constant	9.372***	9.389***	3.164***	3.164***	5.980***	6.091***	6.754***	6.732***	6.732***
Adjusted R^2	0.072	0.072	0.010		0.074	0.077	0.043	0.044	0.043
# municipalities					290				
N					7898				

Notes: *** $p < 0.01$; ** $p < 0.05$

general, more understanding for such actions, particularly for demonstrations and protests via mass media (see Tables 7.1 and 7.2). The "awareness" variable had a significant negative effect on attitudes toward school strikes and teachers' strikes, but had no significant effect on attitudes toward school occupations or parents' visits to politicians' homes. These results provide some support for the "normalization mechanism," that is, the premise that experiencing less disruptive actions might make one more tolerant toward such actions, since those who were aware of protests against school closures responded more positively toward disruptions of public meetings or protesting via media campaigns.

When examining the models "with protest" in Tables 7.1 and 7.2, it is clear that the effect of this study's measure of protest experience is not robust across all forms of action. The experience of large campaigns – that is, the presence of campaigns that involved both petitioning and demonstrations – has some positive effect on targets' understanding for teachers' strikes and of protesting via mass media. Respondents from municipalities that had at least one school strike are, however, less tolerant toward these type of actions. Finally, those who have experienced at least one protest since 2003 also have a lower degree of understanding for parents' visits to their homes and for disturbances of public meetings. One might expect some interaction effect between protest awareness and protest experience, but this was not significant in the majority of cases. It was only for attitudes toward teachers' strikes that some interaction effect was observed.

Although the revealed effect of protest experience is not very clear, it encourages further analysis of targets' reactions to different forms of protest. The result that protest experience relates to a lower understanding for more direct attacks (visits to targets' homes, disruption of public meetings), but to a greater understanding for actions like media campaigns, suggests that the effect of a strategy is mediated via the arguments used during that strategy. In media, groups use more reasoned arguments, while in meetings and direct contacts protests can be very confrontational. Hence, although the "normalization mechanism" may still be at work for the less conflictual cases, in general it is clear that personal characteristics (i.e., gender) or the position of power are much more relevant factors for explaining the varying degrees of understanding for different forms of protest action among the Swedish local elite.

Conclusion

This chapter argued that in order to better understand the consequences of social movements, more knowledge is needed on how targets – the decision-makers – view different protest strategies. This need is motivated by the assumption that politicians who have more understanding for protests would also be more likely to listen to activists' claims and be more responsive to their arguments. Although it is true that the political elite is not expected to have an overly positive response toward protesting, empirical data do demonstrate the variation of targets' attitudes. It is therefore important to ask what explains this variation. Who tolerates petitioning, but not striking, and what is the role of protest experience in this relationship?

Based on prior mass-level studies on attitudes toward protests and participation in protests, it was expected that the variation of understanding for petitioning, demonstrating, striking, occupying public buildings, or attacking targets via media would be explained by targets' personal background variables such as gender and age, ideological leaning, position of power, and experience of protest actions. The expectation was that the effect of protest experience would vary, with a normalization process at work for less contentious actions like petitions, and an amplifying negative effect at work for more contentious actions like strikes and school occupations.

The empirical analysis used data from a survey of Swedish local elite, combined with the knowledge of protest actions against school closures in these same municipalities. The last was done in order to gain a more precise measure of protest experience than was available in the original survey. There are three important findings. First, the effect of protest experience on elite understanding for protests is very small, and varies across the forms of action. Still, the results reveal that an experience of school strikes is negatively related to understanding for school strikes, supporting the expectations of negative amplification effects. Problems with the robustness of the results were shown by the positive relationship between attitudes toward teachers' strikes and experience of large protest campaigns. Nevertheless, protest experience probably plays some role in the attitudes examined here, and the results suggest that future research on this relationship should pay particular attention to the arguments that are used during protests. Targets' understanding for actions that allow activists to use more direct confrontation (visits to homes, protests at meetings) are probably more affected by negative personal experiences during such events.

Second, disentangling the different forms of protest appeared to be important for a better understanding of the targets' varying attitudes toward protests. Otherwise, the interesting gender effect would have been missed: Female decision-makers responded more positively to the use of petitions than their male colleagues; and this gender difference in response was reversed when activists visited politicians at their homes. Social movements often combine various protest strategies, but this study shows that the forms of action matter for some targets. Visiting a female decision-maker at her home might be a counterproductive strategy for activists opposing school closures in Sweden, and the same argument probably applies elsewhere.

Finally, this study supports prior studies that argue that targets' attitudes toward protest depend on their position of power. Incumbents have much less understanding for all protest strategies than opposition members, and this effect does not depend on the ideological or party background of the target. Those with power simply do not like protests. While it is common to expect that left-wing parties, particularly in Sweden, respond more positively to citizens' extra-parliamentary initiatives, the results of this study demonstrate a significant difference between the attitudes of representatives from the Left and from the Social Democratic parties. Still, even the members of Left and Green parties had less understanding for protests while in power. Hence, being a target of protests is a much more important factor for not tolerating such actions than one's personal ideological convictions. Protests against school closures might be a somewhat specific case here, because both left- and right-wing politicians have tried to close some schools in Sweden. If more ideological issues are at stake, it is possible that the role of ideology may become more important than the position of power in explaining the varying attitudes toward protest. Further research is needed to examine this question.

This chapter demonstrated that personal background and the power position of those who are targets of social movement mobilization are important factors for explaining their varying views on protest actions. As protests against school closures often prolong the life of a threatened school (Uba 2014), this study provides better grounds for understanding the varying responses of the targets.

Appendix

Table 7.1.A *Descriptive data of independent variables (N = 7,898,290 municipalities)*

	Mean	Std. Dev.	Min	Max
Female	0.41	0.49	0	1
Age (years)	54.18	11.64	18	96
Incumbent position	0.56	0.49	0	1
Ideology (left (0) - right (10))	4.76	3.03	0	10
Awareness of school protest	0.34	0.47	0	1
% of schools threatened by closure in municipality	17.90	19.87	0	83
Any protests in municipality	0.53	0.50	0	1
Any school strikes in municipality	0.08	0.26	0	1
Any large campaigns in municipality	0.09	0.28	0	1

Table 7.2.A *Descriptive data on attitudes toward protest (dependent variables)*

Form of protests (Scale 0 … 10)	Mean	Std. Dev.	Correlation matrix						
			1	2	3	4	5	6	7
1. Petitioning	7.79	2.43	1.00						
2. Illegal demonstration	3.89	3.20	0.34	1.00					
3. School strike (illegal)	2.70	2.88	0.20	0.49	1.00				
4. Occupation of the school buildings	1.98	2.63	0.20	0.56	0.67	1.00			
5. Illegal teachers' strike	1.67	2.53	0.17	0.49	0.61	0.76	1.00		
6. Parents visit politicians' homes	3.16	3.09	0.15	0.26	0.28	0.30	0.27	1.00	
7. Parents disrupt public meetings	2.97	2.98	0.23	0.44	0.38	0.45	0.43	0.39	1.00
8. Parents attack politicians via media	3.65	3.14	0.24	0.31	0.22	0.28	0.25	0.32	0.45
No. of respondents (municipalities)			7,898 (290)						

Table 7.3.A *Table of factor loadings*

	Factor 1	Factor 2
Petitioning	0.125	**0.555**
Illegal demonstration	**0.642**	0.380
School strike (illegal)	**0.832**	0.122
Occupation of the school	**0.892**	0.170
Illegal teachers' strike	**0.867**	0.129
Parents visit politicians' homes	0.220	**0.616**
Parents disturb meetings	0.418	**0.643**
Parents protest in mass media	0.123	**0.776**

Note: Principal component analysis, varimax rotation, eigenvalues for factor 1 = 6.69 and factor 2 = 1.13. *N* = 7900. Actions forming the single factor are in bold.

References

Abrahamsson, Malina. 2010. "Den responsiva beslutsfattaren? En studie om beslutsprocessen vid skolnedläggningar" [The Responsive Decision Maker? A Study about the Decision Making Process of School Closures]. C-uppsats (BA thesis). Uppsala University.

Althaus, Scott L. and Kevin Coe. 2001. "Social Identity Processes and the Dynamics of Public Support for War." *Public Opinion Quarterly,* 75(1): 65–88.

Amenta, Edwin Amenta, Neal Caren, Elizabeth Chiarello, and Yang Su. 2010. "The Political Consequences of Social Movements." *Annual Review of Sociology,* 36: 287–307.

Arpan, Laura M., Kaysee Baker, Youngwon Lee, Taejin Jung, Lori Lorusso, and Jason Smith. 2006. "News Coverage of Social Protests and the Effects of Photographs and Prior Attitudes." *Mass Communication and Society,* 9(1): 1–20.

Bäck, Hanna, Jan Teorell and Anders Westholm. 2011. "Explaining Modes of Participation: A Dynamic Test of Alternative Rational Choice Models." *Scandinavian Political Studies,* 34(1): 74–97.

Barnes, Samuel and Max Kaase. 1979. *Political Action: Mass Participation in 5 Western Democracies.* Beverly Hills, CA: Sage Publications.

Basu, Ranu. 2007. "Negotiating Acts of Citizenship in an Era of Neoliberal Reform: The Game of School Closures." *International Journal of Urban and Regional Research,* 31(1): 109–127.

Batel, Susana and Paula Castro. 2014. "Collective Action and Social Change: Examining the Role of Representation in the Communication between Protesters and Third-party Members." *Journal of Community & Applied Social Psychology*, published online.

Björklund, Anders, Per-Anders Edin, Peter Fredriksson, and Alan B. Krueger. 2004. "Education, Equality, and Efficiency – An Analysis of Swedish School Reforms During the 1990s," IFAU – Institutet för arbetsmarknadspolitisk utvärdering, Uppsala. Retrieved July, 17, 2012 (www.ifau.se/upload/pdf/se/2004/r04-01.pdf).

Bochel, Catherine. 2013. "Petitions Systems: Contributing to Representative Democracy?" *Parliamentary Affairs*, 66(4): 798–815.

Bohner, Gerd and Nina Dickel. 2011. "Attitude and Attitude Change." *Annual Review of Psychology*, 62: 391–417.

Caren, Neal, R. A. Ghoshal, and V. A. Ribas. 2011. "Social Movement Generation: Cohort and Period Trends in Protest Attendance and Petition Signing." *American Sociological Review*, 76(1): 125–151.

Crozat, Matthew. 1998. "Are the Times a-Changin'? Assessing the Acceptance of Protest in Western Democracies." In David S. Meyer and Sidney Tarrow (eds.), *The Social Movement Society: Contentious Politics for the New Century*. Lanham, MD: Rowman and Littlefield, 59–81.

Detenber, Benjamin H., M. R. Gotlieb, D. M. McLeod, and O. Malinkina. 2007. "Frame Intensity Effects of Television News Stories about a High-Visibility Protest Issue." *Mass Communication and Society*, 10(4): 439–460.

Esaiasson, Peter and Hanne M. Narud. 2013. "Between-Election Democracy: An Introductory Note." In Peter Esaiasson and Hanne M. Narud (eds.), *Between Election Democracy. The Representative Relationship after Election Day*. Colchester: ECPR Press, 1–14.

Gilljam, Mikael, Mikael Persson, and David Karlsson. 2012: "Representative's Attitudes towards Citizen Protests: The Impact of Ideology, Self-interest and Experiences." *Legislative Studies Quarterly*, 37(2): 251–268.

Giugni, Marco. 1998. "Was It Worth the Effort? The Outcomes and Consequences of Social Movements." *Annual Review of Sociology*, 24: 371–393.

Giugni, Marco. 2004. *Social Protest and Policy Change. Ecology, Antinuclear, and Peace Movements in Comparative Perspective*. Lanham, MD: Rowman and Littlefield Publishers, Inc.

Kearns, Robin A., Nicolas Lewis, Tim McCreanor, and Karen Witten. 2010. "School Closures as Breaches in the Fabric of Rural Welfare: Community Perspectives from New Zealand." *Welfare Reform in Rural Places: Comparative Perspectives*, 15: 219–236.

Kriesi, Hanspeter (ed.). 1995. *New Social Movements in Western Europe*. Minneapolis: University of Minnesota Press.

Luders, Joseph. 2006. "The Economics of Movement Success: Business Responses to Civil Rights Mobilization." *American Journal of Sociology*, 111: 963–998.

Marien, Sofie and Marc Hooghe. 2013. "Is Anyone Listening? The Perceived Effectiveness of Electoral and Non-Electoral Participation." In Peter Esaiasson and Hanne Marte Narud (eds.), *Between Election Democracy. The Representative Relationship after Election Day*. Colchester: ECPR Press, 35–52.

Meyer, David S. and Sidney Tarrow (eds.). 1997. *The Social Movement Society: Contentious Politics for a New Century*. Lanham, MD: Rowman & Littlefield Publishers.

Ortiz, David G., Daniel J. Myers, Eugene N. Walls, and Maria-Elena D. Diaz. 2005. "Where Do We Stand with Newspaper Data?" *Mobilization: An International Quarterly*, 10: 397–419.

Polletta, Francesca. 1998. "'It Was like a Fever ...' Narrative and Identity in Social Protest." *Social Problems*, 45: 137–159.

Skrentny, John D. 2006. "Policy-Elite Perceptions and Social Movement Success: Understanding Variations in Group Inclusion in Affirmative Action." *American Journal of Sociology*, 111(6): 1762–1815.

Solevid, Maria. 2009. Voices from the Welfare State: Dissatisfaction and Political Action in Sweden. University of Gothenburg. Kållered: Intellecta Infolog.

Steenbergen, Marco and B. Jones, 2002. "Modeling Multilevel Data Structures." *American Journal of Political Science*, 46(1): 218–237.

Tarrow, Sidney. 1993. "Social Protest and Policy Reform May 1968 and the Loi d'Orientation in France." *Comparative Political Studies*, 25(4): 579–607.

Taylor, Verta and Nella Van Dyke. 2004. "'Get Up, Stand Up': Tactical Repertoires of Social Movements." In David Snow, S. A. Soule, and H. Kriesi (eds.), *Blackwell Companion to Social Movements*. Oxford: Blackwell, 262–293.

Teorell, Jan. 2006. "Political Participation and Three Theories of Democracy: A Research Inventory and Agenda." *European Journal of Political Research*, 45: 787–810.

Teorell, Jan, Paul Sum, and Mette Tobiasen. 2007. "Participation and Political Equality: An Assessment of Large Scale Democracy." In Jan van Deth, Jose Ramon Montero and Anders Westholm (eds.), *Citizenship and Involvement in European Democracies*. London & New York: Routledge, 384–416.

Thomas, Emma and Winnifred Louis. 2013. "When Will Collective Action Be Effective? Violent and Non-Violent Protests Differentially Influence Perceptions of Legitimacy and Efficacy among Sympathizers." *Personality and Social Psychology Bulletin*, online publication, DOI:10.1177/0146167213510525.

Tilly, Chalres. 1999. "Conclusion." In Giugni, McAdam, and Tilly (eds.), *How Social Movements Matter*. Minneapolis: University of Minnesota Press, 253–270.

Turnbull, Maureen. 1973. "Attitude of Government and Administration towards the 'Hunger Marches' of the 1920s and 1930s." *Journal of Social Policy*, 2(2): 131–142.

Uba, Katrin. 2005. "Political Protest and Policy Change: The Direct Impact of Indian Anti-Privatization Mobilizations, 1990–2003" *Mobilization*, 10: 383–396.

Uba, Katrin. 2014. *Postponing the School Closure: Effects of Protests in Swedish Municipalities*. Presented in The Responsive Gov and the MOVEOUT workshop on "Voters, protest and policies: Bridging public opinion, social movement outcomes and policy responsiveness research." June, 2014, University of Leicester, the UK.

Walgrave, Stefaan and Peter van Aelst. 2001. "Who is that (Wo)man in the Street? From the normalisation of Protest to Normalisation of Protester." *European Journal of Political Science*, 39: 461–486.

Witten, Karen, Robin Kearns, Nick Lewis, Heater Coster, and Tim McCreanor. 2003. "Educational Restructuring from a Community Viewpoint: A Case of School Closure from Invercargill, New Zealand." *Environment and Planning C: Government and Policy*, 21: 203–223.

8 FEMINIST MOBILIZATION AND THE POLITICS OF RIGHTS

Joseph E. Luders

On Sunday, March 7, 1965, hundreds of civil rights marchers crossed the Edmund Pettus Bridge on the outskirts of Selma, Alabama, headed for the state capitol in Montgomery. On the other side, state and local police descended on them with tear gas and billy clubs. National news captured shocking images of law enforcement officers beating nonviolent demonstrators who were seeking only the basic element of political freedom: the right to vote. The broadcast of media footage of the melee provoked national and international outrage. This violent episode in Selma, an event that came to be known as "Bloody Sunday," proved to be a decisive catalyst for federal action on voting rights. During the Selma protests, over a hundred members of the House and Senate rose in their respective chambers to denounce lawlessness and the deprivation of fundamental rights (Garrow 1978). Only a week after Bloody Sunday, citing the events in Selma, President Lyndon Johnson announced his intention to submit sweeping voting rights legislation. Although southern Democrats filibustered the bill in the Senate, a bipartisan coalition swept aside their opposition and, five months later, enacted into law the Voting Rights Act of 1965. Because of these events, multiple studies of the civil rights movement document the association between protests, white violence, and government responsiveness to movement demands (Burstein 1979; Garrow 1978; McAdam 1982). Yet, in some ways, this extraordinary movement triumph encourages a faulty impression of how movements achieve political change because incidents such as this, and the public attention they garner, are extraordinarily rare. The far more common setting for social movements is one of broad public disinterest and inattention.

Accordingly, research on the impact of social movements on public policy outcomes presents a much more mixed picture. In their extensive literature review of this topic, Andrews and Edwards (2004) find that, "[advocacy organizations exert] a modest role at best on congressional voting patterns." Casting doubt on the efficacy of protests, Burstein and Sausner (2005) suggest that, given the infrequency of such events, even among the most active movements, it is hardly surprising that evidence for movement impact is uneven. It is implausible, they argue, that congressional majorities would feel impelled to respond to the demands of benefit-seekers active in relatively few localities and engaging in a small number of protests. Nevertheless, others find that movement mobilization does affect government responsiveness and policy outcomes (Amenta 2006). Although the topic of movement impact has received greater attention of late, this research has generated a set of divergent findings with movements sometimes exerting influence on policy-making processes, but other times not. These inconsistent findings highlight the fundamental question: how do social movements and other organized benefit-seekers obtain desired policy outcomes, particularly claims to rights? Or, more precisely, why do the *targets* of these benefit-seekers concede to these demands?

The answer has implications not only for studies of social movement outcome, but more generally for understanding the impact of all organized benefit-seekers. To the extent that movement outcomes have been studied, this research has often highlighted features of movement organizations (spontaneous or organized), tactical differences (violent or nonviolent), or emphasis is placed on external circumstances, such as support from third parties (e.g., Gamson 1975). Yet, as noted above, these studies have often produced contradictory or inconclusive findings (Koopmans and Statham 1999; Giugni 1999). Andrews (2004) argues that there are three basic models for social movement outcome. In brief, for movements to win gains, they can *disrupt* target interests, *persuade* third parties to enter the fray on behalf of the movement, or they can *negotiate* with state actors using conventional institutional tactics. Despite the apparent differences among these models, I suggest that they all share the same basic assumption that targets respond to movement demands based on their exposure to the *costs* that movements and third parties impose upon them. Others have offered variants of this proposition before (Gamson 1975; Lipsky 1968; McAdam 1982; Piven and Cloward 1977; Wilson 1961). However, prior studies have not pushed the theoretical analysis far beyond this general observation, mostly due to the relative underspecification of a target's interests and vulnerabilities (Walsh 1986; Overby and Ritchie 1991). I suggest that variation in exposure to costs is critical to the explanation of the different responses of targets and bystanders. In other words, the same tactics used against identical targets will not necessarily produce uniform responses due to dissimilar cost considerations. And different tactical choices may provide the movement with more or less bargaining leverage *relative* to a specific target.

I develop these points below to delineate a general explanation for the influence of benefit-seekers (social movements and interest organizations alike) on political actors based on a consideration of how targets assess the costs of acceding or resisting. To evaluate the merits of this general perspective, I survey the impact of the contemporary women's movement across multiple demands. Over recent decades, this movement has made multiple and diverse demands upon their targets, won some notable victories in certain areas, and suffered various setbacks in others. Studies of movement outcome, which generally concentrate upon a single aspect of a larger struggle, can reveal causal connections within those specific cases, but they are always vulnerable to the criticism that the circumstances are somehow distinctive and the findings cannot be generalized. A survey of movement agitation across multiple domains provides a more robust test of the imputed causal relations.

Predicting the responsiveness of political targets

As indicated above, the explanation of movement outcome presented here starts with the proposition that cost perceptions shape the behavior of movement targets. In weighing how to respond to movement demands, targets consider two distinct costs: disruption costs and concession costs (Luders 2010). *Disruption costs* are those losses that result directly or indirectly from movement agitation. Movement activities can interfere with a target's realization of desired social, political, or economic objectives. Accordingly, movements have greater leverage to the extent that they can obstruct a target from realizing these valued objectives. *Concession costs* are essentially the social, political, or economic price of conceding movement demands. For elected officials, for instance, voters might punish them for acquiescing to costly or unpopular movement demands. Following the conventional assumption that political actors are motivated principally by electoral concerns (Mayhew 1974; Kingdon 1973), both disruption and concession costs should be understood as grounded in this fundamental electoral calculus. Ultimately, movements are most likely to achieve greater impacts if their disruption costs exceed their concession costs. The key question, then, is: how do political targets assess the impact of movement activities and the acquiescence to movement demands on their electoral fortunes?

Building upon the insights of prior studies on social movement outcomes, interest group influence, and congressional policy making, this investigation highlights the interaction of three main factors that define these costs for targeted politicians: public opinion on the issue in question, mass attentiveness or "salience" (the intensity with which the public holds those preferences), and the electoral leverage of the benefit-seeker and its allies relative to their opponents. The significance of these factors is readily apparent. First, regarding public opinion, elected officials must be preoccupied with the preferences of their constituents if they aspire to be reelected. They are therefore keenly interested in obtaining information of this sort based on opinion polls, constituent mail, town hall meetings, communications with interest organizations, and so on. Next, regarding attentiveness, again due to the reelection imperative, office-seekers will be concerned about the intensity of constituent preferences on the many issues before them. Majorities may care a great deal about a handful of matters (particularly bread-and-butter issues as well as certain hot-button moral topics) but they might be totally unaware of more abstract, technical, or unfamiliar topics. Office-seekers must be actively engaged in responding to constituent preferences on those topics with the greatest salience and representing those views (Page and Shapiro 1983). For issues lacking mass attention, public officials will have a freer hand to react in a manner that suits their own ideological position or, more likely, the preferences of activist minorities. Finally, regarding electoral leverage, in cases in which most citizens are inattentive and benefit-seekers are active, office-seekers must attempt to discern the relative electoral significance of the competitors within their own (re)election coalition. Other things being equal, those benefit-seekers with greater electoral clout should garner preferential treatment. With all of the attention devoted to the contentious aspects of collective action, movement studies are often relatively silent on the less provocative struggles for social change and how specific movement outcomes often depend upon conventional electoral politics (but see Burstein et al., 1995).

Further, instead of treating movements as unitary entities, this approach suggests that different movement goals produce distinctive constellations of public preferences, mass salience, and degrees of organized opposition. To explain movement outcomes, then, it is necessary to disaggregate movement demands to appreciate the distinctive politics associated with each. For instance, in discerning the concession costs for public officials, a key distinction between the Equal Rights Amendment and the Violence Against Women Act was the strong opposition to the former and weak resistance to the latter. For each domain, depending upon the specific combinations of these three factors, a range of divergent outcomes can be predicted, as the different rows in Table 8.1 depict. These different combinations are explicated below.

Across the top and bottom rows, the anticipated outcomes conform to Burstein's (1999) theory of democratic representation in which the strongest predictors for victory or defeat are public opinion and conditions of high mass attentiveness, in which case elected officials adhere to the preferences of interested majoritarian preferences. Simply put, movements are highly likely to succeed if public opinion is both supportive and attentive or fail if the reverse is true. These outcomes are predicted irrespective of movement or countermovement

Table 8.1 *Variation in movement outcomes with political targets*

	Public opinion	Salience	Relative electoral leverage	Predicted outcome
1	Supportive	High	Opponent absent, weaker, or stronger	Success
2	Supportive	Low	Opponent weaker or absent	Success
3	Supportive	Low	Opponent stronger	Defeat or symbolic gains
4	Divided or no opinion	Low	Opponent weaker or absent	Proportionate gains
5	Divided or no opinion	Low	Opponent stronger	Proportionate losses
6	Opposed	Low	Opponent weaker or absent	Limited, concealed gains
7	Opposed	Low	Opponent stronger	Defeat
8	Opposed	High	Opponent absent, weaker, or stronger	Defeat

strength or weakness.[1] However, as suggested at the outset, such cases are exceptional and, in between the two extremes, under circumstances of low salience, there are multiple combinations that are predicted to coincide with other outcomes. Compared to strong public support and high attentiveness, the next most propitious circumstances for movement impact are public support and the absence or relative weakness of organized opposition. Below, I demonstrate that this situation was evident in many of early victories of the feminist movement.

As suggested in the third row, sometimes policy-seekers are overmatched by stronger opponents. If public opinion is supportive but inattentive, elected officials must respond delicately to cater to the preferences of the stronger interest while reducing the threat of repudiation at the ballot box. This triangulation may involve letting proposed legislation die quietly over the course of the policy-making process or enacting policies that are symbolically responsive to the issue, but do not meaningfully threaten the interests of the issue domain's dominant actors. For example, politicians may respond to demands for action on global climate change with promises to invest in new technologies to resolve the problem in the future. This allows officials to claim credit for having done something without antagonizing powerful policy opponents (or arousing the ire of citizens for imposing costs directly upon them). The combination of low attentiveness and the benefit-seeker's weakness is presumed to mean that officials cannot be credibly threatened for inaction or passing policies that are unlikely to substantially address the underlying problem.[2] The outcome may appease mass publics but they often leave the benefit-seekers disenchanted.

The fourth row depicts an organization seeking policy benefits without broader public support, but also without an effective organized opponent. The prediction here is that the degree of success depends on the policy-seeker's overall electoral importance to the target with more expansive benefits possible for larger, more

[1] In the table, additional similar scenarios at the extremes are collapsed into only two by including both absent, weak, and strong movement/countermovements into a single row. As the outcomes are unchanged, this was done to simplify the graphic.
[2] The federal Assault Weapons Ban of 1994, for instance, allowed Congress to take a position on gun control that produced relatively minimal interference with the acquisition of assault weapons that had been only marginally modified to be in compliance.

formidable organizations. Hence, the outcome is described as proportionate gains. This scenario captures conventional interest group politics described by pluralists, as with agricultural lobbies seeking subsidies. Or, before the public paid attention to the repeal of sodomy laws, these changes went forward without opposition as a technocratic reform of states' criminal codes.[3]

The fifth row is the mirror image of the fourth, with the organized opponent capable of overcoming the movement's agenda. The losses are "proportionate" in that the relative size of the competing benefit-seeker affects the overall magnitude of the legislative setback. There are additional nuances to this situation due to the status quo bias of American political institutions. In these contests, the outcome depends in some measure on which side is seeking new benefits or holding the line against change. Due to the commonplace need for supermajorities to overcome legislative obstructionism, interests attempting to thwart policy change will be better positioned to block an interest seeking a new benefit. Whereas a weaker interest seeking new benefits in this situation is poised for failure, a marginally weaker movement attempting to maintain existing benefits may be able to block or reduce the extent of policy retrenchment.

Next, contrary to the thesis that public opinion always rules, the sixth scenario predicts that gains are possible despite mild public opposition. Inattention (and the presumption by policy makers of continued mass inattention) coupled with the weakness of the organized opponent allows a policy-seeker to extract policy concession from targeted officials. I describe these gains as limited and "hidden" because targeted officials will be keenly interested in camouflaging their participation in aiding a disfavored interest. This might necessitate the use of policy instruments to reduce the visibility of "chains of traceability" back to incumbent politicians (Arnold 1990). Hacker and Pierson (2005), for instance, document how tax-cutting Republican lawmakers used "phase-ins" such that average Americans felt their (much smaller) benefits immediately whereas the far more generous and more costly tax reductions for the highest-income citizens were gradually introduced in later years. Thus, even though public opinion opposed tax reductions

---

[3] These gains might involve policies whose material costs are essentially invisible (as with the dispersed cost of agricultural subsidies) or nonexistent, such as elimination of victimless crimes from the penal code (e.g., consensual sodomy).

for highest-income citizens, precisely such tax cuts could be pursued without fear of swift electoral reprisal.

Finally, against public opposition and a more formidable opponent, salience is rendered irrelevant in the seventh scenario as a movement under these circumstances is fated to crushing defeat.

While these different scenarios are presented in schematic fashion, they are nonetheless meant to highlight the proposition that predicted outcomes depend heavily on the convergence of a few crucial variables.[4] An exclusive focus on any single factor, except at the extremes of the continuum, will yield disparate findings. Additional refinements might be suggested. For instance, it is possible that the institutional setting will mediate these expected relationships. Judges with longer terms in office (or lifetime tenure in the case of federal judges) might be more insulated from public preferences and therefore more willing to acquiesce to movement demands based on the legal merits of a movement's specific claims. (Though, by the same token, they are generally insulated from movement disruptions.) That said, state judges in elective positions will be susceptible to the same convergence of factors affecting other office-seekers. While not an exhaustive summary of the refinements that might be devised, I suggest that these theoretical tools enhance explanations of movement outcome. Their actual worth can only be demonstrated in their application to actual movements, which is the principal objective of this chapter.

To recapitulate, this research agenda offers three main contributions. First, this analysis shifts the emphasis from movements to targets and their costs calculations. Second, for political targets, this shift highlights the relevance of three essential factors: public opinion, issue salience, and the relative electoral leverage of competing benefit-seekers. In other words, despite the use of unconventional tactics by movement supporters, conventional political considerations necessarily govern movement outcomes. Finally, depending upon the specific combination of the three main factors, a diverse range of outcomes can be predicted, which is particularly useful in cases of low salience – the most common circumstance in which movements operate.

---

[4] It is possible that, over the course of a struggle between competitors, circumstances will shift from one scenario to another. Such transitions are presumed to be more likely to involve adjacent or nearby rows.

Feminist mobilization

I consider these propositions in brief case studies of the outcomes of feminist agitation concerning multiple issues. This movement has been active for many decades in multiple issue domains and is therefore rich in comparative implications. I adopt a multi-issue focus for several reasons. Too often, movements are treated as if they were unitary entities engaged in the singular aim of promoting equality irrespective of the diverse elements within this general objective. Rather, this movement goal is associated with multiple, distinct issues and variegated combinations of public support, attentiveness, allies, and organized opponents. From the perspective here, it is deceptive to talk about movement outcome in the singular since movements are actually bundles of multiple goals, achieving differing degrees of impact among them. Also, movement studies often derive generalizations about outcome based upon either a single goal or a highly aggregated mixture. By contrast, this perspective suggests that outcomes stem from unique cost configurations associated with specific demands (see also Mucciaroni 2008; Lax and Phillips 2009). A survey of multiple campaigns in a single study promises to elucidate the broader patterns associated with movement outcomes. Thus, from the issues of equal pay to violence against women, the separate cases demonstrate that differing combinations of public opinion, salience, and the relative electoral leverage of competing benefit-seekers account for the observed outcomes. Although the depth of each case is necessarily limited, the evidence is consistent with the general predictions delineated above. The analysis presented here is not meant to be the last word, but rather to introduce a useful analytical perspective and to serve as an invitation to further research.

In the following sections, I briefly describe the development of the contemporary feminist movement, discuss its disruptive capabilities for their political targets, and the variation in concession costs associated with different movement demands. In specific issue-domains addressed below, the movements demanded changes in federal, state, or local government policy and therefore targeted public officials. For elected officials, each movement's disruptive capacities derive largely from their electoral leverage, including their support from broader public and organized third parties. On the other side, the costs associated with acceding to movement demands are contingent upon public preferences, salience, and the extent of organized opposition to move-ment demands. Protests and demonstrations matter insofar as they change public opinion or raise the attentiveness of sympathetic organi-zations and mass publics.[5] After reviewing the cases, I present a more general discussion of these patterns.

Disruption costs

At times, the feminist movement has engaged in lively rallies and protests. Mass rallies, such as "Women's Strike for Equality" in 1970, accentuated the visibility of women's organizations and their demands. The 1968 protest against the Miss America pageant in Atlantic City may be well remembered, but, in actuality, women's social movement organizations have concentrated primarily upon conventional lobbying, the provision of expert information, monitoring implementation of existing statutes, and litigation to bring about social change. "In general, equity-oriented feminists have seen protests as unnecessary in part because other channels of access to the political system were opened without much difficulty in the 1970s and 1980s" (Gelb and Palley 1987: 51). The National Organization for Women (NOW), founded in 1966 and the largest representative of liberal feminism, has a total membership today some-what over 500,000, but, these numbers were far lower in the 1970s at the time the movement achieved a number of important victories. Indeed, in 1971, the combined membership of NOW, the Women's Equity Action League, the National Women's Political Caucus, and the National Abortion Rights Action League was only 75,000–80,000. Thus, liberal feminist organizations often turned for support to the far larger tradi-tional women's organizations such as the nonpartisan League of Women Voters, the American Association of University Women, the General Federation of Women's Clubs, and the National Federation of Business and Professional Women. By 1980, the combined membership of the largest traditional women's organizations totaled more than 2.5 million. In such alliances and, depending upon the issue, with the support of other

[5] For a provocative statistical analysis of some of these propositions, see Costain and Majstorovic (1994). While useful, this piece differs from the approach presented since it uses aggregate measures of public opinion, congressional attention, and legislative action, whereas this analysis suggests that particular measures must be treated sepa-rately to capture their specific cost configurations.

sympathetic organizations, liberal feminist organizations were capable of mustering numbers of electoral significance.

Despite the small size of the new groups, the possibility for liberal feminist organizations to impose disruption costs on political targets depended in some measure on broader public attitudes toward gender equality. These attitudes can be crudely assessed in polling data based on the willingness of respondents to vote for a woman president. In the period from the late 1960s to the early 1970s, stunning changes in the response to this question can be seen. Whereas in 1967, 57 percent of respondents expressed willingness to vote for a woman for president, this figure had risen sharply to 78 percent by 1974 (Geer 2004). Elected officials witnessing this rapid shift in social attitudes might plausibly regard gender equality issues as garnering the support of a growing majority. Lacking clear signs of opposition to this liberalization in attitudes (in the form of contrary polls on certain issues or visible countermobilization by conservative women), supportive public opinion furnished feminist organizations with greater disruptive capabilities based on their potential to elevate constituent attention to emergent women's issues.

Concession costs

The feminist movement declared that "the personal is political." Many activities, particularly among more radical organizations, were concentrated in small "consciousness raising" groups to challenge personal perceptions, question gendered norms, and revalue women. Along with this struggle to bring about cultural change, women's organizations formed to press for the enactment of public policies to redress entrenched gender inequalities. As indicated above, NOW and other liberal feminist organizations, pushed for government action to expand access to paid labor markets and assure reproductive freedom. Later, issues of domestic violence and abuse emerged as additional concerns of the movement, though these are sometimes treated as separate movements. Each of these demands is associated with costs of different magnitudes and visibility and therefore, to explain movement outcome, the overall costs associated with *specific* demands must always be unpacked. For instance, the characteristics of the cost associated with relatively invisible changes in tax law may be quite different than an employer mandate to provide paid maternity leave or abide by standards of comparable worth.

Gelb and Palley (1987) suggest further that the feminist movement has been more successful when the issue can be framed as a matter of equity or basic fairness, rather than as a challenge to gendered identities or "role change." In addition to affecting general public opinion and attentiveness, this insight seems particularly important insofar as public support and the mobilization of third parties factor into the overall assessment of concession costs. Equity demands, which were regarded as culturally unthreatening, produced higher public approval, limited attentiveness, and weak opposition. By contrast, movement demands that were seen as threatening to valued identities met with lower levels of public support, greater attentiveness, and were more likely to precipitate an organized counterreaction.

The movement's best prospects for success, then, depended upon a threatened imposition of disruption costs on vulnerable targets and pursuing goals with low costs, as these are more likely to have public support, lower attentiveness, and limited organized opposition. Indeed, the early feminist movement often benefited from precisely this constellation of factors. By contrast, the struggle for more costly demands likely coincided with weaker public support and greater organized opposition, and a higher likelihood of setbacks or defeat. The case studies below assess feminist mobilization in different domains and the pattern of movement outcomes.

Equal pay and non-discrimination

The Equal Pay Act of 1963 and Title VII of the 1964 Civil Rights Act respectively guarantee equal pay and ban discrimination on the basis of sex. Both measures appear to have been enacted under peculiar circumstances. The Fair Labor Standards Act of 1938 included some provisions banning sex discrimination in compensation; however, the purpose of the policy was principally to protect the wages of men from competition from less well paid women (McBride Stetson 1997). During the Kennedy administration, Esther Peterson of the Women's Bureau in Labor Department proposed "equal pay for comparable work." As administration legislation advanced in Congress, business interests cried out that the proposed standards threatened governmental encroachment in the private sector and the House changed the language to "equal pay for equal work." This change, due to persistent sex segregation in labor markets, reduced the opposition and thus the political cost of accepting this new measure. From congressional comments on the bill, this limitation on the scope of the law was intentional. "Equal pay was ... a perfect compromise," avers Kessler-Harris (2001). "It could be and often was construed as protecting men's jobs by ensuring that women would not undermine male wages ... Even more important was the sense that a rigidly limited equal pay act held less potential for disturbing existing sex roles." Rather than challenging gender roles, the Equal Pay Act actually affirmed them, while insisting upon narrow notions of "justice, fair play, and equity." In other words, public support coupled with the general lack of attentiveness and the absence of an effective women's lobby allowed members of Congress to enact a measure with severe limitations, a largely symbolic gesture with minimal concession costs.

The inclusion of sex under the coverage of the 1964 civil rights bill came from an amendment by Howard Smith (D-VA). Although accounts differ on whether Smith proposed the inclusion of sex in the 1964 civil rights bill in earnest or instead to sink the broader measure, the support from the southern congressional delegation certainly appears to have been actuated by the latter motivation (Gold 1981; Kessler-Harris 2001). Without significant mobilization from women's organizations demanding inclusion in the bill nor countermovement opposition, the insertion of sex in this landmark legislation can be regarded as something of a historical fluke. In the case of the Equal Pay Act, the Congress adopted a measure with limited impact, and significant support for the change to Title VII came from congressional opponents of the larger civil rights bill. For both acts, elite instigation was more significant than external political mobilization. Perhaps more importantly, in the case of the Equal Pay Act, absent independent mobilization, this victory was more symbolic than substantive in that it assisted in furthering legislators' electoral interests without obliging them to offer more costly policy concessions.

Equal Credit Opportunity Act of 1974

The credit industry had a historical aversion to extending credit to women deemed to be risky, such as divorced or widowed women.

Married women, too, lacking a credit history, might be asked "humiliating questions regarding birth-control techniques and intent to bear children" (Gelb and Palley 1987: 66). Single women had more difficulty obtaining credit than single men and the list of inequalities in this arena goes on. Testimony during the 1972 hearings of the National Commission on Consumer Finance addressed these forms of credit discrimination and others, and provided the impetus for action. Women's organizations resolved to push for legislation to protect women from credit discrimination based on sex or marital status. A broad ensemble of women's organizations lobbied for the measure throughout the legislative process. Women's organizations formed a nearly united front in favor of enactment and legislators assumed that the issue had broad appeal among women voters. Nevertheless, despite media attention to credit discrimination, broader public attentiveness was uneven (Costain 1992). On the other side, there was no organized opposition; business supported the enactment of some legislation, and even the credit industry was "not belligerent" (Gelb and Palley 1987: 69). Apart from empowering an enforcement apparatus for alleged infractions, the measure imposed no costs upon the credit industry. In negotiations, women's organizations allowed the penalties stemming from class action suits to be reduced as a concession to the credit industry. In any case, enforcement ultimately depended upon the willingness of plaintiffs to pursue litigation, and the small, diffuse costs that the industry absorbed might be passed onto the consumers essentially without notice. The absence of opposition from the regulated industry or others essentially eliminated concession costs. Framed as a matter of basic fairness for women, the demand offered no challenge to valued gendered identities that might provoke countermobilization from socially conservative organizations.

For representatives with many members of women's organizations among their constituents, the active support from a coalition of benefit-seekers, the absence of organized opposition, and limited public attention produced a cost structure combining modest disruption costs but almost no concession costs, a situation conducive to successful movement outcome. Accordingly, Costain (1992: 90) suggests that "political support for equal credit seemed to stem from the feeling that there was nothing to lose politically by supporting it and potentially a lot to lose by not supporting it." Members without women's organizations of any significance in their states or districts were likely indifferent to the outcome of the legislation, but had no incentive to vote against the bill. With congressional supporters shepherding the measure along, the ensuing negotiations to advance the bill required nominal concessions before going to a floor vote. By October, 1974, the Senate had voted 89 to 0 in favor and the House as well with a similarly lopsided margin of 355 to 1.

Equal Rights Amendment

Since 1923, the Equal Rights Amendment, which promised to enshrine gender equality in the Constitution, had been submitted to almost every session of Congress without success. Finally, in 1972, after nearly five decades, Congress approved the amendment to be sent to the states for ratification. Multiple legislatures in heavily Democratic states acted swiftly to ratify. As the process gathered momentum, intense anti-ERA countermobilization ensued. Ultimately, even after women's groups fought successfully for an extension to the deadline for ratification, the amendment fell three states short of the thirty-eight needed for victory. Several studies address the failure of the Equal Rights Amendment (Mansbridge 1986; Bolce et al 1987; Soule and Olzak 2004). Under the shrewd leadership of Phyllis Schlafly, anti-ERA mobilization signaled strong constituent opposition to ratification. Conservatives argued that the ERA threatened to collapse the traditional distinction between men and women, with possible effects including women being obliged to register for the draft, the banning of sex segregation in sports teams, schools, and bathrooms, as well as an end to protective labor legislation for women. The significant erosion in public support for the measure in states that had not ratified further amplified the concession costs for legislators contemplating voting for the measure (Bolce et al. 1987). Mansbridge (1986: 149) sums up: "These legislators voted against the ERA not because of massive organized lobbying by the insurance industry or large corporate contributions to their campaigns but because the cumulative impact of many influences, including district-based organizing by STOP-ERA, had led them to believe that voting for the Amendment would cause them more trouble that it was worth." Thus, as ERA ratification battles shifted into states with weaker public support for the amendment, more Republican allies in the state legislatures, and stronger anti-ERA organizations, the ratification process faltered (Soule and Olzak 2004). At the end of the day, in the defeated bid to amend the US Constitution, the women's movement lacked sufficient electoral leverage or public backing in enough states to overcome the intense countermobilization of ERA opponents (Klein 1985).[6]

Title IX

By contrast, Title IX of the Higher Education Amendments of 1972, which banned gender discrimination in education, passed without organized opposition. At the outset, the cost implications for educational institutions, particularly in organized sports, were undetected and therefore lacked mass attention. Rep. Edith Green (D-OR) reportedly asked feminist organizations "*not* to testify in behalf of Title IX because she believed that if members of Congress were not aware of what was included in Title IX, they would simply vote for it without paying too much attention to its content or ultimate implications" (italics added; Gelb and Palley 1987: 99). As legislators obtain information from competing benefit-seekers, their presumed ignorance again suggests that no opposition emerged to ascribe unacceptable costs to the bill. Responding to these political circumstances, the legislation passed. Yet, as Health, Education, and Welfare (HEW) began drafting regulations to implement the law, controversy ensued as the NCAA, in particular, lobbied against the application of the law to collegiate sports. A coalition of women's organizations successfully beat back congressional measures to weaken the proposed regulations.

Violence against women

Women suffer from various forms of violence including rape, spousal or partner rape or battery, and sexual assault, all of which have been regarded in the past with greater indifference and sometimes distrust of the victims. Indeed, a husband's right to administer "modest chastisement" to his spouse was historically accepted as legal. Since the 1960s,

---

[6] As countermobilization elements strengthened, five states rescinded their ratification votes for the ERA: Nebraska (1973), Tennessee (1974), Idaho (1977), Kentucky (1978, though vetoed by the acting Governor), and South Dakota (1979). Proponents of a renewed ERA ratification drive argue that the ratification process of the 14th Amendment set a legal precedent that states may not rescind their prior votes.

women's organizations have lobbied states to reform their laws governing domestic violence, rape, police practices, and criminal penalties for various offenses. Although the movement's capabilities to threaten lawmakers with greater disruption costs is comparable to other settings, the costs for conceding to movement demands in this domain are presumed to be significantly lower due to the absence of organized opposition. In particular, public support for the reduction of violence against women is high. A 2000 public opinion survey found that 58% of respondents said that they would be willing to "sign a petition or contact elected officials to urge them to strengthen laws against domestic violence."[7] A 2006 Roper Poll likewise concluded that, "[n]early all women (97%) feel that the issue of domestic violence and sexual assault against women and girls is important and will impact who they vote for in the 2006 mid-term elections." For elected officials, this support meant that public officials might be wary of taking a position that could be construed as insufficiently committed to protecting women, particularly if an organized benefit seeker threatened to draw attention to their roll call votes.

Accordingly, the movement has succeeded in winning numerous policy victories in this domain. Starting in the 1960s, "all fifty states and the District of Columbia eventually established battered women's shelters and passed legislation that criminalized domestic violence" (Harvard Law Review 1993). In some cases, effective litigation against law enforcement agencies has amplified the movement's perceived disruption costs and various policy changes have results, such as the mandatory arrest policy in cases of domestic violence. Many states and localities foster police training to help them in dealing with domestic disturbances. Activism in the 1980s on the criminalization of marital rape prompted states to begin reforming their laws on this point and, by 1993, all states had either through legislative or judicial action proscribed spousal rape.[8] Further, all fifty states have passed stalking statutes that criminalize following or harassing individuals in a threatening manner.[9] Every state has passed "rape shield" laws that limit testimony about the victim's sexual history in rape cases. In 1978 and 1979, opposition from the Morality Majority and other conservatives halted proposed federal grants for centers for

---

[7] By 2007, this figure had climbed to 65%.

[8] In 1981, the supreme courts of Massachusetts and New Jersey ruled that husbands could be held criminally liable for raping their spouses (*CQ Researcher* 2006).

[9] See generally the National Center for Victims of Crime, Stalking Resource Center at www.ncvc.org/src/Main.aspx

abused spouses (Harvard Law Review 1993). These organized opponents "perceived the bills as an attempt to promote radical feminist causes through improper federal intrusion into the private domestic sphere." Nevertheless, in 1984, Congress passed two measures to provide this funding to states and, in most cases, protecting women from violence has not been a partisan issue. Public health professionals and physicians supported further action declaring that the domestic violence had reached "epidemic proportions."[10] By overwhelming margins, in 1994 Congress passed the sweeping Violence Against Women Act that committed $1.6 billion over five years in funding for shelters, police training, stepped up investigation and prosecutions, additional legal remedies for victims, youth education, data collection, and a national hotline.[11] Many other enactments might be cited as well that provide federal resources to state and local governments to promote awareness and provide needed services. Although these measures have not brought an end to violence against women, the number of criminal acts including domestic abuse and rape declined sharply in the 1990s.[12] The combination of public support and the absence of organized opposition have made possible a host of decisive victories for the women's movement.

Reproductive rights

After a number of states had effectively legalized abortion access in the 1960s and early 1970s, the US Supreme Court handed down the landmark decision *Roe v. Wade* (1973), which swept aside abortion

[10] American Medical Association, Diagnostic Treatment Guidelines on Domestic Violence (1992), quoted in *CQ Researcher*, "Violence Against Women" (1993).

[11] The House vote on passage was 421 to 0. On the Senate side, the vote was 61 to 38, largely along party lines. The 2000 VAWA reauthorization passed nearly unanimously in both chambers. The 2013 VAWA reauthorization was more contentious yet passed (286 to 138 in the House and 78 to 22 in the Senate) with much less Republican support, despite huge national majorities (82 percent) in favor of government funding to assist victims of sexual violence.

[12] "Non-fatal, violent victimizations committed by intimate partners (including current or former spouses, girlfriends or boyfriends) against women declined by 49% between 1993 and 2001" and "Incidents of rape are down by 60% since 1992 and attempted rape is down by 57%." Respectively, Intimate Partner Violence, 1993–2001, *Bureau of Justice Statistics*, U.S. Department of Justice, February 2003; National Crime Victimization Survey, *Bureau of Justice Statistics*, U.S. Department of Justice, August 2003.

prohibitions in all fifty states in the first two trimesters of a pregnancy (before fetal viability).[13] This victory stemmed directly from legal mobilization, specifically the activities of Linda Coffee, a member of the Women's Equity Action League, and Sarah Weddington. As Supreme Court justices are not elected and possess lifetime tenure, the political concession costs for the justices in the majority were nil (though defiance of a ruling might arguably reduce the stature of the institution). Since 1973, abortion access spread across the United States, with greater limitations in rural areas due to the paucity of providers. Yet the decision struck some as a lightning bolt and incited a massive countermobilization against the feminist movement and abortion, in particular (Luker 1984). Republican Party activists both courted and facilitated the nascent movement (Oldfield 1996). Within the GOP, anti-abortion activists and conservative Christians more generally are believed to be attentive, single-issue voters with considerable leverage in primary elections. Public opinion on abortion is divided with sharp differences in support depending upon the circumstances. Whereas "hard" reasons, such as cases of rape, incest, or fetal deformity obtain majority support, "soft" economic motivations (i.e., cannot afford to raise a child) do not. Whereas the public is disengaged from most public policy issues, the abortion controversy generates relatively higher levels of mass attentiveness (Abramowitz 1995; Hutchings 2005).

Since 1973, the composition of the Supreme Court and partisan political fortunes have shaped the continuing contours of abortion rights. Pressured by the growing pro-life movement, Congress curtailed abortion access with the enactment of the Hyde Amendment in 1978 that prohibited the use of federal funding to obtain an abortion. The Supreme Court has permitted states to enact additional limitations on unimpeded access (e.g., waiting periods, parental notification, and bans on so-called partial birth abortions) over the opposition of pro-choice organizations.[14] Women's organizations and their opponents continue to struggle to define the issue and place their supporters

---

[13] Thirty-one states permitted abortion only to save the life of the mother and thirteen had enacted more expansive health exceptions.

[14] Research on abortion policy at the state level likewise find a congruence between public opinion and activist mobilization, on the one hand, and public policy outcomes, on the other (see Norrander and Wilcox 1999; Camobreco and Barnello 2008).

in Congress and, more importantly, the White House. At the mercy of presidential politics, the politics of abortion rights depends upon the larger vagaries of national partisan politics or, as social movements theory identifies, changes in the political opportunity structure. With the election of a Republican president in 2000 and congressional control by the same party, the only federal ban on any abortion procedure was enacted – the Partial-Birth Abortion Ban of 2003. When passed, a Gallup survey (Ray 2003) indicated that 70 percent of adults supported the ban. Finally, the addition of two new conservative justices to the Supreme Court upheld this ban in 2007. This defeat should be regarded as a loss stemming in particular from public opposition to this specific abortion procedure, high salience, and the greater electoral leverage of anti-abortion activists within the dominant political coalition. Meanwhile, despite public support for such bans and other impediments to abortion access (e.g., waiting periods), the feminist movement has achieved less visible successes in hindering their enactment in more liberal, Democratic states.

Explaining feminist movement outcomes

In the latter 1960s, the political mobilization of new benefit-seeking organizations coupled with traditional women's organizations provided feminists with a means to impose disruption costs upon political targets. Before that time, policy success might be primarily symbolic (Equal Pay Act) or coincidental (Title VII). Although voter turnout that is stimulated by local notables, media appeals, or party organizations furnishes office-seekers with few incentives to deliver substantive policy benefits, *independent* political action demands attention (Harvey 1997). Insofar as independent benefit-seeking organizations commanded electorally significant blocs of voters (or might behave as instigators to boost public attention to particular issues), elected officials needed to take these disruption costs, and therefore movement demands, seriously. The small size of most women's organizations and their geographic concentration limited their ability to command broad national voting blocs. Yet, a combination of public indifference, the absence of countermobilization, and intense political mobilization can produce policy success, as in the case of the Equal Credit Act. In the case of Title IX, initial passage depended upon stealth such that both public opinion and attentiveness were rendered essentially irrelevant. Insofar as the public might have an opinion, attentiveness matters.[15] Greater attentiveness among women in targeted legislative districts regarding their representative's commitment to gender equity is expected to produce a closer congruence between local opinion and legislative voting behavior. With public preferences on their side and heightened attentiveness, even small organizations can induce targeted legislators to respond favorably. Obviously, in localities in which mass publics are opposed to the movement's agenda, boosting attentiveness is wholly counter-productive.

Concession costs for acceding to movement demands depended on similar factors. Most notably, certain demands had few costs associated with them for either mass publics or discrete interests. In these cases, the movement emerged victorious. Movement victories, embodied in the Equal Credit Act for instance, often shared policy attributes that made them relatively unlikely to carry significant concession costs for supportive legislators. These culturally unthreatening forms of gender equity meant that they were unlikely to be perceived negatively by mass publics, if they were noticed at all (Gelb and Palley 1987). Lacking organized opposition from third parties to signal voter opposition, legislators responded favorably to these movement demands. By contrast, the prospect of government-mandated paid maternity leave provoked business countermobilization against this incursion into the private sector (Bernstein 1997). In a sense, this suggests the conclusion that movements' outcomes will be favorable if movements seek smaller, less costly, incremental changes (Hayes 1992; Szymanski 2003). The reason for this axiom is simple: modest demands keep concession costs low and are less likely to foment organized opposition.

Not only was the mobilization of women in politics as independent benefit-seekers critical, a decisive element in the early successes of the women's movement was the absence or weakness of coherent countermobilization (Harvey 1997). Conservative organizations, such as

---

[15] In the absence of public opinion polls, elected officials regard messages from constituents (offered in town halls and letters) as proxies for constituent views. Lacking any countervailing communications from other constituents, officeholders are presumed to regard public opinion as one-sided. Such communications likewise convey attentiveness. Thus, a relatively small number of organized constituents seeking a policy change without any opposition can signal broader constituent opinion and prospective attentiveness.

Phyllis Schlafly's STOP-ERA, Eagle Forum (formed 1972), the Concerned Women for America (1978), and the Moral Majority (1979), reversed the political logic that had been in favor of concessions. Until these and similar organizations arrived on the political scene, liberal women's organizations largely defined the political field for candidates hoping to appeal to the women's vote. Then, with the onset of this countermobilization sweeping victories ended. In their statistical analysis of state ERA ratification, Soule and Olzak (2004) demonstrate the effectiveness of the STOP-ERA movement. They find that the actuation of these antagonistic elements sharply reduced the prospects for state ERA ratification, particularly if there were more Republicans in the legislature. Certainly, this makes sense. As elements of the Republican base mobilized against the enactment of this new measure, disruption costs mounted for these officials. The further mobilization of evangelical Christians and the ascendance of a Republican majority made new gains exceedingly difficult and some reversals have occurred in the domain of reproductive freedom, as discussed above. Consequently, the victories of the feminist movement were more concentrated in the early 1970s (see Table 8.2).

In all cases, this analysis points to the finding that movement outcomes must be understood as a product of different constellations of public preferences, attentiveness, and the relative electoral leverage of competing benefit-seeking organizations. Table 8.2 summarizes various outcomes of the women's movement, several of which are sketched in the case studies above. A convergence of supportive public opinion, mass attentiveness, and an absent or weak countermovement provides the best prospects for successful policy outcomes. However, as seen below, this particular configuration is extraordinarily uncommon.

By contrast, lack of public support and the presence of formidable opponents doom a movement to certain defeat in majoritarian settings. For example, the fight of women's organizations against restrictions on abortion failed in resisting the federal partial-birth abortion ban, which benefited from substantial public backing. In between these uncommon scenarios, a movement's electoral clout relative to their opponent is critical. Thus, a movement might win concessions from political targets if both the public is indifferent and the opposition is relatively weak. The ban on credit discrimination against women exemplifies this path toward success. Or, even if public opinion is somewhat supportive, a movement might be defeated by an opponent with

Table 8.2 *Overview of feminist movement outcomes*

	Public opinion	Salience	Relative electoral leverage	Feminist movement outcome
1	Supportive	High	Opponent absent, weaker, or stronger	Success. Civil Rights Act of 1964
2	Supportive	Low	Opponent weaker or absent	Success. ERA passed in Congress (1972); Equal Credit Opportunity Act (1974); Pregnancy Discrimination Act (1978); ERA ratification in liberal states; Violence Against Women Act (1994); criminalization of spousal rape; state rape shield laws
3	Supportive	Low	Opponent stronger	Defeat or symbolic gains. Paid maternity leave; Equal Pay Act of 1963; women in combat after 1992, at which time public opinion shifted in favor[a]
4	Divided or no opinion	Low	Opponent weaker or absent	Proportionate gains. Title IX (1973)
5	Divided or no opinion	Low	Opponent stronger	Proportionate losses. Hyde Amendment (1978, limiting federal funding for abortion); ERA failure in non-ratifying states

Table 8.2 (*cont.*)

	Public opinion	Salience	Relative electoral leverage	Feminist movement outcome
6	Opposed	Low	Opponent weaker or absent	Concealed gains. Prevention of adoption of popular abortion restrictions in liberal states
7	Opposed	Low	Opponent stronger	Defeat. Women in combat prior to 1992, at which time public opinion shifts in favor; abortion limits in conservative states[b]
8	Opposed	High	Opponent absent, weaker, or stronger	Defeat. Partial-Birth Abortion Ban Act (2003)

Notes:

[a] Growing public support for women in combat, the erosion of organized opposition, and a supportive Democratic administration are shifting this outcome toward success consistent with the pattern found in the second row.

[b] Although the abortion issue is generally considered to be high salience (particularly among activists), statewide restrictions are assumed here to achieve lower levels of mass attentiveness, in part due to the lower visibility of public policies enacted at the state level.

superior electoral capabilities due to the status quo bias of American institutions, as was the case with the failed ratification of the ERA. This perspective makes sense of outcomes that, based on a consideration of public opinion alone, might otherwise appear perplexing.[16] Along with the specific propositions outlined above, this analysis suggests a few additional observations about public opinion, attentiveness, and countermobilization as well as the interplay among them on policy making.

In particular, conditions of mass indifference – the most common situation in which benefit-seekers find themselves – highlight the significance of countermobilization. In such circumstances, it is the relative electoral clout of the competing organizations within the reelection coalitions of targeted officials that determines policy outcomes (Hansen 1991).[17] In other words, if office-seekers assume public preferences to be essentially irrelevant, then the principal factor affecting their electoral calculations, and ultimate responsiveness, is the presence and effectiveness of countermobilization. The struggles between pro- and anti-ERA organizations transpired against a backdrop of low salience for most voters. Unfortunately, most studies of movement outcome and, for that matter, the interest groups' influence upon public policy, often neglect to address one or more of the three key factors.

Conclusion

Under certain circumstances, social movements and other benefit-seekers can affect the behavior of public officials and shape policy outcomes, including the achievement of new rights. The theoretical approach presented here specifies those circumstances and thereby explains variation in social movement efficacy in extracting concessions from political targets. Beginning with the simple assumption that targets respond to social movements based on their assessment of the relative magnitude of disruption and concessions costs, I added further propositions to elucidate the specific factors shaping these general costs for political actors, in

---

[16] On the contingent impact on public opinion on policy making, see Manza and Cook (2002).

[17] Again, there are simplifications here. Due to the structure of American political institutions, in situations in which competing organizations possess equal electoral leverage, the interest organization attempting to bring about *change* will have greater difficulty next to those seeking to defend the status quo.

particular public opinion, mass attentiveness, and countermobilization. From this specification, I suggested that outcomes depend on the differing configuration of these factors. Instead of attempting to pinpoint a singular route to social movement success, this analysis suggests that there are different paths by which movements can gain concessions from their targets. Indeed, depending upon the peculiar convergence of factors identified above, movements outcomes differ – ranging from decisive victory or proportionate gains to hidden achievements or outright defeat.[18] Contrary to arguments about the sovereignty of public opinion, movements lacking public support can nonetheless achieve gains insofar as they can be hidden, as seen in the passage of Title IX. It is also clear that organized benefit-seekers are crucial elements for the successful achievement of broader social change. Supportive public opinion alone, as the case of Equal Pay Act illustrates, is insufficient to achieve substantive gains in the absence of sufficient mobilization to punish legislators for delivering only symbolic gestures. This analysis also points to the need for a more fine-grained inspection of movements as diverse entities with multiple agendas. Although these case studies are too brief to be definitive, the congruence between the propositions of this analysis and a substantial volume of empirical research suggests that the approach outlined here has merit and warrants further investigation. Also, they indicate that the approaches commonly used to explain movement outcomes suffer from serious shortcomings and need revision. Ultimately, this analysis suggests that social change can be explained, but that accounts must be enriched to include the full ensemble of relevant factors and to capture their subtle interactions.

References

Abramowitz, Alan I. 1995. "It's Abortion, Stupid: Policy Voting in the 1992 Presidential Election." *Journal of Politics*, 57(1): 176–186.
Amenta, Edwin. 2006. *When Movements Matter: The Townsend Plan and the Rise of Social Security*. Princeton, NJ: Princeton University Press.

[18] More research might consider the degree of a benefit-seeker's policy success based on an analysis of the *strength* of legislation enacted to offer a more nuanced measure of movement outcomes (Durden et al. 1991).

Andrews, Kenneth T. 2004. *Freedom is a Constant Struggle: The Mississippi Civil Rights Movement and Its Legacy*. Chicago: University of Chicago Press.

Andrews, Kenneth T. and Bob Edwards. 2004. "Advocacy Organizations in the U.S. Political Process." *Annual Review of Sociology*, 30: 479–506.

Arnold, R. Douglas. 1990. *The Logic of Congressional Action*. New Haven, CT: Yale University Press.

Bernstein, Anya. 1997. "Inside or Out? The Politics of Family and Medical Leave." *Policy Studies Journal*, 25: 87–99.

Bolce, Louis, Gerald De Maio, and Douglas Muzzio. 1987. "The Equal Rights Amendment, Public Opinion, & American Constitutionalism." *Polity*, 19(4): 551–569.

Burstein, Paul. 1979. "Public Opinion, Demonstrations, and the Passage of Antidiscrimination Legislation." *The Public Opinion Quarterly*, 43(2): 157–172.

Burstein, Paul. 1999. "Social Movements and Public Policy." In M. Giugni, D. McAdam, and C. Tilly (eds.), *How Social Movements Matter*. Minneapolis, MN: University of Minnesota Press, 3–21.

Burstein, Paul, Rachel L. Einwohner, and Jocelyn A. Hollander. 1995. "The Success of Political Movements: A Bargaining Perspective." In J. C. Jenkins and B. Klandersman (eds.), *The Politics of Social Protest: Comparative Perspectives of States and Social Movements*. Minnesota: University of Minnesota Press, 275–295.

Burstein, Paul, and Sarah Sausner. 2005. The Incidence and Impact of Policy-Oriented Collective Action: Competing Views. *Sociological Forum*, 20(3): 403–419.

Camobreco, John and Michelle Barnello. 2008. "Democratic Responsiveness and Policy Shock: The Case of State Abortion Policy." *State Politics and Policy Quarterly*, 8(1): 48–65.

Costain, Anne. 1992. *Inviting Women's Rebellion*. Baltimore, MD: Johns Hopkins Press.

Costain, Anne N. and Steven Majstorovic. 1994. "Congress, Social Movements and Public Opinion: Multiple Origins of Women's Rights Legislation." *Political Research Quarterly*, 47(1): 111–135.

Durden, Garey C., Jason F. Shogren, and Jonathan I. Silberman. 1991. "The Effects of Interest Group Pressure on Coal Strip-Mining Legislation." *Social Science Quarterly*, 72(2): 239–250.

Gamson, William A. 1975. *The Strategy of Social Protest*. Homewood, IL: Dorsey Press.

Garrow, David J. 1978. *Protest at Selma: Martin Luther King, Jr., and the Voting Rights Act of 1965*. New Haven, CT: Yale University Press.

Geer, John Gray (ed.). 2004. *Public Opinion and Polling around the World*. New York and Santa Barbara: ABC-CLIO.

Gelb, Joyce, and Marian Leif Palley. 1987. *Women and Public Policies*. Princeton, NJ: Princeton University Press.

Giugni, Marco. 1999. "How Social Movements Matter: Past Research, Present Problems, Future Developments." In M. Giugni, D. McAdam, and C. Tilly (eds.), *How Social Movements Matter*. Minneapolis, MN: University of Minnesota Press, xiii–xxxiii.

Gold, Michael Evan. 1981. "A Tale of Two Amendments: The Reasons Congress Added Sex to Title VII and Their Implication for the Issue of Comparable Worth." *Duquesne Law Review*, 19: 453–477.

Hacker, Jacob S. and Paul Pierson. 2005. *Off Center: The Republican Revolution & the Erosion of American Democracy*. New Haven, CT: Yale University Press.

Hansen, John Mark. 1991. *Gaining Access: Congress and the Farm Lobby, 1919–1981*. Chicago: University of Chicago Press.

Harvard Law Review. 1993. "Developments in the Law: Legal Response to Domestic Violence." 106: 1498–1620.

Harvey, Anna. 1997. "Women, Policy, and Party, 1920–1970: A Rational Choice Approach." *Studies in American Political Development*, 11: 292–325.

Hayes, Michael T. 1992. *Incrementalism and Public Policy*. New York: Longman.

Hutchings, Vincent. 2005. *Public Opinion and Democratic Accountability*. Princeton, NJ: Princeton University Press.

Kessler-Harris, Alice. 2001. *In Pursuit of Equity: Women, Men, and the Quest for Economic Citizenship in 20th-Century America*. New York: Oxford University Press.

Kingdon, John W. 1973 [1989]. *Congressmen's Voting Decisions*, Third edition. Ann Arbor: University of Michigan Press.

Klein, Ethel. 1985. *Gender Politics: From Consciousness to Mass Politics*. Cambridge: Harvard University Press.

Koopmans, Ruud and Paul Statham. 1999. "Ethnic and Civic Conceptions of Nationhood and Differential Success of the

Extreme Right in Germany and Italy." In M. Guigni, D. McAdam, and C. Tilly (eds.), *How Social Movements Matter*. Minneapolis: University of Minnesota Press, 225–251.

Lax, Jeffrey R. and Justin H. Phillips. 2009. "Gay Rights in the States: Public Opinion and Policy Responsiveness." *American Political Science Review*, 103(3): 367–386.

Lipsky, Michael. 1968. "Protest as a Political Resource." *American Political Science Review*, 62(4): 1144–1158.

Luders, Joseph E. 2010. *The Civil Rights Movement and the Logic of Social Change*. New York: Cambridge University Press.

Luker, Kristin. 1984. *Abortion and the Politics of Motherhood*. Berkeley: University of California Press.

Mansbridge, Jane. 1986. *Why We Lost the ERA*. Chicago: University of Chicago Press.

Manza, Jeff and Fay Lomax Cook. 2002. "A Democratic Polity: Three Views of Policy Responsiveness to Public Opinion in the United States." *American Politics Research*, (30): 630–667.

Mayhew, David R. 1974. *Congress: The Electoral Connection*. New Haven, CT: Yale University Press.

McAdam, Doug. 1982. *Political Process and the Development of Black Insurgency, 1930–1970*. Chicago: University of Chicago Press.

McBride Stetson, Dorothy. 1997. *Women's Rights in the USA: Policy Debates and Gender Roles*. New York: Garland.

Mucciaroni, Gary. 2008. *Same Sex, Different Politics: Success and Failure in the Struggles over Gay Rights*. Chicago: University of Chicago Press.

Norrander, Barbara and Clyde Wilcox. 1999. "Public Opinion and Policymaking in the States: The Case of Post-*Roe* Abortion Policy." *Policy Studies Journal*, 27: 707–722.

Oldfield, Duane M. 1996. *The Right and the Righteous: The Christian Right Confronts the Republican Party*. Lanham, MD: Rowman & Littlefield.

Overby, L. Marvin and Sarah Ritchie. 1991. "Mobilized Masses and Strategic Opponents: A Resource Mobilization Analysis of the Clean Air and Nuclear Freeze Movements." *Western Political Quarterly*, 44(2): 329–351.

Page, Benjamin and Robert Y. Shapiro. 1983. "Effects of Public Opinion on Policy." *American Political Science Review*, 77: 175–190.

Piven, Frances Fox and Richard Cloward. 1977. *Poor People's Movements: How They Succeed, Why They Fail.* New York: Pantheon.

Ray, Julie. 2003. "Gallup Brain: Opinions on Partial-Birth Abortions." *Gallup* July 8, Retrieved October 30, 2014. www.gallup.com/poll/8791/gallup-brain-opinions-partialbirth-abortions.aspx.

Soule, Sarah A. and Susan Olzak. 2004. "When Do Movements Matter? The Politics of Contingency and the Equal Rights Amendment." *American Sociological Review*, 69(4): 473.

Szymanski, Ann-Marie E. 2003. *Pathways to Prohibition: Radicals, Moderates, and Social Movement Outcomes.* Durham, NC: Duke University Press.

Walsh, Edward J. 1986. "The Role of Target Vulnerabilities in High-Technology Protest Movements: The Nuclear Establishment at Three Mile Island." *Sociological Forum*, 1(2): 199–218.

Wilson, James Q. 1961. "The Strategy of Protest: Problems of Negro Civic Action." *Journal of Conflict Resolution*, 3: 291–303.

9 REPUTATION, RISK, AND ANTI-CORPORATE ACTIVISM

How social movements influence corporate outcomes

Brayden G. King

Changing corporate practices or policies is an incremental, yet key, step for many social movement agendas (for a review, see King and Pearce 2010). Research about the interactions of movements and corporations has risen in popularity in recent years, in part due to purposeful refocusing efforts by prominent scholars in the field (see, for example, Davis et al. 2005). Spurred by Zald's and Berger's (1978) early formulation of organizations as political entities that are often the focus of internal power struggles and mass movements, scholars have begun investigating the ways in which organizations are sites of employee-led movements (e.g., Lounsbury 2001; Raeburn 2004), shareholder activism (e.g., Davis and Thompson 1994; Rao and Sivakumar 1999), and extra-institutional activism by external constituents (e.g., Schurman 2004; King and Soule 2007).

Underlying much of this research is a fundamental theoretical question: why would corporate decision-makers ever concede to activists who are less powerful, have no access to mechanisms of democratic decision-making within those organizations, and who often represent marginal stakeholders? Employee-led movements usually make up a small proportion of all employees and have grievances that are particular to a specific employee group, as for example when gay and lesbian employees sought same-sex domestic partner benefits from their employers (Raeburn 2004; Briscoe and Safford 2008). Shareholder activists usually have concerns that do not reflect the greater interests of the investor public, such as religious investors whose grievances have a moral rather than an economic rationale (Proffitt and Spicer 2006). External movements are usually focused on particular grievances that fall outside the attention of the majority of employees or investors but that have significance to the greater movement's agenda, such as when the anti-genetic engineering movement protested companies for producing genetically modified organisms (Schurman 2004; Schurman and Munro 2009). In all of these cases, the social movements seeking change were led by activist groups that did not have serious resource advantages over their adversaries, that were outnumbered by the mass market of consumers and investors who affiliated with the companies, and had agendas that were likely seen as radical or marginal by the majority of decision-makers within the firm. And yet, in all of the cases mentioned above, activists were able to win significant concessions from their corporate targets. The gay and lesbian movement set off a wave of changes among Fortune 500 firms in the United States, paving the way for the diffusion of domestic partnership benefits. Religious shareholder activists have become influential voices in contemporary corporate governance, even though they command significantly less capital than non-religious investors. And the anti-genetic engineering movement was successful in convincing major West European supermarkets and food-processing firms to drop genetically modified products.

This chapter offers a theory of social movement effectiveness in corporate campaigns. Drawing on recent empirical research on movements and corporate change, I emphasize two economic mechanisms that give movements leverage to influence corporate targets. First, corporations' concerns with image and reputation make them vulnerable to activist attacks, especially inasmuch as activists are able to generate media attention to their tactics. Second, corporate decision-makers' use of economic risk as a metric for evaluating outcomes gives movements a way to communicate the urgency and importance of their concerns, especially inasmuch as activists' actions become a source of new information to investors and analysts. I first discuss the shortcomings of traditional explanations of movement influence in the contemporary context and then develop the logic behind an alternative explanation.

Mechanisms of tactical effectiveness

Traditional theories of social movement outcomes and institutional change have focused on the ability of activists to disrupt their targets and to create a necessity for change by making it difficult for the organization to carry out its institutional mandates. In Piven's and Cloward's (1977) classic statement on the effectiveness of movements, they argue that even the most powerless actors have the ability to spur institutional change if they violate the rules and norms of the dominant institution, thereby disrupting the resources upon which elites and organizations depend. Further, Piven and Cloward maintained that people could not disrupt institutions "to which they have no access, and to which they make no contribution." It is the withholding of cooperation, the defiant withdrawal of participation that creates the institutional disruption needed to undermine elites' stability. Such institutional disruption also depends on the mass mobilization of defiant participants. Only when the masses mobilize and engage in collective defiance of the system is their disruption of sufficient magnitude to generate the desired influence.

Other social movement scholars have built on this fundamental insight about the link among mass mobilization, institutional disruption, and influence (e.g., Gamson 1990; Gamson and Schmeidler 1984). Although disruption is not always necessary to achieve gains (e.g., Cress and Snow 2000), when a political context is unfavorable and when institutional means of influence are not available, this may be the only option for proponents of change. For this reason, scholars who have studied the impact of movements on corporations and other economic structures, like business communities, have suggested that disruption is necessary. Unlike democratic state institutions, which have routine pathways for expression of grievances and political influence, modern corporations are closed polities that have few "conventional access channels" (Weber et al. 2009: 122) and that exclude most stakeholders from key decision-making processes. Due to their closed nature, the only way that concerned citizens, or even many employees or investors, can influence corporations is through disruption. Walker et al. (2008) find evidence that, in fact, anti-corporate protests are typically more disruptive and contentious.

The classic research on the effects of social movements on business outcomes emphasizes the efficacy of movements that use mass mobilization and disruptive tactics (e.g., Piven and Cloward 1977). For example, the grape boycotts sponsored by the United Farm

Workers initially achieved success because they were able to not only mobilize the local base of migrant farm workers but also because they were able to mobilize political elites and generate support for the boycott among mass consumers (Jenkins and Perrow 1977). As movement organizers used innovative tactics to publicly demonstrate the plight of farmworkers, they gained the support of movement outsiders, leading to a large-scale disruption of the grape industry (Ganz 2000).

Similarly, Luders (2006, this volume) argues that the success of anti-segregationist boycotts in the South were due to the ability of activists to impose costs on local businesses. Businesses that become targets of activists weigh the costs of conceding to activist demands against the costs of failing to take action. In this sense, they are rational actors that seek the least costly path. "[A]ctors weigh the effects of accepting or resisting change, and they accommodate if they regard the costs of resistance as outweighing the costs of acceptance" (Luders 2006: 966). It follows, then, that anti-corporate movements are effective to the extent that they can mobilize sufficient people to disrupt the primary means whereby organizations accrue resources. If they can attack the organization where it is most dependent for its survival, i.e., customer revenue, then the target is more likely to respond.

Most theories about economic disruption of corporate targets follow this logic (e.g., Luders 2006). For corporations to be sensitive to activist demands, activists must mobilize in large numbers in order to be disruptive enough to impose significant costs. However, this depiction of activist influence does not fit the examples of anti-corporate activism described earlier in the paper. In those examples, activism was successful despite the fact that few, relatively marginal actors used tactics that did not garner mass support nor did they seem especially disruptive of the day-to-day routines of their corporate targets. As I discuss below, there are reasons to think that most examples of successful anti-corporate activism do not fit this traditional storyline.

The insufficiency of mobilized disruption as an explanation for movement success

Contemporary activism targeted against corporations is frequently a successful pathway to social change, and yet, many manifestations of these types of movements involve neither mass mobilization nor tactics that lead to the type of institutional disruption described by Piven and

Cloward. Take for instance the prototypical example of the corporate boycott. By design, a boycott seeks to pressure firms to give in to activist demands by diverting a major source of a company's revenue, customer sales. By convincing sympathetic consumers to refuse to purchase a company's products or services, a boycott reduces a target's sales revenue and increases marketing costs. If enough consumers are mobilized to participate, a boycott can be highly disruptive and costly. For example, Luders (2006) argues that the success of anti-segregationist boycotts was a product of activists imposing significant disruption costs and the costs of conceding being fairly low.

However, few boycotts are as capable of mobilizing people to participate as were the civil rights boycotts or the grape boycott sponsored by the Cesar Chavez-led United Farm Workers. Most boycotts fail to attract widespread support from consumers (Ferguson 1997). Summarizing an extensive literature on consumer boycotts, David Vogel says that "there is little evidence to support [the assertion that boycotts change consumer behavior]. There is a major gap between what consumers say they would do and their actual behavior" (2005: 48). Consumers believe they should support companies that share their ideals and value, but their consumption behavior does not always reflect those values. Most consumers do not have strong beliefs about supporting ethical or socially responsible companies (Carrigan and Attalla 2001), but even people who are ideologically aligned with a boycott usually fail to actually change their buying habits. As is true of most habits, consumption is an inertial behavior. We tend to buy what we like and we are not willing to pay a steep price increase to support a boycott that is otherwise consistent with our values (De Pelsmacker et al. 2005). Further, boycott supporters may perceive that the likelihood of a boycott's success is low, which negatively affects their rate of participation (Sankar Sen et al. 2001). Because of these tendencies, even among people who are ideologically aligned with the goals of the boycott, there is low support of consumer boycotts. It is not surprising then that there is little evidence linking boycotts to actual declines in sales revenue (Vogel 2005).

Shareholder activism encounters similar problems. Although the sector for socially responsible investing (SRI) is growing,[1] SRI funds still constitute a minority share of the total marketplace for corporate assets. If

---

[1] A report by the Forum for Sustainable and Responsible Investing claims that SRI funds now manage $3.07 trillion in assets.

an SRI fund is willing to sell their shares in a firm because they are unhappy with a firm's practices, another fund will gladly buy those shares, which means that overall demand for the firm's shares does not decline and does not create a noticeable depreciation in the share price. Shareholder activism for social causes is not widespread. Data on shareholder resolutions submitted between 2006 and 2009 provided by Riskmetrics – the most complete source of resolution data available – show that the median percentage of votes cast for resolutions not related to social issues is 41%, but the median for socially responsible investment resolutions is only 9%.[2] Thus, shareholder activism, in general but especially for social causes, does not garner wide support from other investors.

Given the strong evidence that anti-corporate activism is not supported by mass mobilization, it is surprising that anti-corporate tactics are as effective as they are. Even though the tactics are rarely associated with mass mobilization and disruption, boycotts and shareholder resolutions have fairly high rates of success. Among those corporate boycotts that get at least some minimal amount of national media attention, roughly 25% lead to corporate concessions (Friedman 1999; King 2008). And even though shareholder resolutions for social issues tend to generate less investor support than other resolutions, resolutions sponsored by SRIs are more likely to lead to engagement with corporate decision-makers. Thirty-two percent of shareholder resolutions relating to social issues were withdrawn by their sponsors because corporate leaders decided to engage in discussions on the issue. Only 20% of resolutions related to non-social issues were withdrawn.

The evidence about the effectiveness of anti-corporate tactics sets up an interesting paradox. Why are these tactics relatively successful in creating engagement with corporations if they do not generate mass support and fail to create mobilized disruption of the corporate target? We need a new set of theoretical mechanisms to explain the effectiveness of anti-corporate tactics.

Mechanisms of success in anti-corporate activism

New research has begun to point to an alternative set of mechanisms that may explain why some anti-corporate activists are successful and

---

[2] Percentages tabulated by the author.

others are not. To explain tactical effectiveness we need to better incorporate our understanding of the way the world of business has changed in recent decades. I argue that two major transformations have occurred that give activists new avenues for influence in the corporate world. The first change is an increased emphasis on the intangible resources of companies, especially reputation. As corporate reputation has risen in importance as a marker and potential source of market value, firms have put more effort into managing their image with their various audiences. Reputational sensitivity provides activists with leverage over their corporate targets inasmuch as they are able to create threats against their reputations. The second change is new reliance on risk assessment as a way to calculate the worthiness of particular asset combinations and to gauge the effectiveness of firms' decisions. The language of risk management gives activists a new way to frame their causes. Inasmuch as activists can present their grievances in the language of risk, they become more capable of shaping the corporate agenda.

Corporate reputation as an activist resource

There is no doubt that corporations put a great deal of emphasis on the external perceptions of their various audiences – i.e., customers, suppliers, investors, peers. As these perceptions crystallize as collective judgments about a firm's capabilities, status, and distinctiveness in the marketplace, we can say that a firm has developed a reputation (Fombrun and Shanley 1990). Scholars have shown that reputations have real value for firms, creating trust between the firm and its stakeholders (MacMillan et al. 2005), increasing recruitment and retention of high-quality employees (Podolny 2005), creating brand loyalty (Nguyen and Leblanc 2001), and leading to greater market valuation and financial performance (Roberts and Dowling 2002). Inasmuch as executives perceive that reputation has value for the firm, they make it a strategic priority.

Importantly, corporate reputation has risen in importance as various media outlets and consulting firms have developed new ways to measure and quantify reputation. Rankings, ratings, and awards – the markers of distinction that connote reputation – have proliferated (Fombrun 1998, 2007). These markers of distinction make it easier for audiences to assess a firm's reputation, but they also make organizations hyper-sensitive to their position and status (Espeland

and Sauder 2007; Bermiss et al. 2013). For example, *Fortune* magazine annually puts out a ranking of the world's Most Admired Companies, as determined by surveys administered through industry peers and analysts. The ranking distinguishes firms across industries and conveys firms' relative prestige. Although one can question the scholarly merit of the *Fortune* index, there is no doubt that firm executives use it as an important signal of their broader reputation, especially insofar as it provides a "halo effect" that magnifies other positive qualities of the firm (Black et al. 2000). Such efforts to rank and award firms for their reputations has increased the visibility of corporate reputation and made firms more aware of its importance to their operations. Reputation management has become a major function of corporate public relations (Hutton et al. 2001), and public relations offices appear to be somewhat successful in shaping external perceptions about a firm (Kiousis et al. 2007).

The strategic focus on corporate reputation gives activists an entryway into firm politics. By putting strategic emphasis on their reputations and so much effort into enhancing the way they are perceived, firms become vulnerable to activists who use a "naming and shaming" strategy that seeks to stain a firm's image. Naomi Klein's (1999) influential book, *No Logo*, chronicles the efforts of anti-corporate activists who are dismayed at the expansive influence and pervasiveness of corporate branding. At the same time, corporations' dependence on their images and reputations makes them especially vulnerable targets to attacks on those brands. As activists draw attention to the inappropriate practices of companies that otherwise have stellar reputations, those firms are suddenly face a reputational threat. In other words, by making reputation so critical to their success, firms have given activists a tool that they can use against the firm. Those firms that have invested the most in their reputation have the most to lose.

Evidence provides support to Klein's hypothesis. King and McDonnell (2014; also see Bartley and Child 2007; King 2008, 2011) show that firms that ranked the highest in the *Fortune* Most Admired index are more likely to come under attack by activists. Interestingly, firms that seek to distinguish themselves by doing and advertising socially responsible practices also have an increased likelihood of being targeted by activists. Good firms make good targets. Activists can (1) expose contradictions in how the firm portrays itself in seeking to build a positive reputation and (2) activists are attracted to the public spotlight that already shines on those high-reputation firms. Schurman argues that activists go after established firms with good reputations because "firms that have invested heavily in establishing their reputations and brand names place great value on safeguarding those investments, and perceive the cost of threats to these investments as being very high" (2004: 248–249; see also Sikkink 1986).

King (2011) further showed that firms with high reputational standing are more likely to attract public scrutiny when they become the targets of activist attacks. Boycotts against firms that are ranked highly in the Fortune index receive more media attention compared to boycotts against lower ranked or unranked firms. Whereas many have argued that a company's reputation creates a "halo" of protection around that firm, this research suggests that there is at least one important exception to this belief. Firms with positive reputations attract more attention when activists publicly castigate them. This increased media attention suddenly makes their established reputation susceptible. Bartley and Child (2011) demonstrate that being exposed to an ongoing activist campaign can undercut a firm's reputational ranking.

Boycotts that attract more media attention are also more likely to concede to activists' demands (King 2008). Intense media coverage of this negative event sensitizes the firm to a reputational threat, especially when a firm's reputation has already been damaged in the past. The effect of media attention on concession to a boycott is amplified by past reputational declines. Interestingly, firms that have experienced similar declines in sales revenue are no more likely to respond to a boycott. This finding suggests that firms are primarily concerned about a boycott's impact on its reputation. The possibility of reputational threat makes firms especially sensitive to activists' demands. The impact of activists' influence on reputation is also evident in research that shows that being a boycott target makes a firm focus more on impression management, as it seeks to improve its image as a socially responsible company (McDonnell and King 2013). Firms that are targets of boycotts tend to immediately increase the number of press releases they make about prosocial actions the firm has or will engage in. Usually those prosocial actions are completely unrelated to the substance of the original activist attack. For example, if Wal-Mart is protested because of its unjust employment policies, the company is more likely to release announcements about its sustainability policies. These measures reflect companies' efforts to prevent further erosion to their reputation.

Of course, damage to a company's reputation has material consequences. Firms that suffer from reputational threats may, in certain conditions, experience declines in financial performance. King and Soule (2007) found that firms targeted by protestors experience, on average, a 0.3% decline in stock price during a two-day window around the protest event. Over a twenty-six-day window, protested firms experienced a 1% decline. This negative effect is even stronger for firms that have previously been under-the-radar of media attention. We found that protests have a more negative effect on stock price returns when they present new information about the firm. If a company's reputation for being socially irresponsible is already well-established – e.g., people already know that Exxon engages in practices that hurt the environment – then a protest against that company will have little effect on the public's perceptions and the stock price will remain unchanged. But if the protest conveys new and potentially damaging information, the company's reputation and market value are at risk.

Thus, the literature suggests that one way in which activists can influence firms is by exposing the corporate target to a reputational threat. Firms that have invested heavily in their reputations and/or that are experiencing a reputational decline are more vulnerable to activist attack, making them more likely to concede and more likely to take prosocial actions in the future.

Risk analysis as an activist frame

Increasingly, firms evaluate their practices (and are evaluated by other key audiences) using risk assessment tools. Although risk analysis has been a practice of societies for hundreds of years, it has only been in recent years that advances in science and statistical analysis have made risk management a systematic endeavor (Covello and Mumpower 1985). An entire industry of professional risk analysts has developed around the development of these tools. In addition to the proliferation of tools, increasing complexity in the sorts of problems that corporations must deal with has made risk management a necessary part of any internal decision-making process (Perrow 1984; Short 1984).

The assessment of risk as integral to any decision-making process has seeped into the language of everyday life, but this is especially the case in the corporate world. Perceptions of risk are fundamentally grounded in societal institutions that are what society values as good and worthy of attainment and how people attain those values (Douglas 1985). Moreover, the ability to analyze risk depends on the creation of institutions that facilitate turning basic uncertainties – e.g., there is a possibility that we will cause an oil spill – into estimates of risk – e.g., there is known probability that these actions will lead to an oil spill (Knight 1921). Once professionals developed tools that allowed them to more easily transform inherent uncertainty into risk assessments, the vernacular of risk and the practice of risk analysis become a staple of decision-making. As Giddens (1991: 124) has argued, "thinking in terms of risk and risk assessment is a more or less ever-present exercise, of a partly imponderable character." The pervasiveness of risk analysis has led some to argue that we now live in a "risk society" (Giddens 1991; Beck 1992; Power 2004).

But as Adam, Beck, and van Loon (2000: 2) noted, risk is not "a thing-out-there – risks are necessarily constructed." The perception of risk depends on the presence of actors and technologies that can translate inherent uncertainties into objectively appearing statements of risk. These actors come in two types. First, there are third-party analysts whose professional role is to define and ascertain risk. Insurance actuaries, for example, determine the risk that certain classes of individuals will experience certain events. Professional risk analysts of the corporate world assess the likelihood that certain events, such as a product recall, will occur that expose firms to particular risks, such as being sued by customers. Many of these risk analysts work for ratings agencies, the function of which is to score companies' exposure to risk so that investors have a better idea of the value of their assets. Credit rating agencies, for example, provide scores that rate a firm's asset quality in terms of risk and quality. Other ratings agencies focus exclusively on social issues, such as environmental performance or employment conditions. For example, Innovest, a popular risk management firm, was founded on the idea that "[e]nvironmental and social performance measures [can be used] as leading indicators for management quality and long-term financial performance."[3] Rather than making ethical claims about a company, the purpose of rating a firm is to give investors a quantitative measure of a firm's risk exposure, indicated by environmental and social indicators.

---

[3] This quotation comes from Innovest's methodology document, which can be found online at www.csrwire.com/pdf/Research_Rating_Methodology.pdf.

A second kind of actor that can shape risk analysis is the activist. Unlike third-party analysts, activists are usually motivated by moral or normative frameworks. Risk assessment is not merely an analysis of probabilities and exposure to particular events. Mary Douglas (1985) argued that risk analysis is also inherently based on claims about morality and justice. Risk analysts cannot divorce the objective analysis of probabilities of event occurrences from value-laden assessments about the appropriateness of an action or the desirability of an outcome (Asselt et al. 1996). By injecting claims about injustice or moral inappropriateness into the public debate, activists increase the likelihood that a particular problem or social issue will become seen as a potential risk. The emergence of professional risk managers who focus solely on social issues is a product of this sort of activism. Prior to calls for corporate accountability about the use of sweatshops or about environmental dangers, few risk managers considered social issues very seriously. However, with the rise of the anti-sweatshop movement and the environmental movement in the 1980s, investors and analysts began to respond by tabulating the potential financial dangers morally problematic practices created for their investments (Bartley 2005; Beck and Holzer 2007). By demonstrating how such issues could translate into potential future losses for investors, these social values problems were suddenly given an economic weight they did not previously possess.

We have numerous examples of companies that were taken to task by activists and subsequently paid dearly for their indiscretions. In 2005 the petroleum company Unocal was sued by activist groups who held the company accountable for failing to stop Burmese soldiers from abusing villagers during the construction of a pipeline. They settled out of court for $30 million (*The Economist* 2008). Activists may also consciously translate their concerns in the language of risk. Recently environmental activists, including representatives of Greenpeace and the World Wildlife Fund, raised concerns about a Russian oil company's (Gazprom) drilling in the Arctic region of the country. They argued that doing so would put the company and the country at a substantially greater risk of causing an oil spill that would lead to irrecoverable damage and loss of financial and natural resources (Nataliya 2011). Environmental activism of this type directly raises the profile of a corporate practice that may have previously escaped investor notice while also linking that practice to potential financial losses.

No activists are better positioned to translate social and ethical issues into the language of risk than shareholder activists. Shareholders' interests are already aligned with those of the corporation because they both seek to improve the profitability and market of the value of the firm. This insider position gives activists credibility in the world of risk management that other kinds of activists do not have. Further, shareholder activists are usually experienced investors who share the local vernacular of trading and market valuation. Risk analysis is part of their cultural toolkit. Being able to vocalize their concerns in the language of risk facilitates understanding and leads to a greater likelihood of reaching an understanding with their corporate targets. For example, in 2007 Bart Naylor proposed a shareholder resolution to Weyerhaeuser, a pulp and paper company and one of America's largest owners of timberland, requesting that they suspend a deal to purchase timber in Whiskey Jack Forest in Ontario because he claimed that doing so would infringe on the rights of an aboriginal tribe, the Grassy Narrows First Nation.[4] He explicitly argued that the controversy created by the purchase would "increase the risk to the company of legal liabilities, negative brand identification and decreased market share for Timberstrand LSL." Given that the company was already the object of protests of civil disobedience by the tribe, he urged the company to avoid the possibility of a negative public campaign against the firm and first conduct a thorough risk analysis of the situation. He urged voters to support the resolution because doing so would show that they "agree that further clarification of the company's policy on aboriginal relationships would help the company better manage wood procurement risks." His use of the language of risk throughout the proposal emphasized that the decision to withdraw from the deal should be based not solely on a moral calculation but rather should be grounded in a thorough and rational economic analysis.

In 2009, Ceres, a nonprofit organization that sustains shareholder activism, and the Interfaith Center on Corporate Responsibility, jointly organized a coalition of supporters of shareholder resolutions urging nine companies to be more proactive in disclosing their exposure to climate-related risks. The targeted companies were all considered "climate watch" businesses – or businesses that were in some way overly

---

[4] The resolution can be found online at http://freegrassy.org/wp-content/uploads/2010/ 03/ISSResolutionReport.pdf

exposed to financial risks due to their poor environmental performance. In their press release announcing the resolutions, a Ceres spokesperson said, "Given the political shift in Washington, all companies should be minimizing climate risks and maximizing clean energy opportunities." The president of the New York Pension Fund, one of the institutional investors sponsoring a resolution, said, "Companies in every industry, especially energy sectors, must assess and mitigate climate change risks . . . Investors require full and transparent disclosure of the actions companies are taking to address the risks and opportunities of climate change, so that they can make informed investment decisions."[5] Notably, the shareholder activists framed the logic behind the resolutions by addressing the risks that investors were exposed to due to the companies' stance toward climate change.

Such examples point to the explicit attempt by shareholder activists to influence their fellow investors, analysts, corporate executives by using a shared language of risk. But to what extent are shareholder activists able to influence these audiences? In a recent study, Vasi and King (2012) show that shareholder resolutions have a real effect on the perception that some companies are at greater financial risk than others. We showed that, net of firms' actual environmental performance, companies that faced shareholder resolutions related to environmental concerns were more likely to be rated as having higher environmental risk by independent analysts. Moreover, firms that were rated as having higher environmental risk subsequently had lower financial performance. Shareholder activists indirectly influenced their corporate targets' financial performance by first deflating analysts' views about the financial soundness of the firms' environmental practices. Importantly, the study showed that shareholder activists were able to change perceptions about risk even among firms that were doing the same amount of environmental damage. The paper argues that by drawing attention to previously ignored environmental problems, the activists shaped analysts' risk ratings.

Activists' influence on risk assessments has one additional effect on firms' practices. Godfrey (2005) argues that companies that are exposed to activist-associated risks will seek to ameliorate those risks by engaging in socially responsible practices. By engaging in such

[5] The full press release can be read online at www.iccr.org/news/press_releases/2009/pr_climatewatchlist02.18.09.html

practices, companies purchase "insurance-like positive moral capital" (2005: 790; see also Godfrey et al. 2009). Thus, firms should be more likely to change their practices to the extent that they are seen as risky investments because of association with controversial and potentially crisis-prone practices.

Conclusion

This chapter began with the premise that anti-corporate activists have been successful at influencing firms' behavior in recent years by using a variety of new tactics, including web-based boycotts and shareholder resolutions. However, in the study of social movement outcomes we do not just want to know if, but also *why*, movements create certain types of outcomes. Traditional accounts of movement influence fall short in explaining why many anti-corporate movements produce positive outcomes. Many of these contemporary tactics do not rely on mass mobilization and its associated disruptive effects – staple mechanisms of the classic theories of social movement outcomes in the economic sphere. If activists are not mobilizing mass disruption of their corporate targets, how are they able to influence them? I have posited two mechanisms that may account for the success of anti-corporate tactics: reputational threat and the creation of risk perceptions.

Neither of these mechanisms necessarily requires mass mobilization. Boycotts, for example, can be effective at generating reputational threats insofar as they attract sufficient media attention. The actual number of boycotters and the associated loss of revenue matter little if a boycott is successful at capturing media coverage. A small organization or even a single person can initiate a boycott campaign that grabs national media attention if the organization has the right capabilities. Public relations skills, media savvy, journalist connections, and effective targeting of the opposition may all prove more important to the outcome of the boycott than the organization's ability to mobilize thousands of followers. These capabilities may be especially important in the contemporary age of social media where communications technology like Twitter, Facebook, and blogs allows a single individual to reach tens of thousands from a laptop computer or a mobile phone. To the extent that these social media are successful at helping activists capture a broad audience, this sort of digitally based activism may help to even bypass traditional media and directly attack their targets' reputations. But just as important, skillful use of social media may help activists to more quickly disseminate their messages to mainstream media outlets (as we saw in the Occupy movement). The main point is that activists increasingly have at their fingertips tools that can help them launch effective campaigns against the reputations of corporate targets.

In a similar way, shareholder resolutions are effective tools at creating perceptions of risk, despite not creating a splash in the public eye or massively disrupting their targets' resource acquisition. The success of shareholder resolutions in getting corporations to engage new issues demonstrates the effectiveness of a tactic that changes critical audiences' perceptions. Because corporate executives depend so much on analyst ratings and investor confidence to maintain their own lofty positions in their firms (Khurana 2002), they are especially sensitive to shifts in the perceptions of these audiences. If analysts covering a firm suddenly deem that a company is a risky asset, then executives will listen and be more likely to consider a new issue as part of the legitimate agenda. For this reason, shareholder activists can be relatively successful despite having no real power over the firm.

Before concluding I should note that different tactics obviously seem better suited to causing reputational threat versus shaping risk perceptions. Tactics that are public, theatrical, and that attack highly visible companies are more likely to generate reputational threats (King 2011). This means that boycotts and protests that generate national media are more likely to create reputational threats, whereas shareholder resolutions, due to the credibility of the investor activists themselves, are more likely to shape risk perceptions (Vasi and King 2012).

One of the concerns about relying exclusively on public protest campaigns is that it gives corporations an incentive to merely engage in impression management when reacting to activists and to ignore the more fundamental concerns of the activists. If corporate targets feel that activists represent an immediate reputational threat, they will likely seek to address those concerns in an equally visible and symbolically meaningful way (e.g., giving large donations to a charitable foundation) but they may fail to do anything substantive that would actually change the problems. For this reason, activists may unintentionally push corporate targets to engage in greenwashing, i.e., hollow attempts to bolster their image by associating the firm with socially responsible practices while continuing to engage in the very activities that were cause for concern. Clearly, if activists are to have a real impact on organizational change, they must continue to monitor their targets after the companies have made public promises to alter their practices.

Shareholder activism, in contrast, may convince executives that an issue is worthy of serious consideration, but because resolutions are done in relative privacy and do not attract the broad public attention that boycotts or protests do, firms may not react with urgency to resolutions. Another potential problem is that because a typical reaction to successful shareholder activism is for executives to engage in dialogue with shareholder activists, change may occur quite slowly. Dialogue may be a stalling practice or an attempt to co-opt the agitators.

The two kinds of tactics may be able to complement one another. When used in combination, the two kinds of activism may lead to a greater likelihood of urgent but substantive changes taking place. Future research ought to address this possibility. In the past, research has tended to study these two mechanisms in isolation from one another. Future research ought to examine the extent to which simultaneous shifts in reputation and changes in risk perceptions lead to particular types of corporate outcomes.

References

Adam, Barbara, Ulrich Beck, and Joost van Loon. 2000. *The Risk Society and Beyond : Critical Issues for Social Theory*. London; Thousand Oaks, CA: SAGE.

Asselt, Marjolein, Arthur Beusen, and Henk Hilderink. 1996. "Uncertainty in Integrated Assessment: A Social Scientific Perspective." *Environmental Modeling and Assessment*, 1(1): 71–90.

Bartley, T. 2005. "Corporate Accountability and the Privatization of Labor Standards: Struggles over Codes of Conduct in the Apparel Industry." *Politics and the Corporation*, 14: 211–244.

Bartley, Tim and Curtis Child. 2007. "Shaming the Corporation: Globalization, Reputation, and the Dynamics of Anti-Corporate Movements." *Annual Meeting of the American Sociological Association, New York*, Retrieved March 1, 2009 (www.allaca demic.com/meta/p184737_index.html).

Bartley, T. and C. Child. 2011. "Movements, Markets and Fields: The Effects of Anti-Sweatshop Campaigns on U.S. Firms, 1993–2000." *Social Forces*, 90(2): 425–451.

Beck, Ulrich. 1992. *Risk Society: Towards a New Modernity*. London; Newbury Park, CA: Sage Publications.

Beck, Ulrich and Boris Holzer. 2007. "Organizations in World Risk Society." In Christine M. Pearson, Christophe Roux-Dufort, and Judith Clair (eds.), *International Handbook of Organizational Crisis Management*. Thousand Oaks, CA: Sage, 3–24.

Bermiss, Y. Sekou, Edward J. Zajac, and Brayden G. King. 2013. "Under Construction: How Commensuration and Management Fashion Affect Corporate Reputation Rankings." *Organization Science*.

Black, E. L., T. A. Carnes, and V. J. Richardson. 2000. "The Market Valuation of Corporate Reputation." *Corporate Reputation Review*, 3(1): 31–42.

Briscoe, Forrest and Sean Safford. 2008. "The Nixon-in-China Effect: Activism, Imitation, and the Institutionalization of Contentious Practices." *Administrative Science Quarterly*, 53: 460–491.

Carrigan, Marylyn and Attalla Ahmad. 2001. "The Myth of the Ethical Consumer – Do Ethics Matter in Purchase Behaviour?" *The Journal of Consumer Marketing*, 18(7): 560–577.

Covello, Vincent T. and Jeryl Mumpower. 1985. "Risk Analysis and Risk Management: An Historical Perspective." *Risk Analysis*, 5(2): 103–120.

Cress, Daniel and David A. Snow. 2000. "The Outcomes of Homeless Mobilization: The Influence of Organization, Disruption, Political Mediation, and Framing." *American Journal of Sociology*, 105(4): 1063–1104.

Davis, Gerald F., Doug McAdam, W. Richard Scott, and Mayer N. Zald (eds.). 2005. *Social Movements and Organizational Theory*. Cambridge: Cambridge University Press.

Davis, G. F. and T. A. Thompson. 1994. "A Social-Movement Perspective on Corporate-Control." *Administrative Science Quarterly*, 39(1): 141–173.

De Pelsmacker, Patrick, Liesbeth Driesen, and Glenn Rayp. 2005. "Do Consumers Care about Ethics? Willingness to Pay for Fair-Trade Coffee." *Journal of Consumer Affairs*, 39(2): 363–385.

Douglas, Mary. 1985. *Risk Acceptability According to the Social Sciences*. New York: Russell Sage.

The Economist. 2008. "A Stitch in Time." *The Economist*, London, United States, 12–12.

The Economist. 2012. "The Value of Friendship." *The Economist*, London, UK, 23–26.

Espeland, Wendy Nelson and Michael Sauder. 2007. "Rankings and Reactivity: How Public Measures Recreate Social Worlds." *American Journal of Sociology*, 113: 1–40.

Ferguson, Sarah. 1997. "Boycotts 'R' Us." *Village Voice*, 44–46.

Fombrun, C.J. 1998. "Indices of Corporate Reputation: An Analysis of Media Rankings and Social Monitors' Ratings." *Corporate Reputation Review*, 1(4): 327–340.

Fombrun, Charles J. 2007. "List of Lists: A Compilation of International Corporate Reputation Ratings." *Corporate Reputation Review*, 10(2): 144–153.

Fombrun, Charles J. and Mark Shanley. 1990. "What's in a Name? Reputation Building and Corporate Strategy." *Academy of Management Journal*, 33: 233–258.

Friedman, Monroe. 1999. *Consumer Boycotts: Effecting Change Through the Marketplace and the Media*. New York: Routledge.

Gamson, William. 1990. *The Strategy of Social Protest*. Belmont, CA: Wadsworth.

Gamson, William and Emilie Schmeidler. 1984. "Organizing the Poor." *Theory and Society*, 13: 567–585.

Ganz, M. 2000. "Resources and Resourcefulness: Strategic Capacity in the Unionization of California Agriculture, 1959–1966." *American Journal of Sociology*, 105(4): 1003–1062.

Giddens, Anthony. 1991. *Modernity and Self-Identity: Self and Society in the Late Modern Age*. Stanford, CA: Stanford University Press.

Godfrey, P.C. 2005. "The Relationship Between Corporate Philanthropy and Shareholder Wealth: A Risk Management Perspective." *Academy of Management Review*, 30(4): 777–798.

Godfrey, P.C., C.B. Merrill, and J.M. Hansen. 2009. "The Relationship between Corporate Social Responsibility and Shareholder Value: An Empirical Test of the Risk Management Hypothesis." *Strategic Management Journal*, 30(4): 425–445.

Hutton, James G., Michael B. Goodman, Jill B. Alexander, and Christina M. Genest. 2001. "Reputation Management: The New Face of Corporate Public Relations?" *Public Relations Review*, 27(3): 247–261.

Jenkins, J.C., and C. Perrow. 1977. "Insurgency of Powerless – Farm Worker Movements (1946–1972)." *American Sociological Review*, 42(2): 249–268.

Khurana, Rakesh. 2002. *Searching for a Corporate Savior*. Princeton, NJ: Princeton University Press.

King, Brayden G. 2008. "A Political Mediation Model of Corporate Response to Social Movement Activism." *Administrative Science Quarterly*, 53: 395–421.

King, Brayden G. 2011. "The Tactical Disruptiveness of Social Movements: Sources of Market and Mediated Disruption in Corporate Boycotts." *Social Problems*.

King, Brayden and Mary-Hunter McDonnell. 2014. "Good Firms, Good Targets: The Relationship between Corporate Social Responsibility, Reputation, and Activist Targeting." In Kiyoteru Tsutsui and Alwyn Lim (eds.), *Corporate Social Responsibility in a Globalizing World*. Cambridge: Cambridge University Press, 430–454.

King, Brayden G. and Nicholas Pearce. 2010. "The Contentiousness of Markets: Politics, Social Movements and Institutional Change in Markets." *Annual Review of Sociology*, 36: 249–267.

King, Brayden G. and Sarah A. Soule. 2007. "Social Movements as Extra-Institutional Entrepreneurs: The Effect of Protest on Stock Price Returns." *Administrative Science Quarterly*, 52: 413–442.

Kiousis, Spiro, Cristina Popescu, and Michael Mitrook. 2007. "Understanding Influence on Corporate Reputation: An Examination of Public Relations Efforts, Media Coverage, Public Opinion, and Financial Performance From an Agenda-Building and Agenda-Setting Perspective." *Journal of Public Relations Research*, 19(2): 147–165.

Klein, Naomi. 1999. *No Logo: Taking Aim at the Brand Bullies*. New York: Picador.

Knight, Frank H. 1921. *Risk, Uncertainty and Profit*. Boston and New York.

Lounsbury, Michael. 2001. "Institutional Sources of Practice Variation: Staffing College and University Recycling Programs." *Administrative Science Quarterly*, 46: 29–56.

Luders, Joseph. 2006. "The Economics of Movement Success: Business Responses to Civil Rights Mobilization." *American Journal of Sociology*, 111(4): 963–998.

Luders, Joseph. "Feminist Mobilization and the Politics of Rights." This volume.

MacMillan, Keith, Kevin Money, Steve Downing, and Carola Hillenbrand. 2005. "Reputation in Relationships: Measuring Experiences, Emotions and Behaviors." *Corporate Reputation Review*, 8(3): 214–232.

McDonnell, Mary-Hunter and Brayden G King. 2013. "Keeping Up Appearances: Reputational Threat and Impression Management after Social Movement Boycotts." *Administrative Science Quarterly*, 58(3): 387–419.

Nataliya, Vasilyeva. 2011. "Russia Oil Spills Disastrous to Environment; Annual Leakage is Estimated at 5 Million Tons, Equivalent to a Catastrophe like Deepwater Horizon Every Two Months." *Los Angeles Times*. Los Angeles, CA, A.33–A.33.

Nguyen, Nha and Gaston Leblanc. 2001. "Corporate Image and Corporate Reputation in Customers' Retention Decisions in Services." *Journal of Retailing and Consumer Services*, 8(4): 227–236.

Perrow, Charles. 1984. *Normal Accidents: Living with High-Risk Technologies*. New York: Basic Books.

Piven, Francis Fox and Richard A. Cloward. 1977. *Poor People's Movements: Why They Succeed, How They Fail*. New York: Pantheon Books.

Podolny, Joel M. 2005. *Status Signals: A Sociological Study of Market Competition*. Princeton, NJ: Princeton University Press.

Power, Michael. 2004. *The Risk Management of Everything*. New York: Demos.

Proffitt, W. Trexler and Andrew Spicer. 2006. "Shaping the Shareholder Activism Agenda: Institutional Investors and Global Social Issues." *Strategic Organization*, 4(2): 165–190.

Raeburn, Nicole. 2004. *Lesbian and Gay Workplace Rights: Changing Corporate America from Inside Out*. Minneapolis, MN: University of Minnesota Press.

Rao, H. and K. Sivakumar. 1999. "Institutional Sources of Boundary-Spanning Structures: The Establishment of Investor Relations Departments in the Fortune 500 Industrials." *Organization Science*, 10(1): 27–42.

Roberts, Peter W. and Grahame R. Dowling. 2002. "Corporate Reputation and Sustained Superior Financial Performance." *Strategic Management Journal*, 23: 1077–1093.

Sankar Sen, Zeynep Gürhan-Canli, and Vicki Morwitz. 2001. "Withholding Consumption: A Social Dilemma Perspective on Consumer Boycotts." *Journal of Consumer Research*, 28(3): 399–417.

Schurman, Rachel. 2004. "Fighting "Frankenfoods": Industry Opportunity Structures and the Efficacy of the Anti-Biotech Movement in Western Europe." *Social Problems*, 51(2): 243–268.

Schurman, R. and W. Munro. 2009. "Targeting Capital: A Cultural Economy Approach to Understanding the Efficacy of Two Anti-Genetic Engineering Movements." *American Journal of Sociology*, 115(1): 155–202.

Short, James F., Jr. 1984. "The Social Fabric at Risk: Toward the Social Transformation of Risk Analysis." *American Sociological Review*, 49(6): 711–725.

Sikkink, Kathryn. 1986. "Codes of Conduct for Transnational Corporations: The Case of the WHO/UNICEF Code." *International Organization*, 40(04): 815–840.

Vasi, Ion Bogdan, and Brayden G. King. 2012. "Social Movements, Risk Perceptions, and Economic Outcomes." *American Sociological Review*, 77(4): 573–596.

Vogel, David. 2005. *The Market for Virtue*. Washington, DC: The Brookings Institution.

Walker, Edward T., Andrew W. Martin, and John D. McCarthy. 2008. "Confronting the State, the Corporation, and the Academy: The Influence of Institutional Targets on Social Movement Repertoires." *American Journal of Sociology*, 114(1): 35–76.

Weber, Klaus, Hayagreeva Rao, and L.G. Thomas. 2009. "From Streets to Suites: How the Anti-Biotech Movement Penetrated German Pharmaceutical Firms." *American Sociological Review*, 74: 106–127.

Zald, Mayer N. and Michael A. Berger. 1978. "Social Movements in Organizations: Coup d'etat, Insurgency, and Mass Movements." *American Journal of Sociology*, 83(4): 823–861.

10 TACTICAL COMPETITION AND MOVEMENT OUTCOMES ON MARKETS

The rise of ethical fashion

Philip Balsiger

Scholars of social movements have long ignored the consequences of movements on markets. But in the past decade, a number of studies bridging various disciplines started analyzing how movements interact with corporations and provoke market change (de Bakker et al. 2013; King, Chapter 9; Soule and King 2014; Walker 2012). In a review of this burgeoning literature on the "contentiousness of markets," King and Pearce (2010) distinguish three major approaches through which movements attempt to change markets: contentious actions inside and outside of firms, collaboration, and the developing of new products and categories that constitute new market niches. Many studies have shown how the "success" – i.e., the resulting market change – of given tactics is mediated by contextual conditions (King 2008) and depends on processes involving different actors – movements, firms, states, and other relevant players – trying to shape new markets (Bartley 2007; Weber et al. 2008, 2009).

But while it is possible to assess the outcomes of different tactical approaches individually, they are actually related to one another. Movement organizations are part of "multi-organizational fields" (Curtis and Zurcher 1973) or social movement arenas (Jasper 2011). They pursue similar goals, but use different tactical approaches depending on their social and organizational identities and "cultures of action" (Klawiter 2008). In a dynamic process involving different movement players and their targets, the consequences of one approach may then become an important factor in the contextual "conditions of success" for another one. Focusing on one or the other of these tactical approaches, most studies do not explicitly address this interplay in the transformation of a given market. This is also more generally the case in studies on movement outcomes in the political arena.[1] From an empirical point of view, however, different movement actors very often pursue different approaches concomitantly, and they may be in a competitive or even conflicting relationship. Different tactics such as those of radical and reform-oriented organizations may be complementary and reinforce each other's outcomes, but they may also clash and provoke disputes between movement actors. Given the frequency of such conflicts, studies on movement outcomes have paid surprisingly little attention to their role in achieving change.

This chapter addresses this issue of tactical competition and its role for movement outcomes. How does the interplay of different tactics used by different movement players shape market change such as the emergence of niches? To tackle this question, I study the rise of ethical fashion in Switzerland (Balsiger 2014a). On this market, one observes three kinds of approaches movement actors used to fight for ethical fashion. Some movement organizations launched campaigns targeting fashion brands to push them toward the adoption of codes of conduct and their independent monitoring. Others developed ethical labels, such as for fair trade or organic cotton production, often in collaboration with particular clothing firms or retailers. And some activists and organizations tried to promote an alternative ethical fashion niche, identifying and supporting new producers of ethical clothes. The study shows how the transformations of the clothing market in Switzerland are the result of the interplay between the different approaches. Campaigning put the issue on the agenda of firms and opened the gates for NGOs pursuing collaboration tactics, but collaboration was also a major competitor for the campaigns as it allowed firms to sidestep campaign demands. Attempts at creating an alternative niche, meanwhile, took place in a context shaped by the market transformations that the previous interactions among campaigns, NGOs pursuing collaboration, and firms, had provoked. Focusing on the interplay of tactics enables a better understanding of the process of market transformation and highlights how competing approaches shape movement outcomes.

---

[1] Notable exceptions are Piven and Cloward's study on poor peoples' movements (1977) and studies revealing the so-called radical-flank effect (Haines 1988), which addresses the diverse interplay between moderate and radical groups (see Koopmans 1995).

Social movements and market changes

Authors studying the role of movements in market change (i.e., Davis et al. 2005, 2008; King and Pearce 2010; Rao 2009; Soule 2009; Walker 2012) have pointed out that contentious tactics such as protests are but one way how movements attempt to change markets. Besides such classic movement tactics, movements also collaborate with firms and sometimes act as economic actors themselves, contributing to the creation of new markets. Taking up and slightly modifying King and Pearce's classification (2010) of the contentiousness of markets, Figure 10.1 distinguishes the different roles movements play in market change. Under contention, one finds what is usually considered as classic social movement actions, i.e., mobilization with a goal of social change targeting specific institutions through extra-institutional means, whether from without, through public shaming, boycotts, or the mobilization of consumers (Bartley and Child 2007; den Hond and den Bakker 2007; Weber et al. 2009; King 2008; Balsiger 2010; Dubuisson-Quellier 2009) or from within, through tactics such as shareholder resolutions or the formation of special interest groups (Scully and Segal 2002). The second way movements change markets is through collaboration: movement actors collaborate with corporations to establish new forms of regulation, certification, or labels (Bartley 2003, 2007),

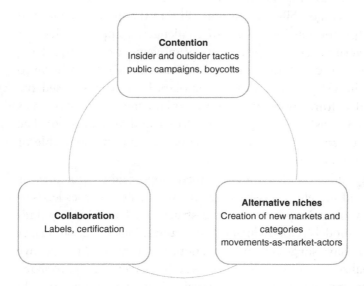

Figure 10.1 Movement approaches to change markets (after King and Pearce 2010).

where practices are assessed against previously established standards. Most of the time, private regulation initiatives involve the participation of social movement or "civil society" actors, firms, and (sometimes) state actors. Finally, movements also contribute to the rise of new market actors and categories. New markets can be the very expression of social movements; activists may become entrepreneurs or give cultural and material resources to entrepreneurs (Hiatt et al. 2009; Weber et al. 2008; McInerney 2014). Here, I term this "alternative niches" to highlight that such new markets, which are the expression of social movements, rise outside of established market actors and can thus be theoretically distinguished from forms of collaboration between movement actors and companies. In this last form, the distinction between movement actions and movement outcomes can also be blurred. Movement actors may promote or favor the establishment of alternative niches, but they may also directly create them, through forms of prefigurative politics (Polletta 1999) as for instance in the case of fair trade shops.

Contexts, movement outcomes, and the dynamic interplay of tactics

Building on political opportunities research, scholars studying movements in markets have highlighted characteristics of corporations (corporate cultures, vulnerabilities, internal allies in the management) and of industries (position as incumbent or challenger, competitiveness, or ties to the government) as determinants of movement outcomes (King 2008; Schurman 2004; Wahlström and Peterson 2006). In addition to corporate or industry characteristics, scholars have also stressed the importance of cultural opportunities to explain movement dynamics and outcomes (Lounsbury et al. 2003; Schurman and Munro 2009). The cultural and structural contexts movements face may be favorable or constitute barriers for movement outcomes.

Most studies in this tradition treat opportunity structures as given, static, and somehow passive contexts. But this sometimes leads to neglecting movements' capacity to change structures. To avoid the pitfalls of structuralist models (Goodwin and Jasper 2004; Fillieule 2006; Jasper 2011), scholars have suggested an interactionist and strategic perspective that conceptualizes a movement's targets as active players that try to shape the further outcome of the interaction to their advantage (Jasper 2011). In such a perspective, "our crisis is our adversary's opportunity, and vice versa" (Jasper 2011: 12). Actors are embedded in structural contexts, but within such contexts, they engage in strategic interaction. And such interaction between movements and their opponents can lead to structural change. Contexts, therefore, are themselves susceptible to be changed by movements. One can speak of "strategic action fields" (Fligstein and McAdam 2012) or interaction arenas with movement players, their opponents, and other relevant players rather than distinguishing between (active) movement actors and their (largely passive) context.

In a perspective attentive of the heterogeneity of movement actors and the conflicts and complementarities between different tactics, one movement player's outcome may thus affect the context of another player's actions. Conflicts between movement actors may arise, for instance, when the actions of movement player B tend to create a more unfavorable environment for movement player A because B's tactics allow A's targets to sidestep demands. This articulation among strategic interactions, the interplay of tactical approaches used by movement players, and contextual factors lies at the heart of the analysis of movement's role in market change proposed here. The perspective enables one to take into account the diversity of tactical approaches and highlights the conflicting and complementary modes of their interplay, without neglecting the role of contextual factors to explain movement outcomes.

What kind of market change

Market boundaries are porous. Markets are best understood as fields where producers occupy specific positions, "observe each other" (White 1981), and guide their actions toward one another (Aspers 2011; Beckert 2010; Fligstein 2001; Fligstein and McAdam 2012). A market is distinct from every other market through its specific set of network structures, cultural framing, and institutional rules (Beckert 2010). New markets or niches can rise at the borders of existing markets. Geographical location, technology (such as new products), or cultural categories (such as framing products as ethical) can lead to the redefinition of field boundaries and the creation of niches, populated by existing firms, new emerging firms, or a combination of both. In turn, the transformation of markets – the potential for the rise of new niches, for example – depends on the configuration of organizational fields, i.e., the structural and cultural characteristics of existing markets (Carroll and Swaminathan 2000; Rao et al. 2000; Sikavica and Pozner 2013).

Through the deployment of various resources, social movements bring grievances to markets that can push corporations to adopt change or serve as cultural templates for the rise of niches. Based on a conception of markets as fields with porous boundaries with specific sets of rules, networks, and cultural frames, one can theoretically conceive of different kinds of change movements can contribute to:

- Market change can mean the change of rules or practices in the existing market. In this case, change concerns all market players equally, either through external coercion (state power) or through normative institutional change
- Market change can mean the rise of new markets/niches that distinguish themselves from existing markets. Such new niches can form
  - around new categories/products developed by existing market actors;
  - around new categories with new emerging producers;
  - around new categories with both new producers and established ones competing.

Just as the tactical approaches used by movements, these market changes are also interrelated. The study of the processes of market transformation can show how they may be in conflict and how specific configurations and interactions produce market change.

Research strategy and methods

The results presented in this chapter draw on fieldwork conducted between 2006 and 2008 on social movements actions on the Swiss market for clothes and on the transformations thereof.[2] The primary

---

[2] The scope of the market transformations studied here is limited in two ways. First, I only discuss market transformations that are directly visible to consumers, in the forms of labels or new ethical brands for example. Everything that leads to clear signals for consumers – what can be called market equipment – is analyzed. This excludes from the study important transformations on the markets for clothes that are not directly visible to consumers, but are clearly linked to movement activity, too. These are market transformation *upwards* the commodity chain; not signaling downwards, from producers to consumers, but moving up the chain from brands to their contractors. In particular, an organizational field around the conduct of social audits has emerged. Second, the scope is limited insofar as I focus on markets for *individual* consumers. The market for clothes also contains an important segment catering to *collective* consumers, notably in the production of uniforms or other working wear. I do not consider this market here.

research goal was to reconstruct social movement activity in the clothing sector and to study the market changes that resulted from this (Balsiger 2014a). The empirical inquiry's starting point was the Swiss branch of the Clean Clothes Campaign (CCC), with the goal of retracing its activities over time. The study thus covers the period from the late 1990s to around 2008. My approach was empirical and inductive. Starting from a first actor – the CCC – I aimed at the identification of all social movement actors active in this field; the field was reconstructed through the information I gathered in interviews. Through interviews with key figures of the CCC as well as the attendance of events organized by the campaign and documentary research on movement initiatives and actions in the garment sector, I identified other social movement actors that intervened. The interviews first led me to follow the lead of the actors involved in the campaign's monitoring initiative. From there, I approached officials from the main label initiatives (Max Havelaar, Helvetas, Coop's Naturaline) as well as some firms. Finally, I participated in a volunteers group of the social movement organization conducting the campaign (the Bern Declaration) while they worked on the creation of a shopping map for ethical clothes, and identified other grassroots initiatives dealing with labor and environmental issues in the garment industry, some doing campaign work, others dedicated to promoting ethical consumption and production. In the latter case, an association based in Lausanne, called NiceFuture, was notably outside of the network linking the other actors identified, and was only found through a detour via the French field of ethical fashion,[3] where I met one of its leaders at an event I attended. As many studies using ethnographic fieldwork (e.g., Klawiter 2008; Péchu 2006), I thus stress the diversity of actors and action forms active in this heterogeneous movement field.

I conducted semi-direct interviews with leaders and grassroots activists of all the identified initiatives. Interviewees were asked to speak about the initiatives of their organization over time and to identify the main difficulties it had faced. I also asked questions, while I progressed with the identification of field actors, about their relationship with one another. Finally, interviews dealt with the social and cultural

---

[3] The research draws on instead of my doctoral thesis, where I compared the fight for ethical fashion in Switzerland and France (Balsiger 2014a).

background of interviewees and their personal trajectories. All in all, twenty-four interviews were conducted, of which twenty were with social movement actors, three with officials from firms, and one with members of the State Secretary for Economic Affairs (seco).

Tactical interplay and the shaping of ethical fashion in Switzerland

In the following empirical discussion, I follow movement activity chronologically and address the interplay of different tactics and their consequences for movement outcomes as they occurred empirically. This means that I first discuss the "clash" between actors pursuing contention and collaboration. In a next step, I look at the attempts at promoting an alternative niche and discuss how this approach related to the two others, and what consequences this had for market change.

Contention and collaboration approaches

On the social movement side, the first actor to raise the issue of production conditions in the clothing sector was the Clean Clothes Campaign (CCC), whose Swiss campaign was launched in the late 1990s. Three organizations were behind the campaign: the Bern Declaration (an advocacy group for development politics founded in the late 1960s) and two development aid NGOs – Bread for all (a protestant organization) and Lenten Fund (a Catholic one). The campaign put pressure on corporations in order to have them adopt codes of conduct about the issue of conditions of production in clothing factories, and urged them to join so-called multi-stakeholder initiatives to independently monitor codes. The targets were the biggest sellers of clothes – two general retailers and many more specialized clothing firms. Through petitions and ratings, the campaign publicly shamed retailers for their practices. But it also gave them positive incentives by educating consumers and giving them the tools to become political consumers (notably through the "ethical ratings" of firms) (Balsiger 2010).

While the CCC was putting pressure on corporations to adopt social standards, some movement actors developed organic and social labels that firms could use to designate parts of their clothes as ethical. Two prominent initiatives of this kind were launched in Switzerland in the early to mid-2000s (that is, several years after the CCC had launched its campaign). The organizations behind both of them came from the development aid sector. The first one, a label for organic cotton developed by the NGO Helvetas, the biggest Swiss development aid organization, was actually a development aid project: producing organic cotton should give farmers in developing countries greater revenues and protect them at the same time from environmental hazards. The project started off once it found commercial partners (the retailer Migros and the clothing firm Switcher) who guaranteed a long-term commitment to buy the organic cotton the project's farmers produce. It was subsidized and supported by the Swiss government. The second such initiative was fair trade cotton labeled and certified by Max Havelaar (MH).[4] It was developed at around the same time. The first MH cotton was sold by Switcher, Migros, and Manor in 2005. In spite of its NGO background (MH Switzerland was created by the country's six most important development aid NGOs, among them Bread for all, Lenten Fund, and Helvetas), the functioning of MH is very much business-oriented. Firms are licensees and have to pay MH a fee in order to carry the label; in exchange, they benefit from the legitimacy and the high profile of the name Max Havelaar. As such, it resembles the Helvetas organic cotton project, with which it actually collaborated since part of the organic cotton was also certified as fair trade by MH.

A third initiative shared some characteristics with these two collaborations, but did not involve the participation of a social movement organization. Coop, the main competitor of Migros in retailing, also developed its own product line of ethical (organic and socially responsible) clothes, called Naturaline. This was not an NGO but a business project, developed by a cotton trading firm. It originated in the early 1990s as a personal project of the owner of the firm. In an interview, he presented himself as someone whose family lives a somewhat alternative lifestyle inspired by the biodynamic principles of the humanist Rudolph Steiner. As the head of the cotton trading firm, he started a small experiment with organic cotton in India – at first, in his own words, as a "hobby." Coop quickly became the project's main economic partner; for the retailer, the mid-1990s corresponded to the time when it started developing its offer in organic food; organic cotton fit well into this

---

[4] Max Havelaar Switzerland is part of Fairtrade Labelling Organization (FLO), the international labeling initiative for fair trade.

strategy. In the course of the years 2000, the cotton trading firm converted fully to organic cotton and launched its own label, called BioRe, which takes into account both organic and social standards. By selling BioRe products, Coop became one of the world's leading outlets for organic clothes.

Contention and collaboration were in many ways distinct tactical approaches. The CCC can be characterized as a classic (if highly professionalized) social movement organization with a contentious action repertoire. Instances of labor abuse are taken up and firms publicly held responsible for it. Solutions for how to deal with the issues were developed, but the core domain of the CCC was contentious targeting and campaign making. The organizations pursuing collaboration, on the other hand, did not use contentious frames or action forms. Instead they developed, often in collaboration with firms, concrete solutions for problems. While both approaches shared a general, abstract goal of improving social and environmental conditions in industrial production, they aimed at different immediate results. In the case of the CCC, the goal was that firms submit their entire production to independently monitored labor standards. In the case of collaboration initiatives, the goal was to certify specific products, and thus to single out value chains that correspond to better standards.

The difference in approaches corresponds to different organizational positioning in the social movement arena and different social backgrounds of the individual actors behind the initiatives. However, one must not overstate the differences: there is actually a lot of overlap between the two "cultures of action." Indeed, it seems more appropriate to speak, in this case, of a continuum between an activist and a business-oriented pole. The overlap is organizational: two development aid organizations were initially part of the CCC. The overlap also concerns action forms: development aid organizations often support campaigns more or less actively, and the CCC wanted to establish a collaboration with firms to monitor codes of conduct. And the overlap also concerns individual actors. Within one organization, one can find more or less "radical" employees with more or less strong activist backgrounds, and there are no recruitment barriers between the two poles. Thus, while campaigning and collaboration are distinct approaches, they were often used concomitantly by the same organizations or by organizations that are associated in a dense network.

Contention and collaboration: interplay effects and outcomes

How did the coexistence of tactics of contentious campaigning and collaborating affect the shaping of the market for ethical fashion? At the core of the analysis, there is a triangular relationship between the CCC, the collaboration initiatives (MH and Helvetas organic cotton), and the firms. The CCC preceded the collaboration initiatives, and it initially faced a relatively favorable environment. In view of its goals, the campaign had some quick successes: most targeted firms adopted codes of conducts (although not exactly the code of conduct advocated by the campaign), and three of them (Switcher, Veillon and Migros) agreed to participate in a pilot project on code monitoring. Several elements favored the establishment of an independent monitoring initiative at this stage. Characteristics of the responding firms and their position in their respective markets certainly played an important role. Two of them saw an opportunity in positioning themselves as "ethical" brands, while the third one (Migros) was in an "ethical" competition with its main competitor on the retail market, Coop. Furthermore, it is likely that the proximity between the campaign actors and the firms was important. In the past, there had been similar campaigns that had opposed the same actors. In the course of these precedents, firm officials and campaign organizations had gotten familiar with each other. Finally, the campaign hit at a time when the market for ethical products had already started to develop in Switzerland (with organic and fair trade goods available at the big retailers, for example), giving signals to retailers that ethical issues may pay off. In sum, there were a number of structural factors that favored campaign outcomes at this early stage.

The collaboration initiatives entered the game at a later stage. Their "environment" was constituted of the same relatively favorable contextual factors that the CCC faced – appeal of "ethical" markets and "ethical" competitions, proximity between social movement actors and firms. One of them – the Helvetas cotton project – furthermore also benefited from state subsidies. But in addition to this, the previous activities of the CCC have to be counted in as an important factor. Through its campaigns on the issue of production conditions in supply chains in the clothing sector, it had put pressure on clothing brands and retailers and raised consumer awareness on ethical issues linked to fashion. Doing so, the campaign had contributed to *creating opportunities* for movement actors that proposed forms of collaboration to retailers. Firms were under public pressure and looked for ways of dealing with the question of production conditions and showing their ethical commitment. Collaboration through labels was a handy way to do so and widely adopted by firms. As we have seen, many of the major companies targeted by the campaign started selling organic or fair trade textile products: Migros (MH and Helvetas), Coop (through its own label), Switcher (MH and Helvetas), or Manor (MH).

In addition to other contextual factors, the collaboration initiatives thus also benefited from the activity of the campaign, which served as a gate-opener; collaboration initiatives promised a market-based solution that allowed firms to partly respond to the pressure put up by the CCC. But while the campaign favored collaboration initiatives, the opposite was true in the other direction, from collaboration to campaign. Once in place, collaboration initiatives changed the configuration of the game for the campaign. From the campaign's perspective, tactics were in conflict since targeted firms could use collaboration as a form of sidestepping the more encompassing demands of the campaign.

For the organizations behind the campaign in Switzerland, the competition between their campaigning approach and the collaboration approach by other NGOs was evident and perceived as a danger. The case of MH textiles most explicitly reveals this conflict between different approaches within the social movement arena. The launching of MH fair trade cotton coincided with the pilot project involving firms and the campaign organizations around code monitoring. The two staff members heading the campaign at the BD at the time were strongly opposed to the launch of certified clothes which, according to one of them, "ruined the campaign": "we were conducting a campaign for all firms to adopt a code of conduct as a basic system for their entire production. In this situation, having MH arriving and saying 'listen, we do not look at everything you do, make a niche, propose 1% of your production, and that's it' – there were big conflicts there." (Interview, campaign official, July 2007).

While campaigning thus opened up opportunities for movement actors pursuing collaboration strategies, the latter had the opposite effect on the former: the development of labels helped firms sidestep campaign demands and made it harder for campaigners to achieve their goals. Figure 10.2 illustrates the interplay between the two tactical approaches, picturing the triangular relationship of campaigners, collaboration initiatives, and firms. The arrow that goes from campaign to collaboration signals that campaigning, by putting the issue on the

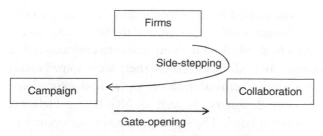

Figure 10.2 Interplay of campaigning and collaboration tactical approaches.

public agenda, opened up gates for collaboration initiatives. The arrow going from firms via collaboration to campaigns illustrates that collaboration forms allowed firms to sidestep the campaign, which had a hampering effect on the latter.

Activists often put forward this potential conflict between contentious campaigning and collaboration forms (see, for example, a report by the Maquila Solidarity Network (2006), a network of anti-sweatshop activists). Not all members of the campaign coalition saw such strong conflict between labels and the campaign; some were more pragmatic and saw both approaches as distinct and complementary. It is a case of the classic debate over the respective merits of radical and reform strategies: for reformers (in this case, collaboration NGOs), small steps can be a first stage to more encompassing change, whereas for more radical groups, they actually prevent broad change from happening. In this case, there is more evidence for the latter than for the former. Initial success of the campaign in the form of a monitoring initiative experienced a drawback when companies developed market-based counter-strategies such as labels. The rise of collaboration initiatives certainly complicated the picture for campaigners and gave firms more possibilities of reacting to campaign demands. However, there are also cases where firms use both labels *and* participate in private regulation through monitoring initiatives. Not all firms, therefore, use collaboration as a form of sidestepping.

Creating an alternative ethical fashion niche

Next to contention and collaboration approaches, other movement actors also attempted to create an alternative niche around new producers embracing ethical fashion. In Switzerland's French-speaking part,

"NiceFuture," which is dedicated to the promotion of a more sustainable lifestyle through different activities, organized the first Swiss ethical fashion show in Geneva in 2008. At this event, some twenty designers, shops, and associations exhibited. Among them there were some brands from France (where a similar ethical fashion show had existed for several years), some Swiss designers, as well as NGOs like Helvetas presenting its organic cotton label. The same year, a similar event had taken place for the first time in Basel in the German-speaking part of the country. Called Green Fashion, it was a section dedicated to ethical fashion within a fair on environment protection and sustainability called "Natur."[5] Finally, the year before a group of activist-volunteers from the NGO Declaration of Berne had created an "ethical shopping map." On this city map, the activists identified all the shops where ethical clothes can be purchased (Balsiger 2014b).

The two initiatives I studied[6] had in common the use of broad criteria for what counted as ethical fashion. The two groups shared a common belief in the role individual change can play in bringing about social change. For the leaders of NiceFuture, a group founded by two young professionals running a "green" communication agency, ecological principles of sustainable development are a matter of individual change. Creating a more sustainable society does not require political and systemic change, or at least this is not the path they privilege. They defend an individualized ecology where a more sustainable society originates from individual and moral change. This individual change, in turn, can be brought about when ethical behavior is presented as easy, hip, and accessible to everyone. In its actions – a festival for sustainability, Facebook groups inciting small gestures for a more sustainable planet, or the ethical fashion show – NiceFuture tries to perpetrate this individualized vision of social change. The volunteers who created the ethical shopping map were driven by similar concerns. Most of the members of this small group were young undergrads or graduate students. In contrast to NiceFuture, they were more integrated into the Swiss social movement field, volunteering for the BD. But they, too, believed individual responsibility should play a part in bringing about social change; in their daily lives, for example, all of them took great

---

[5] *Natur* itself was incorporated into one of Switzerland's biggest commercial fairs taking place yearly in Basel.

[6] I did fieldwork on NiceFuture and the BD's volunteer group, not on the Basel fair.

care to buy ethical products whenever possible. The shopping map reflected this concern, constituting a guide for people allowing them to shop in accordance with their ethical values.

Interplay effects between contention and the promotion of alternative niches

The initiatives aiming at the creation of an alternative niche (or at making such a niche more visible) were drawing on the CCC's anti-sweatshop campaign, as well as on many other movement campaigns that had revealed the "politics behind products." The CCC in particular had raised the issue of ethical production for clothes. Doing so, it had also created a demand for ethical fashion; consumers drawn to the campaign wondered where they could satisfy their desire to buy ethically produced garments. In the case of NiceFuture, the relationship to the campaign was not direct and conscious. The leaders of this group, more distant from the Swiss social movement arena, were more inspired by the French example of a thriving ethical fashion show and market. In the case of the BD volunteers, of course, the link to the CCC was much more present. They had been drawn to the regional volunteer group mostly because they had followed the CCC, were attracted to this particular campaign and wanted to contribute to it. They voiced personal frustration when trying to buy ethical clothes, as well as concerns by friends. One volunteer, for example, said: "I think when one buys clothes it is really stressful. Because somehow you can't just buy items Made in Cambodia and at the same time you don't know where to buy other clothes that you can still afford" (Interview, BD volunteer, August 2007).

For the campaign, the promotion of such a niche – whether it is populated by new emerging firms or by labels from established retailers – may be seen as complementary to the campaign and as a form of inciting not yet ethical producers to join the movement. This is what had happened once the conflict with MH was over; the campaign makers now had to deal with the existence of such a niche market and actually started to value it in their evaluations of brands. Retailers such as Coop or Switcher who had embraced collaboration with NGOs or launched important ethical product lines were listed as good examples in campaign brochures and thus rewarded. Showing up the feasibility of ethical production should serve as a model for other retailers. The ethical shopping map was in the spirit of this strategy and responded to a consumer concern the campaign makers had heard very often.

But in other ways, the development of an ethical fashion niche also ran counter to the interests of the campaigning approach. In relation to campaigning tactics, the stakes are similar to the ones that oppose this tactic to collaboration. The rise of a niche – whether it consists of collaboration of NGOs with established firms or of new emerging firms taking up movement demands – can be seen as a potential obstacle to achieving encompassing change on markets. Again, this was most visible within the CCC itself, as the creation of a shopping map juxtaposed both approaches within the same organization, the Bern Declaration. In spite of the media success of the map and although the volunteers were highly motivated to produce maps for other cities, the campaign leader decided to stop the project. He clearly voiced concerns about demobilization; the existence and promotion of an ethical fashion niche could signify to the campaign's public that action was no longer necessary and lead them to a retreat from public action, opting for exit instead of voice (Hirschman 2004). The existence of such a niche means that concerned consumers (i.e., those who are likely to mobilize in campaigns) can purchase their clothes at ethical stores, while the great majority of consumers do not care about this matter and no global change takes place on the mainstream market. Instead of broad social change, the result would merely be the rise of a small niche for ethical consumers. This perceived trade-off between contentious mobilization and the creating of alternatives characterizes all consumer campaigns and has been observed in many other movements (Balsiger 2014b; Dubuisson-Quellier 2009).

Two kinds of niches: interplay effects and outcomes of collaboration and alternative niches

Did an alternative niche that was distinct from the collaboration between established retailers and SMOs emerge? During the observation period and in the three identified attempts, it is striking that very few small Swiss clothing designers were actually taking part in this niche, whether by participating in one of the fairs or by figuring on the map. Most Swiss designers on the map had been included because they produced in Switzerland, but this did not necessarily mean that they self-identified with the category of ethical fashion. As for the

Geneva show, it was the stated goal of its initiators to show up the potential of ethical fashion to small Swiss designers: for example, one of NF founders told us that the show was also about "showing stylists that natural fabrics exist and that they can work with it, which is why we launch an ethical fashion award" (Interview NiceFuture, February 2008). Thus, the appeal of the "ethical" category was not (yet) self-evident to producers, and cultural work had to be done in order to promote it. This difficulty, I argue, must be linked to the outcome of the previous interplay between campaigns, collaboration initiatives and firms; i.e., the fact that established retailers had already "occupied" the niche for ethical fashion.

Both NF and the BD volunteer group wanted to show that it is possible to buy clothes that are both ethical and respond to esthetic concerns. "What we are interested in was fashion. Something that is contemporary, that men and women of our times appreciate. Nice cuts, textures, and so on" (Interview NiceFuture, February 2008). But rather than encountering small firms that actively embraced this ethical producer identity, the social movement entrepreneurs had a difficult task; indeed, at this stage ethical fashion still had a negative image among Swiss producers. This is what is suggested by a report based on a survey of small clothing brands in the Zurich area. It revealed that the label "ethical fashion" did not serve as a positive form of identification. It was not viewed as an opportunity to reach new consumers, but rather as potentially damaging for business. The designers interviewed for the study associated "green fashion" (Ökomode) and fair trade fashion to a negative image, "certainly not to 'fashion' or 'design'" (Starmanns 2009: 27). None of them actively tried to position their brand as ethical fashion.

It seems that separating ethical fashion from an activist image and making it look fashionable and hip was made more difficult by the fact that big retailers and labels had occupied this niche. In this instance, the actors and frames with which ethical fashion were associated were important. On the one hand, these retailers were not known for making hip clothes and thus associated ethical fashion to mainstream clothing. But more importantly, through the collaborations, ethical fashion continued to be strongly associated with the activist world. Swiss retailers had actively sought out the proximity to movement actors and collaborated with them in order to have legitimacy as providers of ethical clothes. For existing retailers that had been targeted by an anti-sweatshop campaign for their labor conditions, collaboration with

NGOs was the best way of presenting oneself as an "ethically conscious" firm. Doing it without this caution contained important risks, as the campaign would inevitably denounce it.[7] But this also meant that ethical fashion continued to be associated with NGOs and to a particular clothing style as it was sold at big retailers. The cultural meaning of the niche (Carroll and Swaminathan 2000) linked it to an identity that was different from the one promoters of an alternative niche had in mind. This context made it more difficult for a niche built on a different definition of ethical fashion as fashionable to emerge, which may explain the difficulties of social movement entrepreneurs to do so. Previous interactions between social movement actors and firms, resulting in the establishment of organic and fair trade labels and product lines, had thus shaped the opportunities for the initiatives promoting an alternative niche. Of course, this does not mean that different providers for ethical fashion, some catering to fashion-sensitive customers and others offering basic mainstream products, cannot coexist. The case just shows how processes involving different movement actors and firms matter and how they may shape the environment of one another.

Conclusion

Social movements consist of many individual and collective actors that pursue different tactical approaches. Such approaches can be complementary, but they may also be in conflict with one another. This chapter contributes to scholarly discussions on social movement outcomes and more particular social movements' consequences on markets. Regarding social movement outcomes, the chapter suggests a greater emphasis on the interplay of movement actors using different tactics.

[7] This can be seen notably in the case of Coop, which had an ethical product line that was not cautioned by a legitimate NGO. Although the organic and socially responsible *Naturaline* brand preceded NGO-backed labels, it came under attack by social movement actors once the latter got established. They criticized, in particular, Coop's use of the term "fair trade" when advertising *Naturaline*. Coop benefited, however, from a certain credibility within activist circles as a pioneer in retailing organic and fair trade products; it was even awarded a price for its role in the development of the organic market in Switzerland by the Bern Declaration in 2007. This explains why the controversy on Naturaline remained fairly restricted to the "abusive" use – in the eyes of NGOs – of the term fair trade, without questioning the overall legitimacy of the "ethical nature" of this product line.

This not only applies to market contexts, but also to studies on other institutional settings where movements fight for change. Taking into account the diversity within the social movement arena is important when studying movement outcomes because it allows to see how different approaches are sometimes complementary and thus favor movement success, but can also be in competition with one another. In interaction processes involving different movement actors and their targets, the interplay between different approaches shapes outcomes; the outcome of one tactical approach, for example, may become the "political opportunity" for another one.

While a number of studies have increased our understanding of the process of market change through social movements focusing on one approach and treating others as contextual (Bartley 2003, 2007; Weber et al. 2008), addressing their interplay directly promises important future insights into the dynamics of market change. Such an analysis can then reveal, for example, how targets of a given movement may use the diversity of strategies to play out different movement actors against each other. Analyzing the interplay between different approaches also leads to a dynamic view of the process of niche creation. The main effect of the movement for ethical clothes was the creation of market niches, but such niches can take different forms. Collaborations between established firms and social movement actors can enable the creation of niches situated within established firms, with movement players giving legitimacy capital for the identity change. On the other hand, niches can also emerge around new market players that embrace an ethical philosophy and situate themselves at the boundaries between movement actors and market actors.

References

Aspers, Patrick. 2011. *Markets*. Cambridge; Malden MA: Polity Press.

Balsiger, Philip. 2010. "Making Political Consumers: The Tactical Action Repertoire of a Campaign for Clean Clothes." *Social Movement Studies*, 9(3): 311–329.

Balsiger, Philip. 2014a. *The Fight for Ethical Fashion. The Origins and Strategic Interactions of the Clean Clothes Campaign*. Farnham; Burlington VT: Ashgate.

Balsiger, Philip. 2014b. "Between Shaming Corporations and Proposing Alternatives: The Politics of an 'Ethical Shopping Map'." *Journal of Consumer Culture*, 14(2): 218–235.

Bartley, Tim. 2003. "Certifying Forests and Factories: States, Social Movements, and the Rise of Private Regulation in the Apparel and Forest Products Fields." *Politics & Society*, 31(3): 433–464.

Bartley, Tim. 2007. "Institutional Emergence in an Era of Globalization: The Rise of Transnational Private Regulation of Labor and Environmental Conditions." *American Journal of Sociology*, 113(2): 297–351.

Bartley, Tim and Curtis Child. 2014. "Shaming the Corporation: The Social Production of Targets and the Anti-Sweatshop Movement." *American Sociological Review*, 79(4): 653–679.

Beckert, Jens. 2010. "How Do Fields Change? The Interrelations of Institutions, Networks, and Cognition in the Dynamics of Markets." *Organization Studies*, 31(5): 605–627.

Carroll, Glenn R. and Anand Swaminathan. 2000. "Why the Microbrewery Movement? Organizational Dynamics of Resource Partitioning in the American Brewing Industry after Prohibition." *American Journal of Sociology*, 106(3): 715–762.

Curtis, Russel L. and Louis A. Zurcher. 1973. "Stable Resources of Protest Movements: the Multi-Organizational Field." *Social Forces*, 52: 53–61.

Davis, Gerald F., Doug McAdam, et al. (eds.). 2005. *Social Movements and Organization Theory*. Cambridge: Cambridge University Press.

Davis, Gerald F., Calvin Morrill, et al. 2008. "Introduction: Social Movements in Organizations and Markets." *Administrative Science Quarterly*, 53: 389–394.

De Bakker, Frank, Frank den Hond, Brayden King, and Klaus Weber. 2013. "Social Movements, Civil Society, and Corporations: Taking Stock and Looking Ahead." *Organization Studies*, 34(5–6): 573–593.

den Hond, Frank and Frank G. A. de Bakker. 2007. "Ideologically Motivated Activism: How Activist Groups Influence Corporate Social Change Activities." *Academy of Management Review*, 32(3): 901–924.

Dubuisson-Quellier, Sophie. 2009. *La consommation engagée*. Paris: Presses de Sciences Po.

Fillieule, Olivier. 2006. *Requiem pour un concept. Vie et mort de la notion de 'structure des opportunités politiques'. La Turquie conteste.* G. Dorronsoro. Paris: Presses du CNRS.

Fligstein, Neil. 2001. *The Architecture of Markets. An Economic Sociology of Twenty-First-Century Capitalist Societies.* Princeton, NJ; Princeton University Press.

Fligstein, Neil and Doug McAdam. 2012. *A Theory of Fields.* Oxford; New York: Oxford University Press.

Goodwin, Jeff and James M. Jasper. 2004. *Rethinking Social movements: Structure, Meaning, and Emotion.* Lanham, MD; Oxford: Rowman & Littlefield Publishers.

Haines, Herbert H. 1988. *Black Radicals and the Civil Rights Mainstream 1954–1970.* Knoxville, TN: University of Tennessee Press.

Hiatt, Shon R., Wesley D. Sine, et al. 2009. "From Pabst to Pepsi: The Deinstitutionalization of Social Practices and the Creation of Entrepreneurial Opportunities." *Administrative Science Quarterly,* 54: 635–667.

Hirschman, A.O. 2004. *Exit, Voice, and Loyalty: Responses to Decline in Firms, Organizations, and States.* Cambridge, MA: Harvard University Press.

Jasper, James M. 2011. "Introduction: From Political Opportunity Structures to Strategic Interaction." In J. Goodwin and J. M. Jasper (eds.), *Contention in Context. Political Opportunities and the Emergence of Protest.* Stanford, CA, Stanford University Press.

King, Brayden G. 2008. "A Political Mediation Model of Corporate Response to Social Movement Activism." *Administrative Science Quarterly,* 53: 395–421.

King, Brayden G. and Nicholas A. Pearce. 2010. "The Contentiousness of Markets: Politics, Social Movements, and Institutional Change in Markets." *Annual Review of Sociology,* 36.

Klawiter, Maren. 2008. *The Biopolitics of Breast Cancer. Changing Cultures of Disease and Activism.* Minneapolis, London: University of Minnesota Press.

Koopmans, Ruud. 1995. *Democracy from Below: New Social Movements and the Political System in West Germany.* Boulder, CO: Westview.

Lounsbury, Michael, Marc Ventresca, and Paul M. Hirsch. 2003. "Social Movements, Field Frames and Industry Emergence: A Cultural-Political Perspective on US Recycling." *Socio-Economic Review*, 1: 71–104.

Maquila Solidarity Network. 2006. "Is Fair Trade a Good Fit for the Garment Industry?" http://en.maquilasolidarity.org/en/node/215.

McInerney, Paul Brian. 2014. *From Social Movement to Moral Market: How the Circuit Riders Sparked an IT Revolution and Created a Technology Market*. Stanford, CA: Stanford University Press.

Péchu, Cécile. 2006. *Droit au logement, genèse et sociologie d'une mobilisation*. Paris: Dalloz.

Piven, Frances F. and Richard A. Cloward. 1977. *Poor people's Movements: Why They Succeed, How They Fail*. New York: Pantheon Books.

Polletta, Francesca. 1999. "Free Spaces in Collective Action." *Theory and Society*, 28(1): 1–38.

Rao, Hayagreeva. 2009. *Market Rebels. How Activists Make or Break Radical Innovations*. Princeton, NJ; Oxford: Princeton University Press.

Rao, Hayagreeva, Calvin Morrill, et al. 2000. "Power Plays: How Social Movements and Collective Action Create New Organizational Forms." *Research in Organizational Behavior*, 22: 239–282.

Schurman, Rachel. 2004. "Fighting "Frankenfoods": Industrial Opportunity Structures and the Efficacy of the Anti-Biotech Movement in Western Europe." *Social Problems*, 51(2): 243–268.

Schurman, Rachel and William Munro. 2009. "Targeting Capital: A Cultural Economy Approach to Understanding the Efficacy of Two Anti–Genetic Engineering Movements." *American Journal of Sociology*, 115(1): 155–202.

Scully, Maurenn and Amy Segal. 2002. "Passion with an Umbrella." *Research in the Sociology of Organizations*, 19: 125–168.

Sikavica, Katarina and Jo-Ellen Pozner. 2013. "Paradise Sold: Resource Partitioning and the Organic Movement in the US Farming Industry." *Organization Studies*, 34(5–6): 623–651.

Soule, Sarah A. 2009. *Contention and Corporate Social Responsibility*. Cambridge: Cambridge University Press.

Soule, Sarah A. and Brayden King. 2014. "Markets, Business, and Social Movements." In Donatella della Porta and Mario Diani (eds.), *The Oxford Handbook of Social Movements*. Oxford: Oxford University Press.

Starmanns, Mark. 2009. *Ethical Fashion – Made in Switzerland? Eine Marktstudie*. Zürich: Geographisches Institut, Universität Zürich.

Wahlström, Mattias and Abby Peterson. 2006. "Between the State and the Market: Expanding the Concept of 'Political Opportunity Structure'." *Acta Sociologica*, 49(4): 363–377.

Walker, Edward. 2012. "Social Movements, Organizations, and Fields: A Decade of Theoretical Integration." *Contemporary Sociology*, 41(5): 576–587.

Weber, Klaus, Kathryn L. Heinze, and Michaela DeSoucey. 2008. "Forage for Thought: Mobilizing Codes in the Movement for Grass-fed Meat and Dairy Products." *Administrative Science Quarterly*, 53: 529–567.

Weber, Klaus, L. G. Thomas, and Hayagreeva Rao. 2009. "From Streets to Suites: How the Anti-Biotech Movement Affected German Pharmaceutical Firms." *American Sociological Review*, 74(February): 106–127.

White, Harrison C. 1981. "Where Do Markets Come From?" *American Journal of Sociology*, 87: 517–547.

PART III

INSTITUTIONS

PART III

INSTITUTIONS

11 THE IMPACT OF SOCIAL MOVEMENTS ON POLITICAL PARTIES

Daniela R. Piccio

Introduction

> The representative system does not function as representation of
> the people [...]. We do not want to go to a demonstration and
> listen to speeches from party representatives. We want to take our
> future into our hands![1]

The citation from Dutch ecology activists reported above is hardly
exceptional for social movements. They are indeed typical for the way
in which most social movements conceive political parties: as hierarchical organizations, self-insulated, remote from the citizenry and
inattentive to social change. Yet, social movements, including Dutch
ecologists, have established various forms of interaction with parties,
including the establishment of umbrella organizations and the organization of common protest actions. Of course, social movements are
loosely connected informal networks of individuals, groups and organizations (Diani 1995), whose heterogeneity leads to different positions within the movements themselves. Thus, there may be groups
refusing any involvement with parties. Yet, parties play such a critical
role for social movements' political outcomes that they hardly can be
ignored. If they are willing to succeed in influencing and reforming

I am grateful to Jonas Dræge and the editors of this book for comments on an earlier
version of this chapter.

[1] Ecology activists in the Netherlands, cited in Duyvendak and Van Huizen (1983: 83
and 86).

public policy, social movements must broaden their support and be backed by insiders, i.e., mediators and reference groups willing to take up their claims in the institutional arenas (Amenta et al. 1992; Kriesi et al. 1995; Tarrow 1994; Giugni and Passy 1998; Rucht 2004). However, despite the importance of the social movement-party interactions for the movements' outcomes, parties are conspicuously absent from mainstream literature on social movements.

This chapter has two main objectives. The first is to encourage social movement research to pay greater attention to political parties. If having an impact on parties may appear a negligible and unsatisfactory outcome vis-à-vis the broader political objectives that social movements aim to achieve, parties are nonetheless the first and fundamental barrier that social movements' demands have to overcome in order to gain access to the institutional environment. In other words, whether social movements manage to have an impact on parties and the degree to which impact takes place is crucial for the broader political goals of the movements. Second, this chapter explores under which conditions social movements' impact on political parties is more likely to take place. Selectively focusing on two crucial case studies, the ecology movements' impact on the Dutch Social Democratic Party (PvdA) and on the Italian Christian Democratic Party (DC), respectively a most-likely and a least-likely case of social movement impact on parties, the chapter explores the validity of three core conditions explaining social movement-party interactions according to previous research: (i) party electoral vulnerability, and hence the electoral benefits that supporting social movements may imply for parties; (ii) cumulative involvement of party members in social movements' activities; and (iii) affinity between partisan identity and social movements' goals. Impact is measured based on an in-depth analysis of party documents (election manifestos, congress acts, party journals and archival documentation) in the years preceding and following the highest peak of mobilization of the ecology movements in the two countries into consideration.

In the conclusions it is argued that while the above mentioned conditions are indeed relevant to explain the greater impact of the ecology movement on the PvdA as compared to the DC, they are unsatisfactory to explain the complexity of the interactions between social movements and political parties.

Social movements and political parties: an understudied field of research

Tracing the relationship between social movements and political parties in historical perspective, Hanagan (1998) observed how social movements have always fluctuated between integration and independence with respect to political parties' structures. Indeed, the very origin of those that would become the most important party families of the twentieth century in Western Europe (i.e., the Socialists, the Liberals and the Confessional parties) could not be understood without reference to the diverse movements, pressure groups, and associations, which became involved in institutionalized campaigns shaping the configuration of party organizations. Processes of movements' institutionalization have taken place with democratization waves throughout the world (Doowon 2006). However, even when independent, social movements keep intervening in the institutional political process through strategies of confrontation, competition, and cooperation (Della Porta and Rucht 1995; Giugni and Passy 1998). Studies have emphasized that interactions with power holders are a routine part of social movements' activities, and that an ongoing dialogue between social movements and parties exists.

Despite the greater scholarly attention to political outcomes (Giugni 1998; Kolb 2007), and the growing calls to theoretically and empirically bridge the boundaries between so-called institutional and non-institutional politics (Costain and McFarland 1998; McAdam et al. 2001; Goldstone 2003), relatively little research has been conducted on how social movements' mobilizations influence political parties. Several scholars have underlined the methodological challenges and the complexity of observing patterns of exchange and interaction between different actors and different targets in a conflict system (Rucht 2004; Amenta et al. 2010; Bosi and Giugni 2012). Yet, probably the most important reason for the virtual lack of attention to parties in social movement literature is the division of labor that still exists between the two different fields of research (Clemens 1993; Kitschelt 1990; McAdam and Su 2002; Piccio 2011).[2]

---

[2] Moreover, as remarked by McAdam and Su (2002), the two literatures have been drawing different conclusions about the social movements' capacity to bring forward political change: negligible, according to party scholars, influential (to various degrees), according to social movement scholars (see also Piccio 2011).

Such a compartmentalization of political processes in social movement research is surprising, as social movements scholars have stressed the importance of the mediation by political institutions for a very long time. In his seminal work *The Strategy of Social Protest*, Gamson defined social movements as successful *through* the responses they received by political institutions, which granted social movements with "new advantages" and/or "acceptance" (Gamson 1975). If Gamson's definition of social movements' success has been largely criticized (e.g., Giugni 1998), the importance of political institutions as mediators, constraining or facilitating social movements' outcomes, has instead remained unchallenged.

The role of the broader political context for movements' outcomes has become, for example, a central tenet of the "political process approach." The presence of institutional allies supporting social movements was considered as one of the key independent variables constituting social movements' political opportunity structure (POS) (see Kriesi et al. 1995; Tarrow 1994). However, POS scholars have been more interested to observe the movements' broader political outcomes, and have thus more limitedly looked at the specific channels of interaction between social movements and parties. Yet, they developed a number of hypotheses concerning the social movement-party relationship, which I will discuss more at length in the following section. The importance of the interactions between the political context, the strategies of collective action, and their outcomes is also highlighted by those scholars focusing on the impact of social movements on policy change. The latter have observed how political effects of social movements take place at various stages of the policy-making process (i.e., agenda setting, legislation, implementation, see Amenta and Caren 2004; Amenta et al. 2010) and how different rules of the game apply at the different stages of the process (King et al. 2005). However, even when observing social movements' impact on political agenda-setting, admittedly the lowest stage of policy-making activity and the furthest removed from policy impact, empirical studies assessing movement effects on policies have mostly focused on congressional hearings, bills, and legislation, and have left parties out of the policy-making picture (for a review, see Walgrave and Vliegenthart 2012).

In sum, the institutional environment is seen as crucial for social movements' political outcomes, but seldom has research taken parties as dependent variables of social movements' impact (see also the contributions by Peterson [Chapter 13] and by Uba [Chapter 7]). Of course, having an impact on parties is far from the ultimate goal of social movements. As discussed in the introduction to this chapter, the latter tend to think of parties as a substantial part of their problems, or as obstacles for their goals and propositions to be achieved. However, a selective focus on the impact of social movements on parties is essential, for several reasons. First, parties are crucial to the functioning of modern democracies, as they constitute the key institutional channels of political representation, mediating between the citizens, their demands, and the state (Sartori 1976). Due to their centrality, they also constitute a fundamental juncture in the chain of social movements' political outcomes. Focusing on political parties, therefore, adds a fundamental stage to the "complex and multi-staged character of movement impact" (Walgrave and Vliegenthart 2012: 6). Second, focusing on social movement impact on parties improves our knowledge about the broader, possibly longer term societal and political effects that social movements' mobilizations are able to produce. Resistance to change is considered as a tendency among all organizations that reach a certain degree of institutionalization, including parties (Raniolo 2004). As they tend to change more slowly, changes in existing structures and practices of parties are likely to produce broader, long-term societal and political effects (Giugni et al. 1999). Finally, focusing on social movement impact on parties improves the often criticized insularity and "movement-centered" approach of social movement studies (Lofland 1996). Underlying the impact that social movements have on parties is a means through which researchers can shed light on how social movements' demands enter other actors' political agendas and how their demands are treated by other actors, in a mediated form.

Conventional explanations and research design

As argued in the previous section, "political process" scholars suggested a number of factors accounting for social movement-party interactions. In particular, interaction is said to be more likely under three main conditions:

(1) *Electoral vulnerability.* Vulnerability in the parties' electoral environment is seen as a condition favoring social movement-party

interactions (e.g., Kriesi and Wisler 1999; Goldstone 2003; Amenta et al. 2010). The underlying logic is that parties will employ strategies that are beneficial for the maintenance of their organizational survival, which, in representative democracies, translates into the search for electoral support. The presence of electoral competitors at their left, for example, has been considered as an important leverage for social democratic parties to be more open toward social movements (Kriesi et al. 1995).

(2) *Members' cumulative involvement*. Scholars have observed that participation in social movement activities does not exclude participation in political parties' activities, and that political participation in these two venues is cumulative rather than substitutive (Beckwith 2000; Norris 2002). Party members may, therefore, engage in social movement activities themselves, thus promoting and leading to attitudinal changes in the party with respect to those themes at the core of the social movements' mobilizations (Lange 1980).

(3) *Identity coherence*. Finally, for a social movement to be more likely to have an impact on a party, a certain degree of overlap must exist between the party and the social movements' identities. Parties will be more likely to be open to those movements whose cultural and ideological understandings of politics more closely correspond to their own, and whose themes do not contradict their own traditional discourses (Kriesi 1993; Rucht 2004). The importance of maintaining internal coherence with respect to their individual cultural identity has often been underlined in organizational studies as among the most primary goals of organizations (Kraatz and Block 2008). Similarly, cultural identity functions as a filter in parties, discerning from among all theoretically possible actions those deemed politically appropriate for the organization (Raniolo 2004).

Do these conditions indeed explain the way and the degree to which the social movement-party interactions takes place and in particular how social movements' mobilizations impact on parties? In the remaining part of this chapter I will explore the explanatory power of these conditions presenting two critical cases of social movement-party interactions: a most-likely and a least-likely case (Gerring 2007). The first case looks at the impact of the ecology movement in the

Netherlands on the Social Democratic Party (Partij van den Arbeid, PvdA). As I will discuss in greater length below, in the period under consideration the conditions for the ecologists to have an impact on the PvdA were particularly favorable. The second case is opposite to the first: it looks at the impact of the Italian ecology movement on the Christian Democratic Party (Democrazia Cristiana, DC). Here, conversely, the conditions for the ecologists to have an impact were particularly unfavorable.

Impact is operationalized as the effect that social movement mobilizations had on two key dimensions of parties: political discourse and organization. Impact on political discourse is observed as parties take on board social movements' themes of mobilization in their original documents (election manifestos, congress speeches, declarations, and party journals). Impact on party organization is observed as parties introduce changes in their organizational environment, including the formation of internal workgroups focused on themes previously raised by the social movements and the establishment of inter-organizational linkages with social movement groups. Of course, impact can be observed at various stages of party activity, including for example the introduction of law proposals in parliament. However, having an impact on these two dimensions is the bottom line for the fate of the social movements' outcomes, as they constitute the first stage for the representation of the social movements' demands within political parties.

It is important to mention that social movements cannot be considered as the only and primary drive of changes taking place within parties, as parties themselves live in, and are nurtured by, the social environment. The study of social movements' impact on parties is not exempt from the challenges of multi-causality frequently discussed in social movement research (Tilly 1999; Bosi and Giugni 2012). In order to make causal connection robust and avoid "pseudo-outcomes" – that is, political responses related to the political goals of the social movement but that are not caused by the movement (Kolb 2007) – this chapter undertakes a longitudinal qualitative analysis observing the parties' positions before and after the movements' emergence. It is only when changes occur after the movements' emergence and when they relate directly to the goals and ends of the movements that we can make a convincing claim of movement impact (Amenta and Caren 2004; Amenta et al. 2010: 301).

The ecology movement's impact on the PvdA

For the case of the PvdA and the ecology movement all three conditions favoring social movement-party relationship are present. Following the national elections of 1967, the Dutch party system, which was traditionally characterized by stability and predictability of vote distribution (Lijphart 1968; Irwin and Van Holsteyn 1989), witnessed for the first time significant electoral shocks, mostly at the expenses of the traditional political parties. For the PvdA, the turn of the 1970s constituted a particularly challenging electoral environment. The party experienced an unprecedented electoral decline in the 1967 political elections, an internal split-off leading to the formation of a new political party (DS'70), and the electoral growth of smaller New Left parties concurring at its left. The latter, moreover, strongly supported the new social movements' mobilization that emerged in the Netherlands from the second half of the 1960s (Duyvendak and Koopmans 1992). At the same time, the PvdA also had to face internal challenges. A New Left current formed within the party (Nieuw Links) calling for horizontal and participatory decision-making, a more confrontational style of politics, and stressing a notion of "real democracy" being grounded in society and in the activities of action groups. Not only were the New Left core claims very much in tune with the emergent social movements family, but New Left members and a growing number of PvdA members were themselves actively involved in the emergent social movements' protests. Finally, despite their positions (initially) diverged on the nuclear energy issue, the ecology movement and the PvdA had similar positions with respect to environmental problems, the party having claimed for environmental protection and sustainable development since the early 1960s. All in all, as the Dutch ecology movement became a visible political actor in the society, it seemed it could rely on an influential ally in the Dutch party system.

Impact on the PvdA discourse

Even though environmental problems had entered the political discourse of the PvdA already since the 1960s,[3] relevant changes took

---

[3] Most notably, the party published a series of four booklets dedicated to environmental issues (Wiardi Beckman Stichting, 1963–1965. *Om de Kwaliteit van het Bestaan*),

Table 11.1 *Environmental issues in the PvdA election manifestos,*
1971–86 *

Environmental issues	1971	1977	1981	1986
Environmental protection[a]	9	31	30	44
Environmentally aware production[b]	1	2	12	18
Alternative sources of energy[c]	0	1	1	2
Alternative models of growth[d]	0	2	16	16
Stop nuclear energy plans[e]	0	2	8	5
Frequency per document	10	38	67	85

* *Notes:* A score is assigned for each reference to any of the environmental issues found across the documents.

[a] Environmental protection, defense of natural resources and promotion of environmental legislation.

[b] Environmentally aware production methods and ban of polluting means of production.

[c] Promotion, use and/or research on durable resources of energy production (wind, sun, geothermic).

[d] Promotion of alternative models of growth against the quantitative-oriented model.

[e] References against further implementation of nuclear energy and favoring the closure of the existing nuclear factories.

place in the party discourse on these issues after the emergence of the ecology movement. As shown in Table 11.1, which summarizes the number of (positive) references to environmental issues in the PvdA election manifestos from 1971 to 1986, the party's attention to the environment has increased over time, and particularly after 1974, when the ecology movement had become a visible political actor in the society.

Changes are observed both looking at broader, less controversial, environmental themes (such as environmental protection) and, more specifically, at the ecologists' core issues of mobilization (such as alternative models of economic growth and the closure of the existing nuclear factories). It is particularly around the nuclear energy issue – according to Rüdig the best test case to observe the impact of ecology movements on parties (Rüdig 1988) – that the increasing number of

questioning whether economic growth should be positively assessed. The core argument advanced in the four booklets is that limitations should be introduced in the production and the consumption of goods. Indeed, if economic growth had contributed to citizens' improved living conditions, it did so at the expense of the environment. A remarkable statement for a Social Democratic party, traditionally characterized by technological optimism and growth-oriented positions.

references is mostly remarkable and that the impact of the ecologist mobilization appears more pronounced.

Indeed, the PvdA had always been in favor of the nuclear energy option and started from a position that was diametrically opposite to the one of the ecology movement. As Joop den Uyl, party secretary and prime minister from 1973 to 1977, acknowledged:

> I belong to that generation that strongly believed in the revolutionary importance of the application of nuclear energy for peaceful goals.[4]

It was in reaction to the initiatives taken by the PvdA-run government (1973) to participate in the international project for the construction of a nuclear power station in Kalkar and to increase the number of nuclear factories in the Netherlands, that the Dutch ecology movement started its most active mobilization (Duyvendak and Van Huizen 1983). Ecology activists started acts of civil disobedience in a dozen municipalities and formed anti-nuclear action committees in more than eighty cities in the country. These initiatives were not only supported by the smaller left-wing political parties, but also by the local sections of the PvdA and by an increasing number of PvdA members. Party members' participation in the ecology movement's activities constituted an important leverage to change the position of the party on nuclear energy. This reflected in the fifteenth PvdA Congress in 1975, which approved two propositions presented by local party sections: decisions on the further broadening of nuclear energy in the Netherlands had to be postponed and, in the intervening years, available funds should be invested in the research and development of alternative sources of energy (solar, geothermal, and wind energy). A few years later, the party's position overtly turned anti-nuclear:

> No new nuclear power stations shall be built. There shall be no future for Kalkar.[5]

Hence, not only did the PvdA further increase its attention toward environmental issues during the 1970s but it also changed its position

---

[4] J. Den Uyl, cited in Jamison et al. 1990: 153.
[5] PvdA election manifesto (1977). *Voorwaarts, en niet vergeten*. Documentatiecentrum Nederlandse Politieke Partijen (DNPP), Groningen.

with respect to the core issue of mobilization of the Dutch ecology movement. The timing of both changes, which took place a few years after the movement had entered its most visible phase of mobilization, point to the movement's key impact.

The ecology movement's impact, however, did not translate in a full support of the party to the movement's mobilization. The PvdA remained anchored to its anti-nuclear stance, yet it became less confrontational. Against the position expressed by ecology groups, the PvdA agreed to set up a "Wide Social Discussion on Nuclear energy," a society-wide discussion (which ecologists criticized for not being "wide" at all) with the task to formulate a final decision on the future of nuclear energy in the country. On the one hand, this implied to keep postponing the decision to close the two nuclear reactors currently functioning. On the other hand, this also implied a de-politicization of the nuclear energy issue, and hence – in the ecology groups' perspective – a means by which the PvdA was withdrawing from taking political responsibilities.[6] All in all, the party remained anchored to its anti-nuclear stance but it did not support the ecology movement's position to close existing nuclear factories on the Dutch territory, nor, as discussed in the following section, did it provide support to the social protests of the ecology groups.

Impact on the PvdA organization

At the level of the party organization the ecology movement managed to have an impact on the PvdA in at least two ways. First, after the movement's emergence, the party Executive introduced an ad hoc internal workgroup on environmental issues. The Functional Workgroup on Environment and Energy (Functionele Werkgroep Milieu en Energie, FWME) was established in 1978 with two main objectives: provide a platform for discussion of environmental issues within the party and link with the ecology movement's groups. Archival documentation

---

[6] The ecology movement was very critical towards the establishment of the Wide Social Discussion on nuclear energy: "The Wide Social Discussion is and remains an attempt to de-politicize the discussion on nuclear energy, make it less menacing to the citizenry, and turn it in favor of the interests of the bureaucrats and the private undertakings" (Archief PvdA, (1934, 1938–) 1946–96, "Kernenergie en kerncentrale Dodewaard. 1979–1986", inv.nr. 2860, Internationaal Instituut voor Sociale Geschiedenis (IISG), Amsterdam).

shows that the FWME set up several activities with the ecology movement: it drafted booklets, leaflets and reports on environmental matters, organized conferences and meetings, and engaged in a regular written correspondence with several ecology groups.[7] Second, throughout the 1970s, the party Executive guaranteed its support to numerous ecologists' protest actions, and formed a number of broader umbrella organizations with ecology groups and smaller parties of the Left in order to facilitate communication, share ideas and strategies, and organize and promote common social initiatives on environmental matters.

However, as soon as disagreement emerged between the ecology movement and the party on how to deal with the open nuclear factories in the country and as soon as the movement's protest actions became more confrontational, the PvdA did no longer grant its support. While the FWME maintained its formal functions, no support was provided by the party to the two largest ecologist protest actions at the site of the nuclear energy factory Dodewaard in 1980 and 1981, nor to the other actions that followed. For the first time criteria were established for distinguishing between "acceptable" and "unacceptable" social actions:

> The PvdA cannot take part in a social action if not under a number of prerogatives. Social actions must not be violent; they need to have an organizational form with clearly recognizable and controllable representatives; actions need to be discussed beforehand with the authorities; there must be full clearness to all those taking part to the demonstration concerning the beginning, the development and the end of the actions.[8]

Ultimately, the PvdA laid claim to the primacy of institutional politics vis-à-vis protest actions. As the party Executive stated in 1983,

> Social actions cannot impede a certain decision from being taken by the government and that decision from being implemented. There are specific rules and procedures to change the decisions taken by the government.[9]

---

[7] Archief PvdA, "Werkgroep Milieu en Energie," inv.nr. 1378. IISG, Amsterdam.

[8] PvdA Executive (1981). Archief PvdA, "Evaluatie Dodewaard," inv.nr. 2862. IISG, Amsterdam.

[9] PvdA Executive (1983). *Verslagen van het partijbestuur en de kamerfracties over the periode 1982–1984.* DNPP, Groningen.

All in all, the impact of the ecology movement on the PvdA has been substantial, and revealed at both levels of party discourse and organization. The ecologists could benefit from open windows of opportunity within the party: growing electoral volatility, party members' cumulative involvement in movement's activities, and closeness between the movement and the party favored the PvdA's openness and permeability. Yet, the PvdA did not fully stand behind the movement's claims.

The Italian ecology movements' impact on the DC

The case of the Italian Christian Democratic Party is radically different. The party's stable electoral performance, its traditional and conservative character – the party was described as "the conservative party par excellence of the Italian party system" (Caciagli 1992: 11) – and the major cultural and ideological distance between DC party members, its broader constituency, and the Italian ecologists, make this a least-likely case of social movement impact on a political party. Phenomena such as the cumulative involvement of party members in social movements' activities did not take place and the DC had hardly anything to benefit in electoral terms from showing itself as open toward this mobilization. Not least, it was against the DC and its urbanization policies that the first environmental organization in Italy, Italia Nostra, campaigned most energetically, criticizing the party for being responsible for environmental decay and for the depredation of the natural resources of the country (Della Seta 2000). Indeed, the party's position in government at the national and local levels and its strong linkages with the agricultural and industrial sectors of the Italian economy made the DC the most directly accountable party for the "feverish" urban planning of the 1950s. All in all, the conditions for expecting the ecology movement to have an impact on the DC are decidedly unfavorable.

Impact on the DC discourse

While most countries in Western Europe experienced the emergence of ecology movements in the 1970s, in Italy it took up to the turn of the 1980s for the Italian ecology movement to form as a visible social and political actor (Diani 1988). It is from this point, therefore, that we may find traces of impact of the ecology movement on political parties.

Table 11.2 *Environmental issues in the DC election manifestos,*
1976–87*

Environmental issues	1976	1979	1983	1987
Environmental protection[a]	7	0	4	31
Environmentally aware production[b]	0	0	0	6
Alternative sources of energy[c]	0	0	0	1
Alternative models of growth[d]	1	0	1	1
Stop nuclear energy plans[e]	0	0	0	0
Frequency per document	8	0	5	39

* Same as in Table 11.1.

Table 11.2 shows the number of references to environmental issues in the DC election manifestos from 1976 to 1987.

As the table shows, environmental issues received very limited attention in DC manifestos throughout the entire period under consideration, with the relevant exception of the election manifesto presented for the political elections of 1987. This peak in the number of references to environmental issues appears as a reaction to different pressures and should not be read as the result of the ecology movement's impact. Such pressures include the explosion at the nuclear plant in Chernobyl in 1986, which caused sensation in Italian public opinion and led to environmental issues receiving unprecedented attention by the media; the participation, for the first time in 1987, of the Green party to national level elections; the first national referendum on nuclear energy held in the same year. Hence, in this context, which made the elections of 1987 the first environmentally sensitive ones in the history of the Italian Republic, the DC accentuated its environmental profile. Not only can no indication of an increasing attention toward environmental issues be traced in the early 1980s, after the movement's emergence, but the environmental issues that the DC referred to with greater frequency concern general themes (such as environmental protection, pollution, waste reduction, and acknowledgment of the limitation of natural resources), while issues most closely related to the movement's demands (environmentally aware production, halt in nuclear energy, alternative models of economic growth, and investment in durable energy resources) hardly received any attention.

The lack of impact of the ecology movement on the DC discourse reveals in particular on the nuclear energy issue, also in Italy, the ecologists' core issue of mobilization. As stated by the DC Secretary in 1980,

> There is a delay in the implementation of the laws and of the National Energy Plans that have already been approved. [...] Italy needs programs in terms of the construction of nuclear power stations.[10]

The pro-nuclear position of the DC did not change during the whole 1980s decade, as the ecology movement had started its most active and visible phase of mobilization. In the party manifesto presented for the 1983 political elections, the DC urged for the construction "at fast speed" of nuclear power stations in the country. Noticeably, the party did not even change its pro-nuclear position after the nuclear factory explosion of Chernobyl in 1986, the DC being among the few Italian parties that did not campaign for the repeal of nuclear energy for the national referendum promoted by the ecology movement.[11]

Drawing as a conclusion that the ecology movement had no impact at all on the DC discourse would, however, be inappropriate. A closer qualitative analysis of the DC documents reveals, for example, that the DC's manifestos published in the 1980s, after the movement's emergence, all included specific sections dedicated to the environment, previously absent. Another indication of the impact of the ecologist mobilization on the party is the publication of special issues dedicated to the environment in the party's weekly journal *La Discussione*, and the publication, from 1981 onwards, of a thematic page focusing on environmental matters.[12] Here in particular, several articles discussed

---

[10] DC Secretary's opening speech to the 14th DC Congress (1980). *Atti del XIV Congresso nazionale della Democrazia Cristiana*. Rome: Edizioni Cinque Lune, 1982.

[11] The 1987 referendum on nuclear energy comprised three norms that citizens could abrogate. The DC campaigned for one "Yes" and two "No" compared to the three "Yes" demanded by the referendum promoters. The DC agreed that the decision-making power on the location of nuclear power stations should be shifted to a more representative institutional organ (as opposed to the inter-Ministerial Committee that previously held this power). Instead, it voted against the repeal of the second and third referendum questions, thus favoring state support to those regions accepting the location of nuclear power factories on their territory, and Italian participation to international nuclear energy projects.

[12] "Pagina Ambiente" ("Environment page") appeared for the first time in the DC weekly journal *La Discussione* on March 16, 1981.

some of the core claims raised by the ecology movement in Italy, such as the connection between economic progress and environmental quality, the quantitatively oriented model of economic growth, nuclear energy, and durable energy resources. The ecology movement's impact on the DC discourse was marginal, and the party was far from being supportive of the movement's claims. However, the movement's mobilization solicited an internal discussion within the party and brought attention to environmental issues as never before.

Impact on the DC organization

A similar pattern as above emerges when observing the ecologists' impact at the organizational level of the party. Overall, the DC never supported any of the social initiatives of the ecology movement, nor did it create inter-organizational linkages with ecology groups. On the contrary, through statements in the party journals, the party regularly criticized ecology activists, accusing them of being "enemies of progress," "promoters of a counter-productive culture," "emotionally-driven," and scientifically unprepared.[13] Despite not providing its support, however, the DC introduced an internal workgroup, the Ufficio per i Problemi dell'Ambiente (Office for Environmental Problems). The objective of this office, established in 1982, was to conduct research on environmental issues and promote environmental culture within the party.[14] Overall, the office had a very limited role in the internal structure of the party, and scarce were the logistical and human resources it was allocated. However, the establishment of this office points to an internal party change following the ecology movement's emergence, which demanded higher attention from the party to environmental issues.

Conclusions

This chapter does not make the claim that having impact on political parties are the only, or the most relevant, political outcomes of social

[13] Citations from the DC journals *La Discussione* (July 6, 1977; December 16, 1985; April 1, 1986) and *Il Popolo* (May 5–6, 1986).
[14] Archivio della Democrazia Cristiana, "Direzione Nazionale", inv.nr. 57.787. Istituto Luigi Sturzo, Roma.

movements. As underlined in the introduction, to have an impact on parties has hardly ever been an articulated social movement goal, the situation being best described as an unintended outcome of social movements, as by-product lying outside their stated programs (Tilly 1999; Jenkins and Form 2005). Yet, changes in existing practices of parties around the main themes of the movements' mobilizations are highly relevant for the social movements' outcomes in the institutional arena of politics. It is only by entering the parties' agendas that social movements' demands gain wider attention, and are more likely to produce broader, possibly long-term societal and political consequences. Impact, in this perspective, should be seen as the very first stage in the longer chain of interaction between social movements and parties.

Overall, the relationship between social movements and political parties is largely under-theorized. Studies focusing on the relationships between social movements and political parties have traditionally looked at political parties of the left. Indeed, the left-wing parties have been more inclined to take on board social movements' demands and provide their support to the movements' mobilizations. Explanations are conventionally found in the electoral benefits deriving from social movements' support, patterns of cumulative involvement of left-wing party members in social movements' activities, and affinity between the left-wing parties and the social movements' identities. The analysis conducted in this chapter does not challenge the importance of these factors in shaping the interaction between social movements and parties. Among the two cases examined, it is indeed the left-wing PvdA showing higher responsiveness to the ecology movement as compared to the Italian Christian Democrats. However, this chapter has shown that the traditional explanations for the social movement-party interactions are far from exhaustive. First, they fail explaining cases of social movement impact beyond left-wing parties. The case of the Italian Christian Democrats, presented as a least-likely case of social movement impact due to the party's sociological, political and cultural distance from the social movement family, showed that the ecology movement provoked changes – even though marginal and remote from the movement's goals – at both discursive and organizational levels of the party. Second, they fail to explain why social movement impact on parties does not translate into partisan support. The case of the Dutch Social Democratic party, presented on turn as a most-likely case of social movements' impact because of the party's closeness to the social movement family and to environmental issues, showed that despite the fact that the ecology move-ment's impact was significant at both levels of party discourse and orga-nization, the PvdA did not fully embrace the ecologists' positions. Taken together, the two cases reveal a two-fold pattern: that mobilizations are always "worth the effort," as they are able to promote changes across a wider spectrum of party actors than the literature has con-ventionally envisaged; and, at the same time, that even when windows of opportunities are wide open for social movements, parties do not provide indiscriminate support. They will filter social movements' demands, unavoidably distorting and transforming them, through their individual logics and institutional priorities.

To conclude, the relationship between social movements and parties is complex and faces significant challenges at the methodological and theoretical levels. In order to have a more thorough understanding, research should consider the different ways in which social movement and parties interact and explore the different conditions that play a role at each stage of their interaction.

References

Amenta, E. and N. Caren. 2004. "The Legislative, Organizational and Beneficiary Consequences of State-Oriented Challangers." In D.A. Snow, S.A. Soule, and H. Kriesi (eds.), *The Blackwell Companion to Social Movements*. Malden, MA: Blackwell Publishing, Ltd, 461–488.

Amenta, E., N. Caren, E. Chiarello, and Y. Su. 2010. "The Political Consequences of Social Movements." *Annual Review of Sociology*, 36: 287–307.

Amenta, E., B.G. Carruthers, and Y. Zylan. 1992. "A Hero for the Aged? The Townsend Movement, the Political Mediation Model, and U.S. Old-Age Policy, 1934–1950." *American Journal of Sociology*, 98: 308–339.

Beckwith, K. 2000. "Beyond Compare? Women's Movements in Comparative Perspective." *European Journal of Political Research*, 37: 431–468.

Bosi, L. and M. Giugni. 2012. "The Impact of Protest Movements on the Establishment: Dimensions, Models, Approaches." In K. Fahlenbrach, M. Klimke, J. Scharloth, and L. Wong (eds.), *The*

'Establishment' Responds. Power, Politics, and Protest since 1945. New York; London: Palgrave Macmillan, 17–28.

Caciagli, M. 1992. "Doomed to Govern? Christian Democracy in the Italian Political System." In M. Caciagli et al. (eds.), *Christian Democracy in Europe*. Barcelona: Inst. Ciènc. Polit. Soc., 7–27.

Clemens, E.S. 1993. "Organizational Repertoires and Institutional Change: Women's Groups and the Transformation of U.S. Politics, 1890–1920." *American Journal of Sociology*, 98(4): 755–798.

Costain, A.N. and A.S. McFarland (eds.). 1998. *Social Movements and American Political Institutions: People, Passions, and Power*. Lanham, MD: Rowman & Littlefield.

Della Porta, D. and D. Rucht. 1995. "Left-Libertarian Movements in Context: A Comparison of Italy and West Germany, 1965–1990." In J.C. Jenkins and B. Klandermans (eds.), *The Politics of Social Protest: Comparative Perspectives On States and Social Movements*. Minneapolis, MN: University of Minnesota Press, 229–272.

Della Seta, R. 2000. *La difesa dell'ambiente in Italia. Storia e cultura del movimento ecologista*. Milan: Franco Angeli.

Diani, M. 1988. *Isole nell'arcipelago: Il movimento ecologista in Italia*. Bologna: Il Mulino.

Diani, M. 1995. *Green Networks: A Structural Analysis of the Italian Environmental Movement*. Edinburgh: Edinburgh University Press.

Doowon, S. 2006. "Civil Society in Political Democratization: Social Movement Impacts and Institutional Politics." *Development and Society*, 35(2): 173–195.

Duyvendak J.W. and R. Koopmans. 1992. "Protest in een pacificatie-democratie. Nieuwe sociale bewegingen en het Nederlandse politieke systeem." In J.W. Duivendak, H.A. Van Den Heyden, R. Koopmans, and L. Wijmans (eds.), *Tussen Verbeelding en Macht: 25 jaar nieuwe sociale bewegingen in Nederland*. Amsterdam: Sua, 233–256.

Duyvendak, J.W. and R. Van Huizen. 1983. *Nieuwe sociale bewegingen in Nederland, een onderzoek naar de kraakbeweging, de vredesbeweging en de anti-kernenergie beweging*. Zwolle: SVAG-Studies.

Gamson, W.A. 1975. *The Strategy of Social Protest*. Homewood, IL: The Dorsey Press.

Gerring, J. 2007. "Is there a (Viable) Crucial-Case Method?" *Comparative Political Studies*, 40(3): 231–253.

Giugni, M. 1998. "Was it Worth the Effort? The Outcomes and Consequences of Social Movements." *Annual Review of Sociology*, 24: 371–393.

Giugni, M., D. McAdam, and C. Tilly (eds.). 1999. *How Social Movements Matter*. Minneapolis: University of Minnesota Press.

Giugni, M. and F. Passy. 1998. "Social Movements and Policy Change: Direct, Mediated, or Joint Effect?." *American Sociological Association Section on Collective Behavior and Social Movements*, Working Paper Series, 1(4).

Goldstone, J.A. 2003. "Introduction: Bridging Institutionalized and Noninstitutionalized Politics." In J.A. Goldstone (ed.), *State, Parties and Social Movements*. Cambridge: Cambridge University Press, 1–25.

Hanagan, M. 1998. "Social Movements: Incorporation, Disengagement, and Opportunities – A Long View." In M. Giugni, D. McAdam, C. Tilly, and W. Gamson (eds.), *From Contention to Democracy*. Lanham, MD: Rowman and Littlefield Publishers, 3–30.

Irwin, G.A. and J.J.M. Van Holsteyn. 1989. "Towards a More Open Model of Competition." In H. Daalder and G. Irwin (eds.), *Politics in the Netherlands: How Much Change?*. London: Frank Cass, 112–138.

Jamison, A., R. Eyerman, and J. Kramer. 1990. *The Making of the New Environmental Consciousness: A Comparative Study of the Environmental Movements in Sweden, Denmark and the Netherlands*. Edinburgh: Edinburgh University Press.

Jenkins, J.C. and W. Form. 2005. "Social Movements and Social Change." In T. Janoski, R. Alford, A. Hicks, and M.A. Schwartz (eds.), *The Handbook of Political Sociology: States, Civil Societies, and Globalization*. Cambridge: Cambridge University Press, 331–349.

King, B.G., M. Cornwall, and E.C. Dahlin. 2005. "Winning Woman Suffrage One Step at a Time: Social Movements and the Logic of the Legislative Process." *Social Forces*, 83: 1211–1234.

Kitschelt, H.P. 1990. "New Social Movements and the Decline of Party Organisation." In R.J. Dalton and M. Kuechler (eds.), *Challenging the Political Order*. Cambridge: Polity Press, 179–208.

Kolb, F. 2007. *Protest and Opportunities. The Political Outcomes of Social Movements*. Frankfurt; New York: Campus Verlag.

Kraatz, M. and E. Block. 2008. "Organizational Implications of Institutional Pluralism." In R. Greenwood, C. Oliver, R. Suddaby, and K. Sahlin-Andersson (eds.), *Handbook of Organizational Institutionalism*. London: Sage Publication, 243–275.

Kriesi, H. 1993. *Political Mobilization and Social Change: The Dutch Case in Comparative Perspective*. Aldershot: Avebury.

Kriesi, H., R. Koopmans, J.W. Duyvendak, and M. Giugni. 1995. *New Social Movements in Western Europe: A Comparative Analysis*. Minneapolis: University of Minnesota Press.

Kriesi, H. and D. Wisler. 1999. "The Impact of Social Movements on Political Institutions: A Comparison of the Introduction of Direct Legislation in Switzerland and the United States." In M. Giugni, D. McAdam, and C. Tilly (eds.), *How Social Movements Matter*. Minneapolis: University of Minnesota Press, 42–66.

Lange, P. 1980. "Crisis and Consent, Change and Compromise: Dilemmas of Italian Communism in the 1970s." In P. Lange and S. Tarrow (eds.), *Italy in Transition: Conflict and Consensus*. London: Frank Cass, 110–132.

Lijphart, A. 1968. *The Politics of Accommodation: Pluralism and Democracy in the Netherlands*. Berkeley: University of California Press.

Lofland, J. 1996. *Social Movement Organizations. Guide to Research on Insurgent Realities*. New Brunswick, NJ: Transaction Publishers.

McAdam, D., and Y. Su. 2002. "The War at Home: Antiwar Protests and Congressional Voting, 1965 to 1973." *American Sociological Review*, 67(5): 696–672.

McAdam, D., S. Tarrow, and C. Tilly. 2001. *Dynamics of Contention*. Cambridge: Cambridge University Press.

Norris, P. 2002. *Democratic Phoenix: Reinventing Political Activism*. Cambridge: Cambridge University Press.

Piccio, D.R. 2011. "Party Responses to Social Movements. A Comparative Analysis of Italy and the Netherlands in the 1970s and 1980s." Doctoral Dissertation. Florence: European University Institute.

Raniolo F. (ed.). 2004. *Le trasformazioni dei partiti politici*. Soveria Mannelli: Rubbettino.

Rucht, D. 2004. "Movement Allies, Adversaries, and Third Parties." In D.A. Snow, S.A. Soule, and H. Kriesi (eds.), *The Blackwell Companion to Social Movements*. Blackwell Publishing, Ltd, 197–216.

Rüdig, W. 1988. "Peace and Ecology Movements in Western Europe." *West European Politics*, 10(1): 26–39.

Sartori, G. 1976. *Parties and Party Systems: A Framework of Analysis*. Cambridge: Cambridge University Press.

Tarrow, S. 1994. *Power in Movement. Social Movements, Collective Action and Politics.* Cambridge: Cambridge University Press.

Tilly, C. 1999. "From Interactions to Outcomes in Social Movements." In M. Giugni, D. McAdam, and C. Tilly (eds.), *How Movements Matter.* Minneapolis, MN: University of Minnesota Press, 253–270.

Walgrave, S. and R. Vliegenthart. 2012. "The Complex Agenda-Setting Power of Protest: Demonstrations, Media, Parliament, Government, and Legislation in Belgium, 1993–2000." *Mobilization: An International Journal,* 17(2), 129–156.

Wiardi Beckman Stichting (WBS). *Om de kwaliteit van het bestaan* (I – de besteding van groei van het nationaal inkomen'(1963); III – Beter wonen (1963); IV – Luchtverontreiniging (1965)). Amsterdam: N.V. De Arbeiderspers.

Election manifestos & archival sources

PvdA

1971: "Verkiezingsprogramma 1971–1975."
1977: "Voorwaarts, en niet vergeten."
1981: "Weerwerk."
1986: "De toekomst is van iedereen."
(Documentatiecentrum Nederlandse Politieke Partijen, Groningen)
Party archive: Archief Partij van de Arbeid, Internationaal Instituut voor Sociale Geschiedenis (IISG), Amsterdam.

DC

1976: "Il programma della DC."
1979: "La DC chiede maggiori consensi per un'Italia libera e stabile". Il Popolo, May 12, 1979.
1983: "Un programma per garantire lo sviluppo." Il Popolo, May 5–6, 1983.
1987: "Un programma per l'Italia", Il Popolo, April 24–25, 1987.
(Istituto Luigi Sturzo, Rome)
Party archive: Archivio della Democrazia Cristiana, Istituto Luigi Sturzo, Roma.

12 WATERSHED EVENTS AND CHANGES IN PUBLIC ORDER MANAGEMENT SYSTEMS

Organizational adaptation as a social movement outcome

Mattias Wahlström

Research on protest policing has become an important niche within social movement studies. There is widespread acknowledgement in this field that police strategies and tactics are in part an adaptation to contemporary forms of protest and that this adaption has occurred through a process of tactical interaction and gradual institutionalization of different forms of protests (Combes and Fillieule 2011). However, thus far police organizational adaptation has not been explicitly framed as a type of social movement outcome. The argument in this chapter is that analyzing police organizational change in response to protest events as a social movement outcome contributes to a better understanding of both consequences of social movements and developments in protest policing.

Research on social movement outcomes has previously focused on political, cultural, and biographical outcomes (Giugni 2008). Outcomes regarding changes in *institutionalized organizational practices* do not fall neatly into any of these categories and have received considerably less attention (for an exception, see Zald et al. 2005). Furthermore, this type of social movement outcome is largely *unintended* (Tilly 1999). It is related less to the substantial demands and framings of social movements than to the "repertoires of action" (Tilly 1978) associated with movements and protest campaigns.

Historically, government interest in suppressing violent protests during the early to mid-nineteenth century played a significant role in the development of the modern police force. In Britain, concerns about riots and social disorder were used to justify the creation of modern police forces (Reiner 1998, 2000). Similarly, in Sweden the failure of the city guards to contain the March 1848 riots in Stockholm, which resulted in the death of eighteen protesters, constituted a tipping point in a process that led to a modernized Stockholm city police authority (Furuhagen 2004). Presumably, it was not only fear of a popular uprising among the ruling class that contributed to such events. Compared to most other police tasks, large-scale public order policing is a generally far more public and direct measure of police performance. Crowd control failures are difficult to conceal and likely to lead to criticism and political pressure for reform.

Later examples of the impact of protests on police organizations include the development of a "negotiated management" approach to protest policing in response to protests during the late 1960s and early 1970s (McCarthy and McPhail 1998). The massive wave of anti-globalization summit protests since the end of the 1990s also posed policing challenges and gave rise to potentially lasting adaptations in national protest policing styles (cf. della Porta et al. 2006). The present analysis focuses on Denmark and Sweden, where the links between recent watershed events and subsequent reforms are clear-cut and easily traceable. These two cases are compared with three other major contemporary protest events in Italy, the United Kingdom, and the United States, respectively, in order to identify central factors for differences in outcomes. In all cases the police failed spectacularly and were consequently subject to considerable criticism. In Denmark, Sweden, the United Kingdom, and the United States, events led to identifiable changes in protest policing styles; in Italy no significant changes could be linked to the event.

The time frame of the cases is roughly the period of frequent summit protests that began with the 1999 World Trade Organization (WTO) meeting in Seattle. The watershed event in the Danish case occurred earlier, but the new protest policing style developed subsequently was not put to a real test until the 2002 European Union (EU) summit in Copenhagen. Thus the cases are all in the context of the same wave of protests and are interdependent in terms of international learning processes.

This analysis is based on: a review of research on protest policing, an analysis of post-event evaluation reports, and an empirical research project on protest policing in Sweden and Denmark. The latter included observations of police training in protest policing, interviews with political activists, and interviews with police officers of different ranks (Wahlström 2011).[1] Below, the relevant literature on both protest policing and social movement outcomes is reviewed. The five empirical cases are then presented, followed by an analysis of the role of protesters and social movement activists in police organizational change.

Theories about police organizational adaptation and movement outcomes

Protest policing: tactics, styles, and public order management systems

Just as social movements adapt to various forms of repression by authorities, police forces adjust their intervention tactics to the tactical repertoires and scale of political protests. During intensive protest periods, these two tendencies may combine into what McAdam (1983) labelled tactical interaction. From an organizational perspective, such tactical innovations are best understood as elements of police organizations' *continuous* changes in adapting to their environments. However, occasionally police organizations undergo radical *episodic* change (Weick and Quinn 1999) as they undertake fundamental revisions of protest policing strategies. In the academic literature on protest policing, such transformations are conceptualized as changes in "protest policing styles" or, more comprehensively, as introductions of new, or modified, "public order management systems" (POMS) (McCarthy et al. 1999; Noakes and Gillham 2006). The POMS concept includes broad organizational arrangements with five components:

> (1) civilian and/or military police organizations, (2) the public order policies of these organizations, (3) these organizations' programs for recruiting and training personnel (civilian or military) to enact these policies, (4) the actual practices of these policing personnel, and (5) the technology and equipment used while carrying out these practices.
>
> *(McPhail et al. 1998: 64)*

"Protest policing style" focuses attention on the fourth and, to some extent, the second and fifth components. Broadly speaking, most

---

[1] This chapter is based in part on the introduction to the author's doctoral dissertation (Wahlström 2011).

Western democracies have developed during the latter half of the twentieth century from exhibiting a more rigid "escalated force style" of protest policing to a more flexible and facilitating "negotiated management" of protests (McPhail et al. 1998). However, protest policing styles are seldom entirely consistent and there are regional and national cases that diverge from the general pattern (Rafail 2014).

A number of factors have an impact on the predominant style of protest policing. These include: the legal framework; the current configuration of political power; the predominant discourses in mainstream media; the structure, culture, and technology available to the police organization; and the characteristics of contemporary social movements (della Porta and Reiter 1998, 2006b). International factors include structures for coordination and communication between police forces and the degree of openness or closure of international institutions to demands from civil society. Ultimately, global processes such as the rise of the neoliberal economic system may be taken into account (Wood 2014). According to della Porta and Reiter, all factors are filtered through "police knowledge" – i.e., the police officers' collective constructions of external reality (della Porta and Reiter 1998). Related to this is "police philosophy," i.e., the dominant perceptions among police officers of their role in society (Winter 1998). Both police knowledge and police philosophy should be treated as typically being more conscious, variable, and (in the case of police knowledge) practically applied aspects of the broader phenomenon, "police culture" (Loftus 2009; Wahlström 2007).

Several authors have observed that specific "watershed events" sometimes trigger rapid change in police strategies and POMS (e.g., King 2006). Such events typically involve policing failures: spectacular losses of control, injured police officers, and/or wounded demonstrators or onlookers. Generally, organizational changes are preceded by crises and failures because such events force organizations to reconsider practices that have been previously taken for granted (Powell 1991). Reiner (1998) notes that senior police officers portray the tactical and strategic changes in British protest policing as reactions to new public order challenges manifested as failures during specific events (including the 1976 Notting Hill riots and the 1980 Bristol riots). Similarly, in Italy and Germany the protest waves between the 1960s and 1980s contributed to reformation of the old POMS (della Porta 1995). However, we still lack systematic knowledge about how protest events contribute to police organizational change and how characteristics of events might contribute to the character of POMS changes.

Episodic police organizational change as a social movement outcome

Zald and colleagues (2005) provide a rare example of a general analysis of social movements' impact on organizations.[2] The authors identify three factors that affect organizations' response to pressures from social movements: (1) the ideological commitments among the prominent organization members to the movement's goals, (2) the organizational capacity to implement new procedures, and (3) environmental pressures (surveillance and sanctions). Although protesters' influence on police tactics is usually unintended, the factors mentioned by Zald and colleagues can be adapted to fit this class of cases. "Ideological commitment" can in the present case be translated into the dominant police philosophy, as well as the internal evaluations in response to specific events. "Organizational capacity" can be interpreted as financial resources, availability of professional competence, and centralization of police organizations. "Pressure" can be interpreted here as the character of external evaluations and pressure from public opinion.

Major protest events are potential windows of opportunity for social movement activists to influence public opinion about protest policing, or even to direct lobbying for change in the police organization. Della Porta (1999) pointed to the development of more differentiated framing of demonstrators in Italian and German public discourse as a result of protracted protest campaigns between the 1960s and the 1980s. In response to changes in public opinion, police forces adopted differentiated tactics.

Previous research indicates that pressure from public opinion results in policing strategy changes via the police knowledge of high-ranking police officers (della Porta and Reiter 1998) who consider their own interpretation of events, and sometimes also those of lower-ranking officers, politicians, external experts and/or representatives of the security industry (Wood 2014). As in other organizations, external influences have a stronger potential to instigate organizational reform

[2] See also King (2008).

if they are challenges to police organizational *legitimacy* (Ashworth et al. 2009; DiMaggio and Powell 1983). According to Suchman (1995), three general types of organizational legitimacy can be distinguished: *pragmatic* legitimacy (whether important stakeholders regard the activities of an organization as beneficial to them), *moral* legitimacy (whether an organization is perceived by its stakeholders to do the right thing), and *cognitive* legitimacy (whether an organization and its activities are generally understood and even taken for granted). In principle, legitimacy is dichotomous, a matter of either/or, but in practice an organization can be more or less *clearly* or *firmly* legitimate among different actors (Deephouse and Suchman 2008).

The pragmatic legitimacy of the police is related to its capacity to uphold the law and maintain order and security. In non-authoritarian states, the police also need to sustain a general sense of moral legitimacy, which is linked to tolerance of demonstrators and upholding the right to public expression. This aspect of police legitimacy is challenged when protest is violently repressed and people are hurt, provided the protesters and their tactics are generally considered morally acceptable. (From the perspective of the protesters, this is also a question about pragmatic legitimacy.) In modern times, police forces generally have a high degree of cognitive legitimacy, given that most people take the institution completely for granted. Nevertheless, in cases of harsh police repression of peaceful protesters some may begin to question the previously taken-for-granted police legitimacy in maintaining public order. Another aspect of cognitive legitimacy is the comprehensibility of police interventions – that they are not perceived as arbitrary or governed by a hidden agenda.

When reacting to perceived external challenges to organizational legitimacy, actors within police organizations respond in the context of organizational myths (Meyer and Rowan 1977). In order to protect the organization's central myths, organizations may try to rescue established practices through merely revising formal principles while *decoupling* their actual practices, which remain largely unchanged.

As we will see below, the contents of the national POMS reforms are influenced by international diffusion. In line with aspects of DiMaggio and Powell's (1983) theory of institutional isomorphism, McCarthy et al. (1999) pointed to *coercive* and *mimetic* mechanisms of POMS diffusion. In the present cases, mimetic isomorphism

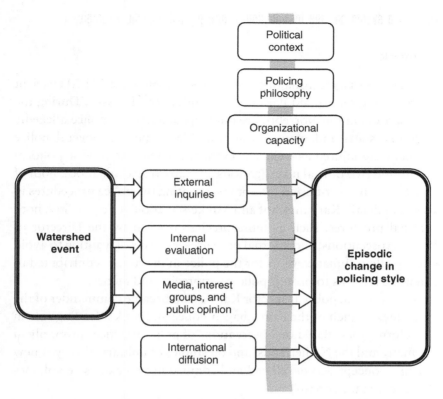

Figure 12.1 Processes leading to episodic change in protest policing styles.

(imitating practices of foreign police forces) may be triggered by traumatic protest events, while coercion (enforced change in practices) is expressed through external evaluations and in top-down implementation of new POMS on a national level. Della Porta and Tarrow (2012) further identify three processes involved in international diffusion of police and protester behavior: active *promotion* of strategies by some police agencies, internal and external *assessments* after failures, and *theorization* of new strategic and operational models.

Figure 12.1 summarizes the main mechanisms outlined in the last two sections. When we turn to the two main cases, and the three complementary cases, the general goals are to determine the role of social movements in instigating police organizational change through protest and how activists' actions, and the character of protest events, may affect the character of change.

Watershed events and the introduction of new protest policing strategies

Denmark

On May 18, 1993, a majority of Danes accepted the EU Maastricht treaty during the second national referendum on the issue. During the ensuing riots in the Nørrebro area in Copenhagen, the police allegedly fired 113 shots and wounded at least eleven people. Several police officers were injured as well. The event was subject to intense political debate and two official investigations (cf. Christrup et al. 2000), both of which have been criticized for not investigating the police procedures in sufficient detail (Karpantschof and Mikkelsen 2008: note 50). Still, both external pressures, such as more precise criticism by the Director of Public Prosecutions, and internal pressures, in terms of wanting to avoid any equally traumatic events for the police in the future, contributed to extensive reforms to protest policing strategies and tactics.

In 1996, police inspector Kai Vittrup became commander of the uniformed branch of the Copenhagen Police and took a leading role in the reform work. Based on observations of police practices primarily in Germany and the Netherlands, and on studies of military history, a new policing concept was developed and codified in two extensive volumes (Vittrup 2003a, 2003b).

Prior to the 1990s, the main developments in Danish protest policing had concerned improved equipment, including the introduction of tear gas. Under new police leadership the goal was to create a more flexible style of policing that, depending on the situation, could become more offensive. A central tenet of the tactical model was to remove law-breaking and disorderly individuals from the crowd by snatch squads. These operational principles were put into practice using armored and lightly armored vehicles already used in the Netherlands, and officers were expected to operate primarily without shields and truncheons to facilitate selective arrests. While stressing the need for negotiations, the model also includes repressive forms of interventions beyond the time and place of the protest. This is expressed through the principles of guerrilla warfare; i.e., to be defensive when the opponent is on the offensive, to be offensive when the opponent is defensive, and to strike when the opponent is weak (Vittrup 2003a: 103).

The new "mobile concept" was put to test in connection with the 2002 EU summit in Copenhagen, which included protecting visiting international leaders. The events at the EU summit in Gothenburg (see below) were used by the Danish police as a cautionary example that contributed to the government's decision to invest additional money in a large number of lightly armored vehicles demanded by the police. During the meeting, there were hardly any violent confrontations between the police and protesters and no serious attempts were made by demonstrators to force the blockades to the EU summit. However, the police operation was marked by a number of repressive proactive strategies, such as checkpoints in the city where people with "suspicious appearances" were frisked, and some blatant shows of force[3] that led to demonstrators feeling criminalized (Peterson 2006; Wahlström and Oskarsson 2006).

Conflicts between police and radical groups escalated in 2006 and 2007, in anticipation of the demolition of the regionally well-known squat and music venue Ungdomshuset (the Youth House) (Karpantschof and Lindblom 2009). In March 2007, the house was evacuated by the police in a military-style operation that was kept secret until its execution. The evacuation ended with several injured demonstrators (Karpantschof 2009: 70). Subsequently, frustrated youth and activists rioted in the streets with little police control.

The United Nations Climate Change Conference hosted by Copenhagen in December 2009 attracted a number of large protests, including a demonstration by 40,000–100,000 participants (Wahlström et al. 2013). While the police generally kept a low profile, a conflict in one section of the march resulted in a much-criticized mass detention of 968 demonstrators, of whom 955 were released later that night without prosecution (Ritzau 2009).

In 2001 the Danish government had changed from a social democratic and liberal government coalition to a liberal conservative government, which passed a number of laws extending the coercive capacities of the police in relation to demonstrators (cf. Karpantschof and Mikkelsen 2008). The "terrorist package" increased the surveillance capacities of the police and introduced lifetime imprisonment as a potential sentence for several activities related to a very imprecise definition of terrorism (Vestergaard 2006). The introduction of "frisking

---

[3] That is, the police tactic of deliberately lining up its resources (i.e., armored vehicles and police officers in protective equipment) in a disciplined way, in order to intimidate potential "troublemakers" (Vittrup 2003a: 97–100).

zones" allows the police to establish zones within which they have unlimited rights to stop and search. Since 2009, the so-called "rascal package" (Dk: lømmelpakken)[4] has allowed police to detain people for up to 12 hours without arrest and has radically increased the sentence for obstructing police work in conjunction with disorder. The 2009 mass detention of demonstrators was clearly facilitated by these laws allowing preventive detentions.

Sweden

The EU summit in Gothenburg took place on June 14–17, 2001, and included a visit by then US president George W. Bush. Whereas the largest protests (one against Bush and two against the EU) turned out to be orderly and peaceful, both on the part of demonstrators and the police, this was not true for other events on their periphery.

The Gothenburg municipality had provided visiting political demonstrators with accommodation at several schools. Coinciding with the arrival of the US president, Thursday, June 14, the commander of the police campaign decided to detain 500 people present at a school. This resulted in violent conflict around the school and a general build-up of tension and frustration among the activists. When, on Friday, a demonstration moving toward the summit venue put pressure on police cordons barring the road, the police made a rather blunt intervention that triggered a riot on the main avenue in Gothenburg. The under-manned police were temporarily forced to retreat from the avenue by a comparatively small number of determined rioters. During the contin-ued clashes with the protesters in a nearby park, the police opened fire and wounded three people.

After initial praise in the media, the police were subject to critical scrutiny not only by researchers and journalists (e.g., Björk and Peterson 2002; Löfgren and Vatankhah 2002) and the Helsinki Committee for Human Rights (Östberg 2002), but also by a Government Official Report (Göteborgskommittén 2002). The police preparations, tactics, and organizing in connection with the summit were criticized. The events during the EU summit were also formally assessed by the police in two reports (West Götaland Police Authority

---

[4] Formal name: "L 49 Forslag til lov om ændring af straffeloven og lov om politiets virksomhed."

2002; Swedish National Police Board 2001). Subsequently, two national projects on tactical development led to a 2004 report (Taktikutvecklingsprojektet 2004) containing a handful of suggestions concerning the adoption of a new "mobile concept" and the creation of a national reinforcement organization. These suggestions led to the introduction of the new "Special Police Tactics" (hereafter SPT).

Activists had a direct influence on this process in at least two ways. First, a large number were interviewed during the official governmental inquiry, providing their versions of events. Second, a few of the protesters were interviewed by officers at the National Police Board in connection with the early drafts of the new concept.

In 2005 SPT was codified in an official instruction manual (Danielsson et al. 2005). Whereas the Danish "mobile concept" directly influenced SPT, in terms of the overall strategic principles and its range of tactical maneuvers, from the start the Swedish concept included further developments, especially concerning its "communicative approach" (Wahlström 2007). The latter aspect of SPT involves prior negotiation with demonstrators, maintenance of openness to communication between individual police officers and demonstrators, and the development of specialized dialogue police units (Holgersson 2010). The Swedish National Police Board later hosted a research project in which the new police tactics were evaluated (Adang 2013; Swedish National Police Board 2010). The project recommendations were based on the "social identity model" in social psychology: to maintain a differentiated approach to the participants in a demonstration, to assure working communication with demonstrators, and to focus on facilitating the protestors' "legitimate" objectives (Reicher et al. 2007).

Following the EU summit, the Swedish police have not, thus far, faced any comparable challenges and the new policing model has been used primarily during sporting events. However, a series of extreme-right mourning marches in the Stockholm suburb Salem during 2001–2010 and concomitant anti-fascist counter-demonstrations serve as a rough indicator of the contemporary developments. Police tactics during these events ranged from reactive violence against anti-racists in 2003, to flexible and tolerant tactics during 2004–2005, followed by occasional proactive repression such as the mass detention of counter-demonstrators in 2008 (Wahlström 2010). The latter incident is a reminder of how the police easily fall back on undifferentiated and hard tactics despite theoretical knowledge and training in dialogue and a differentiated tactical approach.

Between 1994 and 2006 Sweden had a social democratic government and the head of the Gothenburg Committee was also a social democrat: former Swedish prime minister Ingvar Carlsson. In terms of legal innovations, a 2005 law was passed against demonstrators wearing masks as a consequence of debates related to the 2001 Gothenburg riots. So far this law has had very limited practical application. In 2009, another law was introduced that extended the legal capacities of the police to remove participants in a crowd from the location.

The United States

In 1999 protesters managed to temporarily shut down the WTO meeting in Seattle (Gillham and Marx 2000), an event that US police officials have characterized as comparable to Pearl Harbor for the US police forces (Noakes and Gillham 2007: 335). It was followed by a number of evaluations by the Seattle Police Department (2000), the Seattle City Council (2000), the American Civil Liberties Union (2000), and by R.M. McCarthy and Associates (2000). Although the conclusions of the different reports are quite disparate, two general themes can be distinguished: (1) the loss of control over protesters by an undermanned and insufficiently trained police force; and (2) the excessive violence against protesters, including the use of less-lethal weapons, by police officers lacking visible identification. Except for the ACLU report, these evaluations highlighted the need for improving mass arrest techniques for handling unruly protests.

The Seattle events provoked anxiety within US police organizations, perhaps caused not so much by the excessive repression of protesters as by the humiliating loss of control over the streets. Gillham (2011) describes how, in the wake of Seattle, federal and local law enforcement agencies in the United States organized national conferences and training to "develop and share neutralizing strategies useful for undermining the actions of transgressive protesters" (p. 639). Subsequently, new trends of a primarily more repressive type of protest policing could be observed in the United States and Canada, including large no-protest zones, increased use of surveillance, and proactive tactics such as pre-emptive arrests (Noakes and Gillham 2006; Rafail 2010; Vitale 2007; Wood 2007). Noakes and Gillham (2006) propose the label "strategic incapacitation" to characterize the emerging style of protest policing in response to the failures of the previously dominant "negotiated management" approach, harmonizing with contemporary developments in crime policy. Strategic incapacitation is based on a readiness to use harsh repression *selectively* at all stages of protest events in order to incapacitate "risk groups."

One must not underestimate the effects of the September 11 terrorist attacks in 2001 and the introduction of the US Patriot Act on protest policing. The increased tendency of authorities to regard expressions of dissent as a threat to US security appears to have taken the sting out of any post-Seattle concerns for constitutional rights and prepared the ground for the spread of new less-lethal technologies for public order policing, such as pepper spray, Tasers, and flash-bang grenades (Wood 2014). The "protest as threat" discourse is also evident in the federally coordinated monitoring of the Occupy protests in 2011 (The Partnership for Civil Justice Fund 2012). Although these protests were actually met with a relatively tolerant police approach in some cities, they were harshly repressed in other locations (Gillham et al. 2013; Vitale 2012).

Italy

After the Seattle protests, police forces in Europe began adopting new tactics to implement the tactical innovations of the Global Justice Movement (della Porta et al. 2006; della Porta and Tarrow 2012). The 2001 G8 summit in Genoa, which took place about a month after the Gothenburg EU summit, stands out as one of the most violent events, with Italian protester Carlo Giuliani fatally shot by a *carabiniere* (della Porta and Reiter 2006a). Schools inhabited by visiting activists were also brutally raided by Italian police, resulting in a number of seriously injured activists. After a long legal process, twenty-five police officers were found guilty in 2010 of falsifying evidence, grievous bodily harm, and libel (Kington 2012). An Interior Ministry committee report on the Genoa events recommended, inter alia, more extensive police training on relations with protesters and institutionalization of police contact groups (della Porta and Reiter 2006a). However, the Prodi government's proposition to initiate a "full parliamentary commission" was voted down by parliament.

Della Porta and Reiter (2006a) found only limited tactical changes by the Italian police resulting from the G8 experience. With respect to police organizational changes, they argued that "the Genoa events did not lead to a full debate on structural problems but to specific adjustments on the occasion of individual events" (p. 40). In an analysis of a demonstration in Rome on October 15, 2011, della Porta and Zamponi (2013) identified "selective incapacitation tactics typical of the policing of transnational protest in the early 2000s" (p. 78). The apparent failure to initiate any extensive reforms within the Italian police should be seen in the light of (1) the complexity of having three different domestic police organizations which are not perfectly coordinated, as well as (2) the Italian policing philosophy that emphasizes protection of the state from the people (della Porta 1998; della Porta and Reiter 2006a).

The United Kingdom

In 2009, British police forces were shaken by events during protests against the London G20 meeting. This was not the first major protest in the United Kingdom in response to an international summit. Neither was it the first occasion in that decade when the British police used controversial methods of repression, such as "kettling." A media scandal was created by the death of a bystander and video images proving that he was beaten by a police officer just before his collapse (Rosie and Gorringe 2009). The subsequent Home Office report on how to improve British protest policing suggests future emphasis on the facilitation of protest and included a specific chapter on Swedish "dialogue policing" (Her Majesty's Chief Inspector of Constabulary 2010). The UK National Policing Improvement Agency (NPIA) also revised its *Manual of Guidance on Keeping the Peace* (NPIA 2010).

Recent studies indicate that the recommendations in the HMIC report have affected British protest policing – at least in some areas – in terms of a stronger emphasis on the strategic role of specially trained teams of liaison officers who can act as intermediaries and convey a more nuanced picture of activist perspectives to police commanders (Baker 2011; Gorringe et al. 2011; Stott et al. 2013; Waddington 2013). However, this possible trend toward facilitation and dialogue is counterpoised by evidence of increased activist surveillance by police (Gilmore 2010) and increased training in the use of less-lethal weaponry such as "accelerated energy projectiles" (Stott et al. 2013). In other words, it appears that significant adaptations have taken place in response to the 2009 G20 events, albeit reflecting long-standing tension between negotiated management and militarization of British protest policing (Jefferson 1990; Waddington 1994). The development of public order policing in the United Kingdom has likely also been shaped by experiences during subsequent major public order events, such as the student protests and the 2011 London riots.

Summary

Denmark and Sweden underwent the most significant POMS changes, including both increased emphasis on dialogue and facilitation, combined with selective and preemptive coercive strategies. The United Kingdom has shown similar tendencies, although arguably not as radical, whereas the post-Seattle (and 9/11) changes in the US public order policing appear to have been primarily repressive. Italy is the "negative case" where no clear-cut changes in POMS can be identified in response to the G8 protests in Genoa. The five cases are summarized in Table 12.1.

Analysis: watershed events and police reforms

In all but one of these cases, traumatic protest events triggered police organizational reform processes. Interviews with Danish and Swedish senior police officers indicate that without failures of this magnitude any reform processes would not have been initiated. Prior to the respective watershed events, both Danish and Swedish police used strategic and operational approaches to protest policing that appear to have been internally criticized infrequently, if at all. One might argue that *anticipation* of failure could be sufficient for change, exemplified by the international diffusion of police tactics triggered by the diffusion of protest forms (e.g., summit protests). While acknowledging this mechanism on the level of police tactics, I have nevertheless found no examples where a policing failure in one country has by itself triggered extensive organizational reform in other countries. This can be extrapolated into the general proposition that *unless drastic political changes occur, failure during a major protest is a necessary condition for episodic change affecting entire POMS.*

Table 12.1 *An overview of the major crowd control events and subsequent reforms discussed in the chapter*

Event	Policing failures			Mediating factors			Outcome
	Police loss of control over protesters	Dead or seriously injured protesters	Character of inquiry	Government at the time of public inquiry	Nationally predominant policing philosophy	Later events of importance	Reform of police strategies or organization
Maastricht Treaty protests Copenhagen, Denmark, 1993	Yes, extensive rioting exacerbated by police actions.	Yes, 11 shot, yet none mortally wounded.	Vague criticism, later specified by Director of Public Prosecutions.	Social democratic. Replaced by liberal conservatives in 2001.	Strong Bürgerpolizei approach.	New strategies demonstrated during EU summit in 2002.	New POMS. Focus on selectivity, mobility, and proactivity complemented by communicative tactics.
WTO meeting, Seattle, USA, 1999	Yes, major loss during first day of protests.	Excessive use of force but no lethally injured protesters.	A number of contradictory inquiries.	Democratic president, Bill Clinton (replaced by George W. Bush in 2001).	Weak Bürgerpolizei approach. Increasing tendencies toward Staatspolizei approach.	9/11 events. Increased focus on proactive security measures.	Trend toward "strategic incapacitation," including selective proactive repression and surveillance.

EU summit meeting, Gothenburg, Sweden, 2001	Yes, at specific locations.	Yes, three activists shot. One had life-threatening injuries.	Specific criticism in several inquiries. Activist voices in inquiries.	Social democratic.	Strong Bürgerpolizei approach.	No protest events of comparable size or importance.	New POMS inspired by Danish concept. Dialogue policing. Systematic evaluations.
G8 meeting, Genoa, Italy, 2001	Yes, at specific locations.	Yes, one protester shot to death.	Weak criticism. Legal processes against individual police officers.	Right-populist president Berlusconi.	Staatspolizei approach.	No events of comparable importance.	No major changes since Genoa.
G20 meeting, London, UK, 2009	Yes, at specific locations.	One bystander dead after being subject to police violence.	Specific criticism and some concrete proposals.	Labour. Replaced by conservative liberal coalition in 2010.	Strong Bürgerpolizei approach.	Student protests and London urban riots in 2011.	New guidelines. Stronger emphasis on negotiation, facilitation, and selectivity.

However, this type of event is far from sufficient for police organizational change, as exemplified by the Italian case. Several factors influence whether or not a reform process will be initiated. First, one crucial feature is the dominant mode of police philosophy (Winter 1998) within the national police organization(s), and whether the police regard themselves as primarily *Staatspolizei* – protecting the state against the people – or *Bürgerpolizei* – first and foremost protecting the rights of the citizens. This corresponds to Zald et al.'s (2005) notion of an organization's *ideological commitment*. In my interviews with both Danish and Swedish police officers, *Bürgerpolizei* rhetoric is prominent when accounting for change. Using excessive violence contradicts the self-image and outward performance of how police forces should act in predominantly consensual and corporatist societies (Wahlström 2007). The police officers also repeatedly distinguished their domestic police forces from those in other countries and set limits for what activities are possible in Scandinavia. In contrast, the stronger emphasis in Italian policing philosophy on protecting the state arguably made the police forces more resistant to change in response to cases of excessive police violence. In the United States, the 9/11 terrorist attacks also contributed to a stronger *Staatspolizei* approach, resulting in new strategies in which concerns for civil rights became increasingly limited.

Second, the political constellation of power may facilitate or impede change. Even in countries where the police are not tightly linked to the government, police forces remain sensitive to political messages and affected by the laws passed in parliament. Both Denmark and Sweden had social democratic governments when the post-event inquiries were initiated, as did Great Britain in 2009, which may have affected the composition and directives of the inquiry committees. In Italy, the Berlusconi government was not known for expressing liberal attitudes toward popular dissent, and in the United States the federal government has limited influence on police practices at state and city levels.

Third, the character and precision of conclusions from official inquiries appear to be crucial for providing motivation for, and direction of, change. According to the interviewed Danish police officers, some inquiries were neither sufficiently critical, nor precise enough, to instigate any particular reform. In the United States, the contradictions between interpretations in different inquiries led to greater potential for ignoring criticism of excessive violence. Both the political constellation of power and the external inquiries correspond to Zald et al.'s (2005) concept of *pressure*. In terms of *organizational capacity*, there are some indications that organizational centralization might be conductive to change – as in Denmark – while decentralization contributes to the absence of change – as in Italy. Financial resources often tend to become available when political elites consider improvements necessary.

These observations can be summed up in a second proposition: *criticism following extraordinary cases of police repression is more likely to lead to change in POMS if the police are relatively centralized, the national policing philosophy is dominated by a Bürgerpolizei approach, the political opportunity structure is generally open to extra-parliamentary protest groups, and the inquiry committees formulate precise and authoritative criticism of the police.*

In order to approach this as a social movement outcome, we need to know how actions of political protesters affected the initiation of episodic change in POMS. Obviously, no policing failures could occur if nobody staged demonstrations in the first place. Following the events, activists also had a role in formulating public criticism of the police and mobilized to raise public awareness of their version of the events, albeit to varying degrees of success. Also, in the Swedish case protesters were given significant space in the inquiry process and some also had the opportunity to convey their perspectives directly to the police. Consequently: *activists affect the instigation of police strategy and/or POMS change through protest organization and by publicly communicating their interpretations after the events.*

Finally, to explain how the protest events and subsequent inquiries affect the *trajectory* of the reform work, policing failures should be understood as challenges to police legitimacy. In Denmark and Sweden, the experiences of the policing failures were used as a basis for deciding to reform POMS, and the development of new strategies was retrospectively described by senior police officers as attempts to solve prior problems that manifested during the watershed events. The *moral legitimacy* of the police had been challenged by public reactions to blatantly excessive police violence, to the verbal abuse of protesters, and, moreover, to police officers firing live bullets at people. When the police have acted in ways that are regarded as excessive, a way to maintain the moral high-ground is to reorganize protest policing to minimize the risk of playing the role of "the villain" in future protest dramas. Thus, strategy reforms in response to challenges to police moral legitimacy are liable to include more subtle and discretionary tactics, and strategies to increase commanders' control of individual police officers, as well as police officers' self-control (Wahlström 2007). It should be emphasized that improved policing strategies to maintain the moral high-ground are not necessarily less repressive, even though they may be less obviously aggressive, as illustrated by the increasingly proactive strategies adopted in Denmark and Sweden (Peterson 2006; Wahlström 2010). Similarly, in the British case, "facilitation" was emphasized in response to the death of a demonstrator and the much-criticized penning tactics. Conversely, the moral legitimacy of the US police does not appear to have been seriously challenged after the 1999 events in Seattle, and the subsequent discourse of police officers in the United States seems to have become more critical of negotiation with activists (cf. Noakes et al. 2005).

All cases are also examples of challenges to the *pragmatic* legitimacy of the police with respect to its capacity to maintain order and uphold the law. The reforms address this by attempting to increase the effectiveness of crowd control strategies, i.e., improving the repressive capacity of the police. This is reflected in the more offensive aspects of the strategies and in the use of armored vehicles in Denmark and Sweden, and these approaches appear to have dominated American protest policing in the decade following Seattle and the 9/11 bombings.

In Sweden, the police also acknowledged the occasional loss of *cognitive* legitimacy among protesters when motives for police actions were perceived as obscure. The emphasis on negotiation and using dialogue units to continually communicate with protesters is a response to this. However, the general cognitive legitimacy of the police – that it is completely taken for granted as an institution – is typically so strong in democratic societies that it is not a prominent problem in police discourse on strategic development.

In sum, interactions between protesters and police during major protest events may lead to policing failures that challenge the legitimacy of the police in different ways. To the extent that such challenges are acknowledged by the police, their character sets some of the initial parameters for organizational change. In contemporary Western democracies, *significant challenges to the moral legitimacy of the police push reforms toward more differentiated and possibly more communicative approaches, while challenges to their pragmatic legitimacy highlight the need for more coercive strategies. Events that effectively challenge police cognitive legitimacy create incentives for increased transparency and communication.* These adaptive strategies are not mutually exclusive.

It is necessary to consider whether what appear to be substantial changes might simply be various forms of *decoupling* of organizational rhetoric – which easily adapts to maintain organizational legitimacy – from actual organizational practices – which are generally resistant to change (Meyer and Rowan 1977). Do police adaptations to maintain legitimacy involve changes in actual policing practices, or do they mainly amount to changes in rhetoric? No definite answer can be given because of the high degree of situational variation in protest policing strategies and tactics. However, unlike many organizational practices, protest policing is an inherently public activity, which makes it difficult to decouple rhetoric from practices that are often not only easily observable but also increasingly well-documented by activists (Askanius 2013). Therefore, the reforms documented in this chapter should not be dismissed as empty rhetoric. Nevertheless, we should be sensitive to the possibilities that the police may account for discrepancies between myth and practice by blaming the exceptional circumstances of a protest, demonizing a specific group of protesters, or redefining the main goals of an operation.

Because the focus in this chapter has been police organizational changes as a social movement outcome, less attention has been given to the internal organization of the police force and the international learning between countries. Nevertheless, the examples confirm that the Scandinavian police reforms include the learning processes outlined by della Porta and Tarrow (2012): after initial assessments the police commanders looked for models promoted elsewhere and subsequently theorized the more or less hybridized forms of policing strategies and tactics from their different sources of inspiration. However, the Scandinavian cases highlight the importance of national identity and the significance of the "police cultural proximity" of different national police forces for judgements about what constitutes a convincing mode of organizing protest policing. It is not necessarily the best international practices that are adopted, nor those most well promoted; it is those that appear effective while not conflicting with national self-image, domestic laws, and available financial, material, and human resources.

Conclusion

Protest events accompanied by policing failures are crucial triggers of episodic change within police organizations. Yet, events like these are not by themselves sufficient conditions for triggering organizational change; otherwise such changes would be internationally abundant. Furthermore, even though changes in POMS are influenced by a number of external factors, such as political opportunity structures and international learning processes, characteristics of the triggering events themselves also influence the trajectory of change, since they become the warning examples that define the primary problems to be solved. Challenges to different dimensions of police legitimacy contribute to different types of organizational solutions.

This study illustrates that outcomes of social movements may come about in organizations essentially as measures designed to prevent movements from "winning" and to maintain organizational legitimacy in the face of challenges. Such measures can indeed be irrelevant or even contrary to movement goals.

Finally, this study also highlights the potential importance of specific "watershed events" for other types of outcomes of social movements. Changes in political opportunity structures and international learning processes were not enough to induce police organizational change in the cases studied; a traumatic event was necessary. This may apply to other types of social movement outcomes as well. Such outcomes become highly contingent since the characteristics of the events themselves have implications for the direction of further developments, and these characteristics are products of unpredictable interactions, often between several different groups of actors. When studying the development and outcomes of social movements, we must therefore pay careful attention to events that become turning points and to the processes they initiate.

References

Adang, O.M. 2013. "Reforming the Policing of Public Order in Sweden: Combining Research and Practice." *Policing*, 7(3): 326–335.

American Civil Liberties Union. 2000. *Out of Control: Seattle's Flawed Response to Protests Against the World Trade Organization.* Seattle: American Civil Liberties Union of Washington.

Ashworth, R., G. Boyne, and R. Delbridge. 2009. "Escape from the Iron Cage? Organizational Change and Isomorphic Pressures in the Public Sector." *Journal of Public Administration Research and Theory*, 19(1): 165–187.

Askanius, T. 2013. "Protest Movements and Spectacles of Death: From Urban Places to Video Spaces." *Research in Social Movements, Conflicts and Change*, 35: 105–133.

Baker, D. 2011. "A Case Study of Policing Responses to Camps for Climate Action: Variations, Perplexities, and Challenges for Policing." *International Journal of Comparative and Applied Criminal Justice*, 35(2): 141–165.

Björk, M. and A. Peterson (eds.). 2002. *Vid politikens yttersta gräns: perspektiv på EU-toppmötet i Göteborg 2001*. Eslöv: Symposion.

Christrup, H., C. Haagen Jensen, and G. Homann. 2000. *Beretning i henhold til lov nr. 389 af 22. maj 1996 om undersøgelse af Nørrebrosagen*. Retrieved 20 September, 2010, from http://jm. schultzboghandel.dk/upload/microsites/jm/ebooks/redegoerelser/ noerrebrosagen.doc

Combes, H. and O. Fillieule. 2011. "Repression and Protest: Structural Models and Strategic Interactions." *Revue française de science politique (English)*, 61(6): 1–24.

Danielsson, A., O. Wolter, H.-G. Axberger, G. Guvå, R. Hedlund, A. Natri, and M. Bergquist. 2005. *Det mobila insatskonceptet: Utbildningsmaterial*. Solna: Swedish National Police Academy.

Deephouse, D.L. and M. Suchman. 2008. "Legitimacy in Organizational Institutionalism." In R. Greenwood, C. Oliver, R. Suddaby, and K. Sahlin-Andersson (eds.), *The SAGE Handbook of Organizational Institutionalism*. Thousand Oaks: SAGE, 49–77.

della Porta, D. 1995. *Social Movements, Political Violence and the State: Comparative Analysis of Italy and Germany*. Cambridge: Cambridge University Press.

della Porta, D. 1998. "Police Knowledge and Protest Policing: Some Reflections on the Italian Case." In D. Della Porta and H. Reiter (eds.), *Policing Protest: The Control of Mass Demonstrations in Western Democracies*. Minneapolis: University of Minnesota Press, 228–252.

della Porta, D. 1999. "Protest, Protesters and Protest Policing: Public Discourses in Italy and Germany from the 1960s to the 80s." In M. Giugni, D. McAdam, and C. Tilly (eds.), *How Social Movements Matter*. Minneapolis: University of Minnesota Press, 66–96.

della Porta, D., A. Peterson, and H. Reiter (eds.). 2006. *The Policing of Transnational Protest*. Aldershot: Ashgate.

della Porta, D. and H. Reiter. 1998. "The Policing of Protest in Western Democracies." In D. Della Porta and H. Reiter (eds.), *Policing Protest: The Control of Mass Demonstrations in Western Democracies*. Minneapolis: University of Minnesota Press, 1–32.

della Porta, D. and H. Reiter. 2006a. "The Policing of Global Protest: the G8 at Genoa and Its Aftermath." In D. Della Porta, A. Peterson, and H. Reiter (eds.), *The Policing of Transnational Protest*. Aldershot: Ashgate, 13–41.

della Porta, D. and H. Reiter. 2006b. "The Policing of Transnational Protest: A Conclusion." In D. Della Porta, A. Peterson, and H. Reiter (eds.), *The Policing of Transnational Protest*. Aldershot: Ashgate, 175–189.

della Porta, D. and S. Tarrow. 2012. "Interactive Diffusion." *Comparative Political Studies*, 45(1): 119–152.

della Porta, D. and L. Zamponi. 2013. "Protest and Policing on October 15th, Global Day of Action: The Italian Case." *Policing and Society*, 23(1): 65–80.

DiMaggio, P.J. and W.W. Powell. 1983. "The Iron Cage Revisited: Institutional Isomorphism and Collective Rationality in Organizational Fields." *American Sociological Review*, 48(2): 147–160.

Furuhagen, B. 2004. *Ordning på stan: Polisen i Stockholm 1848–1917*. Eslöv: B. Östlings bokförlag Symposion.

Gillham, P.F. 2011. "Securitizing America: Strategic Incapacitation and the Policing of Protest since the 11 September 2001 Terrorist Attacks." *Sociology Compass*, 5(7): 636–652.

Gillham, P.F., B. Edwards, and J.A. Noakes. 2013. "Strategic Incapacitation and the Policing of Occupy Wall Street Protests in New York City, 2011." *Policing and Society*, 23(1): 81–102.

Gillham, P.F. and G.T. Marx. 2000. "Complexity and Irony in Policing and Protesting: The World Trade Organization in Seattle." *Social Justice*, 27(2): 212–236.

Gilmore, J. 2010. "Policing protest: An Authoritarian Consensus." *Criminal Justice Matters*, 82(1): 21–23.

Giugni, M. 2008. "Political, Biographical, and Cultural Consequences of Social Movements." *Sociology Compass*, 2(5): 1582–1600.

Gorringe, H., M. Rosie, D. Waddington, and M. Kominou. 2011. "Facilitating Ineffective Protest? The Policing of the 2009

Edinburgh NATO Protests." *Policing and Society*, 22(2): 115–132.

Göteborgskommittén. 2002. *Göteborg 2001: Betänkande*. Stockholm: Fritzes offentliga publikationer.

Her Majesty's Chief Inspector of Constabulary. 2010. *Adapting to Protest: Nurturing the British Model of Policing*. London: HMIC.

Holgersson, S. 2010. *Dialogue Police: Experiences, Observations and Opportunities. RPS Rapeport 2010:4*. Stockholm: The Swedish National Police Board.

Jefferson, T. 1990. *The Case Against Paramilitary Policing*. Milton Keynes: Open University Press.

Karpantschof, R. 2009. "Ungdomshusoprøret 2006–2008: Baggrund, forløb og konsekvenser." In R. Karpantschof and M. Lindblom (eds.), *Kampen om ungdomshuset: studier i et oprør*. Copenhagen: Frydenlund Monsun, 43–101.

Karpantschof, R. and M. Lindblom (eds.). 2009. *Kampen om Ungdomshuset: Studier i et oprør*. Copenhagen: Frydenlund Monsun.

Karpantschof, R. and F. Mikkelsen. 2008. "Vold, politik og demokrati i Danmark efter 2. Verdenskrig." *Arbejderhistorie*, (1): 56–95.

King, B. 2008. "A Social Movement Perspective of Stakeholder Collective Action and Influence." *Business & Society*, 47(1): 21–49.

King, M. 2006. "From Reactive Policing to Crowd Management? Policing Anti-globalization Protest in Canada." *Jurisprudencija*, 79(1): 40–58.

Kington, T. 2012. "Court Upholds Convictions of Italian G8 Police." *The Guardian*. http://www.guardian.co.uk/world/2012/jul/06/italy-g8-police-appeal

Löfgren, M. and M. Vatankhah. 2002. *Vad hände med Sverige i Göteborg?* Stockholm: Ordfront.

Loftus, B. 2009. *Police Culture in a Changing World*. Oxford: Oxford University Press.

McAdam, D. 1983. "Tactical Innovation and the Pace of Insurgency." *American Sociological Review*, 48(6): 735–754.

McCarthy, J.D. and C. McPhail. 1998. "The Institutionalization of Protest in the United States." In D. Meyer and S. Tarrow (eds.), *The Social Movement Society: Contentious Politics for a New Century*. Oxford: Rowman & Littlefield Publishers, 83–110.

McCarthy, J.D., C. McPhail, and J. Crist. 1999. "The Diffusion and Adoption of Public Order Management Systems." In D. Della Porta, H. Kriesi, and D. Rucht (eds.), *Social Movements in a Globalizing World*. Basingstoke: Macmillan, 71–94.

McCarthy, R.M. and Associates. 2000. *An Independent Review of the World Trade Organization Conference Disruptions in Seattle, Washington, November 29 – December 3, 1999*. San Clemente: R.M. McCarthy and Associates.

McPhail, C., D. Schweingruber, and D. McCarthy. 1998. "Policing Protest in the United States: 1960–1995." In D. Della Porta (ed.), *Policing Protest: The Control of Mass Demonstrations in Western Democracies*. Minneapolis: University of Minnesota Press, 49–69.

Meyer, J.W. and B. Rowan. 1977. "Institutionalized Organizations: Formal Structure as Myth and Ceremony." *American Journal of Sociology*, 83(2): 340–363.

Noakes, J.A. and P.F. Gillham. 2006. "Aspects of the 'New Penology' in the Police Response to Major Political Protests in the United States, 1999–2000." In D. Della Porta, A. Peterson, and H. Reiter (eds.), *The Policing of Transnational Protest*. Aldershot: Ashgate, 97–115.

Noakes, J.A. and P.F. Gillham. 2007. "Police and Protester Innovation since Seattle." *Mobilization*, 12(4): 335–340.

Noakes, J.A., B.V. Klocke, and P.F. Gillham. 2005. "Whose Streets? Police and Protester Struggles Over Space in Washington, DC, 29–30 September 2001." *Policing and Society*, 15(3): 235–254.

NPIA. 2010. *Manual of Guidance on Keeping the Peace*. London: NPIA on behalf of Association of Chief Police Officers and ACPO in Scotland.

Östberg, E. 2002. *Göteborgskravallerna och rätten: Några iakttagelser ur ett människorättsperspektiv*. Stockholm: Swedish Helsinki Committee for Human Rights.

Peterson, A. 2006. "Policing Contentious Politics at Transnational Summits: Darth Vader or the Keystone Cops?" In D. Della Porta, A. Peterson, and H. Reiter (eds.), *The Policing of Transnational Protest*. Aldershot: Ashgate, 43–73.

Powell, W.W. 1991. "Expanding the Scope of Institutional Analysis." In W.W. Powell and P.J. DiMaggio (eds.), *The New Institutionalism in Organizational Analysis*. Chicago: University of Chicago Press, 183–203.

Rafail, P. 2010. "Asymmetry in Protest Control? Comparing Protest Policing Patterns in Montreal, Toronto, and Vancouver, 1998–2004." *Mobilization*, 15(4): 489–509.

Rafail, P. 2014. "Policy Spillover and the Policing of Protest in New York City, 1960–2006." *Policing and Society*. Published online January 13, 2014. doi:10.1080/10439463.2013.878344

Reicher, S., C. Stott, J. Drury, O. Adang, P. Cronin, and A. Livingstone. 2007. "Knowledge-Based Public Order Policing: Principles and Practice." *Policing*, 1(4): 403–415.

Reiner, R. 1998. "Policing, Protest, and Disorder in Britain." In D. della Porta and H. Reiter (eds.), *Policing Protest: The Control of Mass Demonstrations in Western Democracies*. Minneapolis: University of Minnesota Press, 35–48.

Reiner, R. 2000. *The Politics of the Police*, Third edition. Oxford: Oxford University Press.

Ritzau. 2009. Næsten alle aktivister er løsladt *Politiken*. Retrieved from http://politiken.dk/klima/Topmode_i_Kobenhavn/ECE858747/naesten-alle-aktivister-er-loesladt/

Rosie, M. and H. Gorringe. 2009. "What a Difference a Death Makes: Protest, Policing and the Press at the G20." *Sociological Research Online*, 14(5): 4.

Seattle City Council. 2000. *Report to the Seattle City Council WTO Accountability Committee by the Citizens' Panel on WTO Operations*. Seattle: Seattle City Council.

Seattle Police Department. 2000. *The Seattle Police Department After Action Report: World Trade Organization Ministerial Conference, Seattle, Washington, November 29 – December 3, 1999*. Seattle: Seattle Police Department.

Stott, C., M. Scothern, and H. Gorringe. 2013. "Advances in Liaison Based Public Order Policing in England: Human Rights and Negotiating the Management of Protest?" *Policing*, 7(2): 210–224.

Suchman, M.C. 1995. "Managing Legitimacy: Strategic and Institutional Approaches." *The Academy of Management Review*, 20(3): 571–610.

Swedish National Police Board. 2001. *Rikspolisstyrelsens utvärdering av EU-kommenderingen i Göteborg år 2001*. Stockholm: Swedish National Police Board.

Swedish National Police Board. 2010. *Kunskapsutveckling inom Särskild Polistaktik 2007–2010: Slutrapport*. Reg.No. PoA-109-4499/06. Stockholm: Swedish National Police Board.

Taktikutvecklingsprojektet. 2004. *Redovisning av taktikutvecklingsprojektet*. Stockholm: Swedish National Police Board.

The Partnership for Civil Justice Fund. 2012. FBI Documents Reveal Secret Nationwide Occupy Monitoring. Retrieved March 7, 2013, from www.justiceonline.org/commentary/fbi-files-ows.html

Tilly, C. 1978. *From Mobilization to Revolution*. New York: Random House.

Tilly, C. 1999. "From Interactions to Outcomes in Social Movements." In M. Giugni, D. McAdam, and C. Tilly (eds.), *How Social Movements Matter*. Minneapolis: University of Minnesota Press, 253–270.

Vestergaard, J. 2006. "Strafferetlig lovgivning om bekæmpelse af terrorisme." *Tidsskrift for Kriminalret*, (1): 2–13.

Vitale, A.S. 2007. "The Command and Control and Miami Models at the 2004 Republican National Convention: New Forms of Policing Protest." *Mobilization: An International Quarterly*, 12(4): 403–415.

Vitale, A.S. 2012. *Managing Defiance: The Policing of the Occupy Wall Street Movement*. Paper presented at the Politics and protest workshop, CUNY Graduate Center.

Vittrup, K. 2003a. *Operation*, Fifth edition. Copenhagen: Copenhagen Police Authority.

Vittrup, K. 2003b. *Strategi*, Fifth edition. Copenhagen: Copenhagen Police Authority.

Waddington, D. 2013. "A 'Kinder Blue': Analysing the Police Management of the Sheffield Anti-'Lib Dem' Protest of March 2011." *Policing and Society*, 23(1): 46–64.

Waddington, P.A.J. 1994. *Liberty and Order: Public Order Policing in a Capital City*. London: U.C.L.P.

Wahlström, M. 2007. "Forestalling Violence: Police Knowledge of Interaction with Political Activists." *Mobilization*, 12(4): 389–402.

Wahlström, M. 2010. "Producing Spaces for Representation: Racist Marches, Counterdemonstrations, and Public-Order Policing." *Environment and Planning D: Society and Space*, 28(5): 811–827.

Wahlström, M. 2011. *The Making of Protest and Protest Policing: Negotiation, Knowledge, Space, and Narrative.* Gothenburg: Dept. of Sociology, University of Gothenburg.

Wahlström, M. and M. Oskarsson. 2006. "Negotiating Political Protest in Gothenburg and Copenhagen." In D. della Porta, A. Peterson, and H. Reiter (eds.), *The Policing of Transnational Protest.* Aldershot: Ashgate, 117–143.

Wahlström, M., M. Wennerhag, and C. Rootes. 2013. "Framing 'The Climate Issue': Patterns of Participation and Prognostic Frames among Climate Summit Protesters." *Global Environmental Politics,* 13(4): 101–122.

Weick, K.E. and R.E. Quinn. 1999. "Organizational Change and Development." *Annual Review of Psychology,* 50(1): 361–386.

West Götaland Police Authority. 2002. *EU 2001-kommenderingen.* Gothenburg: West Götaland Police Authority.

Winter, M. 1998. "Police Philosophy and Protest Policing in the Federal Republic of Germany, 1960–1990." In D. della Porta and H. Reiter (eds.), *Policing Protest: The Control of Mass Demonstrations in Western Democracies.* Minneapolis: University of Minnesota Press, 188–212.

Wood, L. 2007. "Breaking the Wave: Repression, Identity and Seattle Tactics." *Mobilization,* 12(4): 377–388.

Wood, L. 2014. *Crisis and Control: The Militarization of Protest Policing.* London: Pluto Press.

Zald, M.N., C. Morrill, and H. Rao. 2005. "The Impact on Social Movements on Organizations." In G.F. Davis, D. McAdam, W. R. Scott, and M.N. Zald (eds.), *Social Movements and Organization Theory.* New York: Cambridge University Press, 253–279.

13 THE INSTITUTIONALIZATION PROCESSES OF A NEO-NAZI MOVEMENT PARTY

Securing social movement outcomes

Abby Peterson

Rudolf Heberle (1949) early on maintained that "as a rule, a major social movement tends to form its own political party or at least to affiliate itself with an existing party" (p. 352). However, since Heberle's observation, the relationship between social movements and political parties has been relatively neglected. Doug McAdam and Sidney Tarrow (2010) have in a recent article expressed their concern that the field of social movement research "had become excessively 'movement centric'" (p. 529) giving far too little attention to the relationships between social movements and political parties. In this chapter I address this lacuna by forging a bridge between the literature on social movement institutionalization processes and that on political party institutionalization processes to analyze the Swedish neo-Nazi movement institutionalization in a political party, the Sweden Democrats. In 1989 the Sweden Democrats, at that time a rather obscure sect within the Swedish neo-Nazi movement, was formed as a political party. In 2010 the party successfully mobilized voters and entered the Swedish parliament with 5.7% of the vote in the national election and 612 seats in the municipal councils. In the 2014 election to the European Parliament the party garnered 9.7% of the vote and in the elections to the Swedish Parliament later the same year, SD more than doubled their electoral support mobilizing 12.9% of the vote.

The party building of the Sweden Democrats was a strategic action taken by the neo-Nazi movement to advance their political goals.

Thwarted by the political party system in Sweden and without elite allies the movement actively chose to pursue politics in the electoral arena in order to enter policy-making bodies to effect political outcomes. This social movement strategy – forming a "movement party" as the partisan arm of the movement (Keuchler and Dalton 1990; McAdam and Tarrow 2010; Maguire 1995 introduces the notion of "party of movement") – brings with it inherent dilemmas (Bomberg 1992) in that for the strategy to be successful the movement party must undergo processes of institutionalization. That means that, "no matter how radical their goals, these political challengers are prepared to work within the system because they see government office as the most direct way of achieving their objectives" (Schwartz 2000: 456). Diani (1992) pointed out that social movements that choose to include participation in elections within their action repertoire "will be part of two different systems of action (the party system and the social movement system), where they will play different roles" (p. 15). The way these roles are negotiated and actually shaped is, according to Diani, a crucial area of investigation. While the movement party must effectively institutionalize in order to realize their objectives, at the same time the movement party cannot isolate itself from its movement basis. It must run the gauntlet between the Charybdis of movement commitment and the Scylla of system accommodation.

Background

In 1989 the Sweden Democrat Party elected Anders Klarström as its first president. Klarström and most of the first members of the party executive had backgrounds in the neo-Nazi movement and some with backgrounds in the violent extreme right at that time (Larsson and Ekman 2001: 126; Gestrin 2007: 153). During the 1990s anti-racist activists persistently challenged Sweden Democrat manifestations; for the burgeoning anti-racist movement the Sweden Democrat Party was its focal opponent and the two sides in the "drama of immigration in Sweden" were repeatedly embroiled in violent encounters (Peterson 1997). Despite these confrontations the party began the laborious process of transformation to become a viable electoral party. This work was taken on with new vigor in 1995 when the newly elected party president Mikael Jansson prohibited the wearing of uniforms and Nazi salutes at party manifestations and renounced Nazism in 1999. Initially the party patterned itself after the British National Front and was at this time partially funded by the Front National and joined the European nationalist network (Euro-Nat) (Hellström and Nilsson 2010: 58). It achieved its first electoral successes in 1998 gaining eight seats in municipal assemblies in southern most Sweden. In 2005 the new party leader Jimmy Åkesson continued efforts to reform the party along the lines of the more successful far-right parties in Western Europe (Rydgren and Ruth 2011: 4). The early successful radical right parties across Europe have impacted the developmental dynamics of latecomers such as the Sweden Democrats. Its first major electoral breakthrough came in 2006 when it secured 2.9% of the vote at the national level and representation in approximately half of Sweden's municipalities. The success of the party in the 2006 elections had a springboard effect for their success in 2010 when the party entered parliament and even further with their triumph in the 2014 European Parliamentary and national elections (Peterson and Wallinder 2013). In this chapter I will analyze how an outcome, the institutionalization of the far-right movement in Sweden, has affected the internal dynamics of the movement party *and* the external dynamics of the party political system and the configuration of state power.

Movement institutionalization

Maguire (1995: 200) forcefully argues that the "dichotomy drawn between the world of social movements and that of political institutions is too sharp." In this chapter the focus is upon the interconnections between the far-right neo-Nazi movement in Sweden and political institutions, i.e., social movement institutionalization. Suh (2011: 443) defines movement institutionalization as a process of a social movement traversing the official terrain of formal politics and engaging with state institutions to enhance their collective ability to achieve the movement's goals. In other words, institutionalization is a collective strategic choice of a social movement and not a predestined stage in a movement's historical trajectory. Movements and institutions, social movements and political parties, are not mutually antagonistic nor are political parties degenerate entities emerging out of movements, rather the relationship between movements and political parties is dialectical and multi-polar. Garner and Zald (1987: 312) maintain that parties and movements are closely intertwined, and, I argue, most closely so in a movement party.

Oommen (1990) argues that there is a processual linkage between institutions and movements and that in certain empirical situations we can find an intertwining between movements and institutions perennially present and continuing. This has been the case for the neo-Nazi movement in Sweden. Adopting the tradition of forming political parties from their interwar counter-parts, the movement has formed an array of political party organizations that have to various degrees sought electoral support. Agreed these proto-parties to the Sweden Democrats were extremely marginal, with small member cadres and limited electoral success, they nevertheless call our attention to the assiduous far-right strategy of party building.[1] The Sweden Democrats are just the most electorally successful.

Suh (2011: 445) amongst others claims that in order to understand the process of movement institutionalization one must firstly grasp that the institutionalization process requires that movement actors decide to join the state apparatus *and* that power elites elect to incorporate them and respond positively to their demands (cf. Giugni and Passy 1998). Movement parties as the partisan arm of a social movement may strategically choose to join the political party system and even succeed in gaining entry in legislative bodies, but this does not necessarily mean that the established parties in legislative bodies welcome them. In order to grasp the dynamics between a movement party and established parties in legislative bodies we need to understand the processes of party institutionalization, a neglected perspective in the social movement literature.

Party institutionalization

Political parties are not just political institutions: "they have one foot in the state and the other in civil society" (Maguire 1995: 200; cf. Sartori 1976). It is in this intermediary role that tensions can emerge. Parties in general, and especially movement parties, must constantly confront the dilemmas inherent in adapting to the requirements of the state apparatus and the demands of their members and supporters (cf. Müller-Rommel and Poguntke 1989 on the German Green Party). To capture these interacting

---

[1] Perhaps paradoxically, the far-left in Sweden has been equally eager to organize in a flora of political parties, also with marginal electoral success. Both the far-right and the far-left have persistently chosen the traditional hierarchical organizational structures of political parties.

	Internal	External
Structural	Systemness	Decisional autonomy
Attitudinal	Value infusion	Reification

Figure 13.1 Dimensions of party institutionalization (taken from Randall and Svåsand 2002: 13).

tensions I will employ the notion of party institutionalization. Party institutionalization is a set of processes by which the party becomes established in terms of both integrated patterns of behavior and of attitudes or culture, as well as achieving a degree of recognition in the political system. Randall and Svåsand (2002) have provided a simple analytical model to capture the dimensions of party institutionalization, which includes both internal aspects that refer to developments within the party itself and external aspects that are connected to the party's relationship with the society it is embedded in. Within their model these aspects include structural and attitudinal components, yielding a four-cell matrix. My analysis will proceed from a revised version of their model (see Figure 13.1).

The notion of "*systemness*" refers to the increasing scope, density, and regularity of the interactions, which constitute the party as a structure. In other words, there is a degree of routinization and the development of conventions guiding behavior. The party organization acquires a measure of stability and predictability in its actions. "*Value infusion*" refers to the party's success in creating its own distinctive culture or value system, which brings a cohesive force to the party. Randall and Svåsand (2002: 17) argue that value infusion is likely to be strongest when the party is identified with a broader social movement, in the terms used here a movement party.

"*Decisional autonomy*" refers to the party's freedom of interference in determining its own policies and strategies. In Randall and Svåsand's understanding this means the degree of decisional autonomy from its sponsoring group; in the case here, the Sweden Democrats' autonomy from the wider far-right neo-Nazi movement in Sweden. This is an important aspect in that while the Sweden Democrats are the dominant party of the far-right movement in Sweden, they must differentiate their goals and actions from those pursued by other groups and networks in the movement. However, I will include another aspect of autonomy that refers to the political party system that it wishes to change – the "bargaining" role of the party[2] in the party political system and the degree to which it is included or marginalized. In other words, the power the party wields in political decision-making. Finally, *"reification"* refers to the extent to which the party's existence is established in the public imagination. This is an important dimension in the institutionalization process in that as a party becomes increasingly recognized as a legitimate player in party politics the more likely are the chances that individuals will cast their vote for the party. When this process has become more entrenched even other political actors, i.e. established political parties, will adjust their interactions with the newcomer. This highlights the interconnectedness of the four dimensions. Reification feeds back on autonomy and the internal processes of party institutionalization in turn impact the external processes.

What is lacking in Randall and Svåsand's (2002) analysis is the role of adaptability, which these scholars simply regard as a likely but not inevitable consequence of institutionalization. In contrast, and in line with theories of social movement institutionalization (e.g., Suh 2011), I place adaptability center stage in the analysis. Adaptability is the capacity to control the processes of institutionalization whereby movement parties implement strategies to alter their structures, tactics, goals, ideology, or relations with others. Adaptability, I argue, is necessary if a movement party wants to survive and if a movement party wants to maximize its voter support (cf. Schwartz 2000). Adaptability includes a set of potential strategies to meet internal difficulties and external constraints and opportunities faced by movement parties. In the following sections I will investigate the four dimensions of the institutionalization process in regard to the strategies the Sweden Democrats have employed to control these processes in order to promote and sustain the movement and its message.

Systemness – the search for organizational stability and integrity

The Sweden Democrats have evolved from a movement party firmly rooted in its neo-Nazi movement origins to a party with significant electoral appeal. This evolution has followed with organizational developments that have successively distanced the party from its movement roots.

---

[2] See Burstein et al. 1995 on the bargaining perspective for assessing a social movement's ability to bring about political change.

In order to enhance the appeal of the party among the electorate the party must rid itself of its most radical elements. The Sweden Democrats have undergone many of the internal organizational strategies, which are characteristic of movement parties during a process of reform. As Schwartz (2000: 460) points out, factionalism is a frequent characteristic of movement parties, the result of power struggles and ideological disputes. Factions have formed within the Sweden Democrats between "hardliners" and a new generation of political entrepreneurs bent on transforming the party into a viable alternative in the electoral arena. Factionalism, as a result of the power struggles within the party, led to a split in the party in 2001 when hardliners founded the National Democrats.[3] Left was a new generation of political entrepreneurs ready to take on the challenge of leading the party to parliamentary representation.

This brings us to the theme of leadership for systemness or organizational coherence. The party has undergone three shifts in its leadership – from its hardliner initial leadership core to Mikael Jansson's more moderate leadership in 1995 to its latest shift in 2005 just prior to the 2006 elections. These shifts in leadership have not been uncontested, but they have been more or less orderly, which bears witness to a relatively high level of routinization (cf. Harmel and Svåsand 1997).

The leadership of today's Sweden Democrats is a young and tightly knit leadership core led by the charismatic Jimmie Åkesson, whose name has more or less since his election as party leader in 2005 been synonymous with the party. At his side he has his compatriots since their entry into the party's youth association and early political appointments in local politics in southernmost Sweden. Most importantly, Björn Söder, who is the party secretary and responsible for maintaining party discipline, and Mattias Karlsson, who is press secretary and the chief ideologist of the party, have been responsible for rewriting their party programs since 2002. These three young men are the nucleus of the new party structure and wield considerable power in manning other positions in the party. Their power base is the electoral success that they have brought to the party since the 2006 elections. One of the first measures that the new leadership took was to change the earlier party flag with a burning

---

[3] The National Democrats are a marginal political party with few supporters. So while factionalism can severely weaken and even destroy a movement party, this has not been the case for the Sweden Democrats (cf. Frey et al. 1992: 384 on the deleterious effects of factionalism). It can rather be argued that factionalism was a necessary step in the party's make-over process and helped unify the party behind its new leadership.

torch held in a clinched fist (modified from the British National Front symbol) to its new symbol the hepatica flower (the established parties in Sweden traditionally have flowers as their party symbols). Jimmie Åkesson motivated this change with the following words:

> We have carried out profound changes to the better and we are not the same party we were ten or fifteen years ago. It is logical that these changes are also manifested in our outward symbols (cited in Palani 2011: 26).

The change of the party's symbol heralded in the new leadership; it dramatically announced to the party's members that a new leadership with new goals for the party had taken the helm. The new leadership set out on a strategy of moderation to convince the electorate that it was a viable democratic alternative.

The Sweden Democrats' electoral successes since 2006 have over-extended their movement base and member capacities. After their chock gains in the 2006 local elections, the party was unable to fill all of the local council seats they were awarded. This was also the case after the 2010 elections. Newcomers have streamed in to fill these seats, but the party has not been able to fully socialize the newcomers to the party's prevailing ideological perspectives and tactics. Not all of the newcomers, or for that matter, entrenched neo-Nazi movement activists engaged in the party, have followed the new party line. Maintaining party discipline has become a primary concern. In order to come to terms with the problem of party discipline, the party's central leadership has developed a "communication package" to be distributed to newcomers that will provide them with approved arguments in their interactions with the media and the public. They have promised their supporters that this communication package will help party members meet the arguments of detractors and enable them to better convey the party's messages to potential supporters.[4]

While socializing newcomers at a pace necessary for immediate political appointment is problematic, "housetraining" the entrenched neo-Nazi movement activists to the party's new image of responsible governance has proven even more a problem. Swedish media have been

---

[4] The empirical materials for the analysis were collected from Sweden Television's (SVT) broadcasting of the party's three-day national congress in Göteborg November 2011. During this congress they debated and accepted a new party program. Transcripts were made from relevant speeches and debates.

on the alert for these types of statements and have readily reported on Sweden Democrats' political faux pas. Here we can find the dilemma faced by the new movement party, which on the one hand must distance itself from its more radical and outspoken elements but on the other hand the far-right movement is its mobilizing support base. This dilemma poses a tricky puzzle for the party secretary, who must tame the movement in order to maintain the credibility of the party, but cannot alienate the party from its movement.

Purges or a strategy of purification has been employed to weed out members that have been regarded as jeopardizing the party's integrity. There have been ongoing purges when party officials have been expelled for public statements that have put in question the sincerity of the party's reform process, e.g., overt and offensive racist claims or support for Nazism. In October 2012, party leader Åkesson proclaimed a new policy of zero tolerance in regard to overt racist statements and actions. Shortly afterwards, this new policy was put to test in connection with filmed footage of two parliamentary members marauding on the streets of Stockholm brandishing iron pipes and harassing a well-known ethnic minority comedian with groove racist and sexist language. This time it was not a matter of purging relatively marginal local politicians. The parliamentary members belonged to the leadership core of the party; one was removed from his official party functions and the other, while not expelled, was encouraged to take a "time out." These events brought to a head the problems party leadership is encountering in disciplining party members "to adhere to both the polished party image and common policies" (Hellström and Nilsson 2010: 69). The two politicians found widespread support from the movement, particularly from the youth association, presaging at least the potential of an open division within the party between their grassroots movement supporters and the party leadership bent on convincing the electorate that the party has moved from its neo-Nazi legacy.

If socialization into the party and maintaining party discipline poses one set of problems, the other is recruiting new members and extending and consolidating its grassroots organization. Björn Söderström also challenged party members on this point: "Our party is broadening. We must develop our party's organization in order to better make use of our grassroots supporters. Therefore, we need strong municipal associations" (SVT, 2011 party congress). Carina Herrstedt, chair of the newly formed SD Women's Association, also emphasized the need to broaden their organizational base explaining that the women's association "functions as a plant school for the recruitment of women to hold office … and is a tool to create a better balance (between men and women; men dominate the party and its voter core;) in the party" (SVT, 2011 party congress). Gustav Kasselstrand, chair of the party's youth association, motivated the role of his organization in the party with the following words:

> We are not only building a party, we are building a movement, a folk movement that stands on firm ground and the youth association is a part of that construction.
>
> *(SVT, 2011 party congress)*

Kasselstrand reminded those assembled of the movement nature of the party, emphasizing its movement roots, thereby highlighting the ongoing dilemma of the movement party's institutionalization process – the need to not alienate its movement roots, while making compromises to meet a degree of system accommodation. His speech to the congress was devoid of the new "social conservative" ideology on which the new party program has been built; rather he repeatedly reminded the assembly of the party's nationalist identity and the nationalist movement that he sees as the party's base.

Value infusion – marketing the party for its supporters and prospective supporters

Successful party adaption is understood as a set of changes undertaken in response to changing environmental conditions that improve a party's capacity to gain or maintain electoral office (Burgess and Levitsky 2003: 883). To adapt successfully, movement party leaders must first choose an appropriate strategy and then win support for that strategy from the movement for the movement party, as well as the electorate. Mikael Jansson, former party leader, without expressing a preference, described the two strategic avenues the party could take to maintain a significant level of electoral support.

> Our party is like an opinion rocket that is perpetually rising, but at some point our support will plane out at a certain level. But at what level? This will depend on how we position ourselves politically. If

we are more specific in our political message we will be somewhat smaller, but more distinct in our content. If we are more general we will be somewhat larger, but somewhat less distinct in our politics. However, regardless of which way we choose we will attain a very high level of electoral support.

(*SVT, Mikael Jansson, 2011 party congress*)

The primary adaption strategy undertaken by the Sweden Democrats leadership during the 2000s has been a makeover of the party's ideological basis (cf. Schwartz 2000). While the movement party worked to downplay the party's connection to Nazism and the neo-Nazi movement in the 1990s, during the 2000s the party has step-by-step downplayed its racist and nationalist discourse, choosing the more general diluted avenue Jansson sketched above. This has not been an uncontroversial course in their makeover process. The controversy came to a head during the debates over the new party program during their congress in November 2011. The new party program set in center stage the new party ideology – "social conservatism" – that will convince voters that they offer the "third way" in Swedish politics.

Two major points were raised in the ensuing debate over the new party program, which engaged ten opponents and thirteen supporters. First, opponents to the program were concerned that nationalism as the guiding ideological principle now took on a secondary position. "Redefining our ideology from nationalism to social conservatism is not a broadening of our politics but a step to the side. We do not have the mandate to abandon nationalism" (SVT, Patrik Repo, 2011 party congress). Second, a major bone of contention was the process by which the program had been formulated. "A party with *movement traditions* should have had a longer period to discuss its contents. A political program is not the work of one man" (SVT, Patrik Ehn, 2011 party congress; my emphasis).

It is difficult to assess the robustness of the critique and how well anchored it is among party members. However, it would appear to be at least potentially a source of internal discord, which could lead to a faction of "nationalists" breaking out of the party, thereby weakening its organizational stability.

While the makeover from a primarily nationalist party to a party now identifying itself as "social conservative" has been met with internal discord the makeover is well in line with the populist ideological marketing of its more successful "sister" parties in Europe. The social conservative template was directly imported from the Danish populist Folk Party. Despite raising discord within the party the makeover would appear to be a necessary step to provide additional and appealing meaning to voters and supporters and to achieve their goals of becoming a major political party. We can characterize this shift in their ideological focus as a move by a neo-fascist party to assume what Taggart (1995) called a New Populist orientation.[5] Taggart contends that:

> [t]he muted radicalism of the New Populists has led to great success at entering parliaments and has the potential to transform party systems. As a nascent, but apparently effective force for change – perhaps radical change – the New Populism represents a formidable protest force. It both reflects changes in contemporary society and also is attempting to enact political change.
>
> *(p. 48)*

In Taggart's scheme the neo-fascist party focuses its energies on the streets and is associated with the ideology of the "boot-boy," while the New Populists prefer the parliamentary arena where they are more likely to wear tailored suits than military fatigues. This shift succinctly captures the move of the Sweden Democrats from the uniformed boot-boys of the 1990s to the sober suited party officials of the 2000s. By cashing in on the success of the New Populist ideology, the Sweden Democrat Party has enhanced its voter appeal.

Furthermore, a movement party must also diversify its messages from single issues – in the case of the Sweden Democrats the issues of immigration and multiculturalism – to address the full range of political standpoints expected of a parliamentary party. The party's press secretary and ideologist Mattias Karlsson explained the virtues of the new social conservative ideology at the party congress in 2011.

> We have not abandoned nationalism as our basic outlook, but we have broadened and extended our ideology to include our views on

---

[5] Taggart (1995) has constructed the New Populist party as an ideal type of political party. Some parties in his analysis conform closely to its characteristics, while other parties combine New Populism with neo-fascism and are subsequently a hybrid form, such as the Sweden Democrats, which has taken on most of the characteristics of Taggart's New Populist party but has retained its anti-immigration and nationalist elements.

> mankind, culture, welfare, and the family. We are writing our
> history of ideas. That we stand up for welfare and the people's
> home. .... That we stand up for a democratic nationalism.
>
> *(Mattias Karlsson, 2011 party congress speech)*

In their new party program, the Sweden Democrats hark back to the traditional rhetoric of Swedish Social Democracy invoking a return to an idealized 1950s version of Social Democratic politics. With the broadening of its politics the Sweden Democrats above all promised to enter the electoral struggle in 2014 not only with their anti-multiculturalist message, but also with a focus on law and order issues and issues related to elderly care and pensions. The broadening of their politics proved a success. The Sweden Democrats in particular accomplished a significant mobilization of elderly voters in the 2014 elections.

Autonomy – the consolidation of political power

Party discipline, factional splits, and purges have left the party with considerable decisional autonomy in respect to the wider neo-Nazi far-right movement from which it springs. What the party is now striving to achieve is the recognition of other political parties in Sweden's party political landscape (cf. Harmel and Svåsand 1997; Bale et al. 2010). This has been an uphill struggle.

Swedish politics around the immigration and integration issue has traditionally been consensual and has received limited interest from political parties (Green-Pedersen and Krogstrup 2008: 624–626; Dahlström 2004: 71–78; Borevi 2002: 77–134; Södergran 2000: 7–9). On the national level, the neo-Nazi movement in Sweden and their xenophobic claims have met with "full exclusion" by the Swedish state with neither formal nor informal access to the political system thereby restricting their strategic options vis-à-vis the state. Fridolfsson and Gidlund (2002) maintain that the parliamentary parties in Sweden forged more or less a cartel against extreme right parties. While the movement enjoyed partial success with some concessions in some municipalities in the region of Skåne in southern Sweden during the latter 1980s and 1990s, the Swedish neo-Nazi movement was confronted by a situation in which they could choose continued exclusion *or* make a bid to enter the political system as the most direct way of achieving their goals. In the case of the extreme right in Sweden, without allies in the established political system, it appeared as a logical step to build a party that could successfully compete in the electoral arena as a strategy to impact policy making in the field of immigration.

One strategy of the established political parties has been discursive repression toward the Sweden Democrats – a "strategy of silence." "The general attitude of the established parties can be summarized in the rhetorical figure: *the Sweden Democrats are not like us in any way, shape or form*" (Hellström and Nilsson 2010: 65, emphasis in original). The established parliamentary parties prior to the entry of the Sweden Democrats in the Swedish parliament in 2010 repeatedly refused to meet the party in public debates. Even after their parliamentary entry, the established parties are reluctant to engage with Sweden Democrat representatives in debates and negotiations. Mikael Jansson, former party leader and now Sweden Democrat representative in parliament, claims that "the other political parties' contact anxiety has not abated and the media reinforces this anxiety" (SVT, 2011 party congress).

However, these attempts of closure or discursive repression might have in fact opened the electoral space available to the Sweden Democrats in that a significant proportion of the voters felt that their views were excluded. As the established political parties, even the moderate-right parties, have not occupied anti-immigrant positions within the public discourse, this left a large political space open for the Sweden Democrats thereby enhancing their chances for electoral success (cf. Giugni et al. 2005: 150). Voting for the Sweden Democrats can be regarded as an indication of discontent with the prevailing parties (cf. Ignazi 1996). Schedler (1996) has argued that new extremist parties across Europe have accused established parties of forming an exclusionary cartel, unresponsive and unaccountable to "ordinary citizens." In this political framing, the extremist parties contra-pose the political elite against citizens, on the one hand, and against themselves, on the other.

The Sweden Democrats present themselves as anti-elitist and as representing the views and interests of the ordinary man on the street. By virtue of the fact that none of the other parties has been willing to speak to them, the Sweden Democrat Party has been able to nurture the image of democratic underdogs in Swedish politics. "By being side-stepped, they have been able to portray themselves as friends of the people and, at the same time, sharp critics of a consensual elite that refuses to engage in democratic dialogue and deliberation with SD" (Hellström and Nilsson 2010: 60). The party's message is that "we are the true democrats"

(Rydgren 2002). It can be argued that the strategy of discursive repression has played in the hands of the Sweden Democrats leaving many voters with the feeling that their views are excluded by the political elites, which is underpinned by the established political parties' reluctance to engage with the Sweden Democrats in democratic dialogue.

The other strategy of exclusion employed by the established political parties has been one of institutional exclusion. Suh (2011: 450) points out that when "political power elites feel threatened by a movement, they are more likely to suppress it than admit it to the institutional corridors." This has been the case for the Sweden Democrats. The election in 2010 was a struggle between a newly formed left oppositional alliance including the Social Democrats as the major party, together with the Green Party and the Left Party and a governing moderate/right alliance including the Conservative Party as the major party, together with the Liberal Party, the Centre Farmers' Party, and the Christian Democratic Party. In the 2010 national election, the latter alliance won over the left alliance; however, they did not succeed in collecting a clear majority of the votes. The moderate/right coalition formed a minority government and the Sweden Democrats found themselves in the attractive position of holding the balance of power in the parliament between these two bloc alliances. But how attractive in reality has this position been?

According to Sartori (1976), for a party to be politically relevant in a specific party-system, it must have a "coalition-potential," i.e., the party must be interesting for other parties to collaborate with in creating alliances, or the party must have the capacity for political extortion, "blackmail-potential." The former capacity is an option for small parties in the middle of the political spectrum, for example the Green Party, while the latter option is that available for small extremist parties. The Sweden Democrat Party has not had coalition-potential. Rather the Sweden Democrats have assumed the role of "horse-traders," what Satori calls "blackmail-potential," hoping to gain some concessions for their political goals. So far the Sweden Democrat Party has had little or no success horse-trading for concessions in the field of immigration policy. In Sweden the state imperative is structured along a partisan consensus on the immigration issue (Bevelander and Hellström 2011: 2). Public policy in immigration and multiculturalism issues remain under the sway of state imperatives, subsequently the Sweden Democrats with no state imperative cannot easily acquire the concessions they are seeking (Dryzek 1996: 480).

After the 2014 elections, when the only party that significantly increased their electoral support was the Sweden Democrats, neither the moderate-right bloc nor the center-left bloc are willing to build a majority government with the support of SD. Furthermore, neither bloc wants to find itself voting with the Sweden Democrats, and on more controversial issues what appears to be a governing center-left bloc is at present committed to seeking support across blocs rather than depend upon the support of the Sweden Democrats. According to Hellström and Nilsson (2010: 69), "SD is the card you least want in your hand." Rydgren (2010) argues that the situation of confronting the established political parties not wanting to find themselves in any way associated with the Sweden Democrats has led to a strategy of "cordon sanitaire" with which they choose to answer, or rather not answer, the challenges tendered by the Sweden Democrats. The situation is similar in the municipalities. At least prior to the 2014 elections in none of the local municipalities where the Sweden Democrats have gained mandates, have they been invited to join the governing coalition. Even in municipalities in the southern region of Skåne where the party garnered over 15% of the vote, the Sweden Democrats were not invited by the established parties to join in a governing coalition (Peterson and Wallinder 2013). The established parties have not only taken a strategy of discursive repression they have also assumed a strategy of institutional exclusion in governing bodies. These strategies employed by the established parties to exclude the Sweden Democrats from the party-political space leaves the party with its only alternative of "political blackmail." What is the bargaining power of the Sweden Democrats that can impact the political outcomes of party institutionalization? Mikael Jansson claims that:

> we are rewriting the political map. We are always willing to negotiate in order to acquire concessions. In the parliament we have the balance of power. In the various parliamentary committees we conduct negotiations with both blocs, the right as well as the left. Some times we have achieved successes that have caught the attention of the media and sometimes we influence political decision-making without it showing.
>
> *(SVT, 2011 party congress)*

The remedy proposed by the party leader Jimmie Åkesson to increase their bargaining power is that the party has to increase its electoral mandate by learning to better convey its politics.

We have to grow so much that the other parties can no longer
ignore us. We cannot be satisfied to be a 5 to 6% party; rather in the
long run we must strive to be a 30% party. We cannot allow either
bloc to win a majority. We must guard our position as holding the
balance of power. To do this we must work on our communication
with the voters. We must be able to speak with voters who have not
understood what our party stands for ... A party that aspires to a
position of power cannot be doctrinaire and shout out dogmatic
ideas. We must learn to communicate our politics more softly. We
have to lift up the social in our social conservative party program in
order to attract the voting masses. We must assume responsibility
with humility to achieve our ambition to become a governing party.
(SVT, Jimmie Åkesson, 2011 party congress speech)

A recent change in the Swedish Constitution now requires that
the parliament must vote to elect the prime minister. Appointment as
prime minister, and indirectly then the make-up of the Cabinet, is
contingent upon winning a simple majority vote in parliament. This
change was first put in effect after the 2014 elections. Prior to these
elections Jimmie Åkesson believed that this constitutional change would
significantly impact his party's bargaining power given that the Sweden
Democrats remained in the position of holding the balance of power
between the blocs. "We expect of course that if we give our practical
support to someone, we expect to get something back. In all likelihood
our party holding the balance of power in parliament should become
more interesting in that our support must be actively sought" (*Dagens
Nyheter*. 2012.07.01). This was indeed the case after the 2014 elections.
SD now holds the "absolute balance of power" where neither bloc can
command a majority (i.e., the moderate-right bloc cannot form a majority even with the support of the Environmental Party). This constitutional change, together with their substantial gains in the last elections,
has opened a window of opportunity, which can potentially enhance the
bargaining power of the Sweden Democrats.

Reification – acquiring political legitimacy

Stemming from their initial successes in the 2006 local elections, the
Sweden Democrat Party had then begun the journey to become recognized as a legitimate political party in the eyes of the voters. Since the

2010 elections, the Sweden Democrat Party had consistently maintained, and even increased, its level of popularity in the polls. Despite a series of media scandals in late 2012, the party did not decline in the polls. In the 2014 elections SD accumulated 12.9% of the vote, making it the third largest party in Sweden.

The road to attaining legitimacy in the eyes of the established political parties appears to be more arduous. Mikael Jansson regards the bargaining position of the Sweden Democrats as dependent upon the size of their electoral support. Both the former party leader and the party's present leader see their "blackmail potential" in the number of mandates they are awarded at the polls. The voters hold the key to the success of their institutionalization process in Swedish politics. They reckon that with enough of the vote the established political parties will be forced to allow them full access to the corridors of political power. They have succeeded in acquiring an exceptionally strong position as a wedge between the traditional two blocs. We can conclude that the Sweden Democrats have perhaps irrevocably rewritten the political cartography of Swedish politics undermining the traditional bloc politics, which have prevailed in much of the country's modern political history.

Conclusions: the miraculous metamorphosis of the Sweden Democrats

Over the past twenty-odd years the Sweden Democrats have experienced a miraculous metamorphosis from an obscure neo-Nazi sect to become in 2010 a parliamentary party and in 2014 Sweden's third largest party. During this historical period, the party has actively engaged in processes of institutionalization. Bridging the literature on social movement institutionalization processes with the literature on political party institutionalization processes has allowed for a multidimensional analysis. By recognizing the multidimensional aspects of this process, we can see that this process has been uneven and has as yet not been fully achieved.

In the initial stages of the party's institutional process, the party leaderships have worked to enhance the party's organizational capacity and to transform its political ideology to one that can successfully appeal to voters. While these internal processes have met with some resistance and created rifts among its members and supporters, they have to a large degree achieved their objectives. The party has successively shifted to a more moderate form of nationalist populism, which they call "social conservatism," a relatively radical makeover. Furthermore, they are persistently working with the party's organizational capacity, that is, its grassroots organizational structure and its socialization of its members in the new ideology. It is this latter work that appears to require the most effort. Building up its grassroots organization and socializing the new recruits to the party's more moderate ideology and tactical choices is demanding when the party has extended its governmental mandates at the municipal level well beyond its movement basis. Internally the party has more or less succeeded in its institutionalization endeavors, even if these are ongoing processes that have met with a degree of opposition. However, internal party institutionalization is not enough, party institutionalization also requires external recognition.

Party institutionalization theorists remind us that to become institutionalized is to be regarded as an established party by other relevant external actors, i.e., potential voters and/or other party leaders (i.e., Harmel and Svåsand 1997). The Sweden Democrats appear to have attracted a more or less stable voter base, which is reflected in their substantial success in the 2014 elections. We can conclude that a significant number of voters have recognized the party as a legitimate political player in the electoral arena.

This leaves us with our final dimension in the analysis, which evaluates the impact of the Sweden Democrat Party on other parties in the political system and ultimately the configuration of state power. Rather than trying to "prove" that the Sweden Democrats have "caused" their party political competitors to take a particular line on immigration and integration policy, I will investigate the strategy or combination of strategies that have been chosen.[6] How have the mainstream parties in Sweden responded to the challenge of the Sweden Democrat Party? So far the established parties have stubbornly upheld

---

[6] By focusing on the strategies adopted by the other parties and not a simple causal relation between the challenges of the Sweden Democrats and strategic choices we are recognizing that a number of inter-locking factors influence these choices. For example: the degree to which the party is perceived as siphoning off votes and from which side of the bloc divide; how united the party is on the question of immigration, i.e., the level of internal consensus; the strategies assumed by its bloc fellows; the strategies taken by its bloc competitors, etc.

a "hold and defuse strategy" (Bale et al. 2010), retaining their initial relatively generous approach to immigration and integration ("hold") and refusing to engage with the Sweden Democrats in negotiations on immigration and integration issues ("defuse"). This latter defuse strategy has entailed the cooperation of the other established parties in a general consensus on immigration and integration policy, what Bale et al. call a "conspiracy of silence." However, this tentative consensus is a dicey concord between competitors in the electoral arena. Another party may well feel tempted to fish for votes among an electorate that is concerned about the media-fueled debate on immigration, crime, welfare abuse, and dependency. We can find some indications that there are some cracks in this front; however, we find at this time no indications that the established parties are willing to adopt the politics of the Sweden Democrats. But again, only time will tell. The degree of success that the Sweden Democrats achieve in their institutionalization process will impact the prevailing configuration of power with possible far-reaching outcomes for Swedish politics in the field of immigration and integration policy.

Bevelander and Hellström (2011: 24) found that:

> [d]uring the period 2006–2010, the mainstream parties including the mainstream press acted unanimously against the SD and gradually abandoned their initial *cardon sanitaire* approach. We could, tentatively, find supporting evidence for a re-alignment process, from a sole focus on the socio-economic cleavage dimension to an increased focus on socio-cultural issues, ranging from the Christian Democrats Leader's outburst against the 'new radical elite', to the mobilization against the SD on the immigration issue.

So while there is a strong convergence at the center of the political party system in Sweden around the immigration issue to concede any influence of the Sweden Democrats in national politics, this is not a static situation. What is regarded as "normal" talk about immigrants shifts, even in the mainstream political debate.

Via the electoral arena the Swedish neo-Nazi movement has entered its booted foot, now in brogues, into the corridors of political institutional power. William Gamson (1975) perceived the transition from acting outside of institutionalized politics to being accepted as a legitimate actor in electoral politics as *one* form of social movement success. The key is being accepted as a legitimate electoral actor, which has been argued includes acceptance by *both* the electorate *and* the established political parties. The degree to which the Sweden Democrats can wield bargaining power, i.e., the acceptance they enjoy in the corridors of political power, will impact whether they can achieve their explicit goals. This acceptance will only be fully achieved when and if the party's institutionalization processes are fully developed.

References

Bale, T., C. Green-Pedersen, A. Krouwel, K.-R. Luther, and N. Sitter. 2010. "If You Can't Beat Them Join Them? Explaining Social Democratic Responses to the Challenge from the Populist Radical Right in Western Europe." *Political Studies*, 58(3): 410–426.

Bevelander, P. and A. Hellström. 2011. "Trespassing the Threshold of Relevance: Media Exposure and Opinion Polls of the Sweden Democrats, 2006–2010." *IZA Discussion Paper*. no. 6011.

Bomberg, E. 1992. "The German Greens and the European Community: Dilemmas of a Movement-Party." *Environmental Politics*, 1(4): 160–185.

Borevi, K. 2002. *Välfärdsstaten i det mångkulturella samhället (The Welfare State in the Multicultural Society)*. Uppsala: Acta Universitatis Upsaliensis.

Burgess, K. and S. Levitsky. 2003. "Explaining Populist Party Adaption in Latin America: Environmental and Organisational Determinants of Party Change in Argentina, Mexico, Peru and Venezuela." *Comparative Political Studies*, 36(8): 881–911.

Burstein, P., R. L. Einwohner, and J. A. Hollander. 1995. "The Success of Political Movements: A Bargaining Perspective." In J. C. Jenkins (ed.), *The Politics of Social Protest: Comparative Perspectives on States and Social Movements*. Minneapolis, MN: University of Minnesota Press, 275–295.

Dahlström, C. 2004. *Nästan välkomna (Almost welcome)*. Göteborg: Department of Political Science.

Diani, M. 1992. "The Concept of Social Movement." *The Sociological Review*, 40(1): 1–25.

Dryzek, J.S. 1996. "Political Institutions and the Dynamics of Democratization." *The American Political Science Review*, 90: 475–487.

Frey, S.R., T. Dietz, and L. Kalof. 1992. "Characteristics of Successful American Protest Groups: Another Look at Gamson's Strategy of Social Protest." *American Journal of Sociology*, 98(2): 368–387.

Fridolfsson, C. and G. Gidlund. 2002. *De lokala partierna och den nya politiska kartan.* Örebro: Novemus.

Gamson, W.A. 1975. *The Strategy of Political Protest.* Belmont, CA: Wadsworth.

Garner, R.A. and M.N. Zald. 1987. "The Organisational Economy of Social Movement Sectors." In M.N. Zald and J. McCarthy (eds.), *Social Movements in an Organisational Society.* New Brunswick, NJ: Transactions, 293–318.

Gestrin, H. 2007. *Högerextrema rörelser och deras symboler.* Stockholm: Natur och kultur.

Giugni. M., R. Koopmans, F. Passy, and P. Statham. 2005. "Institutional and Discursive Opportunities for Extreme-Right Mobilization in Five Countries." *Mobilization.* 10(1): 145–162.

Green-Pedersen, C. and J. Krogstrup. 2008. "Immigration as a Political Issue in Denmark and Sweden." *European Journal of Political Research*, 47(3): 610–634.

Guigni, M. and F. Passy. 1998. "Contentious Politics in Complex Societies: New Social Movements Between Conflict and Cooperation." In M. Guigni, D. McAdam, and C. Tilly (eds.), *From Contention to Democracy.* Lanham, MD: Rowman & Littlefield, 81–107.

Harmel, R. and L. Svåsand. 1997. "The Influence of New Parties on Old Parties' Platforms: The Case of the Progress Parties and Conservative Parties in Denmark and Norway." *Party Politics*, 3(3): 315–330.

Heberle, R. 1949. "Observations on the Sociology of Social Movements." *American Sociological Review*, 14(3): 346–357.

Hellström, A. and T. Nilsson. 2010. "'We Are the Good Guys': Ideological Positioning of the Nationalist Party

Sverigedemokraterna in Contemporary Swedish politics." *Ethnicities*, 10(1): 55–76.

Ignazi, P. 1996. "The Crisis of Parties and the Rise of New Political Parties." *Party Politics*, 2(4): 549–566.

Keuchler, M. and R.J. Dalton. 1990. "New Social Movements and the Political Order: Inducing Change for Long-term Stability?" In R.J. Dalton and M. Keuchler (eds.), *Challenging the Political Order*. New York: Oxford University Press, 277–300.

Larsson, S. and M. Ekman. 2001. *Sverigedemokraterna: Den nationella rörelsen*. Stockholm: Ordfront.

Maguire, D. 1995. "Opposition Movements and Opposition Parties: Equal Partners or Dependent Relations in the Struggle for Power and Reform?" In J.C. Jenkins and B. Klandermans (eds.), *The Politics of Social Protest: Comparative Perspectives on States and Social Movements*. Minneapolis: University of Minnesota Press, 199–298.

McAdam, D. and S. Tarrow. 2010. "Ballots and Barricades: On the Reciprocal Relationship between Elections and Social Movements." *Perspectives on Politics*, 8(2): 529–542.

Müller-Rommel, F. and T. Poguntke. 1989. "The Unharmonious Family: Green Paries in Western Europe." In E. Kolinsky (ed.), *The Greens in West Germany*. Oxford: Berg, 11–29.

Oommen, T.K. 1990. "Movements and Institutions: Structural Opposition or Processual Linkage?" *International Sociology*, 5(2): 145–156.

Palani, N. 2011. "Sverigedemokraterna: Från högerextremister till radikala högerpopulister – En idealtypsanalys av partiets politiska program." Unpublished manuscript. Karlstad: C-uppsats i Statsvetenskap.

Peterson, A. 1997. *Neo-Sectarianism and Rainbow Coalitions. Youth and the Drama of Immigration in Contemporary Sweden*. Aldershot, UK: Ashgate.

Peterson, A. and Y. Wallinder. Forthcoming 2013. "An Explorative Study of the Impact of Local Political Opportunity Structures on the Electoral Mobilization of the Far-Right Movement in Sweden." *Mitteilungsblatt des Instituts für Soziale Bewegungen*, Bochum University.

Randall, V. and L. Svåsand. 2002. "Party Institutionalization in New Democracies." *Party Politics*, 8(1): 5–29.

Rydgren, J. 2002. "Radical Right Populism in Sweden. Still a Failure, But for How Long?" *Scandinavian Political Studies*, 26(1): 26–57.

Rydgren, J. 2010. "Radical Right-Wing Populism in Denmark and Sweden: Explaining Party System Change and Stability." *SAIS Review*, Winter-Spring: 57–71.

Rydgren, J. and P. Ruth. 2011. "Voting for the Radical Right in Swedish Municipalities: Social Marginality and Ethnic Competition?" *Scandinavian Political Studies*, 34(3): 202–225.

Satori, G. 1976. *Party and Party Systems: A Framework for Analysis.* Vol. 1. Cambridge: Cambridge University Press.

Schedler, A. 1996. "Anti-Political-Establishment Parties." *Party Politics*, 2(3): 291–312.

Schwartz, M.A. 2000 "Continuity Strategies among Political Challengers: The Case of Social Credit." *American Review of Canadian Studies*, 30(4): 455–477.

Södergran, L. 2000. *Svensk invandrar- och integrationspolitik.* Umeå: Sociologiska institutionen, Umeå universitet.

Suh, D. 2011. "Institutionalizing Social Movements: The Dual Strategy of the Korean Women's Movement." *The Sociological Quarterly*, 52: 442–471.

Taggart, P. 1995. "New Populist Parties in Western Europe." *West European Politics.* 18(1): 34–51.

14 INCORPORATION AND DEMOCRATIZATION

The long-term process of institutionalization of the Northern Ireland Civil Rights Movement

Lorenzo Bosi

It is quite common nowadays in the social movement literature to recognize that "no protest wave ends up where it began" (Koopmans 2004: 22). If this is true, as we believe it is, we should also recognize that in such transformation what changes are the continuous interactions between different actors in the political system, and in particular the interactions between the movement and the state. This changing power relation between the different actors is, more often than not, a critical catalyst for a change in the distribution of power – whether this has positive effects, or results in a backlash for the social movement and its constituency. What we surely can say is that no protest wave leaves the power relation between the movement's constituency and the state unaffected. Thus, the aim of this chapter is to study how political changes (that either benefit or damage the collective good) emerge from the complex interplay of state and social movement, and to study the shifting balance of power relations between them at different stages of the institutionalization process.

By "social movement institutionalization," this chapter means the process of inclusion in the terrain of formal politics of some of its

I would like to thank Gianluca De Fazio, the participants at the international conference "Silence in the Study of Social Movement Outcomes" (Uppsala University, Sweden, September 2012), and the co-editors of this volume for their helpful comments. Donagh Davis has courteously helped with the language. Any errors in the chapter are entirely my own.

ideas (i.e., movement concerns come to be recognized as legitimate within mainstream politics and/or among the general public), personnel (i.e., activists gain positions within political parties, committees, and/or the civil service), or whole movement strands (i.e., sections of the movement establish political parties) (Giugni and Passy 1998; Meyer 2007; Suh 2011). Such a process seems to occur only when two conditions are combined: the willingness of the social movement, in whole or in part, to institutionalize, and the consent of the state for such a path to be pursued (Banaszak 2010; Suh 2011). While both are necessary, they do not need to occur simultaneously. Hence, institutionalization is not a linear process, nor a natural evolution of social movement development, and neither is it structurally determined. Rather it is the result of competing strategic choices: those of a social movement (or parts thereof) to participate in the arena of formal politics, and those of the state to integrate movement activists and their demands into political institutions, under specific, favorable conditions. Thus, social movement institutionalization is not a narrow path leading from social movement mobilization to inclusion within formal politics in a short time span, but a multidimensional and long-term process with multiple causes and uncertain outcomes. It is for this reason that when we study social movement institutionalization, we need to extend the period under investigation far beyond that of a single protest wave.

The research strategy of this chapter employs the method of process tracing (Stinchcome 1995; Mahoney 2000; McAdam et al. 2001; Tilly and Tarrow 2007) in order to seek out those causal mechanisms (identifiable social dynamics recurring across a variety of situations) that, concatenating over time, lead to social movement institutionalization. Different concatenations of mechanisms, broken down themselves in different sets of sub-mechanisms (Alimi et al. 2015), can explain the occurrence of the same process of institutionalization in different episodes of contention against the specificity of several sets of initial conditions. Thus, this chapter takes a middle path between a classically social scientific approach – seeking to identify the conditions that favor certain social movement outcomes across different cases (strategic tactics, the structure of political opportunities, organizational features, resource availability, public opinion) – and one more associated with historians, who for the most part reject causal linkages between social movement activities and social change.

That is, the chapter takes a middle ground between reductionism and idiographic ethnography.[1]

The process tracing research strategy is utilized in order to reconstruct empirically how the wave of contention commencing in late 1960s Northern Ireland with the mobilization of the Northern Ireland Civil Rights Movement (henceforth CRM) gradually institutionalized. This is done by focusing in on that process at intermediate stages up to 1998. Different strands of the CRM institutionalized at different stages of its existence, and even afterwards, while others never took such a path. An initial phase of policy reform and political party formation – what can be called the *incorporation* mechanism – has corresponded in the long term to a transfer of power, and to a change in the character of government and society – what can be called the *democratization* mechanism.[2] As this chapter will demonstrate, the incorporation mechanism was present from early on, and played a part in activating the democratization mechanism. The latter finally came to fruition with the Good Friday Agreement of 1998, which gave the Catholic minority a say in the running of Northern Ireland by institutionalizing a power-sharing system of governance in the region. As Ruane and Todd (2015: 49) point out, the Good Friday Agreement marked the first time in the history of the region that "the British government had disengaged from its dependence on and privileged support for the Protestant community and was creating a political system open to all sections of the population and open to further change."

This is an intriguing empirical episode even for those scholars of contentious politics who are not Northern Ireland specialists, for the reason that very few researchers have analyzed social movement institutionalization in deeply divided societies – preferring, largely, to study "stable" Western democracies.[3] As Nicole Watts writes:

---

[1] For a comprehensive review of critical scholarly debate on the 'mechanism – process' research program, see *Qualitative Sociology* 2008: 31(4) and *Mobilization* 2003: 8(3).

[2] This analysis does not exhaust the list of significant mechanisms at play during thirty years of conflict in Northern Ireland, but rather singles out the ones this chapter deems most important to the process of institutionalization. Where previous studies have looked at the process of radicalization in the same episode, they have highlighted some similar and some different mechanisms (Alimi et al. 2012).

[3] Deeply divided societies are ones in which regimes lack full legitimacy, in which there is an asymmetrical balance of power between the different communities making up the society, and which are prone to widespread political violence, establishment repression, and subcultural divisions based on sociopolitical cleavages that are neither closed nor pacified.

> In liberal democracies the process [of institutionalization of contention] involves a routinization of collective action such that challengers and authorities "adhere to a common script" and challengers often drop their most contentious demands so politics can proceed as normal (Meyer & Tarrow, 1998, p. 21). In cases of ethnic contention in less-than-fully democratic regimes, the seemingly straightforward process of forming an ethnopolitical party and participating in the political system may disrupt "normal" political routines, articulating highly contentious identity claims and challenging the nationalist basis of the state. In addition, the newly elected challengers may view themselves not as politicians but as "activists" working on behalf of their community to carry the cause into the centres of state power.
>
> *(2006: 129)*

However, in spite of the apparent differences between deeply divided societies and "stable" Western democracies, examining processes of social movement institutionalization in the former shows us more clearly the complex relationship between states and social movements.

The chapter is not limited to empirically describing different stages in a process of institutionalization in a deeply divided society. In drawing on secondary and new primary empirical sources (archival data, newspapers, and semi-structured interviews),[4] it also builds on the tenets of a strategic-relational approach and of a process tracing research strategy so as to provide a nuanced understanding of how and when the phenomenon of institutionalization of political mobilization unfolds via particular sequences of mechanisms. The chapter advances an approach to institutionalization based on a theoretical synthesis capable of capturing and explaining the dynamic, relational interplay between social movements and the state.

Analytical approach

Within social movement studies, the process of institutionalization has mainly been addressed via the study of two distinct topics – those of transformation and of outcomes. Scholars who try to understand how

---

[4] A full description and critical reading of the empirical sources used in this chapter are available in Bosi (2006) and (2012).

social movements transform over time have tended to associate movement institutionalization with their decline (Piven and Cloward 1977; Tarrow 1989; Koopmans 1993; Kriesi et al. 1995). Since they see social movements as exclusively extra-institutional, or in competition with institutional structures, they tend to argue that through institutionalization movements de-radicalize – moving toward mostly conventional tactics – and depoliticize. These scholars identify the state's use of divide-and-rule strategies – such as promising concessions and co-optation on the one hand, while employing repressive strategies on the other (Karstedt-Henke 1980) – and point out that these are meant to split social movements between those elements disposed toward accommodation within formal politics, and those others who resist such paths, and who further radicalize. Whether or not these state strategies result in movement decline varies from movement to movement, and from context to context.

On the other hand, a number of scholars who have sought to explain social movement impact have looked at the process of institutionalization as a premeditated action taken by social movements in order to advance their goals (Ruzza 1997; Katzenstein 1998; Giugni 1998; Raeburn 2004; Stearns and Almeida 2004; Meyer 2007; Banaszak 2010; Peterson Chapter 13). For these scholars, the process of institutionalization does not imply its natural decline; rather, in the process of institutionalizing, a social movement or parts thereof can continue "to engage in protest and pursue a radical social change agenda from within the mainstream," in a way that still reflects movement priorities (Ferree and Martin 1995: 18). This is the case, for example, in those episodes whereby activists have entered the institutions and sought to exact change from within, either during or in the aftermath of their movement's lifespan, by increasing the access of previously marginalized groups to the policy-making process (Kim et al. 2013). Institutionalization often comes with a cost for social movements, but it is not inevitably detrimental to them, since the process does not necessarily imply that individuals or groups abandon their goals, or that they lose their shared identity. Social movements' institutionalization does not necessarily make them dependent upon state hegemony. Instead, they can also act from within the institutions to achieve some of their goals, having impact through public policy, lawmaking, and stronger government accountability in policy implementation (Ruzza 1997; Meyer 2007; Rootes 2007; Banaszak 2010; Suh 2011; Peterson Chapter 13).

Whereas those scholars interested in the transformation of social movements have viewed institutionalization as a form of co-optation imposed upon movements by the weight of over-determining structural forces or state strategies (a top-down process) – thus underestimating the will and capacity of some social movements strands to engage in this process on their own terms – those concerned with social movement outcomes tend to do the converse. They read institutionalization as a proactive process which movements undergo in order to pursue their goals (a bottom-up process), thus underestimating the co-optive and assimilative force of the state. Both approaches are valid, and instead of concerning itself with one rather than the other, this chapter tries to combine both from a strategic-relational perspective – an approach to social movement research with the capacity to consider the role of agency both on the part of movement and state (Jasper 2004, 2006).

As we have already stated, the consent of the state (which is not a homogeneous actor – see Johnston 2011; Duyvendak and Jasper 2015) is also necessary for the process of social movement institutionalization. States respond variously toward the mobilization of external contenders, and depending on circumstances may: resist changes and concessions demanded by social movements; attempt to physically repress movements by force; divert social movements or parts thereof toward electoral politics, reformist social organizations or local development initiatives; or, to complicate matters further, respond in any conceivable combination of the above. Like other political actors, states "constantly seek to strategically ameliorate or defend their position of power over material and ideological resources" (Bosi 2008: 243). They are not inclined to open up opportunities or channels of participation unless they consider that they cannot do otherwise, in that the costs for them would be too high to sustain (Piven and Cloward 1977). This happens when they are confronted by overwhelming mobilizations, and when the degree of disruptiveness accruing from this is simply too high. In these cases they may feel threatened by the loss of their legitimacy and authority. In conjunction, third-party actors may constrain (in the case of countermovements) or facilitate (in the case of allies of institutionalizing social movements) states' responses toward social movements' demands (Luders 2010).

Social movements consist of heterogeneous informal networks composed of different groups, organizations, and unaffiliated individuals, which share some general goals and adopt extra-institutional means of collective action. Indeed, different elements within the same social movement might see the prospect of institutionalization somewhat differently, and might propose dissimilar strategic initiatives in order to achieve or avoid it. Different movement components confronted with what they perceive as a change in political opportunities can simultaneously pursue different paths in their struggle for social change; this can mean institutionalizing or radicalizing. Moderate groups, in their internal competition with more radical strands within the movement, may see institutionalization as a safe way to continue their struggle for social change without antagonizing authorities and countermovements, whereas other parts of the movement may prefer to follow more radical repertoires of action when confronted with repression – or even when they want to provoke it. Where movements split over the issue of institutionalization, those groups that do not follow this path may distance themselves from their old allies who now operate inside formal politics. The former see in institutionalization the danger of selling out their key concerns, and it runs against their assumption that it is through unconventional forms of actions that social change will be brought about.

By grounding this conceptual discussion in the solid historical bedrock of the empirical episode at hand, this chapter will, in the following sections, reconstruct how and when two interacting mechanisms, incorporation and democratization, drove the institutionalization process forward over thirty years of conflict in Northern Ireland. Drawing on Marco Giugni's (1998) work, this chapter defines the incorporation mechanism as what happens when a movement, or some of its internal strands, are absorbed into the existing political institutions without changing them. Meanwhile it defines the democratization mechanism as what happens when there is both a transfer of power and a change in the character of government and society, with certain sections of society newly benefiting from enhanced legal rights and state obligations toward them. By way of contextualizing the broader historical and political conditions in which Northern Ireland's wave of contention emerged, a brief overview is given below of the period from 1920 to 1968. The remainder of the chapter is devoted to explaining the two main mechanisms outlined above, which drove the institutionalization process forward over Northern Ireland's thirty years of conflict. The last section summarizes the empirical findings derived from the chapter's process-tracing approach to researching this case.

The mobilization of the Northern Ireland Civil Rights movement

From 1920 to 1972, what Northern Ireland democracy meant in practice was that Protestants could invoke the principle of majority rule to marginalize and exclude the Catholic minority, while Catholics – about one third of the region's population in this period – responded by refusing to accept the legitimacy of the regime. In reality Northern Ireland was a semi-democratic regime, thanks to multiple systematic violations of democratic procedures that put the balance of power between the region's two communities on a thoroughly asymmetrical footing. These included: a system of restrictions on local electoral franchise; the manipulation of ward boundaries and electoral areas; the Protestants' near-monopoly of public appointments; the inequitable allocation of public authority housing, regional development and private jobs; and unfair and frequently partisan policing.

In the post–Second World War settlement the British state had embraced important social welfare reforms, to which Northern Ireland could not remain immune. As a result, the region depended increasingly on subsidies from the British Exchequer. This decreased Northern Ireland's isolation, and also set in motion highly consequential episodes of latent elite contention over how to respond to the postwar reconstruction and its repercussions for the status quo of the region. These structural changes, along with the growth of the mass media, led liberal politics in Britain to become a framework of comparison for Northern Ireland politics, making starker the imbalance of power between Protestants and Catholics and creating new possibilities for collective action (Bosi 2008).

It was in this context that the CRM appeared, emerging out of pre-existing networks of opposition to the unionist establishment, and inspired by the civil rights movement in the U.S. From the outset, the CRM drew on nonviolent repertoires of action to demand the end of the systematic sociopolitical exclusion of the Catholic community. Despite a common agenda of social justice and reform, different strands of the CRM began to focus on very different things. There were those who looked to achieve sociopolitical inclusion of Catholics in the Stormont regime (the "revisionist" constructive nationalist reformers and the laborists), with the intent to make the regional political system more open and fair, and those who sought to campaign for civil rights merely in order to undermine the regime (the socialist republicans and the new left). Left-wing republican thinking at the time held the system to be "irreformable" and unable to survive without systematic discrimination. Asking for civil rights would therefore expose the nature of the system, making its demise, and Irish unification, more likely. But there was also a minority, caught up in the idealism of the international radicalism of the 1960s, who imagined the possibility of building a socialist republic capable of breaking down political divisions and rejecting both "green" and "orange" traditions.

When in the summer of 1968 the CRM started to march in the streets, it was met with harsh state repression, as well as open violent confrontation on the part of a loyalist countermovement.[5] On November 22, after some weeks of mobilization in the streets, Northern Ireland Prime Minister Terence O'Neill announced a five-point program of reforms – his hand forced by the London government, who threatened to suspend the Northern Ireland parliament and impose direct rule from Westminster if he failed to act. The reforms dealt with most of the CRM demands, apart from the principle "one man one vote" in local government elections (see Schumaker 1975 on "agenda responsiveness"). The protest activity of the CRM, together with the local and international media coverage it generated, raised the profile of Northern Ireland's civil rights problem in international public opinion. In turn, the British government felt forced to intervene in the region's policy making on behalf of the Catholic community, for fear of damaging its international legitimacy as the world's first liberal democracy. Terence O'Neill himself was to observe some time later that "the Civil Rights movement brought about reforms which would otherwise have taken years to wring from a reluctant Government" (O'Neill 1972: 111). O'Neill's reforms were not a definitive solution for the region, but they represented an initial recognition of the civil rights issue by the state, and from now on the relationship between the Northern Ireland regime and the Catholic community would be at the top of the political agenda (see Schumaker 1975 on "access responsiveness").

---

[5] Loyalists are generally those prepared to use political violence to protect their community, to defend Protestantism, and to keep Northern Ireland a part of the United Kingdom. Unionists wish to maintain the region's union with the United Kingdom.

Incorporation

In the Northern Ireland case, the incorporation mechanism was, above all, constituted by three sub-mechanisms: *attribution of threat* – or, the construction of a shared definition of the likely negative consequences of possible actions, or failure to act, on the part of some political actor; *boundary activation* – that is, an increase in the salience of the us-them distinction separating two actors (Tilly and Tarrow 2007: 215); and the *radical flank effect* – namely the "detrimental and/or beneficial impacts of radical group actions upon the reputations and effectiveness of more moderate collective actors" (Haines 2013). The threat of the full explosion of a violent communal conflict increased the salience of the boundary between radical and moderate strands within the CRM, which in turn was instrumental in triggering positive radical flank effects for the moderate strands of the movement.

O'Neill's dual strategy of repression and reform was intended to divide the CRM, and indeed led the moderate strands to call in December 1968 for a month-long truce. They promised not to organize any marches in this period, in order to give the government a chance to introduce its promised reforms. Radicals, on the other hand, felt that the reform package was inadequate, and announced that they would stage a march between Belfast and Derry. This initiative was taken with a view to transforming a potential moment of mass anger into a fully fledged political movement against the Northern Ireland system along socialist or republican lines. From start to finish, the march was characterized by loyalist brutality toward the civil rights activists, with the Northern Ireland police doing nothing to protect the marchers from attack. In the aftermath of the Belfast-Derry march, at the beginning of 1969, Northern Ireland was falling progressively into communal disorder, and becoming even more polarized in sectarian terms, according to the traditional ethno-national cleavage.

Fearing that demonstrations could no longer be carried out peacefully, and that the communal violence could explode into a full-scale civil war (reflecting the attribution of threat sub-mechanism), moderate CRM leaders and activists now started to act with considerable caution – either demobilizing, or turning toward the region's existing political institutions in order to pursue change. Quite intentionally, they progressively abandoned street politics, and interpreted the recent openings created by elements of the Northern Ireland establishment as an opportunity to further pursue their goals within a constitutional framework. John Hume, Ivan Cooper, and Paddy O'Hanlon, all of whom were moderate leaders of the CRM, won seats at the February 24th election to the Stormont parliament. Denis Haughey, a civil rights activist and later an MP for the Socialist Democratic and Labour Party (SDLP), later recalled that:

> The march between Belfast and Derry was, in my view, an irresponsible exercise, which would provoke political violence. And it was at that stage that I began to have concern that the sectarian violence, which was provoked by a minority of irresponsible students, was going to distract attention from the real problems of our society, and by the end of 1969 I began to be convinced that the only thing we needed was a coherent political approach, a coherent political party which would work on social justice issues.
> *(Denis Haughey, interview with author, 20th October 2003)*

Moderate activists and leaders felt considerable embarrassment and disappointment at the latest twist of fate for the movement, for which they did not wish to take responsibility (*Irish News*, March 17, 1969). As Eamonn McCann, one of the radical leaders of the CRM, later wrote, it became difficult "to organize a demonstration which did not end in riot" (1974: 57). With badly shaken moderates now asserting that "the appropriate place to present the political demands of the Catholic community was on the floor of the Stormont House of Commons" (McAllister 1977: 24), the stage was set for the creation of a new political party. Thus emerged in August 1970 the SDLP under the leadership of Gerry Fitt, John Hume, Austin Currie, Ivan Cooper, Paddy Devlin, and Paddy O'Hanlon, all central figures within the CRM. Embracing the aims of the CRM, the SDLP provided a political outlet for moderate elements of the Catholic community within the existing political institutions.

The threat attribution induced by the emerging communal conflict, which pushed moderates off the streets and into mainstream politics, was accompanied by a profound deepening of the divide running through the Catholic community. After the riots of summer 1969 and the subsequent deployment of the British Army on the streets of Northern Ireland, many in the Catholic ghettos felt that a different stance needed to be taken in defending their communities, and came to see armed republican militancy as the means to do this. Political violence became an absolutely necessary repertoire of action in protecting Catholic areas from loyalist attack, and from the repressive action of state forces that was simultaneously indiscriminate and discriminatory – that is, catching uninvolved citizens in the crossfire, but falling disproportionately on Catholics. A former republican volunteer – who had taken part in civil rights marches through his involvement in the youth wing of the Nationalist Party in the late 1960s – recalled his passing into the PIRA in this way:

> I decided to join the IRA as I was disillusioned with ordinary politics and how ineffective our politicians were in any sort of change. Then, I believed that an armed conflict could lead to a change in our society. Gradually from 1970 on, for one year, I got more and more radical. Internment had a huge effect on me and I thought then [more] of joining the Irish Republican Army. I discussed [it] with my friends and I was very aware of what an involvement in the Irish struggle meant, but I decided that there was no other option. And I joined late 1971.
>
> *(Interview no. 19) (Bosi 2012: 363)*

Separately from the incorporation of the moderate strands – and partly in consequence – the wave of contention moved progressively into the hands of republicans, who criticized the moderates' retreat from street mobilization as a sellout. These developments within the movement – triggered by the openings created by the Northern Ireland and British authorities to entice the moderates while ramping up repression and re-imposing order by force – further accentuated the already existing and deeply rooted political divisions within the Catholic community. Reflecting the boundary activation sub-mechanism, the fault line between constitutional nationalism and militant, physical force republicanism became more salient than ever – with the former now being represented by the SDLP, and the latter by the Provisional IRA and its political wing, Provisional Sinn Féin (Todd 1990). From 1970 on, the PIRA embarked on a military campaign involving gun and bomb attacks against security forces, commercial premises, militants of rival republican groups, loyalist paramilitaries, and civilians.[6]

---

[6] The Provisional IRA was responsible for over 1,750 deaths between 1970 and 1994.

Under further pressure from London for reform, but at the same time faced with the countervailing pressure of the violent loyalist countermovement against reform (Walker 2004), the Northern Ireland regime attempted from summer 1969 to early 1972 to resolve the conflict by conceding important pieces of legislation (see Schumaker 1975 on "policy responsiveness"). These were congruent with most of the early demands made by the CRM, and were aimed at eradicating the perceived source of unrest and stimulating Catholic participation in the regional institutions.

New measures included:

- The appointment of commissions of inquiry to investigate and report on the causes of the latest protests, and to examine the state bodies implicated in any grievances (Cameron 1969; Hunt 1969; Macrory 1970; Compton 1971; Scarman 1972).
- The abolition of property qualifications pertaining to voting rights, and introduction of universal suffrage in local elections (1969).
- The disarmament of the RUC and replacement of the B Specials by a new, locally recruited part-time security force within the British Army, the Ulster Defence Regiment (UDR) (1969).
- The introduction of a Parliamentary Commissioner for Complaints (1969), in order to deal with complaints regarding discrimination in local administration (ombudsman).
- The institution of both a completely new Ministry of Community Relations and an independent Community Relations Commission (1970), set up to oppose sectarian practices and to promote good community relations.
- The establishment of the Prevention of Incitement to Hatred Act (1970), in order to prosecute people responsible for inciting sectarian sentiment.
- The creation of the Northern Ireland Housing Executive under the Ministry of Development (1971).

If the PIRA was partly responsible for having further stoked the communal conflict in the region, thus moving moderate movement strands out of the streets, it should also be considered that its armed campaign was "useful" in enhancing the bargaining position of the SDLP within the existing institutions (an example of the positive radical flank effect). The British authorities' assumption was that once Catholic grievances had been dealt with, Northern Ireland would quieten down. They put pressure on Stormont to encourage the incorporation of the moderate strands of the CRM within the existing regional institutions, through the integration of most of the movement's demands into public agendas and policies. However, this was not intended to transform the basic rules of the game in the region, or to fundamentally alter its distribution of power in the short to medium term (in keeping with the incorporation mechanism) – with one fear being that of antagonizing the burgeoning loyalist countermovement in the region. Meanwhile, the wave of contention initiated by the CRM was already passing into the hands of the PIRA, with some predictable implications for the future development of the conflict.

Democratization

Democratization operated mainly through the interrelated influence of three sub-mechanisms: *repression* ("action by authorities that increases the cost – actual or potential – of an actor's claim making" (Tilly and Tarrow 2007: 215)); *co-optation* ("incorporation of a previously excluded political actor into some centre of power" (Tilly and Tarrow 2007: 215)); and *incorporated activism* (incorporation of activists into the routine of conventional politics). As will be demonstrated, while repression and co-optation worked in close concert with one another from the outset of the wave of contention, they were also important later on in triggering incorporated activism sub-mechanisms on the part of the PIRA from the early 1980s forward.

The Northern Ireland and British authorities employed wide and indiscriminate repressive measures in the early years of the conflict, with many well-known examples achieving notoriety. During the Falls Road curfew of July 1970, soldiers sealed off a republican area of Belfast for two days, refusing to let people leave their homes during a house-to-house search. On a single morning in August 1971, over 350 people (mostly Catholic) were locked up without trial, marking the introduction of internment. And most importantly of all, on Bloody Sunday in January 1972, British soldiers killed fourteen people and wounded many others at a civil rights march in Derry (O'Dochartaigh 2005). As a consequence of the worsening security situation in the aftermath of Bloody Sunday, the Stormont regime was suspended in March

1972, and direct rule was introduced from Westminster. The stated purpose was for direct rule to be a short-term measure, while a solution was found among the regional actors so that devolution could be reestablished.

From 1974 onwards the PIRA's "all out" armed campaign was mostly contained military by the British armed forces (reflecting the repression sub-mechanism). In response to this, the PIRA attempted to retrieve the initiative through its "Long War" strategy – a campaign of attrition aimed at wearing down the British will to remain in Northern Ireland. It moved away from its traditional structure, modelled on the brigades and battalions of a regular army, toward an emphasis on small, cellular Active Service Units – designed to be more difficult to compromise. In turn, the new republican strategy was put under increasing pressure from the early 1980s on by a multi-level response on the part of the British security forces. This included a more sophisticated intelligence war that utilized informers to penetrate the organization, extradition treaties, increased surveillance, and the development of anti-terrorist technology (Cunningham 2000) – all of which was aimed at increasing the costs of joining and remaining within the PIRA ("pre-emption" and "deterrence").

The British state, under threat from the PIRA's mounting armed campaign, not only acted through counter-insurgency measures, but also employed Keynesian social and economic policies (from housing and planning through to education and employment) in order to reestablish its authority within the Catholic ghettos.[7] Urban, social, and economic development policies were rolled out ("output responsiveness" Schumaker 1975) with the intention of co-opting the broad Catholic community within the framework of the regional institutions, by driving the community into the hands of the moderate, constitutional nationalist SDLP (reflecting the co-optation sub-mechanism). The British endeavor at regional community development and economic regeneration was geared toward undermining the material basis (social disorder, alienation, and social exclusion) of communal violence by bringing Northern Ireland up to "British standards." However, the increasing engagement between the British state and the Catholic community did not eradicate the PIRA from the latter as the authorities

---

[7] This part on the co-optation sub-mechanism heavily relies on the important empirical material provided by the works of Darby (1986), Bean (2007), and Kevlihan (2013).

hoped. Instead, "it actually strengthened the Provisional movement's position within its base areas and facilitated a process of institutionalization" (Bean 2007: 6). Thus, insofar as the British state gradually regained some of its power within the Catholic community, such power had to be shared with the PIRA (Darby 1986). Once the British state tried to use its resources to rebuild its hegemony within Catholic areas, it entered into an important relation with the PIRA, which by the mid-1970s had reoriented itself to some degree toward community development, with a view to maintaining a significant presence in those areas in spite of the heavy repression it suffered (Kevlihan 2013). As Kevin Bean suggests, "community organizations and political structures that had started out as agencies of revolutionary mobilization became gatekeepers between the state and the nationalist community, as well as acting transmission belts for the Provisional movement" (2007: 6).

The attempted co-optation of the broad Catholic community determined the patterns through which republican activists got incorporated within the Northern Ireland institutions (incorporated activism sub-mechanism). Republican leaders were increasingly weary of the counter-productive impact of the armed struggle strategy in a situation of military stalemate with the British state (repression sub-mechanism), and were conscious of losing ground politically to the SDLP (co-optation sub-mechanism). Thus, as a new strategy presented itself via the possibility of challenging the British state's policies toward the Catholic community (what Watts calls "representative contention" in reference to the Turkish/Kurdish case), Sinn Féin MPs and local government councilors started to bargain and mobilize to obtain important concessions for their community by pressurizing institutions from within. This is how a former PIRA activist summarized the situation:

> We have achieved a lot. We knew we were never going to win the
> physical war against the Brits. But as us the Brits were never going
> to win the war against us. Because we were not going to go away. I
> think that this is absolutely fantastic that the war is over. I think it is
> time that the war was over. I think that the leadership direction has
> been great. I think that it was inevitable that this was going to
> happen. Politics had to take over from militarization. People
> wanted it. The movement wanted it and the time wanted it.
>
> *(Interview no. 1)*

By the late 1980s and early 1990s, republican leaders sensed that, through the peace process, they could attain numerous goals: gaining a substantial role in shaping Northern Ireland institutions, with the prospect of achieving greater legitimacy and increased support for Sinn Féin from within the broader Catholic community; eventually taking governmental power north and south; securing prisoners' release; destabilizing and dividing unionism; and, ultimately, playing a central role in history as the political force key to resolving the conflict by assuring that the Catholic community could no longer be treated as second-class citizens in Northern Ireland. On August 31, 1994, the PIRA announced a complete cessation of military activity, thus allowing Sinn Féin to take a seat at the "peace talks" of the following years that led to the Good Friday Agreement of 1998, whereby:

> for the first time the structural relations of Catholic inequality and Protestant power, established by plantation, reconstituted in an urban-industrial setting in the 19th century, and actively maintained by the British state was being dismantled by the British government and ... this was guaranteed internationally.
>
> *(Ruane and Todd 2015)*

Thus the Good Friday Agreement, with its consociational forms of ethnic power-sharing, represented a transfer of power to the Catholic community by guaranteeing them representation in the polity, as well as in the wider social and political sphere (democratization mechanism). The GFA used the practices of the Republicans bargaining with the British state in order to grant to the nationalist community new concession into a new synthesis.

Conclusions

The emergence of a system that gave to the Northern Ireland Catholic minority institutionalized political influence in the region was not inevitable, but rather was contingent on a complex set of interactions within and between different regional actors. Unionists exerted immense pressure against power-sharing throughout the conflict, and without the pressure of the CRM mobilization initially, and subsequently the PIRA armed campaign, the unionists might well have succeeded in preventing full democratic inclusion in decision-making for the marginalized

Catholic community. With the implementation of the Good Friday Agreement, it had ultimately taken almost thirty years to reach a devolved settlement with the support of both the Protestant and Catholic communities. While the Northern Ireland regime and British state were able to incorporate moderate strands of opposition early on in the conflict via their dual strategy of reform and repression, it would take much longer, and much more in the way of concessions (including the provision of social services), to move the radical strands toward incorporation. It is also important, however, to point out that the incorporation of the former (the moderates) made the state more responsive to the claims of the latter (the radicals).

This strategic-relational reading facilitates a long-range, context-sensitive analysis of the process of institutionalization, which avoids falling into the trap of creating a rigid and deterministic vision of development sequences. It also moves toward more dynamic explanations of social movement institutionalization processes via an emphasis on the concatenation of different mechanisms and sub-mechanisms. This chapter shows how institutionalization is a process driven, to a significant extent, by dynamics located within the process itself, in patterns of interactions involving multiple actors within the relational field formed by the political conflict. Therefore, any reading of how and when social movements institutionalize need to pay attention to the shifting and mutually influencing interactions between social movements and the state over an extended period of time that is not limited to a single protest wave, but takes into consideration different types of contention that are strongly interrelated (Maney 2007; Bosi and Malthaner 2013). This means that we need not only to delimit our analysis of the interrelation between social movements and the state authorities at one moment in time, but also to capture their shifting across time in order to yield a fuller explanation of how and when institutionalization processes occur.

Even if it is true that this research is investigative and does not have general application at this stage, however, the dynamic perspective used in this chapter, which considers processes and mechanisms to be key units of analysis, can enhance our understanding of how and when processes of institutionalization unfold as well as allow comparison between different processes of institutionalization across time and space. In the future, comparative research combining quantitative and historical analyses will provide a better assessment of the validity and frequency of conceptualized sequences of social movements' institutionalization.

References

Alimi, Eitan, Lorenzo Bosi, and Chares Demtriou. 2012. "Relational Dynamics and Processes of Radicalization: A Comparative Framework." *Mobilization*, 18(1): 7–26.

Alimi, Eitan, Demetriou Chares, and Lorenzo Bosi. 2015. *The Dynamics of Radicalization. A Relational and Comparative Perspective*. New York: Oxford University Press.

Banaszak, Lee Ann. 2010. *The Women's Movement Inside and Outside the State*. New York: Cambridge University Press.

Bean, Kevin. 2007. *The New Politics of Sinn Féin*. Liverpool: Liverpool University Press.

Bosi, Lorenzo. 2006. "The Dynamics of Social Movements Development: The Northern Ireland's Civil Rights Movement in the 1960s." *Mobilization*, 11(1): 81–100.

Bosi, Lorenzo. 2008. "Explaining the Emergence Process of the Civil Rights Protest in Northern Ireland (1945–1968): Insights from a Relational Social Movement Approach." *Journal of Historical Sociology*, (2): 342–371.

Bosi, Lorenzo. 2012. "Explaining Pathways to Armed Activism in the Provisional IRA, 1969–1972." *Social Science History*, 36(3): 347–390.

Bosi, Lorenzo and Stefan Malthaner. 2013. "A Framework to Analyze Forms of Political Violence Based on Patterns of Socio-Spatial Relations." Unpublished presented at the European University Institute.

Cameron Report. 1969. *Disturbances in Northern Ireland*, Cmd 532. Belfast: HMSO.

Compton Report. 1971. *The Enquiry into Allegations the Security Forces of Physical Brutality in Northern Ireland Arising Out of Events on the 9th August 1971*. Cmd 4823. Belfast: HMSO.

Cunningham, Michael. 2000. *British Government Policy in Northern Ireland*. Manchester: Manchester University Press.

Darby, John. 1986. *Intimidation and the Control of Conflict in Northern Ireland.* Syracuse: Syracuse University Press.

Duyvendak, Jan Willem and James Jasper. 2015. *Breaking Down the State: Protestors Engaged.* Amsterdam: Amsterdam University Press.

Ferree, M.M. and P.Y. Martin. 1995. "Doing the Work of the Movement: Feminist Organizations." In M.M. Ferree and P.Y. Martin (eds.), *Feminist Organizations: Harvest of the New Women's Movement.* Philadelphia, PA: Temple University Press.

Gerges, Fawaz A. 2005. *The Far Enemy: Why Jihad Went Global.* New York: Cambridge University Press.

Giugni, Marco. 1998. "Social Movements and Change: Incorporation, Transformation, and Democratization." In Marco Giugni, Doug McAdam, and Charles Tilly (eds.), *From Contention to Democracy.* Lanham, MD: Rowman and Littlefield, xi–xxvi.

Giugni, Marco and Florence Passy. 1998. "Contentious Politics in Complex Societies: New Social Movements between Conflict and Cooperation." In Marco G. Giugni, Doug McAdam, and Charles Tilly (eds.), *From Contention to Democracy.* Lanham, MD: Rowman & Littlefield, 81–107.

Goldstone, Jack A. 2004. "More Social Movements or Fewer? Beyond Political Opportunity Structures to Relational Fields." *Theory and Society,* 33: 333–365.

Haines, Herbert H. 2013. "Radical Flank Effects." Published online in the Wiley Blackwell Encyclopedia of Social and Political Movements. DOI:10.1002/9780470674871.wbespm174

Hunt Commentary. 1969. *Report Advisory Committee on Police in Northern Ireland.* Cmd 535. Belfast: HMSO.

Jasper, James M. 2004. "A Strategic Approach to Collective Action: Looking for Agency in Social-Movement Choices." *Mobilization,* 9(1): 1–16.

Jasper, James M. 2006. *Getting Your Way: Strategic Dilemmas in the Real World.* Chicago: University of Chicago Press.

Johnston, Hank. 2011. *States and Social Movements.* Cambridge: Polity.

Karstedt-Henke, Susanne. 1980. "Theorien zur Erklä rung terroristischer Bewegungen." In E. Blankenberg (ed.), *Politik der inneren Sicherheit.* Frankfurt am Main: Suhrkamp, 198–234.

Katzenstein, Mary. 1998. "Stepsisters: Feminist Movement Activism in Different Institutional Spaces." In David Meyer and Sidney Tarrow (eds.), *The Social Movement Society*. New York: Rowman and Littlefield Publishers, 195–216.

Kevlihan, Rob. 2013. *Aid, Insurgencies and Conflict Transformation, When Greed is Good*. New York: Routledge.

Kim, Sookyung, Paul Y. Chang, and Gi-Wook Shin. 2013. "Past Activism, Party pressure, and Ideology: Explaining the Vote to Deploy Korean Troops to Iraq." *Mobilization: An International Quarterly*, 18(3): 243–266.

Koopmans, Ruud. 1993. "The Dynamics of Protest Waves: West Germany, 1965 to 1989." *American Sociological Review*, 58(5): 637–658.

Koopmans, Ruud. 2004. "Protest in Time and Space: The Evolution of Waves of Contention." In David Snow, Sarah Soule and Hanspeter Kriesi (eds.), *The Blackwell Companion to Social Movements*. Oxford: Blackwell Publishing Ltd, 19–46.

Kriesi, Hanspeter, Ruud Koopmans, Jan Willem Dyvendak, and Marco G. Giugni. 1995. *New Social Movements in Western Europe: A Comparative Perspective*. Minneapolis: University of Minnesota Press.

Luders, Joseph. 2010. *The Civil Rights Movement and the Logic of Social Change*. New York: Cambridge University Press.

Macrory Report. 1970. *Review Body on Local Government in Northern Ireland*, Cmd 546. Belfast: HMSO.

Mahoney, James. 2000. "Path Dependence in Historical Sociology." *Theory and Society*, 29(4): 507–548.

Maney, Gregory. 2007. "From Civil War to Civil Rights and Back Again: The Interrelation of Rebellion and Protest in Northern Ireland 1955–1972." *Research in Social Movements, Conflict and Change*, 27: 3–35.

McAdam, Doug, Sidney Tarrow, and Charles Tilly. 2001. *Dynamics of Contention*. Cambridge and New York: Cambridge University Press.

McAllister, Ian. 1977. *The Northern Ireland Social Democratic and Labour Party: Political Opposition in a Divided Society*. London: Macmillan.

McCann, Eamonn. 1974. *War and an Irish Town*. Harmondsworth: Penguin Book.

Meyer, David S. 2007. *The Politics of Protest: Social Movements in America*. New York: Oxford University Press.

O'Dochartaigh, Niall. 2005. *From Civil Rights to Armalites: Derry and the Birth of the Irish Troubles*. New York: Palgrave Macmillan.

O'Neill, Terence. 1972. *The Autobiography of Terence O'Neill, Prime Minister of Northern Ireland 1963–1969*. London: Rupert Hart-Davis.

Piven, Frances Fox and Richard A. Cloward. 1977. *Poor People's Movements: Why They Succeed, How They Fail*. New York: Vintage.

Raeburn, Nicole. 2004. *Lesbian and Gay Workplace Rights: Changing Corporate America from Inside Out*. Minneapolis, MN: University of Minnesota Press.

Rootes, Christopher. 2007. "EnvironmentalMovements." In George Ritzer (ed.), *Blackwell Encyclopedia of Sociology*, Vol. III. Malden, MA: Blackwell, 1428–1433.

Ruane, Joseph and Jennifer Todd. 2015. "Multiple Temporalities in Violent Conflict: Northern Ireland, the Basque Country and Macedonia." In Lorenzo Bosi, Niall O'Doghartaigh, and Daniela Pisoiu (eds.), *Political Violence in Context: Time, Space and Milieu*. Fergham: ECPR Press.

Ruzza, Carlo. 1997. "Institutional Actors and the Italian Peace Movement: Specializing and Branching Out." *Theory and Society*, 26: 87–127.

Scarman Tribunal. 1972. *Report of Tribunal of Violence and Civil Disturbances in Northern Ireland in 1969*. Cmnd 566. Belfast: HMSO.

Schumaker, Paul. 1975. "Policy Responsiveness to Protest-Group Demands." *Journal of Politics*, 37: 488–521.

Stearns, Linda Brewster and Paul D. Almeida. 2004. "The Formation of State Actor-Social Movement Coalitions and Favorable Policy Outcomes." *Social Problems*, 51(4): 478–504.

Stinchcome, Arthur L. 1995. *The Logic of Social Research*. Chicago and London: The University of Chicago Press.

Suh, Doowon. 2011. "Institutionalizing Social Movements: The Dual Strategy of the Korean Women's Movement" *The Sociological Quarterly*, 52, 442–471.

Tarrow, Sidney. 1989. *Democracy and Disorder*. Oxford: Clarendon Press.

Tilly, Charles and Sidney Tarrow. 2007. *Contentious Politics*. Boulder, CO: Paradigm Publishers.

Todd, Jennifer. 1990. "Northern Irish Nationalist Political Culture." *Irish Political Studies*, 2(1): 31–44.

Walker, Graham. 2004. *A History of the Ulster Unionist Party*. Manchester: Manchester University Press.

Watts, Nicole. 2006. "Activists in Office: Pro-Kurdish Contentious Politics in Turkey." *Ethnopolitics: Formerly Global Review of Ethnopolitics*, 5(2): 125–144.

CONCLUSION

15 PROTEST ONLINE
Theorizing the consequences of online engagement

Jennifer Earl

Drawing inspiration from protesters who have weathered social stigma, police dogs, rubber bullets, private militias, and even death, social movement scholars collectively hope that when people come together to collectively embody "power in movement" (Tarrow 1994) that this power has some influence or effect. Leaving aside for a moment the varied ability of the field to empirically validate these hopes where traditional, "offline" protest is concerned, many activists and social movement scholars have been far less hopeful about the potential implications of Internet-enabled activism. Instead, scholars and activists have questioned the ability of Internet activism to make change, denigrating online activism by referring to it as "slacktivism," or privileging offline protest as "real protest" (Diani 2000; Rucht 2004; Tarrow 1998) or "'real' actions" (Van Laer and Van Aelst 2010).

But, these negative views are in contrast to what many participants report. For instance, a 2010 survey found that 59% of Americans, and 64% of Internet users, thought that the Internet has had a major impact on the ability of groups to impact society and 49% of Americans, and 52% of Internet users, thought this was true about impacts in their local communities too (Rainie et al. 2011). Likewise, when respondents had participated in the last 12 months in a online group that they judged

I would like to thank the participants of the Berlin MOVEOUT workshop for their comments and insights on the original draft of the chapter, particularly David Meyer and Sidney Tarrow who provided key comments that shaped my revisions. I would also like to thank the Editors for their feedback and hard work on this volume, The John D. and Catherine T. MacArthur Foundation for its support of the Youth and Participatory Politics Research Network (which partially supported this work), and Heidi Reynolds-Stenson for her research assistance.

to be successful, 46% thought that Internet usage played a major role in raising awareness about the issue (Rainie et al. 2011: 3).

I challenge strident dismissals of Internet activism by evaluating the likely range of potential impacts for different kinds of Internet activism. Specifically, I review research on four broad types of Internet activism to evaluate the likelihood of outcomes for each type. I find that one of these types of Internet activism is likely to be ineffective but its offline equivalent is similarly ineffective. For two other types of Internet activism, I find that their potential effects are largely indirect and thus greatly depend on a mediating variable to ultimately determine effectiveness. For the final type of Internet activism, I argue that it might be consequential and therefore examine potential consequences in terms of policy, cultural, internal movement, and biographical impacts. The goal of the chapter is to provide both a more even-handed comparison of offline and online activism and to suggest paths for future research.

Defining offline and online activism

Earl et al. (2010) extensively reviewed research on Internet activism and found that Internet activism includes a wide range of uses of technology and kinds of action, ranging from online information provision, to hacktivism, to culture jamming, to online advertising of offline events, and beyond. This makes it meaningless to discuss "Internet activism" writ large because each version of Internet activism has its own theoretical properties and trends in empirical findings. Instead, they suggest distinguishing between four broad styles of Internet engagement:[1]

(1) brochureware, which involves the distribution of information online but does not directly connect information distribution with opportunities to mobilize either online or offline;
(2) the online facilitation of offline activism (i.e., "e-mobilization"), which primarily uses the Web for recruitment and coordination for offline protest events;

[1] This classification is consistent with other schemes that have paid attention to differences between actions that are supported using the Web versus actions that actually take place through or on the Web (e.g., Vegh 2003; Van Laer and Van Aelst 2010). Of course, in practice, different styles of activism are often combined within larger campaigns and/or within the portfolio of a social movement organization or larger social movement.

(3) online organizing, which involves the organization of entire campaigns and movements online; and

(4) online participation, which occurs when individuals actually engage in activism while online (e.g., in conventional formats such as online petition-signing but also in more controversial forms such as distributed denial of service attacks).

In the sections that follow, I evaluate the likelihood of social movement consequences, and the mechanisms that might drive such consequences, for each of these four ideal types of Internet activism.

The impacts of brochureware

In brochureware, the Internet is used to make information broadly available at low costs. This might happen simply (e.g., plain text on a fairly static website), but can be more dynamic (e.g., including frequent updates or changes) and media-rich (e.g., using videos versus text to provide information). If this kind of Internet activism were to lead to social movement outcomes, the mechanism would be through the power of information because brochureware exists entirely to spread information (see Table 15.1 for a summary of these and other arguments).

But, can information access alone lead to movement outcomes? I argue no, and note that this answer would be the same whether the information was obtained offline or online. In fact, research on offline information provision has found no evidence that information alone is sufficient for motivating participation and/or directly creating actual social change (although it may be a necessary condition). Put in the classic language of resource mobilization, knowledge of grievances and knowledge of a movement are insufficient drivers of participation or movement emergence (McCarthy and Zald 1973, 1977).

At the same time, it is important to not dismiss the social importance of providing access to social movement-relevant information, particularly in less democratic environments. That is, in countries where censorship is severe, information provision through brochureware might be socially notable, even though information alone is not able to drive a social movement or social movement success. For instance, the Chinese government's attempt to limit access to information on protest within China and on specific religious groups, such as the Falun Gong, renders

Table 15.1 *Evaluating the consequences of different styles*
of Internet activism

Type of Internet activism	Mechanism(s)	Likely impact
Brochureware	Information as power	Limited (although information access in censored environments may be socially notable)
Online Facilitation of Offline Activism	Indirect: improving recruitment into offline activism	Dependent on successfulness of offline protests that people are recruited into
	Indirect: online attention drives media coverage	Dependent on whether media coverage has identifiable consequences
Online Organizing	Indirect: increasing online and offline protest opportunities	Dependent on the effects of offline and online protests
	Indirect: online attention drives media coverage	Dependent on whether media coverage has identifiable consequences
Online Participation	Flash flood model of power in movement	Policy impacts are possible in specific scenarios (as is true for offline protest), including: – when clear decision-points exist – for corporate targets and/or elected officials in competitive markets or districts (respectively) – where geographic networks of supporters would otherwise be too diffuse to generate activism Internal impacts are possible, including: – cross-movement and inter-organizational coalition formation – issue spillover across movements – frame diffusion online – tactical diffusion online

Table 15.1 *(cont.)*

Type of Internet activism	Mechanism(s)	Likely impact
		Cultural consequences are possible, including: – influencing public opinion – influencing cultural production Biographical consequences are inconclusive, but given that many known biographical consequences of offline activism are negative, this might not be an issue

covert access to this information quite important. Although Chinese Internet censorship is sophisticated and substantial (Deibert et al. 2008, 2010), a number of engineered routes for accessing banned information exist (Roberts et al. 2010). Information distributed and maintained through these routes may serve as an important lifeline and recruiting tool for movements that cannot lawfully have a public face in their country of origin.

Even in less restrictive countries, information provision can still be socially significant. For instance, in a number of Southeast Asian countries, online activists have used the Web to identify and publicize political corruption, forming entire anti-corruption movements online. In the United States, information provided through Wikileaks has been important to understanding many diplomatic and military operations. But, this social significance is not the same as generating movement consequences.

E-mobilization (online facilitation of offline activism)

The online facilitation of offline mobilization, or what Earl and Kimport (2011) have termed "e-mobilization," uses the Internet to support off-line mobilizations, such as rallies or demonstrations. E-mobilizations are quite common, including Facebook calls to protest that generated widespread protest (e.g., Bloomberg News 2011; Hossain 2013; Rambler 2011), as when an 18-year-old New Jersey student called for school walk-outs that ultimately took place across the state (Heyboer 2010). Social movement organizations (SMOs) have also used Facebook to call for school walk-outs (Gabbatt and Batty 2010) and Facebook-based calls for protest played a role in the Arab Spring (Eltahawy 2010; Tufekci and Wilson 2012) and Occupy Wall Street (Caren and Gaby 2011; Castells 2012). Of course, mobilizations may also be facilitated outside of social media, such as through organizational websites that provide a wide range of online support to would-be attendees, including downloadable banners, rideshare boards, roomshare boards, group travel information, and other logistics information.

I argue that there are two indirect mechanisms that could tie e-mobilization to social movement outcomes (see Table 15.1). First, e-mobilization may increase offline recruitment and participation, and that offline mobilization, in turn, may lead to social movement outcomes. Second, online discussion of offline social movement protests might generate media coverage, which might drive changes in public opinion, affect agenda setting, and/or create pressure for legislative change just as traditional media coverage of social movement protests has been thought to. I evaluate each of these potential mechanisms in turn.

Indirectly courting success: increasing recruitment and mobilization levels

Because e-mobilization is designed to turn people out to offline events, it has been primarily studied as a recruitment tool. That implies that there are two links in the chain between Internet recruitment efforts and movement outcomes: (1) whether Internet recruitment efforts actually result in recruitment; and (2) whether the offline protests that individuals are recruited into "matter." I review research dealing with each of these links in turn.

The Internet as a recruiting tool: In their review of the literature, Earl et al. (2014) find that there is substantially more evidence in favor of the Internet as a powerful recruitment tool than against. For instance, Fisher et al. (2005) examined Web-based recruitment, showing both an integrated and independent effect: in the integrated effect, SMOs used the Internet to contact members, and in the independent effect, participants were only recruited via the Internet. Similarly, Fisher and Boekkooi (2010) also find positive recruitment effects.

Despite the substantial amount of evidence showing that the Internet can be used to recruit into social movement participation, a number of scholars still contest the value or return on Internet-enabled recruitment and mobilization efforts for offline events. One prominent concern is that only face-to-face relationships can support significant enough relationships to pull one into, or sustain, activism, and such notables as Diani (2000), Tarrow (1998), and Rucht (2004) have taken this position. Van Laer and Van Aelst (2010) aptly summarize their collective argument: "the Internet is unable to create the necessary trust and strong ties that are necessary to build a sustainable network of activists" (1163).

I challenge this claim for several reasons. First, empirically it is simply incorrect to argue that there is no effect of Internet usage on recruitment and mobilization to offline protests. It may be that in many cases, the effect of e-mobilization plays only one part in a larger mobilization strategy such that the Internet is not the exclusive method used to mobilize individuals. But, even when compared against other recruitment tools, research shows that online solicitations do enhance offline participation. And, in some instances, the Internet can be the sole recruitment tool for offline protests. For instance, the online group Anonymous's battle with the Church of Scientology has featured large, internationally coordinated offline protest rallies with coordinated messaging, common signs and talking points, and properly obtained protest permits (Beyer 2011). Anonymous does this organizing and recruitment entirely online and through weak, impersonal ties (i.e., all participants in Anonymous are known to one another as Anonymous, offline participants tend to wear Guy Fawkes masks to conceal their individual identities, and having ongoing interpersonal ties between members is discouraged).

Second, the basic foundation of this criticism relies on a faulty assumption: that Internet usage cannot be used to create and maintain strong relationships (which the critics assume are necessary for recruitment and mobilization to take place). To the contrary, substantial amounts of Internet and society research show that the Internet can be used to effectively initiate, grow, and maintain substantial relationships and collaborations across a wide variety of domains (Hampton 2003; Hampton et al. 2011, 2011; Hampton and Wellman 2003; Rainie et al. 2011; Rainie and Wellman 2012). Take, for instance, the most intimate of relationships, marriage: by 2006, 74% of active Internet users who were single had used the Internet to date and 15% of Americans knew someone who met their marriage partner online (Madden and Lenhart 2006). More generally, research shows that people often use the Internet to solicit information and support on major and minor life decisions (Boase et al. 2006). Work groups and business and civic groups have also been impacted by Internet usage, with scholars arguing that Internet usage augments connections and builds robust collaborations (e.g., Shirky 2008). Finally, even when relationships stay entirely online, virtual communities have been shown to hold the capacity to build strong and supportive online relationships that can endure across time (Rheingold 1993).

Third, this criticism treats new media in a fundamentally different way than traditional media has been treated, but does so without explanation or cause. Scholars do not generally doubt that traditional media coverage is sought by movements because of its potential to increase support and participation in movements and to raise pressure on decision-makers. And yet, traditional media has not been argued to create or maintain strong interpersonal relationships. For example, scholarship has not shown that newspapers are used to create and maintain strong interpersonal relationships among activists. Critics of Internet activism have generally not made clear why they believe that traditional media can support activism without developing or maintaining strong interpersonal relationships but online media cannot.

Another prominent concern about the veracity of Internet-based recruiting argues that only already politically active people engage in online activism and therefore there is no new value added in terms of rising participation from online activism. Van Laer and Van Aelst (2010) summarize this concern: "the internet will chiefly serve those activists and groups that are already active, thus reinforcing existing patterns of political participation in society" (1161). However, again, these objections don't fit well with existing evidence.

First, a number of representative surveys have shown that although some people do politically engage both offline and online, many don't. For instance, a Pew Internet and American Life survey from 2009 found that 32% of American adults had signed a petition, with 25% of all adults signing a paper petition and 19% signing an online petition (Smith et al. 2009: 24). Of all petition signers, half had only signed paper petitions, 23% had signed only online petitions, and only 23% had signed both paper and online petitions (Smith et al. 2009: 25).

Second, research suggests that one of the strongest predictors of online political engagement is the level of overall Web engagement, not the level of offline political engagement. That is, people who do many things online, particularly news and information seeking online, are much more likely to be politically and civically engaged online (Smith et al. 2009).

Third, this argument seems to assume that people only expose themselves to politics online when they set out intending to do so – the active search out information online to be active about and the inactive don't. While there is a real ability to tailor information search (offline and online), research suggests that politics is nonetheless more leaky online than this echo-chamber view of the Internet suggests. Wojcieszak and Mutz (2009), for instance, found that political discussions occur in a wide variety of non-political domains online, such as hobby groups. In fact, their research suggests that "on average, roughly half of participation in nonpolitical chats or message boards nonetheless involves some discussion of political topics and controversial public issues" (45). Moreover, while overtly political forums online mirror offline political forums in terms of being relatively ideologically homogenous, online social forums in which political discussions take place are much more heterogeneous and more likely to expose individuals to alternative points of view and information. Political discussion in these more seemingly social forums actually, then, involves high levels of democratic expression and discussion. Additional research on polarization online also suggests that while people may mimic their offline tendencies to search for information that conforms to their views, people who go online often are more likely to have been exposed to different views (Brundidge 2010), and, once confronted with opposing information online, still engage with it nonetheless (i.e., continue to read stories to which they would disagree; Garrett 2009).

Finally, there is some promising evidence that online forms of engagement may help to equalize access to political participation; that is, the Internet might be used as a compensatory technology. A national survey of youth found that contrary to assumptions, African American youth were the most politically engaged group online (Cohen et al. 2012). Groups like the Black Youth Project (blackyouthproject.com) are helping black youth to find their voice online and to participate in institutional and protest politics both online and offline. This is quite important given that African Americans have been relatively shut out of institutional politics and even other social movements (i.e., debates within feminism and LGBTQ movements, among others, about whether the issues of feminists of color or LGBTQ people of color were well-represented). Finding a media that is able to engage so many African American youth is a very important turn and is hardly mobilizing the already politically advantaged.

Do offline protests matter?: Even though the Internet can be used to successfully recruit activists, e-mobilization is still an indirect path to social movement consequences. For enhanced recruitment to actually lead to a social, cultural, or political change, the offline protests and movements that participants are recruited into must still "matter" in order for outcomes to occur. Put differently, since research shows that e-mobilization can increase offline recruitment and mobilization, the question of eventual impact, then, turns on whether offline mobilizations are as effective as social movement scholars imagine them to be! As contributions to this volume have shown, while it is clear that offline protest can matter in some situations, offline protest is far from ubiquitously effective, making offline efforts a potential weak link in the outcomes chain for this kind of online engagement.

Traditional and new media in generating coverage as a mechanism

In addition to buttressing recruitment, e-mobilization may lead to social movement outcomes by driving coverage of protest, which then becomes independently influential. A wide variety of scholarship has been concerned with media coverage of movements (see Gamson 2004 for a recent review). Although some scholars have seen the media as only relevant as a recruitment tool, others have argued that media coverage of protest can independently create pressure for different kinds of outcomes. For instance, Gamson (1995) argued that media coverage could help shape public opinion (see also Gamson and Modigliani 1989; Terkildsen and Schnell 1997). Walgrave and Vliegenthart (2012) argue that media coverage can influence policy outcomes. Other research combines these arguments to suggest that media coverage can shape public opinion and legislative action (Costain and Majstorovic 1994; Gamson and Wolfsfeld 1993). Indeed, some online activists invest substantial time and effort in generating attention for their efforts, both to drive participation in their campaigns and to drive media coverage of them.

If this research is right and media coverage is independently impactful for social movements, then the primary question is whether online protest can generate online and offline media coverage. Fortunately, researchers have already examined this question and found solid evidence that new media coverage can generate extensive crossover coverage in traditional media (Chadwick 2011; Rohlinger et al. 2010). For instance, traditional media coverage of a trial against an abortion provider in the United States was driven by online accusations by right-wing commentators that the traditional media were intentionally ignoring the story because it complicated story lines in the abortion debate (Gabriel 2013). Kreiss (2012) has argued that this crossover is so common that presidential campaigns now have elaborate ways of stoking online media coverage in hopes of producing crossover coverage to traditional media.

Online organizing

Entire campaigns and social movements have been organized online. For instance, Earl and Schussman (Earl and Schussman 2003, 2004; Schussman and Earl 2004) showed that the strategic voting movement was organized entirely online. Gurak (1997) and Gurak and Logie (2003) studied three entirely online campaigns: a campaign against Lotus Marketplace, a campaign against a Geo-Cities terms of service change, and a campaign against the so-called Clipper Chip, which was a NSA-designed tracking program. While the Clipper Chip campaign failed, both of the other campaigns were successful.

Research is also revealing the Internet can be used to create and support protest networks (Bennett 2003a, 2003b, 2004), which may organize protests. This is not surprising given the large and growing amount of work that reveals the Internet can be used to create and grow meaningful and cooperative relationships across time (Rainie and Wellman 2012).

Internet usage is also expanding the range of people involved in online organizing. Empirical research suggests that new kinds of organizers who lack substantial political or activist backgrounds are nonetheless getting involved and organizing their own campaigns and movements online (Earl and Schussman 2003, 2004; Schussman and Earl 2004).

That said, just as was the case with e-mobilization, establishing that it is possible to create online and offline protests and even larger campaigns or movements through online organizing doesn't ensure that protests, campaigns, or movements will ultimately "matter." Similar to my review of e-mobilization efforts above, there are two paths to an eventual social movement outcome (see Table 15.1). First, there is an indirect effect of increasing the number and diversity of protests so that there are more events in which people can participate. That is, research shows that online organizing is effective at increasing what Klandermans (2004) has referred to as the supply side of participation. This creates the potential for more protests that could be effective. But, the ultimate payoff will only be realized if these online and offline events are successful at creating change. In terms of offline protests resulting in change, this is again a paradoxical situation in which critics of Internet activism find that the effectiveness of a form of Internet activism actually hinges on the effectiveness of offline protests it supports. In terms of online protests resulting in change, I discuss the likelihood of this in the next section of the chapter and so defer further consideration until then.

Second, as was true for e-mobilization, there can also be an indirect impact of gaining media attention by organizing online. As pointed out earlier, online efforts can include significant online coverage of events and can generate cross-over coverage in traditional media as well. This significant new or traditional media coverage may impact public opinion, policy, or both, as discussed earlier in the e-mobilization section.

Online participation: in defense of "Slacktivism"

There are a myriad of ways to actually participate in protest while online, from less confrontational protest forms such as online petition signing to more antagonistic and confrontational forms such as politically motivated hacking, which is often referred to as "hacktivism" (see the following for other forms of online engagement: della Porta and Mosca 2009; Van Laer and Van Aelst 2010; Vegh 2003). Most of these forms of online participation accommodate relatively ephemeral forms of participation, such as a signature on an online petition, which has led some to denigrate these activities with such monikers as "slacktivism" and "clicktivism." Despite what might be substantial effort that can go into planning an online opportunity for participation (Zuckerman 2014) and/or the significant effort that might go into publicizing online protests, critics often perfunctorily dismiss this kind of participation precisely because individual participation can be quick and easy if people so choose.

In this chapter, I directly challenge these dismissals. Instead, I argue that this form of activism draws on a very different model of power than offline mobilization – flash activism (Bennett and Fielding 1999) – which likens its disruptive capacities to a flash flood. In fact, there are numerous empirical examples of successful online tactics. For example, in 2007, New York City (NYC) introduced new draft regulations that would have severely limited amateur filmmaking in NYC (see also for a discussion of this campaign: Earl 2010a; Earl and Kimport 2011). The regulations would have required permits and insurance policies for even very limited video shoots. The potential ramifications to the arts and news communities could not have been more substantial. A small group, Picture New York, was formed and it organized primarily using an online petition. Over the course of a few weeks (the draft regulation had a very short review period), the petition garnered over 35,000 signatures against the proposed regulations. The Mayor's Office of Theater, Film, and Broadcasting, which had proposed the regulations, was stunned and backed down. Moreover, even relatively small petitions against corporate targets have succeeded (Earl 2007).

But, anecdotal examples of successful online campaigns and tactics only get the field as far as anecdotal examples of failed campaigns – examples only indicate that failure and success are possibilities; they cannot tell us the relative probability of online forms of participation succeeding or failing. An important starting place to a more systematic analysis of the potential impacts of online participation is the fundamental model for the power of collective action embodied in online participation (see Table 15.1).

Flash activism as a model of power for online participation

Whereas "power in movement" (Tarrow 1994) has typically come from sustained and long-term mobilization, clicktivism and many other forms of online participation tend to draw on a "flash activism" model of power. This model of power in movement sees power as emanating from the very rapid but massive mobilizations that are possible online. Likening the power to the torrents of water that prove so damaging in flash floods, flash activists assert that rapid influxes of participation can be very influential, even if mobilizations also dissipate quickly (Bennett and Fielding 1999). In a flash flood, after all, it is not the long-lasting nature of the flood that is so incredibly powerful, but rather its massive and quick onset.

Social movement scholars are often used to thinking about power emanating from continuous action and influence, even if levels of mobilization rise and fall overtime. That form of power is likely to be important in a variety of settings, a fact that I will further discuss later. But, that this form of power has been successful does not make it the only form of power available to protesters. I argue that instead of thinking of flash-based power as replacing continuous-based power, it would be better to think of flash-based power as offering a new, alternative mode of power for social movements to leverage as well.

Moreover, flash-based power should be very appealing to social movement scholars and SMOs that think deeply about social movement research for several reasons. First, evidence suggests that mobilization levels for more ephemeral online engagements will generally be far larger than could be achieved offline or through more onerous engagements; this is important since the size of mobilization is important to a tactic's likelihood of success (Taylor and Van Dyke 2004). Social movements scholars have a fairly high degree of consensus around the finding that it is easier to get people to engage in lower cost engagements than higher cost engagements. A notable literature on high-risk activism makes this clear (Loveman 1998; McAdam 1986). Research on protest cycles makes the same claim – Tarrow (1994), for instance, argues that as more and more people participate in protest, the marginal cost for each new participant declines, making it easier for the next participant to agree to protest. A core part of the protest cycle dynamic is that the declining costs allow for increasing participation and the protest cycle begins to decline when costs rise, leading participation to drop off. It is quite likely that flash activism drops participation to a cost point low enough that many people who were not going to participate at all will now participate, but only in this form of activism. Research has offered supportive findings of this claim: Earl and Kimport (2011) found that the more websites facilitated activism so that costs were lowered, the higher the participation level.

Despite this evidence, a very prominent concern about online forms of participation has been that, but for more ephemeral action such as flash activism, most people would have otherwise committed themselves to more sustained engagements (Morozov 2011). These scholars see online participation as a net loss for movements because it pulls people away from "thicker" forms of engagement. I refer to this as the substitution hypothesis and argue that while this trade-off has been widely speculated, there is little evidence, or fundamental theoretical reason, to believe that such an effect exists. In fact, a core axiom in social movement scholarship is that even when people are concerned with an issue, by far the most common reaction is to do nothing (Earl 2009). Rigorous social movement scholarship shows that a very small fraction of people actually get involved in activism and the entire sub-area of micro-mobilization research is built to understand what differentiates the relatively few that get involved from \the masses that don't (Klandermans 2004; Oegema and Klandermans 1994). In light of one of the area's most clear findings – that the hard thing to explain is why people do something, not why they do nothing – it is hard to defend an assumption that large troves of people would have defaulted into offline mobilizations save the siren song of slacktivism. Put differently, I am arguing that many people who would not otherwise engage in any activism at all are willing to engage in some flash activism. Instead of a loss for movements, this is a net gain.[2]

A second reason that researchers should be more optimistic about flash activism (or at least more agnostic until more data come in) is that prior research on what makes particular tactical forms effective seems to favor the likely effectiveness of flash activism. Taylor and Van Dyke's (2004) review suggests that key predictors of tactical influence are novelty (see also: McAdam 1983; McCammon et al. 2001) and the size of the mobilization. Cultural resonance is also important, although resonance may be a mediating variable. Applied to online tactics, these trends in research findings actually suggest good news for

---

[2] Closely related to the substitution hypothesis are two other claims: that Internet activism is only useful when it serves as a gateway to offline activism (Zuckerman 2014) and that the role of Internet activism should be to facilitate a climb by participants up a ladder of engagement. See Earl (2014) for a discussion of problems with these claims.

online activists: given the relative newness of online forms of presentation, novelty seems to be on the side of online tactical effectiveness. Moreover, since the main advantage of flash activism is its ability to amass massive levels of participation quickly, size is also on the side of online tactical effectiveness. Although there is no data on cultural resonance, marked interest in new and traditional media in flash activism at least ensures frequent coverage of flash activism and issues raised in such activism.

Do targets discount flash activism?

Countering this model of flash-based power, critics have argued that targets of flash activism – whether government officials or CEOs – are unlikely to take it seriously because it is too "easy" to participate in. This conflation of ephemeral participation with ease has often resulted in critics denigrating flash activism with the label of "slacktivism." Van Laer and Van Aelst (2010) aptly summarize this common reservation:

> Power holders do not believe that a hardly personalized email shows the same commitment as a handwritten letter. Because of this lack of impact also potential subscribers might feel this kind of tactic is not appropriate. More in general, this kind of "keyboard activism" may go at the expense of real actions that demand a higher commitment (1162).

Gladwell (2010) also seemed to raise this concern. In fact, this is perhaps the most ardent and popular of criticisms made against flash activism, but it is also likely wrong.

First, it rests on an unproven assumption – I am unaware of any research that interviews targets of various sorts (state, corporate, etc.), that provides evidence that targets decide how to react to protest in part based on the costliness of the protest acts. Indeed, interview studies that have been done suggest that online contacts are weighed more heavily than actions such as phone calls and that there is not much distinction made by congressional staffers between an electronic letter and a physical letter (Congressional Management Foundation 2011).

Second, if the claim that investment is linearly related to effectiveness were true, several corollaries would follow that have received no research support. For instance, if investment by protesters matters so much, self-immolation and many types of civil disobedience would be incredibly effective since targets could not deny the substantial commitment and self-sacrifice that these tactics involved. Yet, there is no evidence that these tactics are particularly effective (indeed, while these tactics may earn media coverage, there is no evidence showing that they are incredibly effective tactics in targets' minds). To take a contemporary example, the hunger strikes at Guantanamo during 2013 have been incredibly arduous for those participating, but there is no sense that the US government or military is going to actually relent. More generally, I would argue that it is more likely that targets don't care how expensive the tactics are to participate in.

In fact, targets should strategically prefer that challengers choose very time-consuming, risky, or otherwise arduous tactics because such "thicker" engagements would also limit overall participation levels (because so few will be willing to undertake them), decrease the longevity of protest (because so few can persevere), and deplete movement resources. Much as targets might try to repress protest to raise its costs and therefore limit or end it, targets should prefer these thicker engagements because of the strategic advantages it can afford them.[3]

It is also important to note that if arduousness was part and parcel of a target's calculation, this should also affect the outcomes of offline forms of protest. For instance, offline petition signing and boycotting tend to be among the least arduous offline tactics, and thus, under critics' logic, would also be the least effective offline tactics. However, the literature has not treated them as such. In fact, there is a long tradition of studying exactly these tactics in part because of their importance in various movements. Earl and Kimport (2011) review classic social movement research on these tactics, which includes research on petitioning and various revolutions (Zaret 1996, 1999), the abolition movement (Zaeske 2003), the civil rights movement (Andrews 2001), the Dutch peace movement (Kriesi 1988, 1989), and local siting controversies (Lober 1995); boycotts in the civil rights

---

[3] It is important that one not conflate the costliness of participation with disruption from the target's perspective. Arduousness of participation and disruption are orthogonal concepts. Taking the Guantanamo hunger strike example again, it is very arduous for protesters but manageable for jailors. Piven and Cloward (1977), who so famously argued that what really mattered for the power of movements was disruptiveness, have even recognized the disruptive capacity of some types of flash activism (Cloward and Piven 2001).

movement (Barkan 1984) and farm workers' movement (Jenkins and Perrow 1977); and letter-writing campaigns in civil rights movement (Miller et al. 2001) and pro-choice movement (Staggenborg 1988). More recent research on boycotts has confirmed their effectiveness against corporations (King 2011; Vasi and King 2012). Given this research, it is hard to claim that online versions of these tactics would necessarily be so much less effective than the still relatively low-cost offline versions of these tactics.

In sum, this chapter has thus far argued that despite significant naysaying and questioning, it is likely that the most direct impact of online activism would result from online forms of participation. Given that, it is important to evaluate particular kinds of outcomes or consequences, since the impacts of online participation may vary by the type of impact. This is the topic to which the next section turns.

External policy or practice consequences of flash activism

Despite being the most prominent and well-studied area of social movement outcomes research, research on the impacts of activism on policies or practices has made only halting progress toward understanding these dynamics, compared to other significant questions in social movement studies (Amenta and Caren 2004). For instance, causal models that connect movements to external consequences have advanced. Most notably, the political mediation model has received support from a number of studies (e.g., Amenta et al. 1992, 1994). Scholarship has also improved in terms of theorizing about how social movements come to have impacts on policies and practices. For instance, a host of studies on predictors of state-level policy adoption has shown that social movement activities and organizations matter (see Strang and Soule 1998 for a review), teasing apart various patterns of diffusion and influence. Scholars have also disaggregated the policy-making process – moving beyond just thinking about passage – to also studying agenda-setting activities (e.g., Cress and Snow 2000; Johnson 2008; King et al. 2007), the impacts on bringing measures to vote (e.g., McAdam and Su 2002), and social movement effects on the implementation (e.g., Handler 1978) and interpretation of policy (e.g., Edelman 1992).

But, even with these advances, as a field we lack conclusive proof that most of the movements we study "matter" in terms of policy making. I point this out because a reasonable start to a conversation about the external impacts of online participation has to begin by acknowledging that the field cannot simply assume that offline protests do "matter" and cannot assume that the methodological difficulty of tying protest to outcomes is any easier to resolve for online protest than offline protest. Instead, the field must humbly acknowledge that in terms of robust research findings, we know little about when and how offline protests matter and even less about when and how online protests matter.

Moreover, no research to date has attempted to study the policy effects of online protest with such detail. We lack studies on online protest and agenda-setting, legislative passage, and legislative implementation. We also lack accounts of what mechanisms would drive any potential impacts, and whether such mechanisms would be similar or different from mechanisms driving consequences from offline protests. The vast majority of what has been written so far on this topic is theoretical or anecdotal.

In the face of so little research, I argue that instead of belaboring the question of whether online protest matters generally, we should instead discuss alternative questions that could actually move this increasingly stilted debate forward. Specifically, I argue that social movement scholars should ask under what conditions online protest is likely to be effective, under what conditions offline protest is likely to be effective, and under what conditions it is most effective to combine online and offline protest.

Best fit scenarios for online participation

I argue that online organizing and/or participation are likely to be particularly effective when confronting processes that have very clear decision-points, especially if those decision-points occur on specified dates (see Table 15.1). The flash flood model of activism that underlies much of online participation is especially adept at generating substantial amounts of participation in short periods of time. It is this surge in support, not its continuity, that is powerful. Indeed, many of the successful campaigns reported on in the literature have followed this pattern – there were clear decision points and often clear deadlines for making those decisions. Since processes without clear decision-points lack a moment to mobilize around, it would be much harder to focus the concerns of online participants.[4]

I also hypothesize that some kinds of targets might be particularly susceptible to influence from online protest. For instance, it is likely that corporate targets, which tend to be particularly concerned with their online image, are likely to be more responsive to online protest than other targets. It has become relatively commonplace for businesses to monitor their online reputation, including employing customer service representatives who troll twitter posts and social networking sites looking for bad publicity (e.g., Stross 2011). The goal of these employees is to find discontented customers who may have electronically broad networks and address their concerns so that they do not sully the image of the firm. In a context in which businesses are that concerned with their online reputation, well-designed online campaigns against corporations can pose a real threat. Indeed, even a few hundred signatures on an online petition has effectively shaped corporate decisions before (Earl 2007).

However, this is not to suggest that I expect government targets to ignore online protest. To the contrary, I expect that targets in competitive environments generally will be more sensitive to online protest. Thus, I would expect political candidates in competitive districts to be much more responsive to protest in general (and flash activism in particular) than political candidates in relatively safe districts. Similarly, political parties that hold comfortable margins would be expected to be less responsive than parties in more competitive political environments. One could apply the same logic to corporations, where I would expect companies in extremely competitive markets to be much more responsive to online protest, particularly retailers when those protests are from their consumer base.

Because the Internet allows spatially disparate individuals to be drawn together, I also hypothesize that situations in which challengers are geographically dispersed will particularly benefit from online participation. Online participation in such instances might allow for a movement to emerge and succeed where it would otherwise be impossible to do so.

---

[4] However, in such cases, a flood of online activism could be used in an effort to create a clear decision point or deadline where such a focused target was lacking.

Worst fit scenarios for online participation

The foregoing discussion and general tone of this chapter are not to suggest that I think online participation is likely to be appropriate and effective in all situations and for all movements. Quite to the contrary, just as there are kinds of challenges where one might expect online activism would excel, there are also kinds of challenges or goals that would be difficult to gain traction on using only online participation. For instance, when deeply structural problems or culturally revered practices are the focus of contention, online participation might have a more limited effect (e.g., eliminating racism or fundamentally altering gender relations using only online activism would be difficult).

In a balanced view of activism, though, one would be forced to acknowledge that such deep structural and cultural issues have proven difficult to entirely resolve even with substantial and enduring offline mobilizations. While the NAACP, for instance, has inarguably done great good for the civil rights movement and has greatly contributed to the decline in overt racism, very few would argue that decade upon decade of struggle have "solved" racism in America. More generally, these are problems that even long-term offline movements have struggled to successfully address, so this shortcoming of online activism is perhaps less about the qualities of online participation and more about the sheer difficulty of addressing deeply structural or culturally resonant grievances. This is a comparison that many critics of online activism often fail to make. For instance, one of Gladwell's (2010) primary quibbles with Internet activism is that he sees these movements as incapable of long-term and strategic action, which he sees as prerequisites for success. But, he implicitly assumes that offline movements were known to be successful at solving these long-term problems, even though that is not the case.

There are also some processes in which the size of a constituency should not, by design, impact decision-making. In these settings, the ability of flash activism to rapidly mobilize large numbers of participants would likely be an irrelevant capacity. For instance, in the United States, when regulators propose a regulation and make it available for public comment, that public comment period is not designed to be a popularity poll for the regulation. Instead, this period is designed as an opportunity to identify previously unsurfaced concerns. Thus, unique and unforeseen comments have far greater weight in this process than a large number of repetitive messages. It is not surprising, then, that regulators have tried to devise systems that help them detect unique concerns from a flood of correspondence on a proposal regulation (e.g., Shulman et al. 2006). However, this is more about the specific function of public comment periods than it is about online participation.

Finally, online participation might also be likely to be insufficient in situations where the goal of the protest action was to publicly display protesters' commitment to the cause, even if protesters expected that to have no effect on the target. For instance, protesters might engage in actions involving self-harm to show their commitment to the cause, even though they might not reasonably expect these actions to persuade their target. Therefore, where high-commitment protest is an end unto itself, not a means to an end, online forms of participation would seem to be inadequate alternatives.

Internal movement consequences

In addition to policy consequences, online participation might have other effects analogous to the range of effects found for offline activism (see Table 15.1). For instance, it is likely that movements influence one another in a range of ways online. Whittier's (2004) thorough review of research on the consequences that movements have on one another identifies a range of inter-movement impacts based on traditional offline protest. I focus on four, arguing that each is likely to have an online analog.

First, research has shown that movements can build large coalitions for broader issues (Van Dyke and McCammon 2010). Internet usage has been argued by a range of scholars to substantially enhance efforts to build coalitions. Bennett's (2003a, 2004) work is perhaps the most prominent work on this topic. He shows that while Internet usage does not resolve deeply held disagreements between groups, it does allow broad groups to find single issues on which they can come together despite those disagreements and effectively organize. These broad but thin coalitions are often ephemeral, but nonetheless can play a very important role in meso-mobilization and, presumably, in laying the groundwork for future coalitions to emerge again. Van Laer and Van Aelst (2010), who are otherwise far from effusive about the likely impacts of online activism, acknowledge the importance of Internet usage in creating coalitions (see also Gillan 2009; Vasi 2006).

Second, research shows that "spillover" between movements is common and important offline (e.g., Meyer and Boutcher 2007; Meyer and Whittier 1994; Minkoff 1997). It is likely that movements are even more likely to take up nearby or sister issues online. Although theoretically we often imagine neatly segmented movements, Earl (2010b) argues that online there are rarely such neatly segregated political spaces. Instead, an issue central to one movement may nonetheless be discussed on websites related to seemingly distinct movements. For instance, a website ostensibly about the women's movement may also discuss environmental issues, and sometimes even host or link to tactics that are not explicitly feminist in goal.

Third, frames have also spilled over offline (McAdam and Rucht 1993). Given how much of a role online media have played in information diffusion (Ayres 1999; Fisher 1998; Myers 1999), it is quite likely that frames would readily diffuse online. But, thus far there is little research on this point; more research is clearly needed. However, there has been innovative research done using the Internet and computational techniques to study the diffusion of frames in traditional media (Bail 2012).

Finally, tactical innovations have been shown to diffuse offline (Soule 1997). As with the study of frame diffusion, there has only been limited research thus far on the online diffusion of tactics (save work done by Earl and Kimport 2010). Nonetheless, inter-movement impacts appear to be a promising area for future research on the impacts of online organizing and/or online participation.

Cultural consequences

As is true for studies of offline activism (Earl 2004), there is very little research on the cultural consequences of online activism. There is research discussing how online activism engages in things like culture-jamming as tactics (Carty 2002; Lievrouw 2011), but this work by and large doesn't trace through the consequences of these kinds of actions. In the absence of research in this area, I suggest several domains that scholars should consider for future study (see Table 15.1).

First, it is possible that online participation can shape public opinion, or at least issue salience as a component of public opinion. Consider, for instance, the much debated viral circulation of the Kony

2012 video. While many have argued that the video was less than accurate, focused on a strategically poor target, or constructed an overly simplified view of the situation (Zuckerman 2012), it is nonetheless the case that the video was seen by over 100 million viewers. That level of attention likely did impact administration decision-making (Kristof 2012), but even if it did not, it raised awareness about problems in a part of the world that Americans are infamous for ignoring. There are likely very few SMOs or movements that would not want 100 million people to pay attention to their cause for even a few minutes (Earl 2012). More formally, we can expect it raised issue salience and shaped public opinion.

Online participation may also affect the production of culture. Research demonstrates that there are a wide range of issues that people engage online for which they are not engaging offline because of low cost-points (Earl and Kimport 2009). Many of these new claims involve cultural products (e.g., Earl and Schussman 2008), such as petitions about the casting of movie roles and how games and toys should be designed. When these online actions are successful, they directly create cultural change through changes to cultural products due to protest.

Biographical consequences

Giugni (2004) reviewed research on the biographical impacts of (offline) activism and noted several robust findings drawn from research on leftist activists in the 1960s. Chief impacts of activism were continued leftist political leanings, continued movement participation, and a political self-conception that was to the left or radical. However, a career of activism also was found to lead to lower incomes, poorer marital outcomes (e.g., later marriage and earlier divorce), and higher likelihood of sporadic or nontraditional work histories and/or employment in the helping professions (Giugni 2004: 494). Large-scale survey projects confirm some of these effects, even for less committed activists (e.g., marital impacts, see Sherkat and Blocker 1997). However, research on biographical outcomes on right-leaning activists suggests less negative biographical impacts (Klatch 1999).

But, what are likely biographical consequences to online activist engagements, particularly online participation? Much of extant research on online activism seems to imply that there are likely to be few biographical consequences of online activism for several reasons. First, some scholars have argued that online participation engages already active individuals, so any impacts actually owe to their prior activism as opposed to a marginal consequence of online participation. I have discussed this argument about mobilizing the already mobilized above and thus do not reconsider it save to note that there are likely individuals who only participate in online activism, and scholars should consider what biographical consequences befall them.

Second, other scholars have argued that flash activists have lower levels of issue and activist commitment. This lower level of commitment is argued to lead to participation in low-cost forms of action, such as online participation, instead of higher-cost offline activism. Scholars also tend to infer that this lower level of commitment limits the likelihood of biographical consequences as well.[5] In contrast, as I argued above, it is more likely that these individuals would not have engaged in activism but for the ability to engage in flash activism.

Moreover, research suggests that online participation enables people who would otherwise only have a very short connection to a movement to have more enduring connections to movements because they can tune in and out of the movement as their lives permit. For instance, Rohlinger et al. (2009) studied local MoveOn members and found that a major advantage seen by members was the ability to participate when their lives had room for participation and withdraw (temporarily) when they did not have time. Instead of feeling like they had to make a decision about quitting a movement, or ending their involvement entirely, MoveOn members felt their participation could ebb and flow without great consequence and this actually encouraged them to stay involved and get involved again after lapses in participation.

Thus, whether based on ephemeral flash activism or on and off again liaisons with movements, it is important to investigate potential long-term biographical impacts on online participation. This has not

---

[5] Astute readers will notice how the prior argument in the literature and this argument conflict, even though some of the same researchers endorse both. The prior argument claimed that people act both online and offline in tandem, whereas this argument assumes that only the lazy act online and that the lack of commitment limits biographical consequences.

been done in any systematic way thus far, leaving research on this topic sorely needed. However, I would note that if critics are correct and for whatever reason, there are diminished long-term biographical consequences to online participation, this might be a good thing for participants. After all, many of the long-term biographical impacts researchers have found are either neutral or negative (e.g., delayed marriage, reduced career earnings).

Finally, even if there are limited long-term impacts of online participation, this does not mean that there are not short-term positives. For instance, according to a 2010 survey: "internet users are . . . more likely than non-users to say that, in the past 12 months, they have felt really proud of a group they are active in because of something it accomplished or a positive difference it made (62% v. 47%) and that they have accomplished something as part of a group that they could not have accomplished themselves (48% v. 35%)" (Rainie et al. 2011: 5).

Conclusion

Social movement scholarship seems fundamentally ambivalent about the role of the Internet in social movements and protest: on the one hand, there is clear empirical evidence that Internet-enabled tools are increasingly important to organizing, and yet on the other hand, scholars and activists alike frequently worry over the meaningfulness and impact of online protest. In this chapter, I have tried to interject greater nuance into this discussion in three ways.

First, I have followed Earl et al. (2010) and made distinctions between how different types of "Internet activism" might matter. As summarized in Table 15.1, in the case of brochureware, I argued that much like offline information provision, direct movement consequences would be limited. For e-mobilization and online organizing, I argued that two indirect mechanisms could drive impacts: (1) each might lead to more offline protest, and that protest would then directly produce outcomes; and/or (2) each might generate media coverage, that in turn independently produces outcomes. Finally, although critics have widely denigrated online participation, I argued this was likely the kind of Internet activism that would hold the most consequences, although research in this area is still limited.

Second, given that online participation is the most likely form to generate independent consequences, I examined a range of potential consequences for flash activism (see Table 15.1 for a summary). I argued that policy impacts were particularly likely where time-certain decision points existed. I also argued that cultural and inter-movement consequences were quite likely. Joining critics, I questioned the level of biographical consequences, but saw this as a potential positive since so many biographical impacts of activism have tended to be negative (i.e., lower incomes).

Third, for each of these types of consequences for flash activism, I have reviewed what the field already knows (or doesn't know) about the impacts of offline protest. A fair comparison of the effects of online and offline activism must be based on actual research findings as opposed to those stilted by nostalgic desire.

When viewed with this level of nuance, online forms of participation hold the potential to have substantial impacts in some situations. The field will progress more if scholars move away from wholesale condemnation or revelry and instead deeply research the effects of both online and offline activism.

References

Amenta, Edwin and Neal Caren. 2004. "The Legislative, Organizational, and Beneficiary Consequences of State-Oriented Challengers." In D.A. Snow, S.A. Soule, and H. Kriesi (eds.), *The Blackwell Companion to Social Movements*. Oxford: Blackwell Publishing, 461–488.

Amenta, Edwin, Bruce Carruthers, and Yvonne Zylan. 1992. "A Hero for the Aged? The Townsend Movement, the Political Mediation Model, and U.S. Old-Age Policy, 1934–1950." *American Journal of Sociology*, 8: 308–330.

Amenta, Edwin, Kathleen Dunleavy, and Mary Bernstein. 1994. "Stolen Thunder? Huey Long's "Share Our Wealth," Political Mediation, and the Second New Deal." *American Sociological Review*, 59:678–702.

Andrews, Kenneth T. 2001. "Social Movements and Policy Implementation: The Mississippi Civil Rights Movement and the

War on Poverty, 1965 to 1971." *American Sociological Review*, 66: 71–95.

Ayres, Jeffrey M. 1999. "From the Streets to the Internet: The Cyber-Diffusion of Contention." *The Annals of the American Academy of Political and Social Science*, 566: 132–143.

Bail, Christopher A. 2012. "The Fringe Effect: Civil Society Organizations and the Evolution of Media Discourse about Islam since the September 11th Attacks." *American Sociological Review*, 77: 855–879.

Barkan, Steven E. 1984. "Legal Control of the Southern Civil Rights Movement." *American Sociological Review*, 49: 552–565.

Bennett, Daniel and Pam Fielding. 1999. *The Net Effect: How Cyberadvocacy Is Changing the Political Landscape*. Merrifield, VA: e-advocates Press.

Bennett, Lance. 2003a. "New Media Power: The Internet and Global Activism." In N. Couldry and J. Curran (eds.), *Contesting Media Power*. New York: Rowman and Littlefield, 17–37.

Bennett, W. Lance. 2003b. "Communicating Global Activism: Strengths and Vulnerabilities of Networked Politics." *Information, Communication and Society*, 6: 143–168.

2004. "Social Movements Beyond Borders: Understanding Two Eras of Transnational Activism." In D. d. Porta and S. Tarrow (eds.), *Transnational Protest and Global Activism*. New York: Rowman & Littlefield, 203–227.

Beyer, Jessica Lucia. 2011. "Youth and the Generation of Political Consciousness Online." Unpublished Doctoral Dissertation Thesis, Department of Political Science, University of Washington, Washington.

Bloomberg News. 2011. "Facebook Call Prompts Protest Marches in Vietnam Over Dispute With China." Available online at: http://www.bloomberg.com/news/2011-06-05/facebook-call-prompts-protest-marches-in-vietnam-over-dispute-with-china.html, April 27, 2013.

Boase, Jeffrey, John B. Horrigan, Barry Wellman, and Lee Rainie. 2006. "The Strength of Internet Ties." Pew Internet & American Life Project, Washington, D.C.

Brundidge, Jennifer. 2010. "Encountering "Difference" in the Contemporary Public Sphere: The Contribution of the Internet to the Heterogeneity of Political Discussion Networks." *Journal of Communication*, 60: 680–700.

Caren, Neal and Sarah Gaby. 2011. "Occupy Online: Facebook and the Spread of Occupy Wall Street." Available online at: http://dx.doi.org/10.2139/ssrn.1943168, April 27, 2013.

Carty, Victoria. 2002. "Technology and Counter-hegemonic Movements: The Case of Nike Corporation." *Social Movement Studies*, 1: 129–146.

Castells, Manuel. 2012. *Networks of Outrage and Hope: Social Movements in the Internet Age*. Malden, MA: Polity Press.

Chadwick, Andrew. 2011. "Britain's First Live Televised Party Leader's Debate: From the News Cycle to the Political Information Cycle." *Parliamentary Affairs*, 64: 24–44.

Cloward, Richard A. and Frances Fox Piven. 2001. "Disrupting Cyberspace: A New Frontier for Labor Activism?" *New Labour Forum*, Spring/Summer 2001: 91–94.

Cohen, Cathy J., Joseph Kahne, Benjamin Bowyer, Ellen Middaugh, and Jon Rogowski. 2012. "Participatory Politics: New Media and Youth Political Action." MacArthur, Chicago.

Congressional Management Foundation. 2011. "Communicating with Congress: Perceptions of Citizen Advocacy on Capitol Hill." Congressional Management Foundation, Washington, D.C.

Costain, Anne N. and Steven Majstorovic. 1994. "Congress, Social Movements and Public Opinion: Multiple Origins of Women's Rights Legislation." *Political Research Quarterly*, 47: 111–135.

Cress, Daniel M. and David A. Snow. 2000. "The Influence of Organization, Disruption, Political Mediation, and Framing." *American Journal of Sociology*, 105: 1063–1104.

Deibert, Ronald J., John G. Palfrey, Rafal Rohozinski, and Jonathan Zittrain. 2008. "Access Denied: The Practice and Policy of Global Internet Filtering." Boston: MIT.

Deibert, Ronald, John G. Palfrey, Rafal Rohozinski, and Jonathan Zittrain. 2010. *Access Controlled: The Shaping of Power, Rights, and Rule in Cyberspace*. Cambridge: MIT Press.

della Porta, Donatella and Lorenzo Mosca. 2009. "Searching the Net: Web Sites' Qualities in the Global Justice Movement." *Information, Communication & Society*, 12: 771–792.

Diani, Mario. 2000. "Social Movement Networks: Virtual and Real." *Information, Communication and Society*, 3: 386–401.

Earl, Jennifer. 2004. "The Cultural Consequences of Social Movements." In D.A. Snow, S.A. Soule, and H. Kriesi (eds.), *The Blackwell Companion to Social Movements*. Malden, MA: Blackwell Publishing, 508–530.

2007. "Where Have All the Protests Gone? Online." *Washington Post*. Washington, DC, pp. B01.

2009. "When Bad Things Happen: Toward a Sociology of Trouble." *Sociology of Crime, Law, and Deviance*, 12: 231–254.

2010a. "The Dynamics of Protest-Related Diffusion on the Web." *Information, Communication & Society*, 13: 209–225.

2010b. "Spillover as Movement Agenda Setting: How Movement Issues Spillover Online." Paper presented at *MOVEOUT Workshop*, Geneva, Switzerland, February 16, 2010.

2012. "Our Way or the Highway? Policing "Activism" from the Inside." In *The Daily Disruption*, May 1, 2013, Available at: http://mobilizingideas.wordpress.com/2012/04/11/our-way-or-the-highway-policing-activism-from-the-inside/.

2014. "Something Old and Something New: A Comment on 'New Media, New Civics'." *Policy & Internet*, 6: 169–175.

Earl, Jennifer, Jayson Hunt, and R. Kelly Garrett. 2014. "Social Movements and the ICT Revolution." In H.-A. van der Heijden (ed.), *Handbook of Political Citizenship and Social Movements*. Northampton, MA: Edward Elgar Publishing, 359–383.

Earl, Jennifer and Katrina Kimport. 2009. "Movement Societies and Digital Protest: Fan Activism and Other Non-Political Protest Online." *Sociological Theory*, 23: 220–243.

2010. "The Diffusion of Different Types of Internet Activism: Suggestive Patterns in Website Adoption of Innovations." In B. Givans, K. Roberts, and S.A. Soule (eds.), *Dynamics of Diffusion in Social Movements*. Cambridge: Cambridge University Press, 125–139.

2011. *Digitally Enabled Social Change: Activism in the Internet Age*. Cambridge, MA: MIT Press.

Earl, Jennifer, Katrina Kimport, Greg Prieto, Carly Rush, and Kimberly Reynoso. 2010. "Changing the World One Webpage at a Time:

Conceptualizing and Explaining 'Internet Activism." *Mobilization*, 15: 425–446.

Earl, Jennifer and Alan Schussman. 2003. "The New Site of Activism: On-Line Organizations, Movement Entrepreneurs, and the Changing Location of Social Movement Decision-Making." *Research in Social Movements, Conflicts, and Change*, 24: 155–187.

2004. "Cease and Desist: Repression, Strategic Voting and the 2000 Presidential Election." *Mobilization*, 9: 181–202.

2008. "Contesting Cultural Control: Youth Culture and Online Petitioning." In W.L. Bennett (ed.), *Digital Media and Civic Engagement*. 71–95. Cambridge: MIT Press.

Edelman, Lauren B. 1992. "Legal Ambiguity and Symbolic Structures: Organization Mediation of Civil Rights Law." *American Journal of Sociology*, 97: 1531–1579.

Eltahawy, Mona. 2010. "Facebook, YouTube and Twitter are the New Tools of Protest in the Arab World." *Washington Post*. Washington, pp. A13.

Fisher, Dana R. 1998. "Rumoring Theory and the Internet: A Framework for Analyzing the Grass Roots." *Social Science Computer Review*, 16: 158–168.

Fisher, Dana and Marjie Boekkooi. 2010. "Mobilizing Friends and Strangers." *Information, Communication and Society*, 13: 193–208.

Fisher, Dana, Kevin Stanley, David Berman, and Gina Neff. 2005. "How Do Organizations Matter? Mobilization and Support for Participants at Five Globalization Protests." *Social Problems*, 52: 102–121.

Gabbatt, Adam and David Batty. 2010. "Second Day of Student Protests – How the Demonstrations Happened." *The Guardian*, Available online at: http://www.guardian.co.uk/education/2010/nov/24/student-school-pupils-protests-walkout, April 27, 2013.

Gabriel, Trip. 2013. "Online Furor Draws Press to Abortion Doctor's Trial." *New York Times*.

Gamson, William A. 1995. "Constructing Social Protest." In H. Johnston and B. Klandermans (eds.), *Social Movements and Culture*. London: UCL Press, 85–106.

2004. "Bystanders, Public Opinion, and the Media." In D.A. Snow, S. A. Soule, and H. Kriesi (eds.), *The Blackwell Companion to Social Movements*. Oxford: Blackwell Publishing, 242–261.

Gamson, William A. and Andre Modigliani. 1989. "Media Discourse and Public Opinion of Nuclear Power: A Constructionist Approach." *American Journal of Sociology*, 95: 1–37.

Gamson, William A. and Gadi Wolfsfeld. 1993. "Movements and Media as Interacting Systems." *Annals of the American Academy of Political and Social Science*, 528: 114–125.

Garrett, R. Kelly. 2009. "Echo Chambers Online? Politically Motivated Selective Exposure among Internet News Users." *Journal of Computer-Mediated Communication*, 14: 265–285.

Gillan, Kevin. 2009. "The UK Anti-war Movement Online: Uses and Limitations of Internet Technologies for Contemporary Activism." *Information, Communication & Society*, 12: 25–43.

Giugni, Marco G. 2004. "Personal and Biographical Consequences." In D.A. Snow, S.A. Soule, and H. Kriesi (eds.), *The Blackwell Companion to Social Movements*. Oxford: Blackwell Publishing, 489–507.

Gladwell, Malcolm. 2010. "Why the Revolution Will Not Be Tweeted." *New Yorker*, October 4, 2010.

Gurak, Laura J. 1997. *Persuasion and Privacy in Cyberspace: The Online Protests over Lotus MarketPlace and the Clipper Chip*. New Haven: Yale University Press.

Gurak, Laura J. and John Logie. 2003. "Internet Protests, from Text to Web." In M. McCaughey and M.D. Ayers (eds.), *Cyberactivism: Online Activism and Theory and Practice*. New York: Routledge, 25–46.

Hampton, Keith. 2003. "Grieving for a Lost Network: Collective Action in a Wired Suburb. Special Issue: ICTs and Community Networking." *The Information Society*, 19: 417–428.

Hampton, Keith N., Chul-Joo Lee, and Eun Ja Her. 2011. "How New Media Affords Network Diversity: Direct and Mediated Access to Social Capital through Participation in Local Social Settings." *New Media & Society*, 13: 1031–1049.

Hampton, Keith N., Lauren F. Sessions, and Eun Ja Her. 2011. "Core Networks, Social Isolation, and New Media: How Internet and Mobile Phone Use is Related to Network Size and Diversity." *Information, Communication & Society*, 14: 130–155.

Hampton, Keith and Barry Wellman. 2003. "Neighboring in Netville: How the Internet Supports Community and Social Capital in a Wired Suburb." *City & Community*, 2: 277–311.

Handler, Joel F. 1978. *Social Movements and the Legal System: A Theory of Law Reform and Social Change*. New York: Academic Press.

Heyboer, Kelly. 2010. "N.J. Student Protests Showcase Facebook's Role in Mobilizing Social Movements." Available online at: http://www.nj.com/news/index.ssf/2010/04/facebook_student_protest_mobilize.html, April 27, 2013.

Hossain, Ashik. 2013. "Defiant Crowd Battles Propaganda War." *bdnews23.com*, Available online at: http://bdnews24.com/bangla desh/2013/02/11/defiant-crowd-battles-propaganda-war, April 27, 2013.

Jenkins, J. Craig and Charles Perrow. 1977. "Insurgency of the Powerless: Farm Worker Movements (1946–1972)." *American Sociological Review*, 42: 249–268.

Johnson, Eric W. 2008. "Social Movement Size, Organizational Diversity and the Making of Federal Law." *Social Forces*, 88: 967–993.

King, Brayden G. 2011. "The Tactical Disruptiveness of Social Movements: Sources of Market and Mediated Disruption in Corporate Boycotts." *Social Problems*, 58: 491–517.

King, Brayden G., Keith G. Bentele, and Sarah A. Soule. 2007. "Protest and Policymaking: Explaining Fluctuation in Congressional Attention to Rights Issues, 1960–1986." *Social Forces*, 86: 137–163.

Klandermans, Bert. 2004. "The Demand and Supply of Participation: Social-Psychological Correlates of Participation in Social Movements." In D.A. Snow, S.A. Soule, and H. Kriesi (eds.), *The Blackwell Companion to Social Movements*. Oxford: Blackwell Publishing, 360–379.

Klatch, Rebecca E. 1999. *A Generation Divided: The New Left, the New Right, and the 1960s*. Berkeley: University of California Press.

Kreiss, Daniel. 2012. *Taking Our Country Back*. Cambridge: Oxford University Press.

Kriesi, Hanspeter. 1988. "Local Mobilization for the People's Petition of the Dutch Peace Movement." *International Social Movement Research*, 1: 41–82.

1989. "New Social Movements and the New Class in the Netherlands." *The American Journal of Sociology*, 94: 1078–1116.

Kristof, Nicolas D. 2012. "Viral Video, Vicious Warlord." *New York Times*. New York, pp. A35.

Lievrouw, Leah A. 2011. *Alternative and Activist New Media*. Cambridge: Polity Press.

Lober, Douglas J. 1995. "Why Protest? Public Behavioral and Attitudinal Response to Siting a Waste Disposal Facility." *Policy Studies Journal*, 23: 499–518.

Loveman, Mara. 1998. "High-Risk Collective Action: Defending Human Rights in Chile, Uruguay, and Argentina." *American Journal of Sociology*, 104: 477–525.

Madden, Mary and Amanda Lenhart. 2006. "Online Dating." Pew Internet and American Life Project, Washington, D.C.

McAdam, Doug. 1983. "Tactical Innovation and the Pace of Insurgency." *American Sociological Review*, 48: 735–754.

1986. "Recruitment to High Risk Activism: The Case of Freedom Summer." *American Journal of Sociology*, 92: 64–90.

McAdam, Doug and Dieter Rucht. 1993. "The Cross-National Diffusion of Movement Ideas." *Annals*, 528: 56–74.

McAdam, Doug and Yang Su. 2002. "The War at Home: Antiwar Protests and Congressional Voting, 1965 to 1973." *American Sociological Review*, 67: 696–721.

McCammon, Holly J., Karen E. Campbell, Ellen M. Granberg, and Christine Mowery. 2001. "How Movements Win: Gendered Opportunity Structures and U.S. Women's Suffrage Movements, 1866 to 1919." *American Sociological Review*, 66: 49–70.

McCarthy, John D. and Mayer N. Zald. 1973. *The Trend of Social Movements in America: Professionalization and Resource Mobilization*. Morristown, NJ: General Learning Press.

1977. "Resource Mobilization and Social Movements: A Partial Theory." *American Journal of Sociology*, 82: 1212–1241.

Meyer, David S. and Steven A. Boutcher. 2007. "Signals and Spillover: Brown v. Board of Education and Other Social Movements." *Perspectives on Politics*, 5: 81–93.

Meyer, David S. and Nancy Whittier. 1994. "Social Movement Spillover." *Social Problems*, 41: 277–298.

Miller, James A., Susan D. Pennybacker, and Eve Rosenhaft. 2001. "Mother Ada Wright and the International Campaign to Free the

Scottsboro Boys, 1931–1934." *The American Historical Review*, 106: 387–430.

Minkoff, Debra C. 1997. "The Sequencing of Social Movements." *American Sociological Review*, 62: 779–799.

Morozov, Evgeny. 2011. *The Net Delusion: The Dark Side of Internet Freedom*. New York: Public Affairs.

Myers, Daniel J. 1999. "Social Activism through Computer Networks."

Oegema, Dirk and Bert Klandermans. 1994. "Why Social Movement Sympathizers Don't Participate: Erosion and Nonconversion of Support." *American Sociological Review*, 59: 703–722.

Piven, Frances Fox and Richard A. Cloward. 1977. *Poor People's Movements: Why They Succeed, How They Fail*. New York: Vintage Books.

Rainie, Lee, Kristen Purcell, and Aaron Smith. 2011. "The Social Side of the Internet." Pew Internet and American Life Project, Washington, D.C.

Rainie, Lee and Barry Wellman. 2012. *Networked: The New Social Operating System*. Cambridge, MA: MIT Press.

Rambler, Irish. 2011. "Spontaneous Demonstration Called on Facebook Attracts Half a Million in Lisbon." In libcom.org, vol. 2013.

Rheingold, Howard. 1993. *The Virtual Community: Homesteading on the Electronic Frontier*. Reading, MA: Addison-Wesley.

Roberts, Hal, Ethan Zuckerman, Robert Faris, and John Palfrey. 2010. "2010 Circumvention Tool Usage Report." Berkman Center for Internet & Society at Harvard University, Cambridge, MA.

Rohlinger, Deana A., Jordan Brown, and Leslie Bunnage. 2010. "Unpacking Media Strategy: The Case of the Academic Freedom Movement." Paper presented at *Annual Meetings of the American Sociological Association*, Atlanta, GA, August 2010.

Rohlinger, Deana A., Leslie Bunnage, and Jordan Brown. 2009. "Bridging the Gap: The Role of the Internet in US Progressive Politics." Paper presented at *Annual Meetings of the American Sociological Association*, San Francisco, August 2009.

Rucht, Deiter. 2004. "The Quadruple 'A': Media Strategies of Protest Movements Since the 1960s." In W.v.d. Donk, B.D. Loader, P.G. Nixon, and D. Rucht (eds.), *Cyberprotest: New*

Media, Citizens and Social Movements. New York: Routledge, 25–48.

Schussman, Alan and Jennifer Earl. 2004. "From Barricades to Firewalls? Strategic Voting and Social Movement Leadership in the Internet Age." *Sociological Inquiry*, 74: 439–463.

Sherkat, Darren E. and T. Jean Blocker. 1997. "Explaining the Political and Personal Consequences of Protest." *Social Forces*, 75: 1049–1076.

Shirky, Clay. 2008. *Here Comes Everybody: The Power of Organizing Without Organizations.* New York: Penguin Press.

Shulman, Stuart, Jamie Callan, Eduard Hovy, and Stephen Zavestoski. 2006. "Language Processing Technologies for Electronic Rulemaking: A Project Highlight." In *Proceedings of the Seventh National Conference on Digital Government Research*, May 21–24, 2006.

Smith, Aaron, Kay Lehman Scholzman, Sidney Verba, and Henry Brady. 2009. "The Internet and Civic Engagement." Pew Internet & American Life Project, Washington, D.C.

Soule, Sarah A. 1997. "The Student Divestment Movement in the United States and Tactical Diffusion: The Shantytown Protest." *Social Forces*, 75: 855–883.

Staggenborg, Suzanne. 1988. "The Consequences of Professionalization and Formalization in the Pro-Choice Movement." *American Sociological Review*, 53: 585–606.

Strang, David and Sarah A. Soule. 1998. "Diffusion in Organizations and Social Movements: From Hybrid Corn to Poison Pills." *Annual Review of Sociology*, 24: 265–290.

Stross, Randall. 2011. "Consumer Complaints Made Easy. Maybe Too Easy." *New York Times.* New York Times, Pp. 3.

Tarrow, Sidney. 1994. *Power in Movement: Social Movements, Collective Action and Politics.* New York: Cambridge University Press.

———. 1998. "Fishnets, Internets, and Catnets: Globalization and Transnational Collective Action." In M.P. Hanaganm, L.P. Moch, and W. te Brake (eds.), *Challenging Authority: The Historical Study of Contentious Politics.* Minneapolis: University of Minnesota Press, 228–244.

Taylor, Verta and Nella Van Dyke. 2004. "'Get up, Stand up': Tactical Repertoires of Social Movements." In D.A. Snow, S.A. Soule, and

H. Kriesi (eds.), *The Blackwell Companion to Social Movements*. Oxford: Blackwell Publishing, 262–293.

Terkildsen, Nayda and Frauke Schnell. 1997. "How Media Frames Move Public Opinion: An Analysis of the Women's Movement." *Political Research Quarterly*, 50: 879–900.

Tufekci, Zeynep and Christopher Wilson. 2012. "Social Media and the Decision to Participate in Political Protest: Observations from Tahrir Square." *Journal of Communication*, 62: 363–379.

Van Dyke, Nella and Holly McCammon. 2010. "Introduction: Social Movement Coalition Formation." In N. Van Dyke and H. McCammon (eds.), *Strategic Alliances: Coalition Building and Social Movements*. Minneapolis: University of Minnesota Press, xi–xviii.

Van Laer, Jeroen and Peter Van Aelst. 2010. "Internet and Social Movement Action Repertoires." *Information, Communication & Society*, 13: 1146–1171.

Vasi, Ion Bogdan. 2006. "The New Anti-War Protests and Miscible Mobilizations." *Social Movement Studies*, 5: 137–153.

Vasi, Ion Bogdan and Brayden G. King. 2012. "Social Movements, Risk Perceptions, and Economic Outcomes: The Effect of Primary and Secondary Stakeholder Activism on Firms' Perceived Environmental Risk and Financial Performance." *American Sociological Review*, 77: 573–596.

Vegh, Sandor. 2003. "Classifying Forms of Online Activism: The Case of Cyberprotests against the World Bank." In M. McCaughey and M.D. Ayers (eds.), *Cyberactivism: Online Activism and Theory and Practice*. New York: Routledge, 71–95.

Walgrave, Steffan and Rens Vliegenthart. 2012. "The Complex Agenda-Setting Power of Protest: Demonstrations, Media, Parliament, Government, and Legislation in Belgium, 1993–2000." *Mobilization*, 17: 129–156.

Whittier, Nancy. 2004. "The Consequences of Social Movements for Each Other." In D.A. Snow, S.A. Soule, and H. Kriesi (eds.), *The Blackwell Companion to Social Movements*. Oxford: Blackwell Publishing, 531–551.

Wojcieszak, Magdalena E. and Diana C. Mutz. 2009. "Online Groups and Political Discourse: Do Online Discussion Spaces Facilitate Exposure to Political Disagreement?" *Journal of Communication*, 59: 40–56.

Zaeske, Susan. 2003. *Signatures of Citizenship*. Chapel Hill: University of North Carolina Press.

Zaret, David. 1996. "Petitions and the "Invention" of Public Opinion in the English Revolution." *The American Journal of Sociology*, 101: 1497–1555.

1999. *Origins of Democratic Culture: Printing, Petitions, and the Public Sphere in Early-Modern England*. Princeton: Princeton University Press.

Zuckerman, Ethan. 2012. "Unpacking Kony 2012." In *ethanzuckerman.com*, edited by E. Zuckerman.

2014. "New Media, New Civics?" *Policy & Internet*, 6: 151–168.

Index